PEARSON CUSTOM SOCIOLOGY

Formerly published as Intersections, Crossroads & Inequalities

EDITORS

KATHLEEN A. TIEMANN
University of North Dakota
Introduction to Sociology, Social Problems & Issues, Inequalities & Diversity

RALPH B. MCNEAL, JR.
University of Connecticut
Introduction to Sociology

BETSY LUCAL
Indiana University South Bend
Inequalities & Diversity

MORTEN G. ENDER
United States Military Academy, West Point
Inequalities & Diversity

COMPILED BY:

Social Problems

A Custom Edition for
Oregon State University

PEARSON

ISBN 10: 1-269-10093-9
ISBN 13: 978-1-269-10093-9

Table of Contents

The Sociological Approach to Social Problems

From Chapter 1 of *Social Problems, Census Update*, Twelfth Edition. D. Stanley Eitzen, Maxine Baca Zinn, Kelly Eitzen Smith. Copyright © 2012 by Pearson Education, Inc. Published by Allyn & Bacon. All rights reserved.

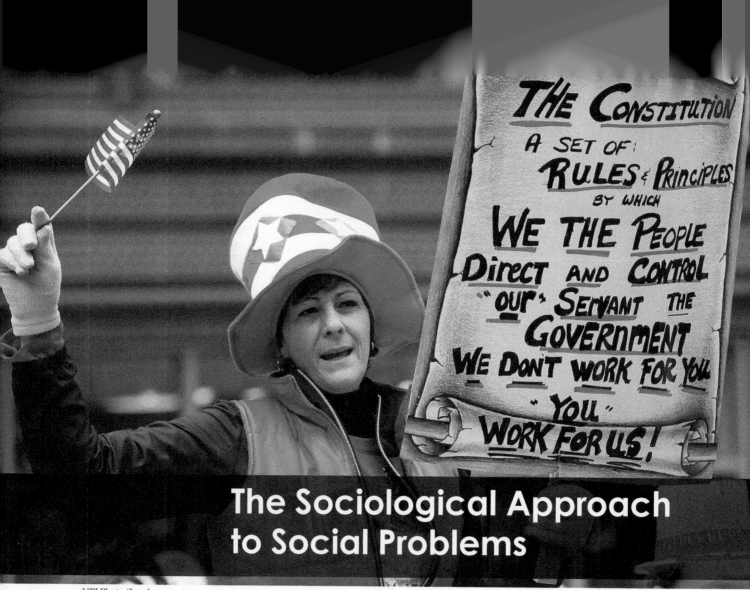

The Sociological Approach to Social Problems

Our most serious problems are social problems for which there are no technical solutions, only human solutions.

—George E. Brown, Jr.

Time magazine declared the first decade of this century "the decade from Hell." "This decade was as awful as any peacetime decade in the nation's entire history" (Serwer, 2009:31). It was a decade defined by terror, war, natural disaster, economic boom and bust, fear, insecurity, division, the decline of the middle class, and the dimming of the American Dream. Here are some indicators of the increasing magnitude of social problems during this tumultuous decade (Serwer 2009; Meyerson, 2009; Hampson, 2009):

- The 2000 presidential election was the most divisive and confusing in American history, with George W. Bush elected, although he had 500,000 fewer votes than Al Gore.

- Islamic terrorists flew hijacked jets into the World Trade Center and the Pentagon, killing nearly 3,000.
- The United States invaded Afghanistan in 2001, and in 2002 Congress authorized military action against Iraq. These wars cost an estimated $2 trillion, the lives of over 5,000 Americans and unknown hundreds of thousands of Iraqis and Afghans, and further destabilized the Middle East.
- Hurricane Katrina ravaged the Gulf Coast in 2005, the largest natural disaster in United States history, causing 1,500 deaths, $100 billion in damages, and the displacement of hundreds of thousands of people. The levees protecting New Orleans were known to be inadequate before the hurricane, and they did not hold. The responses by the federal and state governments were woefully inadequate following the disaster.
- The stock market lost 26 percent during this decade (in 2008 alone, the Dow dropped 34 percent and the S & P 500 declined 38.5 percent, the worst declines since the 1930s).
- Unemployment more than doubled to 10 percent by the end of the decade. The net job creation for the decade was zero (in past decades the average job creation gain was 20 percent; Herbert 2010).
- The median household income dropped from $52,500 in 2000 to $50,303 in 2008 (the most recent available data).
- In 2000, 11.3 percent of Americans were living below the poverty line. By 2008, the rate was 13.2 percent.
- The percentage of Americans without health insurance rose from 13.7 percent to 15.4 percent.
- The housing bubble burst, leaving 23 percent of homeowners owing more than their mortgages were worth. Individual bankruptcies and foreclosures rose sharply.
- Many major corporations such as Kmart, United Airlines, Circuit City, Lehman Brothers, General Motors, and Chrysler went bankrupt.
- During the decade, the price of a barrel of oil went from $25 to $150 and ended 2009 above $70, straining the economy.

In sum, this was a decade of dramatic change, much of it negative. The United States experienced its worst attack by foreigners, its worst natural disaster, its most divisive election, and its worst economic downturn since the Great Depression, and it initiated two wars, both lasting longer than World War II.

The official population of the United States surpassed the 300 million mark at 7:46 a.m. EDT on October 17, 2006. In 2043, when the typical reader of this text is about 52 years old, it is estimated that the United States will have added another 100 million people, reaching 400 million. What will life in the United States be like when you reach middle age with that added 100 million? Will the problems of today be eliminated or reduced, or will they have worsened? Consider these issues:

Immigration and the browning of America. Immigration from Latin America and Asia is fueling the population growth. About half of the last 100 million Americans are immigrants and their U.S.-born children. Half of the next 100 million will be immigrants or their children. Without them, the

Reuters/Jeff Topping/Landov

Immigration, especially illegal immigration, is fueling ethnic animosity in some areas of the United States.

Latino population would total 16 million instead of 44 million today, and Asian Americans would number 2 million, not 13 million (Samuelson 2006). By 2043, the race/ethnicity mix will be such that non-Whites will surpass Whites as the numerical majority. The increasing numbers of non-Whites will likely fuel racial/ethnic unrest among them as they experience discrimination and low-paying, demeaning jobs and among the native-born, who fear that the low wages of recent immigrants either take away their jobs or keep their wages low. With the additional millions of immigrants added in the coming decades, previously White rural areas and small towns will begin to deal with the challenges of new ethnic and racial residents.

The graying of America. After 2030, one of five U.S. residents will be at least 65 (similar to the proportion in Florida today). The increase in the number of elderly will cause problems with funding Social Security and Medicare, placing a greater burden on the young to support the elderly through these programs. This divide between workers who support the old with payroll taxes will have a racial, as well as a generational, dimension because the workers will be increasingly people of color and the elderly overwhelmingly White (Harden, 2006).

The inequality gap. Today the wealth and income of the affluent increases while the income of workers languishes. The inequality gap now is at record levels, resulting in a diminished middle class. In the words of Bill Moyers,

> As great wealth is accumulated at the top, the rest of society has not been benefiting proportionately. In 1960 the gap between the top 20 percent and the bottom 20 percent was 30-fold. Now it is 75-fold. Thirty years ago the average annual compensation of the top 100 chief executives in the country was 30 times the pay of the average worker. Today it is 1,000 times the pay of the average worker. A recent article in The Financial Times *reports on a study by the American economist Robert J. Gordon, who finds "little long-term change in workers' share of U.S. income over the past half century." Middle-ranking Americans are being squeezed, he says,*

"Where did we go wrong?"

because the top 10 percent of earners have captured almost half the total income gains in the past four decades and the top 1 percent have gained the most of all— "more in fact, than all the bottom 50 percent." (Moyers 2006:2)

Globalization and the transformation of the economy. The U.S. economy has undergone a dramatic shift from one dominated by manufacturing to one now characterized by service occupations and the collection, storage, and dissemination of information. As a result of this transformation, relatively well-paid employment in manufacturing products such as automobiles has dwindled and been replaced with jobs in lower-paying service industries. Most of the manufacturing is now done in foreign countries where U.S. corporations produce the same products but with cheaper labor, lower taxes, and fewer governmental controls. Some services, such as research, accounting, and call centers, have also been transferred to overseas companies to increase profits. Currently, these trends have negatively affected U.S. workers by making their jobs more insecure and reducing or eliminating their benefits.

In the coming decades, as 100 million people are added and new technologies enhancing globalization are developed, will the working conditions and standard of living of U.S. workers decline or be enhanced?

The plight of the poor. One of eight Americans is poor. Some 35.9 million Americans received food stamps in 2009, up from 29.1 million a year earlier. Emergency food requests and people seeking emergency shelter are increasing. Some 46.3 million Americans in 2008 were without health insurance, including one in five workers and 7.3 million children. The government considers those with incomes at or below 50 percent of the poverty level to be "severely poor." In 2008, 17.1 million Americans were in this category. Two factors lead to the speculation that the needs of the poor will not be met satisfactorily in the future. First, the trend is for the federal government to reduce "safety net" programs to help the poor,

A CLOSER LOOK

THE HEALTH OF WOMEN AND THEIR CHILDREN

International Comparisons

A few days before Mother's Day 2009, a global relief and development organization, Save the Children, published its "State of the World's Mothers," ranking twenty-six developed nations and ninety-nine countries in the developing world on ten measures related to the health of women and their children, their education, and their political status. Sweden ranked number one as the best place to be a mother, and the United States ranked twenty-seventh. The six indicators of mothers'

well-being are lifetime risk of maternal mortality, percentage of women using modern contraception, percentage of births attended by skilled personnel, percentage of pregnant women with anemia, adult female literacy rate, and participation of women in national government. Among the factors affecting the placement of the United States were the following:

- The U.S. rate of lifetime maternal mortality was 1 in 4,800, compared to 1 in 17,400 for Sweden.

- The United States ranked eighth in under 5 mortality rate per 1,000 live births.
- The United States also lags in the political status of women. Only 17 percent of seats in the U.S. national government were held by women, compared to 47 percent in Sweden, 42 percent in Finland, 41 percent in the Netherlands, 38 percent in Denmark, 37 percent in Finland, and 36 percent in Norway and Spain.
- The United States has a female life expectancy of 81 years. Eighteen nations have a higher life expectancy for women, led by Japan with 86 years.

Source: State of the World's Mothers. 2009. Save the Children, London, UK (May).

such as welfare to single mothers, nutrition programs, Head Start, and the like. Moreover, the national minimum wage was only $7.25 an hour in 2009.

The environmental impact. Currently, the United States, at about 4.5 percent of the world's population, consumes one-fourth of the world's energy, most particularly oil, and is the world's greatest producer of greenhouse gases that result in global warming. More people means more traffic congestion, more suburban sprawl, and more landfills. Population growth means greater demand for food, water, fossil fuels, timber, and other resources. At present, land is being converted for development (housing, schools, shopping centers, roads) at about twice the rate of population growth: about 3,000 acres of farmland are converted to nonagricultural uses daily, up 20 percent from 20 years ago (Knickerbocker 2006). Pollution has made more than 40 percent of the rivers and lakes unsuitable for fishing or swimming (Markham 2006). Adding another 100 million people with today's habits (large houses, gas-guzzling transportation, suburban sprawl, and the consumption of products designed to be obsolete) will lead to an ecological wasteland. But perhaps recognition of the negative environmental impacts of current usage patterns will lead to our reducing waste, finding alternative energy sources, making greater use of mass transit, increasing housing density, and finding other ways to sustain and even enhance the environment. Richard Stengel, managing editor of *Time* put it this way:

> In America, we have always done Big well—big cars, big screens, Big Macs; we're the supersize nation. But now we are being challenged to trade Big for Smart.

*Developers are building greener buildings, scientists talk of a 100-m.p.g. car,
Wal-Mart is testing the use of solar panels. We need to continue growing but
in smarter and more sustainable ways. (Stengel 2006:8)*

At the global level, the earth is warming because of human activities, most prominently the use of oil and other carbons. Global warming will have disastrous effects during this century—coastal flooding, shifting agricultural patterns, violent weather, spread of tropical diseases, and loss of biodiversity, to name a few. The United States is the primary user of petrochemicals, and China will surpass it around 2025.

The growing global inequality. While the United States' population increases by 100 million before midcentury, the world will grow by 50 percent, adding 3 billion (for a total of 9 billion) people. Almost all this growth (the United States is the exception) will occur among the poorest nations. Today, an estimated 1 billion people are undernourished. Most do not have clean water and adequate sanitation. Half of the world's people live on less than $2 a day, one-sixth on less than $1 a day. Hundreds of millions are ravaged by diseases such as malaria, chronic diarrhea, Ebola, dengue, and parasites. At the other extreme, the richest nations live lavish lifestyles, consuming and wasting most of the world's resources. Multinational corporations profit from exploiting the resources and labor of the poorest countries. This gap between the fortunate few and the impoverished, desperate masses continues to widen.

The underdeveloped world, already in dire straits, will face enormous obstacles in providing the minimum of food, water, housing, and medical attention for their peoples as they add billions in population. The result will be ever-greater numbers of desperate people on this planet, making the world less safe. Unless the affluent nations and international organizations make structural changes to aid the underdeveloped countries, conflicts over scarce resources will increase, as will sectarian and tribal violence and acts of terrorism.

An increasingly dangerous world. September 11, 2001, unleashed a chain of negative events. Those terrorist acts on the World Trade Center and the Pentagon caused death and destruction and redirected government policies. The United States responded with a war on Al-Qaeda in Afghanistan and a preemptive war on Iraq, presumably to squelch terrorism and spread democracy throughout the Middle East. To fight the war on terror, the United States suspended the civil rights of prisoners, including their protection from the use of techniques that many would define as torture, and spied on American citizens. Suicide bombers (the "guided missiles" of the militarily weak) have destabilized the Middle East and threaten terror worldwide. There is the growing threat of nuclear proliferation, with North Korea joining the nuclear club in 2006 and Iran threatening to join the club soon. As the world's population soars, with its consequent poverty, hunger, disease, and political chaos, the United States will be increasingly unsafe. Will we face these incredible problems and find solutions? That is the ultimate question.

Although these issues focus on the dark side of social life, our hope is that readers will find this exploration intriguing, insightful, and useful.

HISTORY OF SOCIAL PROBLEMS THEORY

Typically, social problems have been thought of as social situations that a large number of observers felt were inappropriate and needed remedying. Early U.S. sociologists applied a medical model to the analysis of society to assess whether some pathology was present. Using what were presumed to be universal criteria of normality, sociologists commonly assumed that social problems resulted from "bad" people—maladjusted people who were abnormal because of mental deficiency, mental disorder, lack of education, or incomplete socialization. These social pathologists, because they assumed that the basic norms of society are universally held, viewed social problems as behaviors or social arrangements that disturb the moral order. For them, the moral order of U.S. society defined such behaviors as alcoholism, suicide, theft, and murder as social problems. But this approach did not take into account the complexity inherent in a diverse society.

In a variation of the absolutist approach, sociologists in the 1920s and 1930s focused on the conditions of society that fostered problems. Societies undergoing rapid change from the processes of migration, urbanization, and industrialization were thought to have pockets of social disorganization. Certain areas of the cities undergoing the most rapid change, for example, were found to have disproportionately high rates of vice, crime, family breakdowns, and mental disorders.

In the past few decades, many sociologists have returned to a study of problem individuals—deviants who violate the expectations of society. The modern study of deviance developed in two directions. The first sought the sources of deviation within the social structure. Sociologists saw deviance as the result of conflict between the culturally prescribed goals of society (such as material success) and the obstacles to obtaining them that some groups of people face. The other, of relatively recent origin, has focused on the role of society in creating and sustaining deviance through labeling those people viewed as abnormal. Societal reactions are viewed as the key in determining what a social problem is and who is deviant.

Most recently, some sociologists have tried to alert others to the problematic nature of social problems themselves (see Spector and Kitsuse 1987). These theorists emphasize the subjective nature of social problems. They say that what is defined as a social problem differs by audience and by time. Pollution, for example, has not always been considered a social problem. This perspective also examines how particular phenomena come to be defined as social problems, focusing on how groups of people actively influence those definitions.

This brief description reveals several issues that must be addressed in looking at social problems. First, sociologists have difficulty agreeing on an adequate definition of social problems. Second, there is continuing debate over the unit of analysis: Is the focus of inquiry individuals or social systems? Related to the latter is the issue of numbers: How many people have to be affected before something is a social problem? In this regard, C. Wright Mills (1962) made an important distinction: If a situation such as unemployment is a problem for an individual or for scattered individuals, it is a "private trouble." But if unemployment is widespread, affecting large numbers of people in a region or the society, it is a "public issue" or a "social problem."

TOWARD A DEFINITION OF SOCIAL PROBLEMS

There is an objective reality of social problems: there are conditions in society (such as poverty and institutional racism) that induce material or psychic suffering for certain segments of the population; there are sociocultural phenomena that prevent a significant number of societal participants from developing and using their full potential; there are discrepancies between what a country such as the United States is supposed to stand for (equality of opportunity, justice, democracy) and the actual conditions in which many of its people live; and people are fouling their own nest through pollution and the indiscriminate use of natural resources (Eitzen 1984). This normative approach assumes that some kinds of actions are likely to be judged deleterious in any context. Therefore, one goal is to identify, describe, and explain situations that are objective social problems.

There are several dangers, however, in defining social problems objectively. The most obvious is that subjectivity is always present. To identify a phenomenon as a problem implies that it falls short of some standard. But what standards are to be used? Will the standards of society suffice? In a pluralistic society such as the United States, there is no uniform set of guidelines. People from different social strata and other social locations (such as region, occupation, race, and age) differ in their perceptions of what a social problem is and, once defined, how it should be solved. Is marijuana use a social problem? Is pornography? Is the relatively high rate of military spending a social problem? Is abortion a social problem? There is little consensus in U.S. society on these and other issues. All social observers, then, must be aware of differing viewpoints and respect the perspectives of the social actors involved.

In looking for objective social problems, we must also guard against the tendency to accept the definitions of social problems provided by those in power. Because the powerful—the agencies of government, business, and the media—provide the statistical data (such as crime rates), they may define social reality in a way that manipulates public opinion, thereby controlling behaviors that threaten the status quo (and their power). The congruence of official biases and public opinion can be seen in several historical examples. Slavery, for instance, was not considered a social problem by the powerful in the South, but slave revolts were. In colonial New England, the persecution of witches was not a social problem, but the witches were (Szasz 1970). Likewise, racism was not a social problem of the Jim Crow South, but "pushy" Blacks were. From the standpoint of U.S. public opinion, dispossessing Native Americans of their lands was not a social problem, but the Native Americans who resisted were.

Thus, to consider as social problems only those occurrences so defined by the public is fraught with several related dangers. First, to do so may mean overlooking conditions that are detrimental to a relatively powerless segment of the society. In other words, deplorable conditions heaped on minority groups tend to be ignored as social problems by the people at large. If sociologists accept this definition of social problems as their sole criterion, they have clearly taken a position that supports existing inequities for minority groups.

Second, defining social problems exclusively through public opinion diverts attention from what may constitute the most important social problem: the existing social order (Liazos 1972). If defined only through public opinion, social problems are limited to behaviors and actions that disrupt the existing social order. From this perspective, social problems are manifestations of the behaviors of abnormal people, not of society; the inadequacies and inequalities perpetuated by the existing system are not questioned. The distribution of power, the system of justice, how children are educated—to name but a few aspects of the existing social order—are assumed to be proper by most of the public, when they may be social problems themselves. As Skolnick and Currie noted,

> *Conventional social problems writing invariably returns to the symptoms of social ills, rather than the source; to criminals, rather than the law; to the mentally ill, rather than the quality of life; to the culture of the poor, rather than the predations of the rich; to the "pathology" of students, rather than the crisis of education. (Skolnick and Currie 1973:13)*

By overlooking institutions as a source of social problems (and as problems themselves), observers disregard the role of the powerful in society. To focus exclusively on those who deviate—the prostitute, the delinquent, the drug addict, the criminal—excludes the unethical, illegal, and destructive actions of powerful individuals, groups, and institutions in U.S. society and ignores the covert institutional violence brought about by racist and sexist policies, unjust tax laws, inequitable systems of health care and justice, and exploitation by the corporate world (Liazos 1972).

TYPES OF SOCIAL PROBLEMS

Consider two main types of social problems: (1) acts and conditions that violate the norms and values present in society and (2) societally induced conditions that cause psychic and material suffering for any segment of the population.

Norm Violations

Sociologists are interested in the discrepancy between social standards and reality for several reasons. First, this traditional approach directs attention to society's failures: the criminals, the mentally ill, the school dropouts, and the poor. Sociologists have many insights that explain the processes by which individuals experience differing pressures to engage in certain forms of deviant behavior because of their location in the social structure (social class, occupation, age, race, and role) and in space (region, size of community, and type of neighborhood). A guiding assumption of our inquiry here, however, is that norm violators are symptoms of social problems, not the disease itself. In other words, most deviants are victims and should not be blamed entirely by society for their deviance; rather, the system they live in should be blamed. A description of the situations affecting deviants (such as the barriers to success faced by minority group members) helps explain why some categories of persons participate disproportionately in deviant behavior.

Another reason for the traditional focus on norm violation is that deviance is culturally defined and socially labeled. The sociologist is vitally interested in the social and cultural processes that label some acts and persons as deviant and others as normal. Because by definition some social problems are whatever the public determines, social problems are inherently relative. Certain behaviors are labeled as social problems, whereas other activities (which by some other criteria would be a social problem) are not. People on welfare, for example, are generally considered to constitute a social problem, but slumlords are not; people who hear God talking to them are considered schizophrenic, but people who talk to God are believed perfectly sane; murder is a social problem, but killing the enemy during wartime is rewarded with medals; a prostitute is punished, but the client is not; aliens entering the country illegally constitute a social problem and are punished, but their U.S. employers are not. The important insight here is that "deviance is not a property *inherent* in certain forms of behavior; it is a property *conferred upon* these forms by the audiences which directly or indirectly witness them" (Schur 1971:12). The members of society, especially the most powerful members, determine what is a social problem and what is not.

Powerful people play an important role in determining who gets the negative label and who does not. Because there is no absolute standard that informs citizens of what is deviant and what is not, our definition of deviance depends on what behaviors the law singles out for punishment. Because the law is an instrument of those in power, acts that are labeled deviant are so labeled because they conflict with the interests of those in power. Thus, to comprehend the labeling process, we must understand not only the norms and values of the society but also what interest groups hold the power (Quinney 1970).

Social Conditions

The second type of social problem emphasized in this text involves conditions that cause psychic and material suffering for some category of people in the United States. Here, the focus is on how the society operates and who benefits and who does not under existing arrangements. In other words, what is the bias of the system? How are societal rewards distributed? Do some categories of persons suffer or profit because of how schools are organized or juries selected, because of the seniority system used by industries, or because of how health care is delivered? These questions direct attention away from individuals who violate norms and toward society's institutions as the generators of social problems.

Social problems of this type generate individual psychic and material suffering. Thus, societal arrangements can be organized in a way that is unresponsive to many human needs. As a benchmark, let us assume, with Abraham Maslow, that all human beings have a set of basic needs in common: the fundamental needs for shelter and sustenance, security, group support, esteem, respect, and self-actualization (the need for creative and constructive involvement in productive, significant activity; Maslow 1954). When these needs are thwarted,

> *individuals will be hostile to society and its norms. Their frustration will be expressed in withdrawal, alcohol or other drugs, or in the violence of crime, terrorism, and aggression. People will take up lives outside of the pale of social control and normative structure; in so doing they will destroy themselves and others. They will rightly be condemned as "bad" people, but this is so because they have lived in bad societies. (Doyle and Schindler 1974:6; emphasis added)*

When health care is maldistributed, when poverty persists for millions, when tax laws permit a business to write off 50 percent of a $100 luncheon but prohibit a truck driver from writing off a bologna sandwich, when government is run by the few for the benefit of the few, when businesses supposedly in competition fix prices to gouge the consumer, when the criminal justice system is biased against the poor and people of color, then society is permitting what is called institutionalized deviance (Doyle and Schindler 1974:13). Such a condition exists when the society and its formal organizations are not meeting the needs of individuals. But these conditions often escape criticism and are rarely identified as social problems. Instead, the focus has often been on individuals who vent their frustration in socially unacceptable ways. A major intent of this text is to view individual deviance as a consequence of institutionalized deviance.

In summary, here we consider social problems to be (1) societally induced conditions that cause psychic and material suffering for any segment of the population and (2) acts and conditions that violate the norms and values found in society. The distribution of power in society is the key to understanding these social problems. The powerless, because they are dominated by the powerful, are likely to be thwarted in achieving their basic needs (sustenance, security, self-esteem, and productivity). In contrast, the interests of the powerful are served because they control the mechanisms and institutions by which the perceptions of the public are shaped. By affecting public policy through reaffirming customs and through shaping the law and its enforcement, powerful interest groups are instrumental in designating (labeling) who is a problem (deviant) and who must be controlled. Our focus, then, is on the structure of society—especially on how power is distributed—rather than on "problem" individuals. Individual deviants are a manifestation of society's failure to meet their needs; the sources of crime, poverty, drug addiction, and racism are found in the laws and customs, the quality of life, the distribution of wealth and power, and the accepted practices of schools, governmental units, and corporations. As the primary source of social problems, society, not the individual deviant, must be restructured if social problems are to be solved. (See the panel titled "Social Problems in Global Perspective," which compares the United States with other nations on social problems, and the panel titled "Social Policy," which shows how societies can be designed to minimize social problems.)

THE SOCIOLOGICAL IMAGINATION

Sociology is the discipline that guides this inquiry into the sources and consequences of social problems. This scholarly discipline is the study of society and other social organizations, how they affect human behavior, and how these organizations are changed by human endeavors. C. Wright Mills (1916–1962), in his classic *The Sociological Imagination* (1959), wrote that the task of sociology is to realize that individual circumstances are inextricably linked to the structure of society. The sociological imagination involves several related components (Eitzen and Smith 2003:8):

- The sociological imagination is stimulated by a willingness to view the social world from the perspective of others.
- It involves moving away from thinking in terms of the individual and her or his problem and focusing rather on the social, economic, and historical circumstances that produce the problem. Put another way, the sociological imagination is the ability to see the societal patterns that influence individuals, families, groups, and organizations.
- Possessing a sociological imagination, one can shift from the examination of a single family to national budgets, from a poor person to national welfare

SOCIAL PROBLEMS IN GLOBAL PERSPECTIVE

SOCIAL WELFARE STATES: A MIXTURE OF CAPITALISM AND SOCIALISM

The nations of Western Europe, Scandinavia, and Canada have generous welfare policies for their citizens, certainly much more generous than those available in the United States (the description here is general, characterizing all the nations to a degree, although there are variations among them). These nations are capitalistic, permitting private property and privately owned businesses. To a much greater degree than in the United States, these nations have publicly owned enterprises and some nationalization of industry, typically transportation, mineral resources, and utilities.

Most important, these nations provide an array of social services to meet the needs of their citizens that is much greater than in the United States. These services include a greater subsidy to the arts (symphony orchestras, art exhibitions, artists, auditoriums), more public spaces (parks, public squares, recreation facilities), more resources for public libraries, universal preschool education, free public education through college, universal health insurance, housing subsidies to help low-income families, paid leave for new parents (mother and father), the provision of safe government child care facilities, extended unemployment benefits, paid vacations, and excellent retirement benefits, including paid long-term care if necessary.

These services are expensive, resulting in relatively high taxes, almost double the rate in the United States. But as Joe R. Feagin and Clairece Booher Feagin point out in their discussion of Sweden,

If we were to add to the taxes Americans pay, the cost of the private medical insurance carried by many Americans . . . as well as the cost of medical care not covered by insurance and the cost of private social services such as day care centers, [the taxes of the social welfare states] and U.S. "taxes" are much more nearly equal. Much of what [they] pay for through the tax system, Americans buy, if they can get it at all, from private enterprise— and they often get less adequate health care, child care, and other services as a result. Indeed, Americans probably pay more per capita for all such support services than do [those in the social welfare states]—and Americans receive less. (Feagin, Feagin, and Baker 2006:483)

As a result of these extensive social services, the people in the social welfare states have several advantages over those living in the United States: longer life expectancy, lower infant and maternal mortality, greater literacy, less poverty and homelessness, lower rates of violent crime, a lower proportion of single-parent households, and a proportionately larger middle class.

Are the people in these countries less free than Americans? There is freedom of speech and freedom of the press in each of the nations. The governments in these countries, for the most part, permit greater individual freedom than is found in the United States for personal behaviors (greater acceptance of homosexuality, legalization of prostitution, few restrictions on abortion, and the like).

Is there a downside? These countries are not immune to economic problems such as recessions, high unemployment, and citizen unrest over high taxes. In the past few years, the governments in these countries have reduced some of their social programs, but they are still much more generous than the United States (which has also curbed its more meager welfare programs). Typically, government leaders in each of these countries have argued that more austere programs are needed to stimulate the economy and permit the government to pay its bills. These measures have been met with citizen protest, particularly from the labor unions, which are much stronger than in the United States. It will be interesting to see how reduction in the welfare state plays out. If the austerity measures hold, will the countries follow the U.S. example and become more unequal, experience increased social unrest, see a rise in social problems? Or, as conservatives argue, will more capitalism and less socialism make these nations more efficient and more prosperous?

SOCIAL POLICY

SOCIAL PROBLEMS AND SOCIAL POLICY

The political-social-economic system of a society does not simply evolve from random events and aimless choices. The powerful in societies craft policies to accomplish certain ends, within the context of historical events, budgetary constraints, and the like. Addressing the issue of inequality, Claude Fischer and his colleagues from the sociology department at the University of California–Berkeley say,

> The answer to the question of why societies vary in their structure of rewards is more political. In significant measure, societies choose the height and breadth of their "ladders." By loosening markets or regulating them, by providing services to all citizens or rationing them according to income, by subsidizing some groups more than others, societies, through their politics, build their ladders. To be sure, historical and external constraints deny full freedom of action, but a substantial freedom of action remains. . . . In a democracy, this means that the inequality Americans have is, in significant measure, the historical result of policy choices of Americans—or, at least, Americans' representatives. In the United States, the result is a society that is distinctly unequal. Our ladder is, by the standards of affluent democracies and even by the standards of recent American history, unusually extended and narrow—and becoming more so. (Fischer et al., 1996:8)

In other words, America's level of inequality is by design (Fischer et al., 1996:125).

Social policy is about design, about setting goals and determining the means to achieve them. Do we want to regulate and protect more, as the well-developed welfare states do, or should we do less? Should we create and invest in policies and programs that protect citizens from poverty, unemployment, and the high cost of health care, or should the market economy sort people into winners, players, and losers based on their abilities and efforts? Decision makers in the United States have opted to reduce the welfare state. Are they on the right track? Can those policies that the generous welfare states have adopted be modified to reduce the United States' social problems? If societies are designed, should the United States change its design?

Source: D. Stanley Eitzen. 2007. "U.S. Social Problems in Comparative Perspective." In D. Stanley Eitzen (Ed.), *Solutions to Social Problems: Lessons from Other Societies,* 4th ed. Boston: Allyn & Bacon, pp. 9–10.

policies, from an unemployed person to the societal shift from manufacturing to a service/knowledge economy, from a single mother with a sick child to the high cost of health care for the uninsured, and from a homeless family to the lack of affordable housing.

- To develop a sociological imagination requires a detachment from the taken-for-granted assumptions about social life, and establishing a critical distance (Andersen and Taylor 2000:10–11). In other words, one must be willing to question the structural arrangements that shape social behavior.

When we have this imagination, we begin to see the solutions to social problems not in terms of changing problem people but in changing the structure of society.

SOCIAL STRUCTURE AS THE BASIC UNIT OF ANALYSIS

There is a very strong tendency for individuals—laypeople, police officers, judges, lawmakers, and social scientists alike—to perceive social problems and prescribe remedies from an individualistic perspective. For example, they blame the individual for being poor, with no reference to the maldistribution of wealth and other

© Jim Richardson/Corbis

Are families to blame for their poverty or are the institutions of society to blame for their plight by not providing jobs, adequate wages, and health care?

socially perpetuated disadvantages that blight many families generation after generation; they blame African Americans for their aggressive behavior, with no understanding of the limits placed on social mobility for African Americans by the social system; they blame dropouts for leaving school prematurely, with no understanding that the educational system fails to meet their needs. This type of thinking helps explain the reluctance of people in authority to provide adequate welfare, health care, and compensatory programs to help the disadvantaged.

The fundamental issue is whether social problems emanate from the pathologies of individuals (person-blame) or from the situations in which deviants are involved (system-blame), that is, whether deviants are the problem itself or only victims of it. The answer no doubt lies somewhere between the two extremes, but because the individual- or victim-blamers have held sway, we should examine their reasoning (Ryan 1976).

Person-Blame Approach versus System-Blame Approach

Let us begin by considering some victims, such as the children in a slum school who constantly fail. Why do they fail? The victim-blamer points to their cultural deprivation.* They do not do well in school because their families speak different dialects, because their parents are uneducated, because they have not been exposed to the educational benefits available to middle-class children (such as visits to the zoo, computers in the home, extensive travel, attendance at cultural events, exposure to books). In other words, the defect is in the children and their families. System-blamers look elsewhere for the sources of failure. They ask, What is there about the schools that make slum children more likely to fail? The answer is found in the irrelevant curriculum, class-biased IQ

---

*Cultural deprivation is a loaded ethnocentric term applied by members of the majority to the culture of the minority group. It implies that the culture of the group in question is not only inferior but also deficient. The concept does remind us, however, that people can and do make invidious distinctions about cultures and subcultures. Furthermore, people act on these distinctions as if they were valid.

tests, the tracking system, overcrowded classrooms, differential allocation of resources within the school district, and insensitive teachers, whose low expectations for poor children create a self-fulfilling prophecy.

Ex-convicts constitute another set of victims. Why is their recidivism rate (reinvolvement in crime) so high? The victim-blamer points to the faults of individual criminals: their greed, their feelings of aggression, their weak control of impulse, their lack of conscience. The system-blamer directs attention to very different sources: the penal system, the scarcity of employment for ex-criminals, and even the schools. For example, 20 to 30 percent of inmates are functionally illiterate; that is, they cannot meet minimum reading and writing demands in U.S. society, such as filling out job applications. Yet these people are expected to leave prison, find a job, and stay out of trouble. Illiterate ex-criminals face unemployment or at best the most menial jobs, with low wages, no job security, and no fringe benefits. System-blamers argue that first the schools and later the penal institutions have failed to provide these people with the minimum requirements for full participation in society. Moreover, lack of employment and the unwillingness of potential employers to train functional illiterates force many to return to crime to survive.

The inner-city poor are another set of victims. The conditions of the ghetto poor, especially African Americans, have deteriorated since the mid-1960s. Some observers believe that this deterioration is the result of the transplantation of a southern sharecropper culture (Lemann, 1986), welfare programs (Murray, 1984), and laziness. The more compelling system-blame argument, however, is made by William J. Wilson (1987). He claims that the ghetto poor endure because of the disappearance of hundreds of thousands of low-skill jobs, those mainly involving physical labor, in the past 40 years or so. Wilson's contention, supported by research, is that the pathologies of the ghetto (such as teenage pregnancy, illegitimacy, welfare dependency, and crime) are fundamentally the consequence of too few jobs.

The strong tendency to blame social problems on individuals rather than on the social system lies in how people tend to look at social problems. Most people define a social problem as behavior that deviates from the norms and standards of society. Because people do not ordinarily examine critically the way things are done in society, they tend to question the exceptions. The system not only is taken for granted but also has, for most people, an aura of sacredness because of the traditions and customs with which they associate it. Logically, then, those who deviate are the source of trouble. The obvious question observers ask is, Why do these people deviate from norms? Because most people view themselves as law-abiding, they feel that those who deviate do so because of some kind of unusual circumstance, such as accident, illness, personal defect, character flaw, or maladjustment (Ryan 1976:10–18). The flaw, then, is a function of the deviant, not of societal arrangements.

Interpreting social problems solely within a person-blame framework has serious consequences. First, because societal causes are not addressed, social problems remain in place (Davis-Delano 2009). Second, it frees the government, the economy, the system of stratification, the system of justice, and the educational system from any blame:

> [B]laming the poor [for example] is still easier than fixing what's really wrong with America: segregated schools, unjust wages, inadequate health care, and other such complicated matters. (Vogel 1994:31)

This protection of the established order against criticism increases the difficulty of trying to change the dominant economic, social, and political institutions. A good example is the strategy social scientists use in studying the origins of poverty. Because the person-blamer studies the poor rather than the nonpoor, the system of inequality (buttressed by tax laws, welfare rules, and employment practices) goes unchallenged. A related consequence of the person-blame approach, then, is that the relatively well-off segments of society retain their advantages.

A social-control function of the person-blame approach is that troublesome individuals and groups are controlled in a publicly acceptable manner. Deviants—whether they are criminals, mentally ill, or social protesters—are incarcerated in prisons or mental hospitals and administered drugs or other forms of therapy. This approach not only directs blame at individuals and away from the system, but it also eliminates the problems (individuals).

A related consequence is how the problem is treated. A person-blame approach demands a person-change treatment program. If the cause of delinquency, for example, is defined as the result of personal pathology, then the solution must clearly lie in counseling, behavior modification, psychotherapy, drugs, or some other technique aimed at changing the individual deviant. The person-blame interpretation of social problems provides and legitimates the right to initiate person-change rather than system-change treatment programs. Under such a scheme, norms that are racist, sexist, or homophobic, for example, go unchallenged.

The person-blame ideology invites not only person-change treatment programs but also programs for person-control. The system-blamer would argue that this emphasis, too, treats the symptom rather than the disease.

A final consequence of a person-blame interpretation is that it reinforces social myths about the degree of control individuals have over their fate. It provides justification for a form of social Darwinism: that the placement of people in the stratification system is a function of their ability and effort. By this logic, the poor are poor because they are the dregs of society. In short, they deserve their fate, as do the successful in society. Thus, in this viewpoint, little sympathy exists for government programs to increase welfare to the poor. (See the insert on William Graham Sumner for an example of this ideology.)

Reasons for Focusing on the System-Blame Approach

We emphasize the system-blame approach in this text. We should recognize, however, that the system-blame orientation has dangers. First, it is only part of the truth. Social problems are highly complex phenomena that have both individual and systemic origins. Individuals, obviously, can be malicious and aggressive for purely psychological reasons. Clearly, society needs to be protected from some individuals. Moreover, some people require particular forms of therapy, remedial help, or special programs on an individual basis if they are to function normally. But much behavior that is labeled deviant is the end product of social conditions.

A second danger of a dogmatic system-blame orientation is that it presents a rigidly deterministic explanation of social problems. Taken too far, this position views individuals as robots controlled totally by their social environment. A balanced view acknowledges that human beings may choose between alternative courses of action. This issue raises the related question of the degree to

William Graham Sumner and Social Darwinism

William Graham Sumner (1840–1910), the sociologist who originated the concepts of folkways and mores, was a proponent of social Darwinism.

This doctrine, widely accepted among elites during the late nineteenth and early twentieth centuries, was a distorted version of Charles Darwin's theory of natural selection. From this viewpoint, success is the result of being superior. The rich are rich because they deserve to be. By this logic, the poor also deserve their fate because they are biological and social failures and therefore unable to succeed in the competitive struggle.

Social Darwinism justified not only ruthless competition but also the perpetuation of the status quo. Superior classes, it was believed, should dominate because their members were unusually intelligent and moral. The lower classes, on the other hand, were considered inferior and defective. Their pathology was manifested in suicide, madness, crime, and various forms of vice.

On the basis of this philosophy, Sumner opposed social reforms such as welfare to the poor because they rewarded the unfit and penalized the competent. Such reforms, he argued, would interfere with the normal workings of society, halting progress and perhaps even contributing to a regression to an earlier evolutionary stage.

which people are responsible for their behavior. An extreme system-blame approach absolves individuals from responsibility for their actions. To take such a stance would be to argue that society should never restrict deviants; this view invites anarchy.

Despite these problems with the system-blame approach, it is the guiding perspective of this text for three reasons. First, because average citizens, police officers, legislators, social scientists, and judges tend to interpret social problems from an individualistic perspective, a balance is needed. Moreover, as noted earlier, a strict person-blame perspective has many negative consequences, and citizens must recognize these negative effects of their ideology.

A second reason for using the system-blaming perspective is that the subject matter of sociology is not the individual—who is the special province of psychology—but society. Because sociologists focus on the social determinants of behavior, they must make a critical analysis of the social structure. An important ingredient of the sociological perspective is the development of a critical stance toward social arrangements. Thus, the sociologist looks behind the facades to determine the positive and negative consequences of social arrangements. The sociologist's persistent questions must be, Who benefits under these arrangements? Who does not? For this reason, there should be a close fit between the sociological approach and the system-blaming perspective.

A final reason for the use of the system-blame approach is that the institutional framework of society is the source of many social problems (such as racism, pollution, unequal distribution of health care, poverty, and war). An exclusive focus on the individual ignores the strains caused by the inequities of the system and its fundamental intransigence to change. A guiding assumption of this text is that because institutions are made by human beings (and therefore are not sacred), they should be changed whenever they do not meet the needs of the people they were created to serve. As Skolnick and Currie stated,

Democratic conceptions of society have always held that institutions exist to serve people, and not vice versa. Institutions therefore are to be accountable to the people whose lives they affect. Where an institution—any institution, even the most "socially valued"—is found to conflict with human needs, democratic thought holds that it ought to be changed or abolished. (Skolnick and Currie 1973:15)

SOCIOLOGICAL METHODS: THE CRAFT OF SOCIOLOGY

The analysis of social problems depends on reliable data and logical reasoning. These necessities are possible, but some problems must be acknowledged. Before we describe how sociologists gather reliable data and make valid conclusions, let us examine the kinds of questions sociologists ask and the two major obstacles sociologists face in obtaining answers to these questions.

Sociological Questions

To begin, sociologists try to ascertain the facts. For example, let's assume that we want to assess the degree to which the public education system provides equal educational opportunities for all youngsters. To determine this, we need to conduct an empirical investigation to find the facts concerning such items as the amount spent per pupil by school districts within each state and by each state. Within school districts we need to know the facts concerning the distribution of monies by neighborhood schools. Are these monies appropriated equally, regardless of the social class or racial composition of the school? Are curriculum offerings the same for girls and boys within a school? Are extra fees charged for participation in extracurricular activities, and does this affect the participation of children by social class?

Sociologists also may ask comparative questions—that is, how does the situation in one social context compare with that in another? Most commonly, these questions involve the comparison of one society with another. Examples here might be the comparisons among industrialized nations on infant mortality, poverty, murder, leisure time, or the mathematics scores of sixteen-year-olds.

A third type of question that a sociologist may ask is historical. Sociologists are interested in trends. What are the facts now concerning divorce, crime, and political participation, for example, and how have these patterns changed over time? Figure 1 provides an example of a trend over time by examining the divorce rate in the United States from 1860 to 2005.

The three types of sociological questions considered so far determine the way things are. But these types of questions are not enough. Sociologists go beyond the factual to ask why. Why have real wages (controlling for inflation) declined since 1973 in the United States? Why are the poor, poor? Why do birthrates decline with industrialization? Why is the United States the most violent (as measured by murder, rape, and assault rates) industrialized society?

A sociological theory is a set of ideas that explains a range of human behavior and a variety of social and societal events. "A sociological theory designates those parts of the social world that are especially important, and offers ideas about how the social world works" (Kammeyer, Ritzer, and Yetman 1997:21). The late Michael Harrington said this regarding the necessity of theory: "The data of society are, for all practical purposes, infinite. You need criteria that will provisionally permit you to bring some order into that chaos of data and to distinguish

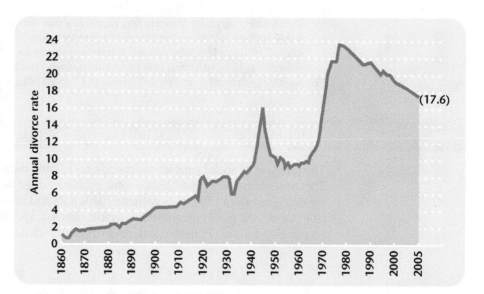

FIGURE 1

Annual Divorce Rates, United States, 1860–2005 (Divorces per Thousand Married Women Age 15 and Over)

Sources: Cherlin, Andrew J. *Marriage, Divorce, Remarriage.* Cambridge, MA: Harvard University Press, 1981, p. 22; Levitan, Sar A., Richard S. Belous, and Frank Gallo, *What's Happening to the American Family?* Rev. ed. Baltimore: Johns Hopkins University Press, 1988, p. 27; and current U.S. Census Bureau douments.

between relevant and irrelevant factors" (Harrington 1985:1). Thus, theory not only helps us to explain social phenomena, but it also guides research.

Problems in Collecting Data

A fundamental problem with the sociological perspective is that bane of the social sciences—objectivity. We are all guilty of harboring stereotyped conceptions of such social categories as Muslims, hard hats, professors, gays and lesbians, fundamentalists, business tycoons, socialists, the rich, the poor, and jocks. Moreover, we interpret events, material objects, and people's behavior through the perceptual filter of our religious and political beliefs. When fundamentalists oppose the use of certain books in school, when abortion is approved by a legislature, when the president advocates cutting billions from the federal budget by eliminating social services, or when the Supreme Court denies private schools the right to exclude certain racial groups, most of us rather easily take a position in the ensuing debate.

Sociologists are caught in a dilemma. On the one hand, they are members of society with beliefs, feelings, and biases. On the other hand, though, their professional task is to study society in a disciplined (scientific) way. This latter requirement is that scientist–scholars be dispassionate, objective observers. In short, if they take sides, they lose their status as scientists.

This ideal of value neutrality (to be absolutely free of bias in research) can be attacked from three positions. The first is that scientists should not be morally indifferent to the implications of their research. Alvin Gouldner has argued this in the following statement:

> *It would seem that social science's affinity for modeling itself after physical science might lead to instruction in matters other than research alone. Before Hiroshima, physicists also talked of a value-free science; they, too, vowed to make no value judgments. Today many of them are not so sure. If we today concern ourselves exclusively with the technical proficiency of our students and reject all responsibility for their moral sense, or lack of it, then we may someday be compelled to accept responsibility for having trained a generation willing to serve in a future Auschwitz.*

Granted that science always has inherent in it both constructive and destructive potentialities. It does not follow from this that we should encourage our students to be oblivious to the difference (Gouldner 1962:212).

Or, put another way, this time by historian Howard Zinn, explaining his style of classroom teaching:

I would start off my classes explaining to my students—because I didn't want to deceive them—that I would be taking stands on everything. They would hear my point of view in this course, that this would not be a neutral course. My point to them was that in fact it was impossible to be neutral. You Can't Be Neutral on a Moving Train [the title of Zinn's memoir] means that the world is already moving in certain directions. Things are already happening. Wars are taking place. Children are going hungry. In a world like this—already moving in certain, often terrible directions—to be neutral or to stand by is to collaborate with what is happening (quoted in Barsamian 1997:37–38).

The second argument against the purely neutral position is that such a stance is impossible. Howard Becker, among others, has argued that there is no dilemma—because it is impossible to do research that is uncontaminated by personal and political sympathies (Becker 1967; see also Gould 1998:19). This argument is based on several related assumptions. One is that the values of the scholar–researcher enter into the choices of what questions will be asked. For example, in the study of poverty, a critical decision involves the object of the study—the poor or the system that tends to perpetuate poverty among a certain segment of society. Or, in the study of the problems of youth, we can ask either of these questions: Why are some youths troublesome for adults? Or, Why do adults make so much trouble for youths? In both illustrations, quite different questions will yield very different results.

Similarly, our values lead us to decide from which vantage point we will gain access to information about a particular social organization. If researchers want to understand how a prison operates, they must determine whether they want a description from the inmates, from the guards, from the prison administrators, or from the state board of corrections. Each view provides useful insights about a prison, but obviously a biased one. If they obtain data from more than one of these levels, researchers are faced with making assessments of which is the more accurate view, clearly another place in the research process where the values of the observers have an impact.

Perhaps the most important reason why the study of social phenomena cannot be value free is that the type of problems researched and the strategies used tend either to support the existing societal arrangements or to undermine them. Seen in this way, social research of both types is political. Ironically, however, there is a strong tendency to label only the research aimed at changing the system as political. By the same token, whenever the research sides with the powerless, the implication is that the hierarchical system is being questioned—thus, the charge that this type of research is biased. Becker has provided us with the logic of this viewpoint:

When do we accuse ourselves and our fellow sociologists of bias? I think an inspection of representative instances would show that the accusation arises, in one important class of cases, when the research gives credence, in any serious way, to the perspective of the subordinate group in some hierarchical relationship. In the case of deviance, the hierarchical relationship is a moral one. The superordinate parties in the relationships are those who represent the forces of approved and official morality; the subordinate parties are those who, it is alleged, have violated that morality. . . . It is odd that, when we perceive bias, we usually see it in these circumstances. It is odd because it is easily ascertained that a great many more studies are biased in the direction of the interests of responsible officials than the other way around. (Becker 1967:240, 242)

In summary, bias is inevitable in the study and analysis of social problems. The choice of a research problem, the perspective from which one analyzes the problems, and the solutions proposed all reflect a bias that either supports the existing social arrangements or does not. Moreover, unlike biologists, who can dispassionately observe the behavior of sperm and the egg at conception, sociologists are participants in the social life they seek to study and understand. As they study homelessness, poor children, or urban blight, sociologists cannot escape from their own feelings and values. They must, however, not let their feelings and values render their analysis invalid. In other words, research and reports of research must reflect reality, not as the researcher might want it to be. Sociologists must display scientific integrity, which requires recognizing biases in such a way that these biases do not invalidate the findings (Berger 1963:5). When research is properly done in this spirit, an atheist can study a religious sect, a pacifist can study the military-industrial complex, a divorced person can study marriage, and a person who abhors the beliefs of the Ku Klux Klan can study that organization and its members.

In addition to bias, people gather data and make generalizations about social phenomena in a number of faulty ways. In a sense, everyone is a scientist seeking to find valid generalizations to guide behavior and make sense of the world. But most people are, in fact, very unscientific about the social world. The first problem, as we have noted, is the problem of bias. The second is that people tend to generalize from their experience. Not only is one's interpretation of things that happen to him or her subjective, but there also is a basic problem of sampling. The chances are that one's experience will be too idiosyncratic to allow for an accurate generalization. For example, if you and your friends agree that abortion is appropriate, that does not mean that other people in the society, even those of your age, will agree with you. Very likely, your friends are quite similar to you on such dimensions as socioeconomic status, race, religion, and geographic location.

Another instance of faulty sampling leading to faulty generalizations is when we make assumptions from a single case. An individual may argue that African Americans can succeed economically in this country as easily as Whites because she or he knows a wealthy African American. Similarly, you might argue that all Latinos are dumb because the one you know is in the slowest track in high school. This type of reasoning is especially fallacious because it blames the victim (Ryan, 1976). The cause of poverty or crime or dropping out of school or scoring low on an IQ test is seen as a result of the flaw in the individual, ignoring the substantial impact of the economy or school.

Another typical way that we explain social behavior is to use some authority other than our senses. The Bible, for example, has been used by many people to support or condemn activities such as slavery, capital punishment, war, homosexuality, or monogamy. The media provide other sources of authority for individuals. The media, however, are not always reliable sources of facts. Stories are often selected because they are unusually dramatic, giving the faulty impression of, for example, a crime wave or questionable air safety.

Our judgments and interpretations are also affected by prevailing myths and stereotypes. We just "know" certain things to be true, when they actually may be contradicted by scientific evidence. As examples, six common beliefs about the poor and racial minorities are presented and discussed.

1. *Most homeless people are disabled by drugs, mental disease, or physical afflictions.* The facts show, however, that the homeless, for the most part, are not "deficient and defective" but rather not much different than the nonhomeless. Most people are not homeless because of their individual flaws but because of structural arrangements and trends that result in extreme impoverishment and a shortage of affordable housing (Timmer, Eitzen, and Talley 1994).

2. *African American and Latino youth are more likely than White youth to smoke tobacco and be heavy binge drinkers of alcohol.* The facts belie this myth (Centers for Disease Control study, report in McClam 2000).

3. *Welfare makes people dependent, lazy, and unmotivated.* Contrary to this image, however, the evidence is that most daughters of welfare recipients do not become welfare recipients as adults (Sklar 1993). Put another way, most women on welfare did not receive welfare as children (Center on Social Welfare and Law 1996).

4. *Welfare is given more generously to the poor than to the nonpoor.* Farm subsidies, tax deductibility for taxes and interest on homes, low-interest loans to students and victims of disasters, and pork-barrel projects are examples of government welfare and even the dependency of nonpoor people on government largesse. Most important, these government handouts to the nonpoor are significantly greater than the amounts given to the poor.

5. *African Americans are similar in their behaviors.* Blacks are not a monolithic group, with members acting more or less alike. A study by the Rand Corporation, for example, found that about 1 in 100 young, high-ability, affluent Black women from homes with two parents become single, teenage mothers (for White women in this category, the chances were 1 in 1,000, explained, in part, by the much greater willingness to use abortion). In contrast, a poor Black teenager from a female-headed household who scores low on standardized tests has a 1 in 4 probability of becoming an unwed teenage mother (for White women in this category, the odds were 1 in 12) (cited in Luker 1991:76–77). In the words of Kristin Luker, "Unwed motherhood thus reflects the intersecting influences of race, class, and gender; race and class each has a distinct impact on the life histories of young women" (Luker 1991:77).

6. *Unmarried women have babies to increase their welfare payments.* Three facts show that this belief of political conservatives is a myth (Males 1996): (a) From 1972 to 1996, the value of the average Aid to Families with Dependent Children (AFDC) check declined by 40 percent, yet the ratio of out-of-wedlock births rose in the same period by 140 percent; (b) states that have lower welfare benefits usually have more out-of-wedlock births than states with higher benefits; and (c) the teen out-of-wedlock birthrate in the United States is much higher than the rate in countries where welfare benefits are much more generous.

Conventional wisdom is not always wrong, but when it is, it can lead to faulty generalizations and bad public policy. Therefore, it is imperative to know the facts, rather than accept myths as real.

A similar problem occurs when we use aphorisms to explain social occurrences. The problem with this common tactic is that society supplies us with ready explanations that fit contradictory situations and are therefore useless. For instance, if we know a couple who are alike in religion, race, socioeconomic status, and political attitudes, that makes sense to us because "birds of a feather flock together." But the opposite situation also makes sense. If partners in a relationship are very different on a number of dimensions, we can explain this by the obvious explanation: "opposites attract." We use a number of other proverbs to explain behavior. The problem is that there is often a proverb or aphorism to explain the other extreme. These contradictory explanations are commonly used and, of course, explain nothing. The job of the sociologist is to specify under what conditions certain rates of social behaviors occur.

Sources of Data

Sociologists do not use aphorisms to explain behavior, nor do they speculate based on faulty samples or authorities. Because we are part of the world that is to be explained, sociologists must obtain evidence that is beyond reproach. In addition to observing scrupulously the canons of science, four basic sources of data yield valid results for sociologists: survey research, experiments, observation, and existing data. We describe these techniques only briefly here.

- **Survey Research.** Sociologists are interested in obtaining information about people with certain social attributes. They may want to know how political beliefs and behaviors are influenced by differences in sex, race, ethnicity, religion, and social class. Or sociologists may wish to know whether religious attitudes are related to racial antipathy. They may want to determine whether poor people have different values from other people in society, the answer to which will have a tremendous impact on the ultimate solution to poverty. Or they may want to know whether voting patterns, work behaviors, or marital relationships vary by income level, educational attainment, or religious affiliation.

To answer these and similar questions, the sociologist may use personal interviews or written questionnaires to gather the data. The researcher may obtain information from all possible subjects or from a selected sample (a representative part of a population). Because the former method is often impractical, a random sample of subjects is selected from the larger population. If the sample is selected scientifically, a relatively small proportion can yield satisfactory results—that is, the inferences made from the sample will be reliable about the entire population. For example, a probability sample of only 2,000 from a total population of 1 million can provide data very close to what would be discovered if a survey were taken of the entire 1 million.

Typically with survey research, sociologists use sophisticated statistical techniques to control the contaminating effects of confounding variables to determine whether the findings could have occurred by chance, to determine whether variables are related, and to see whether such a relationship is a causal one. A variable is an attitude, behavior, or condition that can vary in magnitude and significance from case to case.

A special type of survey research, longitudinal surveys, has special promise. This type of research collects information about the same persons over many years and in doing so has "given the social sciences their Hubble telescope. Both allow the observing researcher to look back in time and record the antecedents of current events and transitions" (Butz and Torrey 2006:1898). For example, the Panel Study of Income Dynamics at the University of Michigan has followed the same people for 40 years, "documenting the importance of accumulated life experience in causing transitions from health to infirmity; from work to unemployment or retirement; and across the states of marriage, family structure, and wealth" (Butz and Torrey 2006:1898).

- **Experiments.** To understand the cause-and-effect relationship among a few variables, sociologists use controlled experiments. Let us assume, for example, that we want to test whether White students in interracial classrooms have more positive attitudes toward African Americans than Whites in segregated classrooms have toward them. Using the experimental method, the researcher would take a number of White students previously unexposed to Blacks in school and randomly assign a subset to an integrated classroom situation. Before actual contact with the Blacks, however, all the White students would be given a test of their racial attitudes. This pretest establishes a benchmark from which to measure any changes in attitudes. One group, the control group, continues school in segregated classrooms. (The control group is a group of subjects not exposed to the independent variable.) The other group, the experimental group, now has Blacks as classmates. (The experimental group is a group of subjects who are exposed to the independent variable.) Otherwise, the two groups are the same. Following a suitable period of time, the Whites in both groups are tested again for their racial attitudes. If this post-test reveals that the experimental group differs from the control group in racial attitudes (the dependent variable), then it is assumed that interracial contact (the independent variable) is the source of the change. (The dependent variable is a variable that is influenced by the effect of another variable. The independent variable is a variable that affects another variable.) As an example of a less-contrived experiment, a researcher can test the results of two different treatments on the subsequent behavior of juvenile delinquents. Delinquent boys who had been adjudicated by the courts can be randomly assigned to a boys' industrial school or a group home facility in the community. After release from incarceration, records are kept on the boys' subsequent behavior in school (grades, truancy, formal reprimands) and in the community (police contacts, work behavior). If the boys from the two groups differ appreciably, then we can say with assurance, because the boys were randomly assigned to each group, that the difference in treatment (the independent variable) was the source of the difference in behavior (the dependent variable).

- **Observation.** Famed baseball great Yogi Berra once said in his unique way: "You can observe a lot by just watching." The researcher, without intervention, can observe as accurately as possible what occurs in a community, group, or social event. This type of procedure is especially helpful in understanding such social phenomena as the decision-making process, the stages of a riot, the attraction of cults for their members, or the depersonalization of patients in a mental hospital. Case studies of entire communities have been very instrumental in the understanding of power structures and the complex interaction patterns in cities. Longtime participant observation studies of slum neighborhoods and gangs have been insightful in showing the social organization present in what the casual observer might think of as disorganized activity.

- **Existing Data.** The sociologist can also use existing data to test theories. The most common sources of information are the various agencies of the government.

Data are provided for the nation, regions, states, communities, and census tracts on births, deaths, income, education, unemployment, business activity, health delivery systems, prison populations, military spending, poverty, migration, and the like. Important information can also be obtained from such sources as business firms, athletic teams and leagues, unions, and professional associations. Statistical techniques can be used with these data to describe populations and the effects of social variables on various dependent variables.

One goal of this text is to help the reader understand the social nature of social problems. Accepting the system-blame perspective is a necessary first step in efforts to restructure society along more humane lines. The job of social scientists in this endeavor should be to provide alternative social structures (based on theory and research) for those about which we complain. To do this job, social scientists must ask very different research questions from those posed in the past, and they must study not only the powerless but also the powerful.

Many aspects of social problems are conditions resulting from cultural and social arrangements. It therefore requires examining the fundamental organization of U.S. society. This includes elaborating on the political economy of social problems, emphasizing the political and economic organization of society and its impact on social problems. The focus is on power because the powerful, by making and enforcing the laws, create and define deviance. They determine which behaviors will be rewarded and which ones punished. The powerful influence public opinion, and they can attempt to solve social problems or ignore them. Through policies for taxation and subsidies, the powerful determine the degree to which wealth is distributed in society. They also determine which group interests will be advanced and at whose expense.

The economy is equally important. The particular form of the economy establishes a distribution process not only for wealth but also for goods and services. In many important ways, Karl Marx was correct: The economy is the force that determines the form and substance of all other institutions—the church, school, family, and polity.

Critical scrutiny of the polity and the economy provides clues for the bias of society. It helps explain the upside-down qualities of society whereby the few benefit at the expense of the many; how reality gets defined in contested issues; how political and economic processes affect what is currently being done about social problems; and thus, why so many social policies fail.

Also to consider is the context of social problems in the United States, such as world population and global inequality, environmental degradation globally and domestically, two major population changes in the United States: the browning and the graying of America, and the problems of location: urban, suburban, and rural. A crucial element of U.S. social structure is the various manifestations of social inequality based on wealth, race/ethnicity, gender, sexual orientation, and disability.

Consider also the impact of social structure on individuals. **Deviant behavior** is activity that violates the norms of an organization, community, or society. Consequently, deviance is culturally defined and socially labeled. Certain behaviors are also labeled as deviant because they conflict with the interests of the powerful in society. Public policy, then, reflects the values and interests of those in power and is codified into law. Members of society are also taught how to respond to deviants. The law and these structured responses to deviants are societal reactions that establish deviance in social roles; paradoxically, the degraded status that results from societal reactions reinforces the deviance that society seeks to control. Deviance, then, is fundamentally the result of social structure. Examine these processes in relation to two types of deviance: crime and drug use.

We must also look at the problems found within five representative institutions. First, address the allocation and remuneration of jobs. The number and types of jobs are undergoing a major shift with globalization and as society deindustrializes and moves toward a service economy. Although the resulting changes bring many opportunities, they also bring many problems, such as the widening gap between the haves and the have-nots and the emergence of a new form of poverty. Second, look at the family-related problems of child care, violence, and divorce. Third, consider how education, although necessary as the source for transmitting the necessary skills and shared understandings to each generation, is also a generator of social problems. Thus, it shows once again how social problems (in this case, inequality) originate in the basic structure of society. Fourth, study the reasons for the high cost of health care in the United States and the effort to reform the health care system. Last, analyze the policies of national security, especially the threat of terrorism.

What do we do about social problems? The solutions come from the bottom up—that is, people organize through human agency to change social structures (Eitzen and Stewart 2007). Solutions also come from the top down—social policies determined by the powerful (Eitzen and Sage 2007). Both of these forces and the interaction between the top and the bottom need to be explored.

■ CHAPTER REVIEW

1. Historically, U.S. sociologists have viewed social problems in terms of social pathology: "bad" people were assumed to be the sources of social problems because they disturbed the prevailing moral order in society.

2. In the 1920s and 1930s, sociologists focused on the conditions of society, such as the rapid changes accompanying urbanization and industrialization, as the sources of social problems.

3. More recently, many sociologists have returned to a study of problem individuals—deviants who violate the expectations of society. The modern study of deviance has developed in two directions. The first sought the sources of deviation within the social structure. The other, of relatively recent origin, has focused on the role of society in creating and sustaining deviance through labeling those viewed as abnormal. In this view, societal reactions are assumed to determine what a social problem is and who is deviant.

4. There is an objective reality to social problems; some conditions or situations do induce material and psychic suffering. There are several dangers, however, in defining social problems objectively. Subjectivity cannot be removed from the process. A standard must be selected, but in a pluralistic society, there are many standards. Moreover, social scientists not only disagree on what a social

problem is but also cannot escape their own values in the study of social problems. Most important, the objective approach to social problems entails acceptance of the definitions provided by the powerful. The acceptance of these definitions diverts attention away from the powerful and toward those the powerful wish to label negatively, thus deflecting observations away from what may constitute the most important social problem—the existing social order.

5. Examine two types of social problems: (a) acts and conditions that violate the norms and values of society and (b) societally induced conditions that cause psychic and material suffering for any segment of the population. The key to understanding both types of social problems is the distribution of power.

6. The sociological imagination involves (a) a willingness to view the social world from the perspective of others; (b) focusing on the social, economic, and historical circumstances that influence families, groups, and organizations; (c) questioning the structural arrangements that shape social behavior; and (d) seeing the solutions to social problems in terms not of changing problem people but of changing the structure of society.

7. The focus is on the structure of society rather than on "problem" individuals. A guiding assumption of our inquiry is that norm violators are symptoms of social problems. These deviants are, for the most part, victims and should not be blamed entirely for their deviance; the system in which they live should also be blamed.

8. The person-blame approach, which we do not use, has serious consequences: (a) The social sources of social problems are ignored. (b) It frees the institutions of society from any blame and efforts to change them. (c) It controls "problem" people in ways that reinforce negative stereotypes. (d) It legitimates person-control programs. (e) It justifies the logic of social Darwinism, which holds that people are rich or poor because of their ability and effort or lack thereof.

9. The system-blame orientation also has dangers. Taken dogmatically, it presents a rigidly deterministic explanation for social problems, suggesting that people are merely robots controlled by their social environment.

10. Sociology depends on reliable data and logical reason. Although value neutrality is impossible in the social sciences, bias is minimized by the norms of science.

11. Sociologists use a variety of methods: surveys, experiments, observation, and the use of existing data sources.

■ KEY TERMS

Subjective nature of social problems. What is and what is not a social problem is a matter of definition. Thus, social problems vary by time and place.

Objective reality of social problems. Some societal conditions harm certain segments of the population and therefore are social problems.

Self-actualization. The assumed need (by Maslow) of individuals for creative and constructive involvement in productive, significant activity.

Institutionalized deviance. When a society is organized in such a way as to disadvantage some of its members.

Social problems. Societally induced conditions that harm any segment of the population, and acts and conditions that violate the norms and values found in society.

Sociological imagination. C. Wright Mills's term emphasizing that individual troubles are inextricably linked to social forces.

Person-blame. The assumption that social problems result from the pathologies of individuals.

System-blame. The assumption that social problems result from social conditions.

Cultural deprivation. The assumption by the members of a group that the culture of some other group is not only inferior but also deficient. This term is usually applied by members of the majority to the culture of a minority group.

Recidivism. Reinvolvement in crime.

Social Darwinism. The belief that the place of people in the stratification system is a function of their ability and effort.

Deviant behavior. Activity that violates the norms of a social organization.

Sociological theory. A set of ideas that explains a range of human behavior and a variety of social and societal events.

Sample. A representative part of a population.

Variable. An attitude, behavior, or condition that can vary in magnitude and significance from case to case.

Longitudinal surveys. The collection of information about the same persons over many years.

Control group. The subjects not exposed to the independent variable.

Experimental group. The subjects exposed to the independent variable.

Dependent variable. The variable that is influenced by the effect of another variable.

Independent variable. A variable that affects another variable.

■ SUCCEED WITH mysoclab www.mysoclab.com

Experience, Discover, Observe, Evaluate
MySocLab is designed just for you. This chapter features a pre-test and post-test to help you learn and review key concepts and terms.

Experience sociology in action with dynamic visual activities, videos, and readings to enhance your learning experience. Complete the following activities at www.mysoclab.com.

Social Explorer is an interactive application that allows you to explore Census data through interactive maps.

- Explore the Social Explorer Map: *Create Your Own "Hypothetical Subway Ride"*

The Core Concepts in Sociology video clips offer a real-world perspective on sociological concepts.

- Watch *Anti-Abortion March*

MySocLibrary includes primary source readings from classic and contemporary sociologists.

- Read Babbie, *The Importance of Social Research;* Adler & Adler, *The Promise and Pitfalls of Going into the Field;* Coontz, *How History and Sociology Can Help Today's Families*

Wealth and Power: The Bias of the System

From Chapter 2 of *Social Problems, Census Update*, Twelfth Edition. D. Stanley Eitzen, Maxine Baca Zinn, Kelly Eitzen Smith.

Wealth and Power: The Bias of the System

We can have a democratic society or we can have the concentration of great wealth in the hands of a few. We cannot have both.

—Justice Louis Brandeis

The thesis of this text is that the problems of U.S. society result from the distribution of power and the form of the economy. This chapter begins the analysis of U.S. social problems by looking at the political and economic realities of interest groups and also at power, powerlessness, and domination. As we discuss, the state is not a neutral agent of the people but is biased in favor of those with wealth—the upper social classes and the largest corporations. As we analyze the bias of the system, we begin to see that, contrary to popular belief, the U.S. system does not produce a society that is democratic, just, and equal in opportunity. Rather, we find that the United States is an upside-down society, with the few benefiting at the expense of the many. Finally, we see how our society itself is the source of social problems.

The study of social problems requires the critical examination of the structure of society. Some readers will find this approach uncomfortable, even unpatriotic. In this regard, introducing his critical analysis of the United States, Michael Parenti said,

> If the picture that emerges in the pages ahead is not pretty, this should not be taken as an attack on the United States, for this country and the American people are greater than the abuses perpetrated upon them by those who live for power and profit. To expose these abuses is not to denigrate the nation that is a victim of them. The greatness of a country is to be measured by something more than its rulers, its military budget, its instruments of dominance and destruction, and its profiteering giant corporations. A nation's greatness can be measured by its ability to create a society free of poverty, racism, sexism, imperialism, and social and environmental devastation, and by the democratic nature of its institutions. Albert Camus once said, "I would like to love my country and justice too." In fact, there is no better way to love one's country, no better way to strive for the fulfillment of its greatness, than to entertain critical ideas and engage in the pursuit of social justice at home and abroad. (Parenti 1995b:6)

This chapter is divided into three sections. The first describes the U.S. economy, with its concentration of corporate and private wealth. The second examines the political system and its links to the economic elites. The final section shows how the politicoeconomic system is biased in favor of those who are already advantaged.

U.S. ECONOMY: CONCENTRATION OF CORPORATE WEALTH

The U.S. economy has always been based on the principles of capitalism; however, the present economy is far removed from a free enterprise system. The major discrepancy between the ideal system and the real one is that the U.S. economy is no longer based on competition among more-or-less equal private capitalists. It is now dominated by huge corporations that, contrary to classical economic theory, control demand rather than respond to the demands of the market. However well the economic system might once have worked, the increasing size and power of corporations disrupt it. This development calls into question what the appropriate economic form is for a modern industrialized society.

Monopolistic Capitalism

Karl Marx, more than 125 years ago, when bigness was the exception, predicted that capitalism was doomed by several inherent contradictions that would produce a class of people bent on destroying it (see the insert on Karl Marx and "self-destruct" capitalism). The most significant of these contradictions for our purposes is the inevitability of monopolies. Marx hypothesized that free enterprise would result in some firms becoming bigger and bigger as they eliminate their opposition or absorb smaller competing firms. The ultimate result of this process is the existence of a monopoly in each of the various sectors of the economy. Monopolies, of course, are antithetical to the free enterprise system because they, not supply and demand, determine the price and the quality of the product.

Karl Marx and Self-Destruct Capitalism

Karl Marx (1818–1883) was one of history's greatest social theorists. His ideas have fueled revolutionaries and revolutions. His writings have had an enormous impact on each of the social sciences. His intellectual contributions to sociology include (1) elaboration of the conflict model of society, (2) the theory of social change based on antagonisms between the social classes, (3) the insight that power originates primarily in economic production, and (4) concern with the social origins of alienation.

Marx believed that the basis of social order in every society is the production of economic goods. What is produced, how it is produced, and how it is exchanged determine the differences in people's wealth, power, and social status. Marx argued that because human beings must organize their activities to clothe, feed, and house themselves, every society is built on an economic base. The exact form this organization takes varies among societies and across time. The form that people chose to solve their basic economic problems would, according to Marx, eventually determine virtually everything in the social structure, including polity, family structure, education, and religion. In Marx's view, all these social institutions depend on the basic economy, and an analysis of society will always reveal its underlying economic arrangements.

Because it owns the means of production, the social class in power uses the noneconomic institutions to uphold its position. Thus, Marx believed that religion, the government, and the educational system are used by the powerful to maintain the status quo.

Marx argued that every economic system except **socialism** produces forces that eventually lead to a new economic form. In the feudal system, for example, the market and factory emerged but were incompatible with the feudal way of life. The market created a professional merchant class, and the factory created a proletariat. Thus, new inventions create a tension with the old institutions, and new social classes threaten to displace old ones. Conflict results, and society is rearranged with a new class structure and an alteration in the division of wealth and power based on a new economic form. Feudalism was replaced by capitalism; land ownership was replaced by factories and the ownership of capital.

Capitalism, Marx maintained, also carries the seeds of its own destruction. Capitalism will produce a class of oppressed people (the proletariat) bent on destroying it. The contradictions inherent in capitalism are (1) the inevitability of monopolies, which eliminate competition and gouge consumers and workers; (2) lack of centralized planning, which results in overproduction of some goods and underproduction of others, encouraging economic crises such as inflation, slumps, and depressions; (3) demands for labor-saving machinery, which force unemployment and a more hostile proletariat; (4) employers will tend to maximize profits by reducing labor expenses, thus creating a situation where workers will not have enough income to buy products, thus the contradiction of causing profits to fall; and (5) control of the state by the wealthy, the effect of which is passage of laws favoring themselves and thereby incurring more wrath from the proletariat. All these factors increase the probability that the proletariat will build class consciousness, which is the condition necessary to class conflict and the ushering in of a new economic system.

Sources: Robert J. Werlin. 1972. "Marxist Political Analysis." *Sociological Inquiry* 42 (Nos. 3–4):157–181; Karl Marx. 1976. *Karl Marx: Selected Writings in Sociology and Social Philosophy* (T. B. Bottomore, Trans.). New York: McGraw-Hill, pp. 127–212. See also Michael Harrington. 1976. *The Twilight of Capitalism.* New York: Simon & Schuster.

For the most part, the evidence in U.S. society upholds Marx's prediction. Less than 1 percent of all corporations produce over 80 percent of the private-sector output. Most sectors of the U.S. economy are dominated by a few corporations. Instead of one corporation controlling an industry, the typical situation is domination by a small number of large firms. When four or fewer firms supply 50 percent or more of a particular market, a shared monopoly results, which performs much as a monopoly or cartel would. Most economists agree that above this level of concentration—a four-firm ratio of 50 percent—the economic costs of shared monopoly are most manifest. Government data show that a number of industries are highly concentrated (e.g., each of the following industries has four or fewer firms controlling at least 60 percent: light bulbs, breakfast cereals, milk supply, turbines/generators, aluminum, cigarettes, beer, chocolate/cocoa, photography equipment, trucks, cosmetics, film distribution, soft drinks, snack foods, guided missiles, and roasted coffee; Mokhiber 2010).

This trend toward ever-greater concentration among the largest U.S. business concerns has accelerated because of two activities—mergers and interlocking directorates.

- **Megamergers.** There are thousands of mergers each year as giant corporations become even larger. In 2006, $1.45 trillion worth of mergers and acquisitions occurred in the United States, and in 2007, there were $1.21 trillion worth. The ten largest mergers in U.S. history have occurred in the past 15 years (i.e., Time, Inc., and AOL joining with Warner Communications; Disney merging with Capital Cities/ABC; the combining of Wells Fargo and First Interstate Banks; the merger of NationsBank and BankAmerica; Philip Morris taking over Miller Brewing; the AT&T buyout of Tele-Communications, Inc.; Citicorp merging with Travelers Group; Texaco buying out Getty Oil; Exxon merging with Mobil Oil; Exxon merging with XTO, and MCI World.Com's acquisition of Sprint). In the first three months of 2009, major mergers took place in the pharmaceutical industry as Pfizer bought Wyeth, Merck merged with Schering-Plough, Roche purchased Genentech, and Gilead Sciences merged with CV Therapeutics. There have also been megamergers combining U.S. and foreign firms (e.g., Daimler and Chrysler, British Petroleum and Amoco, and Deutsche Bank and Bankers Trust). The federal government encouraged these mergers by relaxing antitrust law enforcement on the grounds that efficient firms should not be hobbled.

  This trend toward megamergers has at least five negative consequences: (1) it increases the centralization of capital, which reduces competition and raises prices for consumers; (2) it increases the power of huge corporations over workers, unions, politicians, and governments; (3) it reduces the number of jobs (for example, when Qwest combined with US West, 11,000 jobs were eliminated); (4) it increases corporate debt; and (5) it is nonproductive. Elaborating on this last point, mergers and takeovers do not create new plants, products, or jobs. Rather, they create profits for chief executive officers, lawyers, accountants, brokers, bankers, and big investors.

- **Interlocking Directorates.** Another mechanism for the ever-greater concentration of the size and power of the largest corporations is interlocking directorates, the linkage between corporations that results when an individual serves on the board of directors of two companies (a direct interlock) or when two companies each have a director on the board of a third company (an indirect interlock). These arrangements have great potential to benefit the interlocked companies by reducing competition through the sharing of information and the coordination of policies.

In 1914, the Clayton Act made it illegal for a person to serve simultaneously on corporate boards of two companies that were in direct competition with each other. Financial institutions and indirect interlocks, however, were exempt. Moreover, the government has had difficulty determining what constitutes "direct competition." The result is that, despite the prohibition, over 90 percent of large U.S. corporations have some interlocking directors with other corporations. When directors are linked directly or indirectly, the potential exists for cohesiveness, common action, and unified power. Clearly, the principles of capitalism are compromised when this phenomenon occurs.

Despite the relative noncompetitiveness among the large corporations, many of them devote considerable efforts to convincing the public that the U.S. economy is competitive. Many advertisements depict the economy as an Adam Smith–style free market with competition among innumerable small competitors. This, however, is a myth. Competition does exist among the mom-and-pop stores, but they control only a minute portion of the nation's assets. The largest assets are located among the very large corporations, and competition there is minimal.

CASE STUDY   Media Monopolies

The media, through movies, television, radio, books, magazines, newspapers, and advertising, are major players in the creation of the culture, shaping what we think and do. The media play an influential role in a democracy because a democracy hinges on whether there is an informed electorate. The people need unbiased information and the push-and-pull of public debate if they are to be truly informed. These conditions become problematic, however, when the sources of information are increasingly concentrated in a few huge conglomerates guided only by commercial and bottom-line values. In 1983, fifty corporations controlled media in the United States. Now there are five—News Corporation, General Electric, Disney, Time Warner, and Viacom. Consider the range and scope of their media holdings (*The Nation* 2006:23–26):

- Viacom owns CBS, UPN, Simon & Schuster, Pocket Books, Scribner, Free Press, Paramount Pictures, DreamWorks, MTV, Nickelodeon, Nick at Night, *The Daily Show with Jon Stewart,* TV Land, CMT, VH1, Showtime, Movie Channel, Sundance Channel, Flick, Black Entertainment, and Comedy Central, to name a few of their holdings.
- Some of Time Warner's holdings include *Time, People, Sports Illustrated, Fortune, Entertainment Weekly, Popular Science,* AOL, CompuServe, Netscape, CNN, Cinemax, NASCAR.com, Warner Brothers Pictures, Warner Brothers Cable, TBS, TNT, Cartoon Network, HBO, The Movie Channel, and Court TV.
- A sample of News Corporation's media holdings includes Fox News, Fox Sports, Fox Business Network, National Geographic Channel, 175 newspapers worldwide, Speed, Twentieth Century Fox, 28 television stations in the United States, *New York Post, The Wall Street Journal, Weekly Standard, TV Guide, Barron's,* HarperCollins, ReganBooks, Zondervan Publishing, FX, and My Space.
- Disney's media affiliates are ABC, ESPN, The Disney Channel, E! Entertainment, The History Channel, Disney Publishing, Hyperion Books, ABC Radio (73 stations), Walt Disney Pictures, Miramax Films, Buena Vista Productions, and Pixar.
- Some of General Electric's media holdings are NBC, 14 television stations in major markets, Telemundo, Universal Pictures, Universal Studios, CNBC, MSNBC, Bravo,

AP Images/Peter Cosgrove

In addition to amusement parks, Disney has media holdings including ABC, ESPN, The Disney Channel, Hyperion Books, ABC radio, Walt Disney Pictures, Miramax Films, Buena Vista Productions, and Pixar.

USA Network, and A & E. Late in 2009, Comcast attempted a merger with NBC Universal, "marrying" the largest cable company and the biggest residential Internet server provider. Should this merger be approved, the resulting Comcast/NBC would own 52 cable channels including the Golf channel, PBS Kids, E!, and the NBC channels listed earlier, 27 local TV stations, and the NBC network.

In addition to these media giants, ten companies broadcast to two-thirds of the nation's radio audience. One of these, Clear Channel Communications, owns more than 1,200 radio stations, each day reaching 54 percent of all people in the United States ages 18 to 49. Clear Channel also owns 42 television stations and a substantial number of billboards and other outdoor advertising.

Three-quarters of cable channels are owned by six corporate entities, four of which are the major TV networks

Pearson Higher Education is the world's largest publisher of college textbooks. Included among its subsidiaries are Addison-Wesley (Allyn and Bacon, the publisher of this text, is part of that organization), Prentice Hall, Scott Foresman, and Penguin. College textbook publishing in the United States is dominated by Pearson, Thomson, and McGraw-Hill.

In 1965, there were 860 owners of daily newspapers. Today there are fewer than 300. Many cities now have only one major newspaper. The most important newspapers are (1) the *New York Times,* which also owns the *Boston Globe* and 15 other daily newspapers, as well as television and radio stations, and (2) the *Washington Post,* owner of *Newsweek,* as well as other newspapers and TV and cable stations.

These examples show the extent to which a few major corporations control what we see, hear, and read. What does it mean when the information and entertainment we receive are increasingly under monopolized control? First, the media help to define reality by determining what is important and, conversely, what is not. This shapes our understanding of what is a social problem. For instance, the evening news focuses much more on street crime, using a disproportionate number of images of people of color as perpetrators, than it does on white-collar and corporate crime.

Second, diverse opinions are rarely heard. Because a few media giants control the content and distribution of programming, smaller companies with distinctive viewpoints are increasing rare. The content of talk radio, for example, leans heavily to the political right, as evidenced by the views of Rush Limbaugh, Glenn Beck, G. Gordon Liddy, Oliver North, Sean Hannity, Armstrong Williams, Michael Savage, Bob Grant, and Laura Ingraham. In a nation that is divided more or less equally politically, there are few, if any, progressive voices on the radio.

Third, reporting is sometimes compromised by conflict of interest. For example, did NBC, when it was owned by General Electric, report extensively on the long-term contamination of the Hudson River by a GE plant? Similarly, media corporations might shy away from news that is too critical of the government because of the corporation's political leanings, they do not want to offend customers, or they depend on government subsidies and favorable legislation.

Fourth, a media giant may, through its subsidiaries, push a political stance. For example, Clear Channel Communications, with more than 1,200 radio stations, used its considerable market power to drum up support for the war in Iraq. Following the 9/11 terrorist attacks, songs such as Cat Stevens's "Peace Train" and John Lennon's "Imagine" were blacklisted in the corporation's stations. The network sponsored prowar rallies and a continuous barrage of uncritical comment (Marshall 2003). When one of the Dixie Chicks said that she was ashamed that President Bush came from Texas, Clear Channel Communications banned the Dixie Chicks' music from its country music stations (as did Cumulus Media).

Fifth, big stories (war, corruption, the economy, legislation) are often pushed aside in favor of "hot" stories, such as kidnappings and murders, and salacious stories about celebrities, such as the philandering behavior of Tiger Woods, that entice audiences with their sensationalism.

Finally, the messages we hear and see tend to focus on problem individuals rather than on problems with structural origins. Thus, the media pull us away from sociological interpretations—with critical consequences for social policy.

Transnational Corporations

The thesis of the previous section is that there is a trend for corporations to increase in size, resulting eventually in huge enterprises that join with other large companies to form effective monopolies. This process of economic concentration provides the largest companies with enormous economic and political power. If, for example, we compare government budgets with gross corporate revenues, in 2003, the total sales of Wal-Mart, British Petroleum, and ExxonMobil each exceeded the gross domestic product of Indonesia (the fourth most populous country in the world). Combining these three transnational corporations, their sales revenues were more than the combined economies of the world's poorest 118 countries (Teller-Elsberg, Folbre, and Heintz 2006:15).

Another trend—the globalization of the largest U.S. corporations—makes their power all the greater. This fact of international economic life has very important implications for social problems, both at home and abroad.

A number of U.S. corporations have substantial assets overseas, with the trend to increase these investments rapidly. In 2008, five of the top ten multinationals in sales were U.S.-based corporations (*Forbes* 2009a:130). Why are U.S. corporations shifting more and more of their total assets outside the United States? The obvious answer is that the rate of profit tends to be higher abroad. Resources necessary for manufacture and production tend to be cheaper in many other nations. Most significant, U.S. corporations increase their profits by moving their production facilities from high-wage situations to low-wage nonunion countries. Moreover, foreign production costs are lower because labor safety laws and environmental protection laws are much more lax than in the United States.

The consequences of this shift in production from the United States to other countries are significant. Most important is the reduction or even drying up of many semiskilled and unskilled jobs in the United States. The effects of increased unemployment are twofold: increased welfare costs and increased discontent among people in the working class.

Another result of the twin processes of concentration and internationalization of corporations is the enormous power wielded by gigantic transnational corporations. In essence, the largest corporations control the world economy. Their decisions to build or not to build, to relocate a plant, or to start a new product or scrap an old one have tremendous impacts on the lives of ordinary citizens in the countries they operate from and invest in and on their disinvestment in U.S.-based operations.

Finally, transnational corporations tend to meddle in the internal affairs of other nations to protect their investments and maximize profits. These activities include attempts to overthrow governments considered unfriendly to corporate interests and payment of millions of dollars in bribes and political contributions to reactionary governments and conservative leaders in various countries.

Concentration of Wealth

The other discrepancy between free enterprise in its real and ideal states is the undue concentration of wealth among a few individuals and corporations. This imbalance makes a mockery of claims that capitalism rewards the efforts of all enterprising individuals.

- **Concentration of Corporate Wealth.** Wealth in the business community is centralized in a relatively few major corporations, and this concentration is increasing. In 2008, for example, the U.S. corporation with the most assets ($2.175 trillion) was JPMorgan Chase; the top corporation in sales—Wal-Mart— had $405.6 billion in revenues; and the greatest producer of profits was Exxon-Mobil at $45.22 billion (*Forbes* 2009a:128-133). The following examples show just how concentrated wealth is among the major U.S. corporations:

  - Less than 1 percent of all corporations account for over 80 percent of the total output of the private sector.
  - Of the 15,000 commercial U.S. banks, the largest 50 hold more than one-third of all assets.
  - One percent of all food corporations control 80 percent of all the industry's assets and about 90 percent of the profits.
  - Six transnational corporations ship 90 percent of the grain in the world market.

- **Concentration of Private Wealth and Income.** Capitalism generates inequality. Wealth is concentrated not only in the largest corporations but also among individuals and families. For example, in 2009, according to *Forbes* (2009b), the two wealthiest were Bill Gates, head of software giant Microsoft, with an estimated fortune of $50 billion, and Warren Buffett of Berkshire Hathaway, with

"Hold it! We almost forgot your backdated stock options."

$40 billion. Each of the four heirs to the Wal-Mart fortune was worth from $19.0 billion to $21.5 billion.

The concentration of wealth is greatly skewed. Consider the following facts:

- The combined net worth of the 400 richest Americans in 2009 was more wealth than the total for the bottom 155 million Americans (DeGraw, 2010).
- In 2007, the latest year for data from the Federal Reserve Board, the richest 1 percent of U.S. households owned 33.8 percent of the nation's private wealth. That is more than the combined wealth of the bottom 90 percent (Kennickell, 2009).
- From 1980 to 2006 the richest 1 percent of Americans tripled their after-tax percentage of the nation's total income, while the income of the bottom 90 percent dropped by over 20 percent (DeGraw, 2010).

The data on wealth always show more concentration than do income statistics, but the convergence of money among the few is still very dramatic when considering income. The share of the national income of the richest 20 percent of households was 50.3 percent, while the bottom 20 percent received only 3.4 percent of the nation's income in 2009. The data in Table 1 show that income inequality is increasing in U.S. society. Especially noteworthy is the sharp gain in the Gini index, which measures the magnitude of income concentration from 1970 to 2009. (See Table 1.)

Another measure of this increasing gap is the difference in earnings between the heads of corporations and the workers in those corporations. In 1960, the average chief executive officer (CEO) of a *Fortune* 500 corporation was paid 40 times more than the average worker. By 2007, it had risen dramatically to 344 times more. The top 50 hedge fund and private equity managers received more than 19,000 times as much as typical workers earned.

The inequality gap has risen dramatically for a number of reasons. The gain at the top reflects the increased tax benefits received by the affluent from changing tax laws. Another factor explaining this inequality gap is the changing

			Percentage Distribution of Aggregate Income			
Year	Lowest Fifth	Second Fifth	Third Fifth	Fourth Fifth	Highest Fifth	Gini* Index
2009	3.4	8.6	14.6	23.2	50.3	.468
1990	3.9	9.6	15.9	24.0	46.6	.428
1980	4.3	10.3	16.9	24.9	44.7	.403
1970	4.1	10.8	17.4	24.5	43.3	.394

TABLE 1

Share of Aggregate Income by Each Fifth of Households, 1970, 1980, 1990, 2009

*The income inequality of a population group is commonly measured using the Gini index. The Gini index ranges from 0, indicating perfect equality (i.e., all persons having equal shares of the aggregate income), to 1, indicating perfect inequality (i.e., where all of the income is received by only one recipient or one group of recipients and the rest have none). The increase in the Gini index for household income between 1970 and 2009 indicates a significant increase in income inequality.

Sources: U.S. Bureau of the Census, Current Population Surveys. Online. Available: http://www.census.gov/hhes/www/incineq.html. U.S. Census Bureau, Current Population Survey, 2009 and 2010 Annual Social and Economic Supplements.

SOCIAL POLICY

GOVERNMENT POLICIES EXACERBATE WEALTH INEQUALITY

Government policies have the power to expand or reduce the gap between the haves and the have-nots. Consider what we could do to lift up the underserved:

We could truly address the disgraceful truth that in this rich nation one in six children is raised in poverty and deprived of the healthy, fair start vital to equal opportunity. Now we have the resources to rebuild an aging and overburdened infrastructure—witnessed daily in power blackouts, collapsing sewers and aged water systems, overburdened airports, deferred toxic waste cleanups. Now we can redress the growing shortage of affordable housing and insure that every American has access to healthcare. (Borosage 2001:5).

All these actions are within our reach, but the decision makers have ruled them out, making the reduction of taxes paramount, which increases the inequality gap, already the most unequal by far among the industrialized nations. Economist Paul Krugman argued that current government policies entrench the advantages of the haves. Examples (Krugman, 2004:17):

- Getting rid of the estate tax so that large fortunes can be passed on to the next generation.
- Reducing tax rates both on corporate profits and on unearned income such as dividends and capital gains so that the wealthy can more easily accumulate even more.
- Reducing tax rates on people with high incomes, shifting the burden to the payroll tax and other revenue sources that bear most heavily on people with lower incomes.
- On the spending side, cutting back on health care for the poor, on the quality of public education, and on state aid for higher education. This makes it more difficult for people with low incomes to achieve upward mobility.

The affluent, by paying less in taxes, will, in effect, withdraw their support from programs that help those who are poor, those who do not have health insurance, and those who cannot afford decent housing. Former secretary of labor Robert Reich argues that what is really at issue here is the sorting of America, where our society is becoming more rigidly stratified. Reich says,

There's only one way to reverse the sorting mechanism. . . . We have to rededicate ourselves to strong public institutions that are indubitably public because they work well for everyone. Of course this means more money and higher performance standards. But it also requires a renewed public spiritedness—a we're-all-in-this-together patriotism that says it's good for Americans to transcend class, race, education, health, and fortune, and to participate together. (Reich 2000b:64)

© 2005 Matt Wuerker. Used with the permission of Matt Wuerker and the Cartoonist Group.

job structure as the economy shifts from manufacturing to service and as U.S. jobs are exported. At the upper end, corporate executives added handsomely to their incomes while downsizing their domestic workforces. Congress has increased this upper-class feast by reducing taxes on capital gains (taxes on the profits from the sale of property) and by allowing the affluent to place as much of their income as they wish in special tax-deferred pay plans not available to the less well-to-do. Most significant were the tax cuts in 2001 and 2003. Since 2001, they resulted in $491 billion going to the richest 1 percent (Drucker 2008). To illustrate, in the 2008 tax year, households in the bottom 20 percent received $26 from these tax cuts while households in the top 1 percent received $50,495, and households in the top 0.1 percent received $266,151 in tax savings. See the "Social Policy" panel for more government policies that increase the inequality gap.

The recent tax policies have four major consequences. First, they exacerbate the unequal distribution of wealth in the United States, which is already the most unequal in the Western world. Second, the huge tax cuts are in place at the very time that the U.S. is conducting two costly wars in Iraq and Afghanistan and spending huge amounts to get the country out of the greatest economic disaster since the Great Depression. The result is a dramatic increase in the national debt. This leads to the third consequence: the ever-increasing debt will have the effect of reducing government spending for programs that help the less fortunate, and it will weaken public institutions that benefit society. As the late political observer Molly Ivins has put it,

The . . . reason it's dumb to cut taxes for the rich is the problem of social justice.
We're already in trouble because the income gap between the rich and the rest
of us keeps getting worse and worse. The rich buy their way out of our public

institutions—schools, hospitals, parks—and then contribute money to politicians who let the public infrastructure go to hell. It doesn't work. (Ivins 2003:39A)

Ivins points to the fourth negative consequence of the widening gap between the haves and the have-nots—the increasing political influence of the wealthy, which is the topic of the next section.

POLITICAL SYSTEM: LINKS BETWEEN WEALTH AND POWER

In many ways, the U.S. government represents the privileged few rather than the majority. Although the government appears democratic, with elections, political parties, and the right to dissent, the influence of wealth prevails. This influence is seen in the disproportionate rewards the few receive from the politicoeconomic system and in government decisions that consistently benefit them. Senator Bernie Sanders argues that the United States is, increasingly, an oligarchy. An **oligarchy** is a government ruled by the few. In Sanders's words, "Oligarchy refers . . . to the fact that the decisions that shape our consciousness and affect our lives are made by a very small and powerful group of people" (Sanders 1994:B1). Other critics have taken this a step further, suggesting that the United States is a **plutocracy** (a government by or in the interest of the rich; e.g., Parenti 2008: 27–39). In the words of Kevin Phillips, a conservative scholar,

By 2000 the United States could be said to have a plutocracy. . . . Compared with 1990, America's top millennial fortunes were three or four times bigger, reflecting the high-powered convergence of innovation, speculation, and mania in finance and technology. Moreover, the essence of plutocracy, fulfilled by 2000, has been the determination and ability of wealth to reach beyond its own realm of money and control politics and government as well. (Phillips 2002:xv; emphasis added)

Government by Interest Groups

Democracy may be defined as a political system that is of, by, and for the people. It is a system under which the will of the majority prevails, there is equality before the law, and decisions are made to maximize the common good. The principles that define a democracy are violated by the rules of the Senate (see "A Closer Look," The Structure of the Senate as a Barrier to Democracy), special-interest groups, which by deals, propaganda, and the financial support of political candidates attempt to deflect the political process for their own benefit. Individuals, families, corporations, unions, professional associations, and various other organizations use a variety of means to obtain tax breaks, favors, subsidies, favorable rulings, and the like from Congress and its committees, regulatory agencies, and executive bureaucracies. Among the means used to accomplish their goals are the following:

[A]long with the slick brochures and expert testimony corporate, lobbyists offer the succulent campaign contributions, the "volunteer" campaign workers to help members of Congress get reelected, the fat lecture fees, easy-term loans, prepaid vacation jaunts, luxury resorts, four-star restaurants, lush buffets, lavish parties with attractive escorts, stadium suites at major sporting events, and the many other hustling enticements of money. (Parenti 2008:213).

A CLOSER LOOK

THE STRUCTURE OF THE SENATE AS A BARRIER TO DEMOCRACY

The U.S. Senate is designed to thwart popular will in at least two ways: the filibuster and the disproportionate power of small states.

The filibuster is a self-imposed rule not found in the Constitution. It is the practice of holding the Senate floor to prevent a vote on a bill. In 1917 the Senate adopted a rule that allowed the Senate to end a debate with a two-thirds majority vote for "cloture." For the next 50 years, the Senate tried to invoke cloture but usually failed to gain the necessary two-thirds votes. Filibusters were used primarily by segregationists seeking to derail civil rights legislation. South Carolina's Strom Thurmond, for example, filibustered for 24 hours and 18 minutes (the all-time record) against the Civil Rights Act of 1957. The southern senators tried to stymie antilynching legislation in the Civil Rights Act of 1964, but failed when cloture was invoked after a fifty-seven-day filibuster. In 1975, the Senate reduced the number of votes required for cloture from two-thirds (67) to three-fifths (60). That is the rule now in place.

The political composition of the Senate in 2010 was 57 Democrats, 2 Independents who caucus with the Democrats, and 39 Republicans. Despite the public's election of a Democratic president in 2008 and adding enough Democrats to have large majorities in Congress, the Democrats have not been able to get legislation passed for two reasons: the Republicans vote as a bloc to block the agenda of the Democrats and the difficulty in garnering 60 votes to defeat a filibuster. The use of the filibuster

or the threat of a filibuster, once a relatively rare parliamentary move, has become commonplace. Political scientist Barbara Sinclair has found that in the 1960s, extended-debate-related problems affected only 8 percent of major legislation. By the '80s this had risen to 27 percent. Since 2006, when Republicans became a minority, it was 70 percent (reported in Krugman, 2009b). As a result, the health reform package was watered down and a few wavering centrist Democrats were allowed to shape the bill to their liking.

The majority, which won so conclusively in 2008 should be able to make major changes. As Paul Krugman has said:

We need to deal with climate change. We need to deal with our long-run budget deficit. What are the chances that we can do all that . . . if doing anything requires 60 votes in a deeply polarized Senate? . . . . Our current situation is unprecedented: America is caught between severe problems that must be addressed and a minority party determined to block action on every front. Doing nothing is not an option—not unless you want the nation to sit motionless, with an effectively paralyzed government, waiting for financial, environmental and fiscal crises to strike. (Krugman 2009b, para 12)

Added to the filibuster is that the Senate is designed to thwart popular will by giving extraordinary power to small states (the following is from MacGillis 2009). For example, the key senators drafting health reform legislation,

the so-called "Gang of Six" (three Democrats and three Republicans) came from the least-populous states, states with few voters who swept Obama to victory and with so few uninsured people. In total these states hold 8.4 million people—less than New Jersey—and represent only 3 percent of the U.S. population. Climate change legislation, which passed the House, faces tough odds in the Senate because the states dominated by agriculture, coal, and oil, which are typically underpopulated states, are opposed. The coal state of Wyoming has a single vote in the House, compared to New York's 29 and California's 53. In the Senate, each state has two. North and South Dakota with a combined population of 1.4 million has twice as many in the Senate as Florida (18.3 million) or Texas (24.3 million) or Illinois (12.9 million). A few additional inequities with each state having two senators, regardless of population size:

- California is 70 times as large as the smallest state, Wyoming.
- The 10 largest states have more than half the people in the United States, yet have only a fifth of the votes in the Senate.
- The 21 smallest states combined have fewer people than California, yet they have 42 senators, while California has only two.

Although three small states (Vermont, Delaware, and Rhode Island) favor the Democrats, most of the states with small populations and large land areas are staunchly Republican. Thus, the Senate structure is not only unequal, it has a built-in bias. Is this what the founders of the United States had in mind when they wrote the Constitution?

Special interests (e.g., National Rifle Association [NRA], the pharmaceutical industry, labor unions, dairy farmers) hire lobbyists to persuade legislators to vote their way. At the national level, lobbying in 2008 was a $3.3 billion business. There were twenty-three lobbyists for each member of Congress in 2008 (Eggen 2009b). Lobbyists for the health industry alone, for example, outnumbered the members of Congress by 3,300 to 535 and spent more than $1 million a day trying to influence legislation on health-related issues (Kroll 2009).

Interested parties lobby because there can be a significant payoff. In 2003 and 2004, for example, 840 U.S. corporations lobbied Congress to change the tax laws enabling transnational companies to bring home their overseas earnings at a tax rate of 5.25 percent instead of 35 percent (the following is from Belsie 2009). They succeeded, accruing benefits through the new law—the American Jobs Creation Act of 2004. These benefits were stunning. For every dollar spent on lobbying for the tax break, corporations reaped a $220 benefit on their U.S. taxes—*a 22,000 percent return on their investment*. For those corporations spending more than $1 million on tax lobbying did even better—a 24,300 percent return. For example, Eli Lilly & Co. spent $8.52 million lobbying for this bill. It reaped more than $2 billion in return.

The argument supporting lobbying is that on various issues, there are lobbyists on both sides. Thus, it is argued, there is a balance of viewpoints that legislators weigh in their decision making. The evidence, however, does not support such a cheerful view (Parenti 2008:215). The existence of lobbyists does not ensure that the national interest will be served but only that the interests of the powerful typically get their way. For instance, from 1998 to 2008 the financial sector spent more than $5 billion on campaign contributions (Nader 2010). With these contributions, along with the efforts of as many as 3,000 lobbyists, the business community was able to get Congress and executive agencies to reduce or eliminate regulatory restraints and to not enforce rules that were in place. Combined, these deregulatory moves helped pave the way for the current financial meltdown (Weissman 2009), and the massive oil leakage along the Gulf coast. Moreover, the interests of the powerless are not heard. Who, for example, speaks for the interests of minority groups, the poor, the mentally retarded, children, renters, migrant workers—in short, who speaks for the relatively powerless? And if there is a voice for these people, does it match the clout of lobbyists backed by immense financial resources?

Financing of Political Campaigns

Perhaps one of the most undemocratic features (at least in its consequences) of the U.S. political system is how political campaigns are financed. (See A Closer Look for the other undemocratic features.) Campaigns are becoming increasingly expensive, with money needed to pay for staff, direct-mail operations, phone banks, computers, consultants, and media advertising. The cost of the presidential and congressional election in 2008 was $5.3 billion (up from $2.2 billion in 1996), including monies from the federal government, individuals, political parties, and organizations outside political parties. Candidate Barack Obama raised $750 million for his presidential campaign in 2008, a record amount. Compare this with the $650 million that President Bush and Senator John Kerry collected together for their campaigns in 2004.

The cost of winning a seat in Congress is enormous. In 2008, the average winning House race cost $1.1 million, and the average winning Senate race

A CLOSER LOOK

UNDEMOCRATIC ELECTIONS IN A DEMOCRACY?

A democracy is a political system that is of, by, and for the people. Democratic principles include (1) fair and open elections; (2) access by the people to accurate information; (3) accountability of the governors to the governed; (4) political equality among all citizens; and (5) due process of law. The United States claims to be a democracy. Is it?

The short answer is that the United States is a democracy in theory but not always in practice. We focus here on elections. Indian novelist Arundhati Roy has said this about elections: "I think it is dangerous to confuse the idea of democracy with elections. Just because you have elections doesn't mean you're a democratic country" (cited in Mickey Z 2006:7). Consider the following undemocratic practices in U.S. elections.

First, the writers of the Constitution framed what they considered a democracy, but they allowed voting only for White male property owners, which, of course, excluded women, Native Americans, Blacks, and renters. Senators were not popularly elected. Clearly, most of the governed had no power. The framers also set up the Electoral College, a device that gave the ultimate power of electing the president to the elite in each state and gave extraordinary power to the least populous states. Now most of these undemocratic principles have been overturned by amendments to the Constitution. But the Electoral College remains, allowing for a president to be elected with fewer votes than his or her opponent (e.g., George W. Bush was elected in 2000 with 539,893 *fewer* votes than

Al Gore). The Electoral College gives *all* electoral votes from a state to the winner in that state (e.g., in 2000 with nearly 3 million votes cast in Florida, George W. Bush won by a disputed margin of 537 votes and received *all* of Florida's electoral votes, giving Bush a majority in the Electoral College). And, to top it all, an electoral vote in Wyoming (in 2004) corresponded to 167,081 persons, while an electoral vote in California represented 645,172 persons (because the number of electors is determined by the number of senators and representatives in that state, giving states with small populations disproportionate votes). In short, the Electoral College may or may not reflect the popular will. Clearly, "the democratic faith in majority rule sustains and validates every other form of American election, but the election of the president takes place in an

cost $6.5 million. Obviously, candidates must either be wealthy or accept money from various sources to finance their expensive campaigns. These costly campaigns favor incumbents, who have an easier time raising money.

In 2002, Congress passed the Bipartisan Campaign Reform Act (also known as the McCain-Feingold law). This law limited the use of "soft money" in federal elections. Before this act was passed, individuals, corporations, unions, and other organizations were allowed to give unlimited amounts of money to political parties at the national, state, and local levels or to other private organizations that are technically independent of the candidates. Because this tactic was not covered by the election laws, the amounts raised were unlimited. This loophole was used by wealthy persons to contribute to the Republican and Democratic national parties (and indirectly to the presidential candidates).

McCain-Feingold did eliminate soft money in federal elections (buttressed by a favorable Supreme Court decision in 2003), but it did not limit the giving of large sums to affect election outcomes. A number of ways were employed to navigate the system and give large donations to build support among Democrat or Republican voters. The loophole used is called 527s, which are advocacy groups, tax exempt under Section 527 of the Internal Revenue Code, that finance political advertisements while not directly calling for the election or

alternative universe" (Lapham 2004:8).

The winner-take-all system means that minorities may not be represented. Assume that a state has five districts, each electing a representative to the House of Representatives. If this state is predominantly Republican, it could have all five Republican representatives even though 40 percent (in this hypothetical case) are Democrats. Also, what if 30 percent of the state is Latino? It is possible that their voice will not be heard in Washington. Similarly, a city may have a seven-member city council elected at large by majority vote. The usual result is that not one council member represents a poor section of the city.

Disenfranchisement also occurs when state legislatures under partisan control deliberately shape congressional districts (called *gerrymandering*) to increase their advantage. By moving the district boundaries (made all the easier these days with computers), the party in power can take an area that is overwhelmingly composed of their party members and move some of them to a neighboring area that is more evenly split. In this way, they can make both districts *their* districts. This rigging of the system means, in effect, that the public is denied a choice. "By trying to fix the outcomes of House races before Election Day, professional partisans are effectively disenfranchising voters" (*USA Today* 2002b:13A).

The two-party system that has emerged in the United States (political parties are not mentioned in the Constitution) is a major impediment to democracy. Corporations, special interests, and wealthy individuals sponsor both parties. The federal government subsidizes the two major parties, which keeps the strong parties strong and the weak parties weak. Third-party candidates are often excluded from political debates because, it is argued, they have no chance of winning. The election laws also make it difficult for third parties to get on the ballot. "How can U.S. elections be deemed truly democratic when only 'major' candidates are allowed to participate in televised debates and only those accepting inordinate amounts of cash from wealthy/corporate donors are considered 'major' candidates?" (Mickey Z 2006:7).

Finally, as shown in this chapter, money makes the difference in politics. The people get to vote between candidates selected by the wealthy (corporations, interest groups, or individuals), which means that voting does not always express the public will. As Mark Green says: "Because average voters pull levers but big donors pull strings, often public sentiment wants one thing while political elites deliver something else" (Green 2006:6). Thus, when public sentiment is at odds with the moneyed interests, the public often loses.

defeat of specific candidates (Dwyer 2004). Democrats, for example, created such organizations as the Media Fund and America Coming Together. Working through these organizations, billionaires George Soros and Peter Lewis pledged a total of $15 million, creating among other strategies the liberal Internet organization MoveOn.org. Republicans have set up comparable groups, such as the Leadership Forum, a fund-raising group headed by Washington lobbyists.

McCain-Feingold also limited maximum contributions to $2,300 per election cycle. While technically adhering to this limitation, corporate executives, lobbyists, and other insiders could maximize their political influence by a sophisticated system of bundling—the pooling of a large number of contributions. This tactic is used by both political parties.

Another method to raise money is through contributions to a "foundation" or to the favorite charity. Through this loophole, donors could give unlimited contributions to a candidate. For example, during the 2008 campaign, four major defense contractors—Northrop Grumman, General Dynamics, Boeing, and Lockheed Martin—donated hundreds of thousands of dollars to the symphony orchestra in Johnstown, Pennsylvania. Why? Well, the orchestra is a favorite charity of Representative John Murtha, the chairman of the congressional committee that gives out lucrative defense contracts (Hernandez and

'...with liberty and justice for sale.'

Chen 2008). Similarly lobbyists can donate to favorite causes of the legislator, such as $336,224 that Representative James Clyburn received for his James E. Clyburn Research and Scholarship Foundation (Schouten and Overberg 2009). A fourth way to funnel special interest money legally is to honor members of Congress. In 2008 special interests donated $35.8 million to honor legislators. A fifth source of money is the contributions to the political conventions. In 2008, for example, the cost of the Democratic convention in Denver was underwritten by such entities as Quest Communications ($3 million), Molson Coors Brewing ($1 million), the American Federation of Teachers ($750,000), and the American Federation of State, County and Municipal Employees $500,000 (Schouten and O'Driscoll 2007; Schouten 2008). The Republican convention in Minneapolis received many millions as well from special interests. Similarly, corporations and wealthy individuals spent millions to fund Obama's inauguration in 2009. Although technically not a political contribution, the parties and candidates are beholden to the contributing corporations.

- **The Supreme Court Decision (*Citizens United v. Federal Election Commission*) in 2010.** As noted, while McCain-Feingold attempted to control spending, it was not always successful because of various ways to evade the law. With a Supreme Court decision in 2010, however, these efforts to get around McCain-Feingold were no longer necessary. By a landmark 5–4 decision the Supreme Court struck down the laws of 22 states and the federal government. It invalidated part of the McCain-Feingold campaign finance reform law that sought to limit corporate influence by ruling that the constitutional guarantee of free speech means that corporations, labor unions, and other organizations can spend unlimited sums to help elect or defeat political candidates.* These organizations

---

*It is important to point out that although labor unions have the same right as corporations to spend freely in elections, they are no match to the corporations. The Center for Responsive Politics provides the data from the 2007–2008 election cycle: (1) corporations gave $1.964 billion in federal campaign contributions, compared to labor, which spent $74.8 million—a 15–1 disadvantage for labor (cited in Bybee, 2010); and (2) business and corporate interests accounted for 70.8 percent of the total political contributions, while only 2.7 percent came from labor (cited in Chapin 2010).

In 2010 by a 5–4 vote, the Supreme Court gave organizations the right to use unlimited funds to sway prospective voters.

UPI/Gary Fabiano/Pool/Landov

are still barred from making direct contributions to politicians but they can now legally give unlimited amounts for ads to sway voters, as long as the ads are produced independently and not coordinated with a candidate's campaign. In effect, Exxon can spend millions to defeat an environmentalist candidate or Goldman Sachs could fund the entire cost of every congressional campaign in the United States (Alter 2010). As the *New York Times* editorialized: "The court's conservative majority has paved the way for corporations to use their vast treasuries to overwhelm elections and intimidate elected officials into doing their bidding" (*New York Times* 2010a, para 1).

This ruling has changed the political landscape. Small donors, who played a major role in the 2008 presidential election, have become irrelevant, being unable to match corporate treasuries. Somehow money has been interpreted by a majority of the Supreme Court to be a form of speech, and big money trumps small money. So the "speech" of the well-heeled is more important than the "speech" of ordinary citizens. Future elections will likely be inundated by a flood of corporate spending. What will be the effects of this newly unleashed torrent of attack advertisements? Will the United States be a functioning democracy with this triumph of corporate power?

Candidate Selection Process

Closely related to the financing of campaigns is the process by which political candidates are nominated. Being wealthy or having access to wealth is essential for victory because of the enormous cost of the race. Consider the cost for a run at the presidency. In the first three months of 2006, 18 months before the 2008 presidential election, three candidates had each raised more than $20 million—Democrats Hillary Clinton ($26 million), Barack Obama ($25 million), and Republican Mitt Romney ($23 million). And that was only the beginning. By the end of the 2008 presidential campaign, Obama had raised $750 million. Thus, the candidates tend to represent a limited constituency—the wealthy.

The two-party system also works to limit choices among candidates to a rather narrow range. Each party is financed by the special interests—especially business. As William Domhoff puts it,

> Campaign donations from members of the corporate community and upper class are a central element in determining who enters politics with any hope of winning a nomination. . . . It is the need for a large amount of start-up money—to travel around the district or the country, to send out large mailings, to schedule radio and television time in advance—that gives members of the power elite a very direct role in the process right from the beginning and thereby provides them with personal access to politicians of both parties. (Domhoff 1978:225)

Affluent individuals and the largest corporations influence candidate selection by giving financial aid to those candidates sympathetic with their views and withholding support from those whose views differ. The parties, then, are constrained to choose candidates with views congruent with the monied interests.

BIAS OF THE POLITICAL SYSTEM

Most people think of the machinery of government as a beneficial force promoting the common good, and it often is. But although the government can be organized for the benefit of the majority, it is not always neutral (Parenti 1978). The state regulates; it stifles opposition; it makes and enforces the law; it funnels information; it makes war on enemies (foreign and domestic); and its policies determine how resources are apportioned. In all these areas, the government is generally biased toward policies that benefit the business community. In short, power in the United States is concentrated in a power elite, and this elite uses its power for its own advantage.

Power in the United States is concentrated among people who control the government and the largest corporations. This assertion is based on the assumption that power is not an attribute of individuals but rather of social organizations. The elite in U.S. society are those people who occupy the power roles in society. The great political decisions are made by the president, the president's advisers, cabinet members, members of regulatory agencies, the Federal Reserve Board, key members of Congress, and the Supreme Court. Individuals in these government command posts have the authority to make war, raise or lower interest rates, levy taxes, dam rivers, and institute or withhold national health insurance.

Formerly, economic activity was the result of many decisions made by individual entrepreneurs and the heads of small businesses. Now, a handful of companies have virtual control over the marketplace. Decisions made by the boards of directors and the managers of these huge corporations determine employment and production, consumption patterns, wages and prices, the extent of foreign trade, the rate at which natural resources are depleted, and the like.

The few thousand people who form this power elite tend to come from backgrounds of privilege and wealth. It would be a mistake, however, to equate personal wealth with power. Great power is manifested only through decision making in the very large corporations or in government. We have seen that this elite exercises great power. Decisions are made by the powerful, and these decisions tend to benefit the wealthy disproportionately. But the power elite is not formally organized; there is no conspiracy per se.

The interests of the powerful (and the wealthy) are served, nevertheless, through the way in which society is structured. This bias occurs in three ways: by the elite's influence over elected and appointed government officials at all levels, by the structure of the system, and by ideological control of the masses.

As noted earlier, the wealthy receive favorable treatment either by actually occupying positions of power or by exerting direct influence over those who do. Laws, court decisions, and administrative decisions tend to give them the advantage over middle-income earners and the poor.

More subtly, the power elite can get its way without actually being mobilized at all. The choices of decision makers are often limited by what are called systemic imperatives; that is, the institutions of society are patterned to produce prearranged results, regardless of the personalities of the decision makers. In other words, a bias pressures the government to do certain things and not to do other things. Inevitably, this bias favors the status quo, allowing people with power to continue to exercise it. No change is easier than change. The current political and economic systems have worked and generally are not subject to questions, let alone change. In this way, the laws, customs, and institutions of society resist change. Thus, the propertied and the wealthy benefit, while the propertyless and the poor remain disadvantaged. As Parenti has argued,

The law does not exist as an abstraction. It gathers shape and substance from a context of power, within a real-life social structure. Like other institutions, the legal system is class-bound. The question is not whether the law should or should not be neutral, for as a product of its society, it cannot be neutral in purpose or effect. (Parenti 1978:188)

In addition to the inertia of institutions, other systemic imperatives benefit the power elite and the wealthy. One such imperative is for the government to strive to provide an adequate defense against our enemies, which stifles any external threat to the status quo. Thus, Congress, the president, and the general public tend to support large appropriations for defense and homeland security, which in turn provide extraordinary profit to many corporations. In addition, the government protects U.S. transnational companies in their overseas operations so that they enjoy a healthy and profitable business climate. Domestic government policy also is shaped by the systemic imperative for stability. The government promotes domestic tranquility by squelching dissidents.

Power is the ability to get what one wants from someone else, by force, authority, manipulation, or persuasion. In Parenti's words, "The ability to control the definition of interests is the ability to define the agenda of issues, a capacity tantamount to winning battles without having to fight them" (Parenti 1978:41). U.S. schools, churches, and families possess this power. The schools, for instance, consciously teach youth that capitalism is the only correct economic system. This indoctrination to conservative values achieves a consensus among the citizenry concerning the status quo. Each of us comes to accept the present arrangements in society because they seem to be the only options that make sense. Thus, there is general agreement on what is right and wrong. In sum, the dominance of the wealthy is legitimized. Parenti observes, "The interests of an economically dominant class never stand naked. They are enshrouded in the flag, fortified by the law, protected by the police, nurtured by the media, taught by the schools, and blessed by the church" (Parenti 1978:84).

Finally, popular belief in democracy works to the advantage of the power elite, as Parenti has noted:

> *As now constituted, elections serve as a great asset in consolidating the existing social order by propagating the appearances of popular rule. History demonstrates that the people might be moved to overthrow a tyrant who shows himself provocatively indifferent to their woes, but they are far less inclined to make war upon a state, even one dominated by the propertied class, if it preserves what Madison called "the spirit and form of popular government." Elections legitimate the rule of the propertied class by investing it with the moral authority of popular consent. By the magic of the ballot, class dominance becomes "democratic" governance. (Parenti 1978:201)*

Consequences of Concentrated Power

Who benefits from how power is concentrated in U.S. society? At times, almost everyone does; but often the decisions made tend to benefit the wealthy. Whenever the interests of the wealthy clash with those of other groups or even of the public at large, the interests of the former are served. Consider how the president and Congress deal with the problems of energy shortages, inflation, or deflation. Who is asked to make the sacrifices? Where is the budget cut—are military expenditures reduced or are funds for food stamps slashed? When Congress considers tax reform, after the clouds of rhetoric recede, which groups benefit from the new legislation or from the laws that are left unchanged? When the economy was on the verge of collapse in 2008, who was bailed out by the government—the unemployed? The newly bankrupt? Those who lost their homes through foreclosure? No, the government spent many hundreds of billions of dollars to lift up the banks and insurance companies. When a corporation is found guilty of fraud, violation of antitrust laws, or bribery, what are the penalties? How do they compare with the penalties for crimes committed by poor individuals? When there is an oil spill or other ecological disaster caused by a huge enterprise, what are the penalties? Who pays for the cleanup and the restoration of the environment? The answers to these questions are obvious: the wealthy benefit at the expense of the less well-to-do. In short, the government is an institution run by people—the rich and powerful or their agents—who seek to maintain their advantageous positions in society.

Two journalists, Donald Bartlett and Steele, argue that there are two ways to get favorable treatment by Congress and the White House: contribute generously to the right people and spend lavishly on lobbying (Barlett and Steele, 2000:40-42). If you do you will get, for example, favorable tax rates, immunity from certain laws, government subsidies, and even a government bail out if needed. If you do not make generous political contributions and have lobbyists to make your case, then you will, according to Barlett and Steele, pay a disproportionate share of taxes, pay higher prices for a range of products, be compelled to pay all of your debts, and you will see legislation for the social good weakened or killed. In essence, we have a political system where spending money for political purposes makes a huge difference, dividing Americans into the fortunate few and second-class citizens.

The bias of the system today is nothing new. Since the nation's founding, the government's policy has primarily favored the needs of the corporate system. The founding fathers were upper-class holders of wealth. The Constitution they wrote gave the power to people like themselves—White, male property owners.

This bias continued throughout the nineteenth century as bankers, railroad entrepreneurs, and manufacturers joined the landed gentry as the power elite. The shift from local business to large-scale manufacturing during the last half of the nineteenth century saw a concomitant increase in governmental activity in the economy. Business was protected from competition by tariffs, public subsidies, price regulation, patents, and trademarks. When there was unrest by troubled miners, farmers, and laborers, the government invariably sided with the strong against the weak. Militia and federal troops were used to crush railroad strikes. Antitrust laws, though not used to stop the monopolistic practices of business, were invoked against labor unions.

During this time, approximately one billion acres of land in the public domain (almost half the present size of the United States) were given to private individuals and corporations. The railroads in particular were given huge tracts of land as a subsidy. These lands were and continue to be very rich in timber and natural resources. This active intervention by the government in the nation's economy during the nineteenth century was almost solely on the behalf of business. Parenti noted, "The government remained laissez-faire affording little attention to poverty, unemployment, unsafe work conditions, child labor, and the spoliation of natural resources" (Parenti 2008:56).

The early twentieth century was a time of great government activity in the economy, which gave the appearance of restraining big business. However, the actual result of federal regulation of business was to increase the power of the largest corporations. The Interstate Commerce Commission, for instance, helped the railroads by establishing common rates instead of ruinous competition. Federal regulations in meat packing, drug manufacturing, banking, and mining weeded out the weaker cost-cutting competitors, leaving a few to control the markets at higher prices and higher profits. Even the actions of that great trustbuster, Teddy Roosevelt, were largely ceremonial. His major legislative proposals reflected the desires of corporation interests. Like other presidents before and since, he enjoyed close relations with big businessmen and invited them into his administration (Parenti 2008:57).

World War II intensified the government bias on behalf of business. Industry was converted to war production. Corporate interests became more actively involved in the councils of government. Government actions clearly favored business in labor disputes. The police and military were used against rebellious workers; strikes were treated as efforts to weaken the war effort and therefore as treasonous.

The New Deal is typically assumed to be a time when the needs of people impoverished by the Great Depression were paramount in government policies. But as Parenti has argued, "The central dedication of the Franklin Roosevelt administration was to business recovery rather than social reform" (Parenti 1980:74). Business was subsidized by credits, price supports, bank guarantees, stimulation of the housing industry, and the like. Welfare programs were instituted to prevent widespread starvation, but even these humanitarian programs also worked to the benefit of the big business community. The government's provision of jobs, minimum wages, unemployment compensation, and retirement benefits obviously aided people in dire economic straits. But these programs were actually promoted by the business community because of the benefits to them. The government and business favored social programs not because millions were in misery but because violent political and social unrest posed a real threat.

Two social scientists, Frances Fox Piven and Richard A. Cloward, in a historical assessment of government welfare programs, determined that the government institutes massive aid to the poor only when the poor constitute a threat (Piven and Cloward 1971). When large numbers of people are suddenly barred from their traditional occupations, they may begin to question the legitimacy of the system itself. Crime, riots, looting, and social movements aimed at changing existing social, political, and economic arrangements become more widespread. Under this threat, the government initiates or expands relief programs to defuse the social unrest. During the Great Depression, Piven and Cloward contend, the government remained aloof from the needs of the unemployed until there was a surge of political disorder. Added proof for Piven and Cloward's thesis is the contraction or even abolition of public assistance programs when stability is restored.

The historical trend for government to favor business over less powerful interests continues in current public policy. This bias is perhaps best seen in the aphorism enunciated by President Calvin Coolidge and repeated by subsequent presidents: "The business of America is business."

Subsidies to Big Business

A general principle applies to the government's relationship to big business: Business can conduct its affairs either undisturbed by or encouraged by government, whichever is of greater benefit to the business community. The government benefits the business community with $125 billion in subsidies annually. Corporations receive a wide range of favors, tax breaks, direct government subsidies to pay for advertising, research and training costs, and incentives to pursue overseas production and sales (Gillespie 2003). The following are examples of governmental decisions that were beneficial to business.

- State and local governments woo corporations with various subsidies, including tax breaks, low-interest loans, infrastructure improvements, and relatively cheap land. In 2006, for example, Mississippi offered Kia, the Korean automaker, $1 billion in incentives to build a plant (Georgia offered Kia $400 million). Similarly, to keep the New York Stock Exchange in New York City, the city and state of New York offered an incentive package worth more than $1 billion. To which Ralph Nader replied: "It would be hard to script a more brazen and shameless corporate giveaway from a city where nearly one in three children lives in poverty, and public investment necessities go begging" (Nader 2001:26). Citizens for Tax Justice argued that when these subsidies occur, corporations manage to shield as much as two-thirds of their profits from state corporate income taxes. "The result: Money that could be spent on real economic development opportunities flows instead into the pockets of executives and the bill gets passed along to small taxpayers—local businesses and workers" (Singer 2006:6).
- The government installs price supports on certain commodities, increasing the profits of those engaged in those industries and simultaneously costing consumers. For example, sugar price supports cost consumers $3 billion a

year; dairy and milk price supports increase the annual cost to consumers by $9 million (Green 2002:161).

- Eleven days after the terrorist attacks of September 2001, Congress rushed through a $15 billion bailout of the airlines. Congress did not provide any relief to the 140,000 fired airline workers or to the 2 million people employed by the hotel industry whose jobs were imperiled (Hightower 2002a).

- In 1996, instead of auctioning off leasing or auctioning off the rights, Congress *gave* broadcasters spectrum rights to broadcast one channel of superhigh-resolution digital programs or several channels that could be used for digital interactive services or TV programs of high, but not super-high, resolution—to which the *New York Times* editorialized, "By giving the new spectrum away instead of auctioning it off to the highest bidders, Congress deprived the treasury, and thus taxpayers, of tens of billions of dollars" (*New York Times* 2000c:1).

- The government often funds research and develops new technologies at public expense and turns them over to private corporations for their profit. This transfer occurs routinely with nuclear energy, synthetics, space communications, and pharmaceuticals. Although the pharmaceutical industry, for example, argues that it must charge high prices on drugs to recoup its costly research, the Joint Economic Committee of Congress found that public research led to 15 of the 21 drugs considered to have the highest therapeutic value introduced between 1965 and 1992 (reported in Goozner 2000). Three of those drugs—Capoten, Prozac, and Zovirax—have sales of more than $1 billion each.

- Congress subsidizes the timber industry by building roads for logging at an annual cost of $173 million (Zepezauer 2004). Under an 1872 law, mining companies need not pay for the $2 billion worth of minerals they extract from public lands (Scher 2000). The government subsidizes corn growers and its processors by mandating the use of ethanol (a corn-based fuel product) in gasoline.

- Transnational corporations are permitted to set up tax havens overseas to make various intracompany transactions from a unit in one foreign country to another, thus legally sheltering them from U.S. taxes.

- In 2003, Congress passed the Medicare Prescription Bill. The pharmaceutical industry, using 675 lobbyists from 138 firms, nearly 7 lobbyists for each senator, was successful in achieving favorable treatment in the legislation, including (1) a prohibition on the Medicare program from using its bargaining clout to directly negotiate deep drug-price discounts (one estimate is that prohibition will increase profits by $139 billion over 8 years) and (2) a ban on the reimportation of prescription drugs from Canada, which cost about 50 percent less than in the United States (*Public Citizen* 2003).

- Perhaps the best illustration of how business benefits from government policies are the benefits provided by the tax code. The 2001 and 2003 tax cuts slashed an estimated $175 billion in corporate taxes through 2004. Moreover, the tax code provides corporations with numerous ways to avoid taxes through generous exemptions, credits, and deductions. Corporations legally escape much of the tax burden through such devices as the investment tax credit, accelerated depreciation, capital gains, and locating in tax havens overseas. The key point is that Congress has allowed the tax burden to shift from corporations to individuals—in 1940, companies and individuals each paid about half the federal income tax collected; in 2003 the companies paid 13.7 percent and individuals 86.3 percent (Byrnes and Lavelle 2003).

- The more than $700 billion in government bailouts to the banks and financial firms in 2008 actually rewarded them for their reckless behavior.

Trickle-Down Solutions

Periodically, the government is faced with finding a way to stimulate the economy during an economic downturn. One solution is to spend federal monies through unemployment insurance, government jobs, and housing subsidies. In this way, the funds go directly to the people most hurt by shortages, unemployment, inadequate housing, and the like. Opponents of such plans contend that the subsidies should go directly to business, which would help the economy by encouraging companies to hire more workers, add to their inventories, and build new plants. Subsidizing business in this way, the advocates argue, benefits everyone. To provide subsidies to businesses rather than directly to needy individuals is based on the assumption that private profit maximizes the public good. In effect, proponents argue, because the government provides direct benefits to businesses and investors, the economic benefits indirectly trickle down to all.

Opponents of "trickle-down" economics argue that this is an inefficient way to help the less-than-affluent.

> One way to understand "trickle-down" economics is to use a more graphic metaphor: horse-and-sparrow economics—that is, if you feed the horse well, some will pass on through and be there on the ground for the sparrow. There is no doubt that sparrows can be nourished in this manner; and the more the horses get fed, the more there will be on the ground for the sparrows to pick through. It is, however, probably not a very pleasant way for sparrows to get their sustenance, and if one's primary goal is to feed the sparrows, it is a pretty silly—and inefficient—way to do the job. . . . Why waste the money on the horses when it might go directly to the sparrows? (MacEwan 2001:40)

There are at least two reasons government officials tend to opt for these trickle-down solutions. First, because they tend to come from the business class, government officials believe in the conservative ideology that says that what is good for business is good for the United States. The second reason for the probusiness choice is that government officials are more likely to hear arguments from the powerful. Because the weak, by definition, are not organized, their voice is not heard or, if heard, not taken seriously in decision-making circles.

Although the government most often opts for trickle-down solutions, such plans are not very effective in fulfilling the promise that benefits will trickle down to the poor. The higher corporate profits generated by tax credits and other tax incentives do not necessarily mean that companies will increase wages or hire more workers. What is more likely is that corporations will increase dividends to the stockholders, which further increases the inequality gap. Job creation is also not guaranteed because companies may use their newly acquired wealth to purchase labor-saving devices. If so, then the government programs will actually have widened the gulf between the haves and the have-nots.

The Powerless Bear the Burden

Robert Hutchins, in his critique of U.S. governmental policy, characterized the basic principle guiding internal affairs as follows: "Domestic policy is conducted according to one infallible rule: the costs and burdens of whatever is done must be borne by those least able to bear them" (Hutchins 1976:4). Let us review several examples of this statement.

When threatened by war, the government sometimes institutes a military draft. A careful analysis of the draft reveals that it is really a tax on the poor. During the height of the Vietnam War, for instance, only 10 percent of men in college were drafted, although 40 percent of draft-age men were in college. Even for those educated young men who ended up in the armed services, there was a greater likelihood of their serving in noncombat jobs than for the non-college-educated. Thus, the chances of getting killed while in the service were about three times greater for the less educated than for the college educated (Zeitlin, Lutterman, and Russell 1977). Even more blatant was the practice that occurred legally during the Civil War. The law at that time allowed the affluent who were drafted to hire someone to take their place in the service. In the Afghanistan and Iraq wars beginning in 2003, the government decided not to have a draft. Instead, the forces were made up of volunteers. This meant, in effect, that the battles were fought overwhelmingly by young men and women from the working and lower classes. As one critic put it: "If this war is truly worth fighting, then the burdens of doing so should fall on all Americans. . . . If it's not worth your family fighting it, then it's not worth it, period" (Broyles 2004:A25).

The poor, being powerless, can be made to absorb the costs of societal changes. In the nineteenth century, the poor did the backbreaking work that built the railroads and the cities. Today, they are the ones pushed out of their homes by urban renewal and the building of expressways, parks, and stadiums.

Following the devastation from Hurricane Katrina in Louisiana and Mississippi in 2005, priorities were set by decision makers as to where rebuilding should be initiated and where it should be delayed or ignored. In New Orleans, the bulk of the money spent first went to the business community and for repairing the Superdome (home field for the New Orleans Saints). Left behind were low-income families. Although Congress required that half of federal grant money help low-income people, some 90 percent of $1.7 billion in federal money spent in Mississippi went to repair condominiums for the affluent, rebuild casinos and hotels, and expand the Port of Gulfport (Eaton 2007).

The government's attempts to solve economic problems generally obey the principle that the poor must bear the burden. A common solution for runaway inflation, for example, is to increase the amount of unemployment. Of course, the poor, especially minorities (whose rate of unemployment is consistently twice the rate for Whites), are the ones who make the sacrifice for the economy. This solution, aside from being socially cruel, is economically ineffective because it ignores the real sources of inflation—excessive military spending, excessive profits by energy companies (foreign and domestic), and administered prices set by shared monopolies, which, contrary to classical economic theory, do not decline during economic downturns (Harrington 1979).

More fundamentally, a certain level of unemployment is maintained continuously, not just during economic downturns. Genuine full employment for all job seekers is a myth. But why is it a myth, since all political candidates extol the work ethic and it is declared national policy to have full employment? Economist Robert Lekachman (1979) has argued that it is no accident that we tolerate millions of unemployed persons. The reason is that a "moderate" unemployment rate is beneficial to the affluent. These benefits include the following: (1) people are willing to work at humble tasks for low wages; (2) the children of the middle and upper classes avoid military service as the unemployed disproportionately join the volunteer army; (3) the unions are less demanding; (4) workers are less likely to demand costly safety equipment; (5) corporations do not have to pay their share of taxes because local and state governments give them concessions to lure them to their area; and (6) the existing wide differentials between White males and the various powerless categories such as females, Latinos, and African Americans are retained.

Foreign Policy for Corporate Benefit

The operant principle here is that "foreign policy seems to be carried on in the light of the needs of the munitions makers, the Pentagon, the CIA, and the multinational corporations" (Hutchins 1976:4). For example, military goods are sold overseas for the profit of the arms merchants. Sometimes, arms are sold to both sides in a potential conflict, the argument being that if we did not sell them the arms, then someone else would, so we might as well make the profits.

The government has supported foreign governments that are supportive of U.S. multinational companies, regardless of how tyrannical these governments might be.

U.S. rulers mainly have been interested in defending the capitalist world from social change—even when the change has been peaceful and democratic. They overthrew reformist governments in Iran, Guatemala, the Congo, the Dominican Republic, Brazil, Chile, and Uruguay. Similarly, in Greece, the Philippines, Indonesia, and at least ten Latin American nations, military oligarchs—largely trained and financed by the Pentagon and the CIA—overthrew popular governments that pursued egalitarian policies for the benefit of the destitute classes. And in each instance, the United States was instrumental in instituting right-wing regimes that were unresponsive to popular needs and wholly accommodating to U.S. investors (Parenti 2008:85).

The U.S. government has directly intervened in the domestic affairs of foreign governments to protect U.S. corporate interests. As Parenti has characterized it,

> Sometimes the sword has rushed in to protect the dollar, and sometimes the dollar has rushed in to enjoy the advantages won by the sword. To make the world safe for capitalism, the United States government has embarked on a global counter-revolutionary strategy, suppressing insurgent peasant and worker movements throughout Asia, Africa, and Latin America. But the interests of the corporate elites never stand naked; rather they are wrapped in the flag and coated with patriotic appearances. (Parenti 1988:94)

Reprise: The Best Democracy Money Can Buy

Billions are spent on each federal election campaign. The consequence of this flood of money in elections is that it sabotages democracy in several ways. First, it makes it harder for government to solve social problems.

> How can we produce smart defense, environmental, and health policies if arms contractors, oil firms, and HMOs have a hammerlock over the committees charged with considering reforms? How can we adequately fund education and child care if special interests win special tax breaks that deplete public resources? (Green 2002:4)

Second, and related to the first, the have-nots of society are not represented among the decision makers. Moreover, because the successful candidate must either be wealthy or be beholden to the wealthy, they are a different class of people from a different social world than most Americans. Thus, the money–politics connection is undemocratic because "democracy requires diversity in its legislatures in order to reflect the popular will" (Green 2002:18).

> *Since cash is the currency of elections, candidates troll for money where it is concentrated: in largely white, wealthy neighborhoods. . . . When a small, wealthy group in effect decides which candidates will have enough money to run a viable campaign, it is no great surprise that the agenda of policymakers is skewed toward its interests and not those of people of color and other underserved communities. (Gonzalez and Moore 2003:23A)*

Third, the money chase creates part-time elected officials and full-time fund-raisers. It now takes an average of $1.1 million to win a seat in the House of Representatives and $6.5 million to become or remain a senator. Senators have to raise an average of $20,833 a week every week of their 6-year term to raise the necessary capital.

Fourth, money diminishes the gap between the two major political parties because the candidates and parties seek and receive funds from the same corporate sources and wealthy individuals. Democrats in need of funds, even though they are more inclined than Republicans to support social programs and raising taxes, must temper these tendencies or lose their monetary support from wealthy interests. As Robert Reich has observed, "It is difficult to represent the little fellow when the big fellow pays the tab" (Reich 1989:A29).

Fifth, the money chase in politics discourages voting and civic participation (of the twenty-four Western democracies, the United States ranks twenty-third in voting turnout). In the 2000 presidential election, 49 percent of those who could have voted did not vote. This meant in effect that George W. Bush was elected by 24 percent of the electorate.

Sixth, big money in politics means than special interests get special access to the decision makers and receive special treatment from them.

> *The pay-to-play mentality has so seeped into our system that there now exist two classes of citizens. There are those for whom tax breaks, bailouts, and subsidies are granted; for whom running for and winning office is plausible; and with whom elected officials take time to meet. And then there are the rest of us—the non-donors for whom taxes go up, consumer prices rise, and influence evaporates. (Green 2002:148)*

In sum, the current politicoeconomic system is biased. It works for the benefit of the few at the expense of the many. Because the distribution of power and the organization of the economy give shape and impetus to the persistent social problems of U.S. society, the analysis of these problems requires a politicoeconomic approach.

■ CHAPTER REVIEW

1. The state is not a neutral agent of the people but is biased in favor of the upper social classes and the largest corporations.
2. Marx's prediction that capitalism will result in an economy dominated by monopolies has been fulfilled in the United States. But rather than a single corporation dominating a sector of the economy, the United States has shared monopolies, whereby four or fewer corporations supply 50 percent or more of a particular market.

3. Economic power is concentrated in a few major corporations and banks. This concentration has been accomplished through mergers and interlocking directorates.

4. Private wealth is also highly concentrated. Poverty, on the other hand, is officially dispersed among 39.8 million people (2008); many more millions are not so designated by the government but are poor nonetheless.

5. The inequality gap in the United States is the widest of all the industrialized nations. The gap continues to grow especially because of tax benefits for the affluent.

6. These tax policies, in addition to increasing the unequal distribution of wealth, increase the national debt, reduce government spending for programs to help the less fortunate, and weaken public institutions that benefit society. The widening gap increases the political influence of the wealthy.

7. The government tends to serve the interests of the wealthy because of the influence of interest groups and how political campaigns are financed.

8. Democracy is a political system that is of, by, and for the people. Democracy is undermined by special interests, which use money to deflect the political process for their own benefit.

9. The powerful in society (those who control the government and the largest corporations) tend to come from backgrounds of privilege and wealth. Their decisions tend to benefit the wealthy

disproportionately. The power elite is not organized and conspiratorial, but the interests of the wealthy are served, nevertheless, by the way in which society is organized. This bias occurs through influence over elected and appointed officials, systemic imperatives, and ideological control of the masses.

10. The government supports the bias of the system through its strategies to solve economic problems. The typical two-pronged approach is, on the one hand, to use trickle-down solutions, which give the business community and the wealthy extraordinary advantages; and, on the other hand, to make the powerless bear the burden and consequently become even more disadvantaged.

11. Business benefits from governmental actions through foreign policy decisions, which typically are used to protect and promote U.S. economic interests abroad.

12. The flood of money to support political parties and candidates sabotages democracy in several ways: (a) it makes it more difficult to solve social problems; (b) the interests of the have-nots are not served; (c) the money chase creates part-time legislators and full-time fund-raisers; (d) money diminishes the gap between the two major parties because both seek and receive funds from the same corporate and individual sources; (e) it discourages voting and civic participation; and (f) big money in politics leads to a bias in the laws passed and the subsidies provided.

■ KEY TERMS

Shared monopoly. When four or fewer companies control 50 percent or more of an industry.

Interlocking directorate. The linkage between corporations that results when an individual serves on the board of directors of two companies (a direct interlock) or when two companies each have a director on the board of a third company (an indirect interlock).

Oligarchy. A political system that is ruled by a few.

Plutocracy. A government by or in the interest of the rich.

Democracy. A political system that is of, by, and for the people.

Power elite. People who occupy the power roles in society. They either are wealthy or represent the wealthy.

Systemic imperatives. The economic and social constraints on political decision makers that promote the status quo.

Power. The ability to get what one wants from someone else.

■ SUCCEED WITH mysoclab www.mysoclab.com

Experience, Discover, Observe, Evaluate

MySocLab is designed just for you. This chapter features a pre-test and post-test to help you learn and review key concepts and terms.

Experience sociology in action with dynamic visual activities, videos, and readings to enhance your learning experience. Complete the following activities at www.mysoclab.com.

Social Explorer is an interactive application that allows you to explore Census data through interactive maps.

- Explore the Social Explorer Map: *Max Weber: Property, Power, and Prestige*

The Core Concepts in Sociology video clips offer a real-world perspective on sociological concepts.

- Watch *Democracy: Those Who Don't Participate*

MySocLibrary includes primary source readings from classic and contemporary sociologists.

- Read Clawson & Weller, *Dollars and Votes: How Business Campaign Contributions Subvert Democracy*; William, *Who Rules America? The Corporate Community and the Upper Class*; Weber, *The Characteristics of Bureaucracy*

World Population and Global Inequality

From Chapter 3 of *Social Problems, Census Update*, Twelfth Edition. D. Stanley Eitzen, Maxine Baca Zinn, Kelly Eitzen Smith. Copyright © 2012 by Pearson Education, Inc. Published by Allyn & Bacon. All rights reserved.

World Population and Global Inequality

If the global village were reduced to 1,000 who proportionately represent the world's population, 584 would be Asians, 124 Africans, 84 Latin Americans, 95 eastern/western Europeans, 55 from the former Soviet Union, 52 North Americans, four Australians and two would be from New Zealand. . . . Rich folks call the shots in the global village. One-fifth of the people control three-quarters of the wealth. Another fifth of the population receive only 2 percent of the wealth. Only 70 people own automobiles. Only one-third of the population have access to clean drinking water. Fewer than 20 have a college education.

—Brigada

The countries of the world vary widely in levels of material conditions. Some nations are disproportionately poor with rampant hunger, disease, and illiteracy. Other nations are exceptionally well off, with ample resources. Table 1, using an index based on life expectancy, educational attainment, and real income, ranks the world's nations on "livability." Notice that the bottom twenty

TABLE 1

Most and Least Livable Countries: UN Human Development Index, 2007

"Most Livable" Countries, 2007

1. Iceland	11. Finland
2. Norway	12. United States
3. Australia	13. Spain
4. Canada	14. Denmark
5. Ireland	15. Austria
6. Sweden	16. United Kingdom
7. Switzerland	17. Belgium
8. Japan	18. Luxembourg
9. Netherlands	19. New Zealand
10. France	20. Italy

"Least Livable" Countries, 2007

1. Sierra Leone	11. Burundi
2. Burkina Faso	12. Côte d'Ivoire
3. Guinea-Bissau	13. Zambia
4. Niger	14. Malawi
5. Mali	15. Benin
6. Mozambique	16. Angola
7. Central African Republic	17. Rwanda
8. Chad	18. Guinea
9. Ethiopia	19. Tanzania
10. Congo	20. Nigeria

Source: United Nations Human Development Index, 2007. Online: http://www.hdr.undp.org

countries are all in sub-Saharan Africa, a region where 50 percent of the people live below the poverty line.

Here are some facts concerning the uneven distribution of the world's wealth:

- The richest 2 percent of adults own more than half of the world's household wealth.
- The poorest half of the world's adult population own barely 1 percent of global wealth.
- The top ranks in wealth are dominated by the Americans, Japanese, and Europeans.

The reasons for such global inequality include, as one might suspect, the degree of geographic isolation, climate, overpopulation, and natural resources. Another key determinant is the effect of power. The poor are poor, as we discuss, because they have been and continue to be dominated and exploited by powerful nations and corporations that have extracted their wealth and labor. This continuing domination of the weak by the powerful has resulted in an ever-widening gap between the rich and poor nations.

This chapter examines the plight of the poorest countries and the role of the richest—especially the United States—in maintaining global inequality. The first section focuses on world population growth, examining in particular the variables affecting why some nations have high growth and others do not.

The second part examines poverty throughout the world and the social problems generated by impoverishment, such as hunger, unhealthy living conditions, and economic/social chaos. The third part explores the relationship of the United States with the poor nations, historically through colonialism and currently through the impact of multinational corporations and official government policies.

WORLD POPULATION GROWTH

The number of people on this planet constitutes both a major problem and potential future calamity. The world population in mid-2009 was estimated to be 6.8089 billion, and at its current rate of growth, the net addition annually is 75 to 80 million people (the equivalent of adding a city the size of San Francisco every three days, or a New York City every month, or the combined populations of France, Greece, and Sweden every year). According to the latest projections, the world's population will increase to 7 billion in the latter half of 2011 and reach 9 billion in 2050 (Population Reference Bureau 2009).

> *The jump from six billion to nine billion is the equivalent of the impact of adding 33 more Mexicos to the world. And 33 additional Mexicos is the appropriate metaphor, because essentially all of the projected increase will occur in developing nations, the very places that strain to accommodate those already present. (Easterbrook 1999:23)*

To put the population growth curve in perspective: it took all of human history until about 1830 to reach the first billion. The next billion took 100 years (1930); the third billion, 30 years (1960); the fourth billion, 15 years (1995); the fifth billion, 12 years (1987); the sixth billion, 12 years (1999); and the next billion will also take about 12 years.

Most significant, 99 percent of the current population growth occurs in the less-developed nations, where poverty, hunger, and infectious disease are already rampant. There is a strong inverse relationship between per capita GNP and population growth rates—the lower the per capita GNP, the higher the population growth. For example, the less-developed nations are expected to increase in population from 5.6 billion in 2009 to 8.2 billion in 2050, whereas the more developed countries are projected to grow from 1.2 billion to just 1.3 billion (Bremer et al., 2009). This is a consequence of differential fertility (differences in the average number of children born to a woman by social category). To illustrate, the fertility rate in the more developed countries in 2009 was 1.7, compared to 4.6 in the least developed countries. These differences in fertility rate (the average number of births per woman) reveal a future world population that will be overwhelmingly from the developing countries (see Figure 1).

The population growth rates in the poor countries make it difficult to provide the bare necessities of housing, fuel, food, and medical attention. Ironically, there is a relationship between poverty and fertility: the greater the proportion of a given population living in poverty, the higher is the fertility of that population. This relationship is not as irrational as it first appears. Poor parents want many children so that the children will help them economically and take care of them in their old age. Because so many children die, the parents must have a large number to ensure several surviving children. Large families make good economic sense to the poor because children are a major source of labor and income.

*World Population
Growth Is Now Almost
Entirely Concentrated in
the World's Poorer
Countries*

Source: UN Population
Division, *World Population
Prospects: The 2008 Revision,*
medium variant (2009).

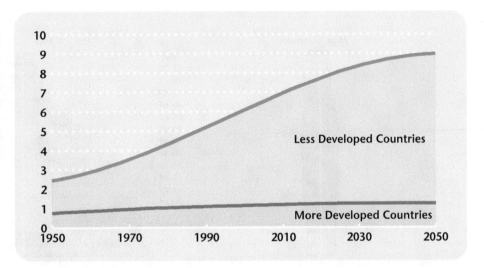

How can the nations of the world deal with the problems of expanding population? Basically, there are three ways to reduce fertility—through economic development, family-planning programs, and social change.

Demographic Transition

Historically, as nations have become more urban, industrialized, and modernized, their population growth has slowed appreciably. Countries appear to go through three stages in this process, which is known as the modern demographic transition. In the agricultural stage, both birth and death rates are high, resulting in a low population growth rate. In the transition stage, birthrates remain high, but the death rates decrease markedly because of access to more effective medicines, improved hygiene, safer water, and better diets. Many nations are presently in this stage, and the result for them is a population explosion. Much later in the process, as societies become more urban and traditional customs have less of a hold, birthrates decline, slowing the population growth and eventually stopping it altogether (as is now occurring in many nations of Europe and Japan). Figure 2 shows the population pyramids for less-developed countries where population growth is booming, and the more developed, where population growth is slow. Especially important to population growth is the "critical cohort" of those under age 20. There are more than 2 billion in this category in the developing countries. These young people will soon become parents (400 million are already between 15 and 19). What will be the fertility of this critical cohort? If the growth rate is to continue to slow, the demographic transition with its accompanying urbanization, medical advances, and the liberation of women from traditional gender roles will have worked.

The concept of a demographic transition is supported empirically. For example, birthrates in the developed world are down dramatically. Peter Drucker summarizes the situation:

> In the developed countries the dominant factor in [the near future] will be something to
> which most people are only just beginning to pay attention: the rapid growth in the
> older population and the rapid shrinking of the younger generation. . . . In every single

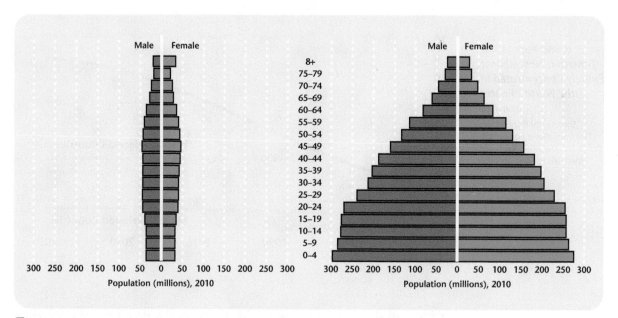

FIGURE 2

(a) **More Developed Countries Have Fewer Young People**

(b) **Less Developed Countries Have More Young People**

Source: UN Population Division, *World Population Prospects: The 2008 Revision* (2009).

developed country, but also China and Brazil, the birth rate is now well below the replacement rate of 2.2 live births per woman of reproductive age. (Drucker 2001:3)

For example, not a single country in Europe is producing enough children to replace itself. According to the United Nations, approximately 43 percent of the world's peoples live in countries at or below the replacement rate of 2.1.

The problem, of course, is that the modern demographic transition experienced in Europe took about 200 years. With relatively high growth rates in the less-developed world plus a huge cohort in, or soon to be in, the child bearing category, this length of time is unacceptable because the planet cannot sustain the massive growth that will occur while the demographic transition runs its course. But the fertility rate is dropping more quickly than expected, even in the less-developed countries. For example, in sub-Saharan Africa, where the fertility rate is the highest, it has fallen from 6.7 children per woman in 1950 to 5.3 now. Worldwide, the use of contraception has risen from 10 percent of married women in the 1960s to 62 percent in 2009 (Bremer et al., 2009). The global fertility rate (2.6 in 2009) will continue to decline, but with so many women of childbearing age in the less-developed countries, the world's population is projected to increase by 2.4 million over the next 40 years to about 9.2 billion in 2050, at which it will stabilize.

Family Planning

Beginning in the 1960s, international organizations such as the World Health Organization and UNICEF incorporated reproductive health into their missions. National governments, beginning with India in 1951, began to adopt

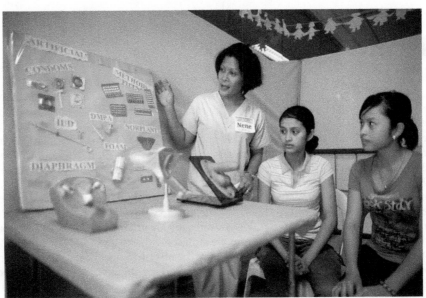

The World Bank estimates that it would take $8 billion to make birth control readily available globally.

family-planning policies (see the "Social Problems in Global Perspective" panel for a description of the mildly successful family-planning effort in India). As a result, fertility rates have fallen. Worldwide, the average number of children per woman fell from 5.0 in 1950 to 2.6 in 2009. Declines were most significant in Asia, Latin America, and the Caribbean. Only in sub-Saharan Africa did the average remain well above 5. The nations with the least use of modern contraceptives are largely rural and agricultural with very low per capita incomes. But with the continuing migration of the poor to the cities, there is less incentive to have large families.

The United Nations estimates that about 200 million worldwide would like to prevent pregnancy, but are not using effective contraception either because they cannot afford it or are not knowledgeable about it (cited in Francis 2009). The World Bank estimates that it would take $8 billion to make birth control readily available on a global basis. Such availability would reduce the projected world population from 10 billion to 8 billion during the next 60 years. The important point is that family-planning programs do work. Beginning in the late 1960s, the United States and the United Nations began funding such programs.

Formal policies by the United States, beginning with the Reagan and Bush administrations (1980–1992), have not supported the efforts of international organizations to promote contraceptive use. Because of popular opposition to abortion and the use of the drug RU-486 (a pill that induces a relatively safe miscarriage in the early stages of pregnancy), the United States withdrew aid from the United Nations Population Fund and the International Planned Parenthood Federation. President Clinton reversed these policies. President George W. Bush cut off U.S. contributions to the fund and defunded a British charity focusing on AIDS programs because it cooperated with the U.N. Population Fund (*Los Angeles Times* 2004). President Obama, however, restored U.S. funding for the United Nations Population Fund and rescinded the antifamily policy of the Bush administration (going back to President Reagan) that required all nongovernmental organizations that receive federal funds to refrain from performing abortions or citing abortion services offered by others.

SOCIAL PROBLEMS IN GLOBAL PERSPECTIVE

POPULATION GROWTH IN INDIA

More than one-third of the world's population live in either China or India. In mid-2009, China's population was 1.331 billion and India's was 1.171 billion (Population Reference Bureau 2009). If current growth rates continue, India will surpass China as the country with the world's largest population before 2030. China has reduced its population growth significantly by placing limits on family size (one child per urban couple while rural residents may have two children). India's population policy is to encourage small family size through family planning (53 percent of married women use contraceptives), female literacy programs, and sterilization, which has reduced the birthrate over the past 50 years from six births for each woman of childbearing age to 2.9. Still India grows by 48,000 every day.

Although India has had birth control programs since the early 1950s and public education at virtually no cost, the population continues to grow, especially in poor rural areas.

In poor rural areas—such as Bihar state, where women's literacy rates are lowest and family sizes are largest—girls are often married by the age of 15 and pressured to produce children quickly—especially sons who will one day provide for their elders and light their fathers' funeral pyres, a ritual central to Hinduism.

"Many women do not want large families any more, but this is still a patriarchal society, where men make the decisions on reproduction," says Saroj Pachauri, who heads the local branch of the Population Council, an international nonprofit group. "Ask a woman in Bihar if she

wants more children, and she will say no. Ask her if she is using [birth control], and she will also say no."

Another obstacle is the popular notion, especially in the countryside, that more children mean more hands to work—rather than mouths to feed—and that larger clans mean mightier defenses (Constable 1999:16).

India, roughly one-third the geographical size of the United States, has more than four times as many people. The national literacy rate is 65 percent (75 percent for males and 54 percent for females). More than 260 million survive on less than one dollar a day. Nearly half of India's children below age six are undernourished. Resources such as arable land and water are strained to the limit. That is the situation now. What will it be like when they add another 500,000 million people in the next half century?

Societal Changes

The third strategy to reduce population growth involves societal changes. Ingrained cultural values about the familial role of women and about children as evidence of the father's virility or as a hedge against poverty in old age must be changed.

Religious beliefs, such as the resistance of the Roman Catholic hierarchy and of fundamentalist Muslim regimes such as in Saudi Arabia to the use of contraceptives, are a great obstacle to population control. However, religion is not an insurmountable barrier. Despite the Catholic hierarchy's resistance to family planning, some nations with overwhelming Catholic majorities have extremely low birthrates. As examples, Italy had a fertility rate of 1.4 in 2009, Spain a rate of 1.5, and Chile had a 1.9 rate, each below the average of 2.11 needed to sustain a stable population. And some Muslim countries have instituted successful family planning. For example, Iran and the United Arab Emirates each had a 2.0 fertility rate in 2009. Perhaps the most significant social change needed to reduce fertility is to change the role of women. When women are isolated from activities outside the home, their worth depends largely on their ability to bear and rear children. Conversely, fertility rates drop when women gain opportunities and a voice in society (Sen 2000). Women need to be included in the formal education process. Research has shown that increasing education is one of the most effective ways to reduce birthrates. Educated women are more likely than uneducated women to use effective methods of family planning (*New York Times* 2002a).

Unplanned social change, such as economic hard times, also affects birthrates. Recent data show that economic difficulties for individual families in less-developed countries can cause couples to delay marriage and to be more likely to use contraceptives. When enough families are affected negatively by an economic downturn, the fertility rate can fall for a nation. This is opposite the usual relationship of declining birthrates accompanying long-term economic success (the demographic transition).

Thus, in the long run, the population problem may abate, perhaps even reducing economic inequality and altering the balance of power among nations. However, for those living now, their lives will be negatively affected by the current population growth in developing nations, environmental degradation, and the overwhelming poverty of billions.

> *Chaos is the increasingly real result of trying to support more than 6 billion people on this planet, spawning desperate mass migrations, wars over rights to fresh water, medical epidemics, bloody riots and crime waves nurtured in teeming shantytowns.*
>
> *The war on terrorism, too, cannot logically be divorced from the struggle for population sanity. Refugee camps and hopeless slums steadily churn out alienated, landless young men and women who are perfect cannon fodder for ambitious religious and political zealots. (Scheer 2002:1)*

POVERTY

According to the World Bank, 1.4 billion people are living below the poverty line, defined as living on less than $1.25 a day. More than one-fourth of the developing world's population are living in this extreme poverty, with 50 percent in sub-Saharan Africa, and 42 percent Indian people found below this poverty marker (reported in the *New York Times* 2008). The global inequality gap is enormous. Consider, for example, that the global Gini index of inequality is 0.892. Recall that the Gini coefficient in the United States is 0.451 and that the closer the coefficient is to 1.00, the greater the inequality gap).

The underdeveloped and developing nations are not only characterized by poverty, hunger, and misery but also by relative powerlessness because most of them were colonies and remain economically dependent on developed nations and transnational corporations, especially those of North America and Europe. These nations are also characterized by rapid population growth, high infant mortality, unsanitary living conditions, high rates of infectious diseases, low life expectancy, and high illiteracy. This section documents hunger, squalor, and marginality of life in these countries.

There is a striking maldistribution in life chances (the chances throughout one's life cycle to live and experience the good things in life) between the developed and developing nations. The significance of worldwide poverty and its concentration in the developing-world nations cannot be overstated. The gap between the rich and poor countries is increasing, and the gap between the rich and poor in the poor countries is increasing. Those in absolute poverty suffer from disease, malnutrition, squalor, stigma, illiteracy, unemployment, and hopelessness. These deplorable conditions will likely lead to extreme solutions such as terrorist movements and government policies of military expansion.

Food and Hunger

The Food and Agricultural Organization maintains that the world's agriculture produces enough food to provide every person with at least 2,720 kilocalories every day for the world's population (cited in Cain 2004). Actually, if everyone adopted a vegetarian diet and no food was wasted, current production would feed 10 billion people, more than the projected population for 2050 (Bender and Smith 1997:5). Food production, however, is unevenly distributed, resulting in about 1 billion being malnourished (one in six people), about one in every three of the world's inhabitants being food insecure, and around 9 million people dying of malnutrition each year. How can we explain these chilling figures?

An obvious source of the problem is rapid population growth, which distorts the distribution system and strains the productive capacity of the various nations. The annual increase of 75 to 80 million people requires an enormous increase in grain production just to stay even. A number of factors are shrinking the productive land throughout the world, in rich and poor countries alike. The earth loses 24 billion tons of topsoil each year. Irrigation systems that tap underground reserves are dropping water tables to dangerously low levels in many areas, causing the land to revert to dry-land farming. Air pollution and toxic chemicals have damaged some crops and water sources. The rising concentration of greenhouse gases is changing the climates negatively. Each year millions of acres of productive land are converted to housing and roads. A growing number of people in developing countries are affluent enough to eat like Westerners; that is, they are eating more meat (Krugman 2008). The result is that a good deal of grain is diverted to feed livestock (it takes about 8 pounds of grain to produce a pound of beef; 6 pounds of grain to produce a pound of pork). Another important diversion of grains away from the food chain is the government subsidized conversion of crops into fuel (e.g., corn into ethanol)

Most significant, of course, is that almost all the population increase is occurring in regions and countries that are already poor. Because of low levels of economic development, the various levels of government, farmers, and others in these countries lack adequate money and credit for the machinery, fertilizer, pesticides, and technology necessary to increase crop production to meet the always increasing demand. The high cost of oil has an especially devastating effect on food production in poor nations. Food production in developing-world nations is also more adversely affected by natural disasters (floods and droughts) than it is in more affluent nations because these countries are less likely to have adequate flood control, irrigation systems, and storage facilities. As a result,

> most of the world's hungry [are] concentrated in two regions: the Indian subcontinent and sub-Saharan Africa. In India, with more than a billion people, 53 percent of all children are undernourished. In Bangladesh, the share is 56 percent. And in Pakistan, it is 38 percent. . . . In Ethiopia, 48 percent of all children are underweight. In Nigeria, the most populous country in Africa, the figure is 39 percent. (Brown 2001:44)

Another way to explain the food problem is to view it as a poverty problem. Food supplies are adequate, but people must have the resources to afford them.

Because the poor cannot afford the available food, they go hungry. Although this view of poverty is correct, it has the effect of blaming the victims for their plight. To do so ignores the political and economic conditions that keep prices too high, make jobs difficult to obtain and poorly paid, and force too many people to compete for too few resources.

The major problem with food shortages is not food production, although that is exceedingly important, but the political economy of the world and of the individual nations. Economic and political structures thwart and distort the production and distribution of agricultural resources. (The following discussion is adapted from Lappe and Collins, 1979, 1986; and Murdoch, 1980.) The primary problem is inequality of control over productive resources. In each country in which hunger is a basic problem, most of the land is controlled by a small elite, and the rest of the population is squeezed onto small plots or marginal land or is landless. For example, although colonial rule ended in southern Africa decades ago, the small White minority still controls most of the arable land. The evidence is that when the few control most of the agriculture, production is less effective than when land is more equally apportioned among farmers. Yields per acre are less, land is underused, wealth produced is not reinvested but drained off for conspicuous consumption by the wealthy, and credit is monopolized. Most important, monopoly control of agricultural land is typically put into cash crops that have value as exports but neglect basic local needs.

Agriculture controlled by a few landowners and agribusiness interests results in investment decisions made on the basis of current profitability. If prices are good, producers breed livestock or plant crops to take advantage of the prices. This approach results in cycles of shortages and gluts. Small farmers, on the other hand, plant crops on the basis of local needs, not world prices.

The way food surpluses are handled in a world in which more than a billion people are chronically hungry is especially instructive. The grain surplus is handled by feeding more than a third of the world's production to animals. Crops are allowed to rot or are plowed under to keep prices high. Surplus milk is fed to pigs or even dumped to keep the price high. The notion of food scarcity is an obvious distortion when the major headaches of many agricultural experts around the world are how to reduce mountains of surplus and keep prices high.

From this point of view, then, the problem of food scarcity lies in the social organization of food production and distribution. The solution to hunger is to construct new forms of social organization capable of meeting the needs of the masses. The problem, though, goes beyond the boundaries of individual countries. The policies of the rich nations and multinational corporations are also responsible for the conditions that perpetuate poverty in the developing world. The United States, for example, supports the very conditions that promote hunger and poverty. The last section of this chapter documents this role.

Sickness and Disease

Chronic malnutrition, an obvious correlate of greater numbers of people and poverty, results in high infant mortality rates, shorter life expectancies, and a stunting of physical and mental capacities.

> *Malnutrition takes its heaviest toll on children, and the health damage can begin before birth. Pregnant women who receive inadequate nourishment are likely to have underweight babies, who are especially vulnerable to infections and parasites that can*

lead to early death. Children who survive but receive inadequate food in the first five years of life are susceptible to the permanent stunting of their physical growth. (Bender and Smith 1999:6)

We know that protein deficiency in infancy results in permanent brain damage. "When protein is not available in the diet to supply the amino acids from which brain proteins are synthesized, the brain stops growing. Apparently it can never regain the lost time. Not only is head size reduced in a malnourished youngster, but the brain does not fill the cranium" (Ehrlich and Ehrlich 1972:92).

Vitamin deficiencies, of course, cause a number of diseases such as rickets, goiter, and anemia. Iron deficiency is a special problem for hungry children: some 25 percent of men and 45 percent of women (60 percent for pregnant women) in developing countries are anemic, a condition of iron deficiency (Gardner and Halweil 2000). Almost one-third of the world's people do not get enough iodine from food and water, causing goiters, dwarfism, and mental slowness (Kristof 2008).

Vitamin deficiencies make the individual more susceptible to influenza and other infectious diseases. Health in overpopulated areas is also affected by such problems as polluted water and air and inadequate sewage treatment.

Malnourishment also causes a low level of energy. Not only lack of food but also intestinal disorders commonly associated with poverty cause general lassitude in the afflicted.*

The United Nations estimates that 1.1 million people do not have access to safe water and that 2.6 billion live in unsanitary squalor. This lack of a safe water supply and sanitation results in millions of cases of water-related diseases and more than 5 million deaths every year (DeSouza, Williams, and Meyerson 2003). Polluted water, contaminated food, exposure to disease-carrying insects and animals, and unsanitary living conditions make the world's poor highly vulnerable to, among other diseases, chronic diarrhea, tuberculosis, malaria, Ebola, dengue, hepatitis, cholera, and parasites (see A Closer Look). More than half of the annual deaths in sub-Saharan Africa are caused by infectious and parasitic diseases. In addition to these diseases, one has emerged in the last 30 years or so with devastating effects—HIV.

HIV, the virus that causes AIDS, is transmitted through the exchange of bodily fluids, usually through sex, but also from contaminated needles, contact with tainted blood, or during birth for an infant born of an infected mother. Since the start of the AIDS pandemic (a worldwide epidemic) some three decades ago, some 60 million people have been stricken with AIDS worldwide, and 25 million have died. By the end of 2008, in addition to the deaths, 33.4 million were infected with HIV, two-thirds of them in sub-Saharan Africa, where 5.2 percent of the population were living with HIV/AIDS (Avert 2009).

HIV/AIDS is the worst epidemic in human history. The Black Death that ravaged Europe in 1348 killed approximately 25 million, and the United Nations Programme on HIV/AIDS predicts that AIDS will claim 68 million lives by 2020 (cited in Sternberg 2002). Two-thirds of those infected with HIV worldwide live in sub-Saharan Africa, where AIDS is the leading cause of

---

*Although low energy levels are a result of poverty, many persons have blamed poverty on an inherent lack of energy, or "drive" in the poor—a classic example of blaming the victim.

A CLOSER LOOK

THE BILL AND MELINDA GATES FOUNDATION'S WAR AGAINST MALARIA

Bill Gates, the cofounder of Microsoft, and his wife, Melinda, founded the Bill and Melinda Gates Foundation. The foundation is richly endowed with money from Bill Gates, the richest person in the United States, plus the bulk of the fortune of the second wealthiest person in the United States, Warren Buffett. In October 2008, the foundation had an endowment of $35.1 billion. The amount it donates each year more than doubles the annual budget of the United Nations Educational, Scientific, and Cultural Organization (UNESCO; O'Brien and Saul 2006).

The efforts of the foundation are directed at three main problems: global health, global development, and programs in the United States to improve education. We focus here on one part—the eradication of malaria, which the foundation, working with other organizations, hopes to eradicate by 2015.

Malaria is a disease of the developing world, mostly in sub-Saharan Africa and Asia. The disease is caused by a parasite transmitted by certain types of mosquitoes. As many as 2.7 million people a year die from malaria annually, 75 percent of them African children. Bill Gates feels that the corporate world is not working on the problem because the potential profits are few. "More money is being spent finding a cure for baldness than developing drugs to combat malaria. The market does not drive scientists, thinkers, and governments to do the right things" (quoted in Gardner 2009). The Bill and Melinda Gates Foundation seeks to fill the void. It funds research to discover, develop, and clinically test malaria vaccines; it develops new malaria drugs that are more effective and affordable; it develops improved methods for malaria control (effective pesticides, insecticide-treated bed nets that protect against mosquitoes); it distributes insect nets and other protective gear; and it works to develop greater public awareness about malaria and advocate for effective research and control (Bill and Melinda Gates Foundation n.d.).

death. The high death rate is the result of poor people in these regions not being able to afford the costly drugs to fight the disease.

> More than 2 million children in Africa under age 15 are living with HIV. . . . Of these youngsters, perhaps 660,000 are sick enough to require medical intervention. Yet only 1 in 20 children who need ARVs [antiretroviral drugs] get them. In addition, fewer than 1 in 10 HIV-positive mothers receive the drugs they need to keep from transmitting the virus to newborns. (Gorman 2006:96)

The New Slavery

"In almost every culture and society there has been, at one time or another, slavery" (Bales 2000:xiii; this section is dependent largely on Bales [1999, 2000], Re [2002], and Cockburn, [2009]). Typically, slaves were captured by the powerful to work the rest of their lives for the benefit of their captors. Often slavery was legalized with people bought and sold as property to work at the whim of their owners. Slavery was outlawed in the United States with the ratification of the Thirteenth Amendment in 1865.

By conservative estimate, there are 27 million slaves in the world today, and the number is growing. Slavery today (the new slavery), just as slavery in other times, means the loss of freedom, the exploitation of people for profit, and the control of slaves through violence or its threat. But today's forms of slavery also differ from the past. First, slavery is no longer a lifelong condition, as the slave typically is freed after he or she is no longer useful (e.g., a prostitute who has AIDS). Second, sometimes individuals and families become slaves by choice—a choice forced by extreme poverty. The population explosion in the poorest nations has created a vast supply of potential workers who are desperate and vulnerable, conditions that sometimes translate into enslavement. Often the poor must place themselves in bondage to pay off a debt. Faced with a crisis (crop failure, illness), an individual borrows money, but having no other possessions uses his or her family's lives as collateral. The slave must work for the slaveholder until the slaveholder decides the debt is repaid. This situation is problematic because many slaveholders use false accounting or charge very high interest, making repayment forever out of reach. Sometimes the debt can be passed to subsequent generations, thus enslaving offspring. Debt bondage is most common in South Asia.

Impoverishment may also lead desperate parents to sell their children (often told that the children will have good jobs) to brokers who in turn sell them to slaveholders. This practice is common in Thailand as the conduit for young girls to end up as prostitutes in brothels against their will. The United Nations Children's Fund estimates that 200,000 children in West and Central Africa are sold into slavery annually by their parents. Most come from the poorest countries, such as Benin, Burkina Faso, or Mali, where up to 70 percent of the people live on less than $1 a day. Faced with grinding poverty, parents may sell their children to traders for as little as $15, in the hope that the children will find a better life. Girls end up as domestic workers or prostitutes while boys are forced to work on coffee or cocoa plantations or as fishermen. Sometimes poor young people with little prospect for success may deal directly with a broker who promises legitimate jobs, but once they are away from their homes, violence is used to take control of their lives.

There is an international traffic in slavery, involving forced migration, the smuggling of illegal immigrants, and criminal networks. The Central Intelligence Agency (CIA) estimates that 900,000 people are sold across international borders each year, yielding an annual income to the perpetrators of $7 billion (Hardy 2004). These migrants who end up as slaves come from Asia, Africa, Latin America, Eastern Europe, and the nations of the former Soviet Union, where as many as two-thirds of women live in poverty. The antitrafficking program at Johns Hopkins University estimates that 1 million undocumented immigrants are trapped in the United States in slavelike conditions (Bowe 2007). The State Department estimates that as many as 50,000 women and children (and a smaller number of men) are smuggled into the United States each year to be forced into prostitution (about 40,000), domestic service, or as bonded labor in factories and sweatshops. Immigrants pay as much as $50,000 (in debt bondage) to get smuggled into the United States with false promises of decent jobs. Once in this country, most find their passports are stolen, and they are forced to work as prostitutes or maids, on farms, or in sweatshops. They may be locked up, but even if not, they are trapped because they fear violence by the slaveholders, and they fear the police because they are illegals and because they are strangers in a strange land.

Concentration of Misery in Cities

In 1800, just 3 percent of the world's population lived in cities. In 2007, for the first time, more people were city dwellers than rural dwellers. And, by 2050,

Reuters/Andrew Biraj/Landov

Often the poor must place themselves in debt bondage, using one's family as collateral, thus enslaving their children.

when the planet's population reaches 9 billion, two-thirds will likely live in cities, some of them huge cities.

In 1950, only one city in the developing countries, Shanghai, had a population of more than 5 million. By 2009, there were five cities in the developing world with populations exceeding 20 million.

A major problem is that the infrastructure of these cities are overwhelmed by the exploding population growth. A second problem is providing employment for their citizens. The special problem is to find employment for new immigrants to the cities—the farmers pushed off the land because of high rural density and the resulting poverty. The people who migrate to the cities are, for the most part, unprepared for life and work there. They do not possess mechanical skills; they are illiterate; they are steeped in tradition. The cities, too, are unprepared for them. Aside from the obvious problems of housing, schools, and sanitation, the cities of the developing nations do not have the industries that employ many workers. Because their citizens are usually poor, these countries are not good markets for products, so there is little internal demand for manufactured goods.

Another massive problem of the cities in the developing world is the mushrooming of squatter settlements ("shantytowns"), where 1 billion struggle to survive without clean water, sanitation, schools, and other infrastructure.

The immediate question for these immigrants is where to live. They have little choice but to create houses out of scraps (tin, plywood, paper) on land that does not belong to them (in streets, alleys, or ravines or on hillsides). Often they literally "live in shit" because the lack of sanitation forces excrement to pile up, creating serious health dangers (Montgomery 2009). Shantytowns are the fastest-growing sections of cities of the developing countries.

How do squatters react to their deplorable situation? They are unemployed or work at the most menial of tasks. They are hungry. Their children remain illiterate. They suffer the indignities of being social outcasts. Will their alienation lead to terrorism and/or revolutionary activity? Some observers believe that for those experiencing abject poverty, the struggle is for the next meal, not for a redistribution of power. Others see the growing squatter settlements as breeding grounds for riots, terrorism, and radical political movements. Thomas Friedman says that "the growth of third world cities occurs in the countries least able to sustain it, and that will create a situation that will likely fuel instability and extremism—not just in those areas, but beyond them as well" (Friedman 2008:29).

The prospects for the cities of the developing countries are bleak. Their growth continues unabated. Unbelievable poverty and hunger are common. The inequality gap between the rich and poor is staggering. Jobs are scarce. Resources are limited and becoming more scarce as the number of inhabitants increases. The capital necessary for extensive economic development or for providing needed services is difficult to raise.

In sum, the high growth rates of cities, combined with the high concentration of people who are poor, unemployed, angry, hungry, and miserable, magnifies and intensifies other problems (such as racial and religious animosities, resource shortages, and pollution).

U.S. RELATIONS WITH THE DEVELOPING WORLD

There is a huge gap between the rich and poor nations of the world. About 75 percent of the world's people live in the overpopulated and poverty-afflicted developing world, yet these nations produce only one-tenth of the world's industrial output and one-twelfth of its electric power output.

The nations of the developing world are underdeveloped for a number of reasons, including geography, climate, lack of arable land and minerals, and a history of continuous warfare; but the rich nations are also responsible. The developing world economies are largely the result of a history of colonialism and of economic domination by the developed nations in the postcolonial era.

As recently as 1914, approximately 70 percent of the world's population lived in colonies (in those areas now designated as the developing world). As colonies of superpowers, their resources and labors were exploited. Leadership was imposed from outside. The local people were treated as primitive and backward. Crops were planted for the colonizer's benefit, not for the needs of the indigenous population. Raw materials were extracted for exports. The wealth thus created was concentrated in the hands of local elites and the colonizers. Population growth was encouraged because the colonizer needed a continuous supply of low-cost labor. Colonialism destroyed the cultural patterns of production and exchange by which these societies once met the needs of their peoples. Thriving industries that once served indigenous markets were destroyed. The capital generated by the natural wealth in these countries was not used to develop local factories, schools, sanitation systems, agricultural processing plants, or irrigation systems. Colonialism also promoted a two-class society by increasing land holdings among the few and landlessness among the many.

Although the process began centuries ago and ended, for the most part, in the 1960s and 1990s, the legacy of colonialism continues to promote poverty today. In short, the heritage of colonialism that systematically promoted the self-interest of the colonizers and robbed and degraded the resources and the lives of the colonized continues. Vestigial attitudes, both within and outside these countries, and the continued dependency of developing nations on the industrialized superpowers, exacerbate their problems. As a result, the gap between the developing world and the industrial nations continues to widen.

This section explores the relationship of the United States to the developing world, focusing on the economic mechanisms that maintain dependency and the political policies that promote problems within these countries.

Transnational Corporations

Gigantic transnational corporations, most of which are U.S.-based, control the world economy. Their decisions to build or not to build, to relocate a plant, to begin marketing a new product, or to scrap an old one have a tremendous impact on the lives of ordinary citizens in the countries in which they operate and in which they invest.

In their desire to tap low-wage workers, the multinational corporations have tended to locate in poor countries. Although the poor countries should have benefited from this new industry (by, say, gaining a higher standard of living and access to modern technology), they have not for the most part. One reason is that the profits generated in these countries are mostly channeled back to the United States. Second, global companies do not have a great impact in easing the unemployment of the poor nations because they use advanced technology whenever feasible, which reduces the demand for jobs. Also, the corporations typically hire workers from a narrow segment of the population—young women.

The global corporations have enormous advantages over local competition when they move into an underdeveloped country. Foremost, they have access to the latest technology in information technology, machinery, or genetic engineering. Second, they receive better terms than local businesses when they borrow money. They are preferred customers because their credit is backed by their worldwide financial resources. Moreover, global banks and global corporations are closely tied through interlocking directorates and shared ownership. Thus, it is in the interest of these banks to give credit under favorable conditions to their corporate friends. Finally, the global corporations have an enormous advantage over local companies through their manipulation of the market, influence over local government officials, and their control of workers.

An important source of the developing countries' current dependency on the United States and on other industrialized countries is their growing public and private debt. This debt, which is more than half the collective GNP of these countries, is so large for some nations that they cannot spend for needed public works, education, and other social services. Available monies must be spent, rather, on servicing the debt. Thus, the debt treadmill stifles progress. This situation is further exacerbated by the toll on the natural resources of the developing countries as they overexploit their resources to pay foreign creditors.

The United States, as a lender nation, is also negatively influenced. First, the United States is encouraged to buy imports and reduce exports, which eliminates domestic jobs. Second, to the degree that foreign governments default on their loans, the U.S. banks that made the bad loans are subsidized by American taxpayers, ensuring the banks' profit. This occurred, for example, in Mexico's 1995 financial crisis and in the 1998 financial crises in a number of Asian nations. Although this money shored up a teetering economy, in reality it protected the assets of U.S. banks that were in danger of losing their investments in Mexico and Asia.

Two activities by transnationals are highly controversial because they have negative costs worldwide, especially to the inhabitants of developing nations—arms sales and the sale of products known to be harmful.

- **Arms Sales.** The wealthy nations sell or give armaments to the poorer nations. Since the end of the Cold War, the United States has sold well over $100 billion worth of weapons abroad. In 2008, global arms sales by the United States totaled $37.8 billion. In 2008, for the sixteenth straight year, the United States was the number one seller of arms abroad, accounting for 68.4 percent of all weapons sales (followed in order by Italy, Russia, and France). The United States was not only the leader worldwide but also in sales to the developing world (76 percent of its sales went to nations in the developing world) (Shanker 2009).

  The United States is actively engaged in promoting and financing weapons exports through 6,500 full-time government employees in the Defense, Commerce, and State Departments. These sales efforts are motivated by what was deemed to be in the national interests of the countries involved and by the profit to the manufacturers (in the United States, the multinationals most involved are Lockheed Martin, General Motors/Hughes, Northrop Grumman, General Electric, and Boeing). Not incidentally, the top ten arms-exporting companies give millions in political contributions (political action committees and soft money) during federal election campaigns.

  There are several important negative consequences of these arms sales. First, they fan the flames of war. The United States sells weapons to countries actively engaged in military conflict. So rather than working to promote stability in already tense regions, the search for profits exacerbates the situation. Second, the United States has become an informal global shopping center for terrorists, mercenaries, and international criminals of all stripes (Bergman and Reynolds 2002). These gun sales are made through retail stores (not corporations), as the United States has such a lax system of controls over gun dealers and transactions at gun shows. September 11 and the subsequent war on terrorism have not changed U.S. gun control policies.

  A third consequence is that arms sales can boomerang; that is, they can come back to haunt the seller—for example, the United States has sold armaments to Iraq to aid in their fight with Iran, only to have those weapons used against its forces in the Gulf War in 1990 and the Iraq War of 2003 and beyond. Similarly, the United States aided the freedom fighters in Afghanistan as they fought the Soviets, only to have those weapons used later by Al-Qaeda and the Taliban against the United States after the terrorist attacks of September 11, 2001.

  Fourth, the United States, in its zeal to contain or defeat regimes unfriendly to its interests, has sold arms to countries that are undemocratic and that violate human rights.

- **Corporate Sales That Endanger Life.** Corporate dumping, the exporting of goods that have either been banned or not approved for sale in the United States because they are dangerous, is a relatively common practice. Most often the greatest market for such unsafe products is among the poor in the developing world. These countries often do not bar hazardous products, and many of their poor citizens are illiterate and therefore tend to be unaware of the hazards involved with the use of such products.

The United States and other industrialized nations continue to use the nations of the developing world as sources of profits as nations purchase these unhealthy products. For example, the Dalkon Shield intrauterine device was sold overseas in forty-two nations after the manufacturer, A. H. Robins, withdrew it from the U.S. market because of its danger to women. Similarly, after the Consumer Product Safety Commission forced children's garments with the fire retardant called tris phosphate off the domestic market because it was found to be carcinogenic, the manufacturer shipped several million garments overseas for sale.

Chemical pesticides pollute water, degrade the soil, and destroy native wildlife and vegetation. The use of the most potent pesticides is banned in the United States. This ban, however, does not pertain to foreign sales: 25 percent of the pesticides exported by the United States are restricted or banned by the Environmental Protection Agency for domestic use.

Another form of corporate dumping, in the literal sense of the word, is the practice of shipping toxic wastes produced in the United States to the developing world for disposal. This practice is attractive to U.S. corporations because the Environmental Protection Agency requires expensive disposal facilities, whereas the materials can be dumped in developing-world nations for a fraction of the cost. The host nations engage in such potentially dangerous transactions because they need the money.

Some companies dump workplace hazards as well as hazardous products and waste materials in poor nations. Governmental regulations often require U.S. corporations to provide a reasonably safe environment for their workers. These requirements, such as not exposing workers to asbestos, lead, or other toxic substances, are often expensive to meet. Thus, many corporations move their manufacture (and unsafe working conditions) to a country with few or no restrictions. This move saves the companies money and increases their profits, but it disregards the health and safety of workers outside the United States.

Corporate dumping is undesirable for three reasons. First, and most obvious, it poses serious health hazards to the poor and uninformed consumers of the developing world. Second, the disregard of U.S. multinational corporations for their workers and their consumers in foreign lands contributes to anti-U.S. feelings in the host countries. Third, many types of corporate dumping have a boomerang effect; that is, some of the hazardous products sold abroad by U.S. companies are often returned to the United States and other developed nations, negatively affecting the health of the people in those countries. For example, the United States imports about one-fourth of its fruits and vegetables, and some of this produce is tainted with toxic chemical residues.

UNITED STATES IN THE GLOBAL VILLAGE

In the global economy, the fate of the world's poorest nations and the poor within these nations are of crucial importance to all nations and the people within them. Huge gaps in income, education, and other measures of the quality of life make the world less safe. And, as the population growth surges in the developing world, the inequality gap will widen and the world will become less stable. Unless wealthy nations do more to help the poor nations catch up, the twenty-first century will witness Earth split into two very different planets, one inhabited by the fortunate few, and the other by poverty-stricken, desperate masses.

What can the wealthy nations do to help the impoverished nations? First, the affluent nations can pledge more resources targeted for development aid. The United Nations set a goal for the rich nations to give 0.7 percent of Gross National Income (GNI) to alleviate poverty in the poor nations. There are two major problems with this. First, the rich nations have failed to meet this obligation, giving instead around 0.2 to 0.4 percent, falling more than $100 billion short each year. Second, the type of aid often is not helpful. Rather than targeted to meet the needs of the poor, it is sometimes designed to meet the strategic and economic interests of the donor countries (for a nongovernmental approach to solving poverty, see the Social Policy panel); the aid benefits powerful domestic interest groups; and too little aid reaches those who most desperately need it (Shah 2009). For example, in 2008, the U.S. government spent $26 billion in foreign aid to address the plight of the world's poor. Much of this aid, however, was for armaments not humanitarian aid. In the case of Egypt, the United States

SOCIAL POLICY

ARE MICROLOANS THE ANSWER FOR THE WORLD'S POOR?

The 2006 Nobel Peace Prize was awarded to Muhammad Yunus, an economics professor from Bangladesh. Since the 1970s, Yunnis, through his Grameen Bank, has been offering very small loans (usually under $100) to the impoverished to start activities such as buying a dairy cow or a mobile phone that villagers can pay to use. Since then, the Bank has disbursed more than $5.3 billion to nearly 7 million borrowers who have no collateral. They pay a high interest rate (as much as 20 percent) to service these small loans, but 98 percent of the loans are paid off. Ninety-six percent of these loans are to women because traditionally, banks in the developing world lend only to men.

This model for helping the world's poorest has attracted funds from various foundations (e.g., Michael and Susan Dell Foundation, Google.org, Bill and Melinda Gates Foundation) and from the World Bank, which grants loans of as little as $1,000 for enterprises such as brick making. Through these foundations, 113 million borrowers received microloans in 2005. The goal of the Micro-credit Summit Campaign is to reach 175 million of the world's poorest families by 2015.

Without question, this microcredit movement has helped many poor women and their families. The trouble, as Alexander Cockburn has put it, "is that microloans don't make any sort of macrodifference" (2009:9). In other words, "Loans to the poor have not yet had a demonstrable effect on aggregate poverty levels" (Bruck 2006:67). Bangladesh and Bolivia, for example, have two of the most successful microcredit programs in the world, but they also remain two of the poorest countries of the world.

Two plans should be added to the microcredit program. At the microlevel, lending should be combined with other initiatives, such as education and health care. And foremost, the structural causes of poverty in these impoverished nations must be addressed. Economist Robert Pollin says that poor countries need publicly subsidized macrocredit programs to support "manufacturing, land reform, marketing cooperatives, a functioning infrastructure, and, most of all, decent jobs" (quoted in Cockburn 2009:9). "What poor countries need most, then, is not more microbusinesses. They need more small-to-medium sized enterprises . . . companies that are relatively rare in the developing world" (Surowieki 2008:35).

"Governments like microloans because they allow them to abdicate their most basic responsibilities to poor citizens. Microloans make the market a god" (Cockburn 2009:9). The market, however, is a major source for the abject poverty in the world. Although microloans do help many individuals, they must be combined with structural societal reforms necessary to reduce overall poverty.

gave $1.3 billion in 2008 to buy weapons; only $103 million for education, and $74 million for health care (O'Brien 2008).

According to the chief economist of the World Bank, Nicholas Stern, "If the rich nations increased aid to 0.7 percent of their economic output, it would add $100 billion a year in assistance" (quoted in Memmott 2001:3B). What could be accomplished with an additional $100 billion?

- The global relief agency Oxfam argues that about $8 billion more each year is needed in spending for education in the world's poorest countries to fulfill a pledge by 155 nations that every child on earth have a basic level of literacy by 2015 (Briscoe 1999).
- The world's poor countries owe the rich ones trillions of dollars. The annual interest owed on this debt exceeds the amount spent on health and education in the poor countries. Some poor countries spend 40 percent of their income for interest on a foreign debt that will never be repaid (much like the contract debt that enslaves poor individuals). The rich countries must provide debt relief to the poor countries. Currently, there is a partial debt relief plan whereby the United States pays 4 percent of the wealthy nation's total, or $920 million over 4 years. Each dollar contributed to this plan produces $20 in debt relief.
- There could be a frontal assault by the World Health Organization and the developed countries to reduce the incidence and spread of infectious diseases such as tuberculosis, malaria, and meningitis. Eradication of diseases for which the technology is already available (poliomyelitis, leprosy, tetanus, Chagas' disease, and dracunculiasis) and the disorder of iodine deficiency could be reached. Education programs need to be instituted to warn about sexually transmitted diseases and how to protect against them.
- Meeting the basic nutrition and health needs of the world's poorest people would cost $13 billion a year (Cain, 2004).
- When Kofi Annan was secretary-general of the United Nations, he argued that an annual expenditure of $7 billion to $10 billion (five times the current expenditure) sustained for many years is needed to defeat AIDS in the developing world. Other estimates are that a comprehensive AIDS program would exceed $20 billion annually. Specifically, the money would be used for prevention through education, providing medicines to prevent the transmission from mother to child, care and treatment of those infected, and protection of those left most vulnerable (widows and orphans; Annan, 2006).

The wealthy nations can provide humanitarian aid to the developing nations with three provisos: (1) that it is truly humanitarian (such as technology, medical supplies, food, inoculation programs, family planning, agricultural equipment, sewage treatment systems, water treatment) and not military aid; (2) that the aid reaches the intended targets (those in need), not the well-off elites; and (3) that the governments in the impoverished nations have sensible plans for using the new resources, such as spending on health (e.g., the vaccination of children) and education, especially for women (Sen 1999).

How much commitment should the United States make to bringing poor nations up to a minimum standard? Many citizens, corporations, and politicians are indifferent to the plight of the poor, hungry, and sick far away. Many have misgivings about helping corrupt governments. Others are opposed to our support of family planning and the funding of abortion.

The ultimate interest of the United States is best served if there is peace and stability in the developing world. These goals can be accomplished only if population growth is slowed significantly, hunger and poverty alleviated, and the extremes of inequality reduced.

If the United States and other developed nations do not take appropriate steps, human misery, acts of terrorism against affluent nations, tensions among neighbors, and wars—even nuclear war—will increase. The last factor becomes especially relevant given that a number of developing nations have nuclear bomb capabilities. Moreover, a number of developing-world countries have been alleged to have used chemical weapons. The ultimate question is whether the way these steps are implemented will help the developing world reduce its dependence on the more developed nations, the hunger and misery within their countries, and in the process, international tensions. We ignore the poor of the developing world at our peril.

■ CHAPTER REVIEW

1. The term *developing world* refers to the underdeveloped and developing nations where poverty, hunger, and misery are found disproportionately. These nations also are characterized by relative powerlessness, rapid population growth, high infant mortality, unsanitary living conditions, and high rates of illiteracy.

2. In mid-2009, the world population exceeded 6.8089 billion and was increasing by 75 to 80 million annually. About 99 percent of the population growth occurs in the developing world, where food, housing, health care, and employment are inadequate to meet present needs.

3. While world population is growing rapidly, the amount of productive land is shrinking in rich and poor countries alike because of the loss of topsoil, the lowering of water tables from irrigation and overgrazing, and pollution.

4. Within the nations experiencing the most rapid population growth, cities are growing much faster than are rural areas. The problems of survival for individuals and families are increased dramatically in cities: food is too expensive, jobs are scarce and poorly paid, and sanitation problems increase the likelihood of disease. The concentration of the poor in the limited space of cities increases tensions and the probability of hostility.

5. There are three ways to reduce high fertility in the developing world: (a) economic development (modern demographic transition), (b) familyplanning programs, and (c) social change, especially through the changing of traditional women's roles.

6. Poverty is a special problem of the developing world: 1.3 billion people have inadequate diets, high infant mortality, low life expectancy, and high rates of illiteracy. Poverty also contributes to high fertility.

7. Hunger is a worldwide problem, especially in the developing world, but even there food production is adequate to meet the needs of all of the people. The problem of hunger results from high prices, unequal distribution of food, overreliance on cash crops, and concentration of land ownership among very few people—all the consequences of the political economy in these nations and the world.

8. The developing world is underdeveloped for a number of reasons, the most important of which is a heritage of colonialism. Colonialism destroyed local industries and self-sufficient crop-growing patterns, drained off resources for the benefit of the colonizers, and promoted local elites through concentration of land ownership among the few. In the postcolonial era, the dependency of the developing world and its control by outside forces continue.

9. A huge worldwide problem, especially among the poor in the developing world, is HIV/AIDS. Since 1980 some 60 million people have contracted this disease worldwide, with 25 million deaths.

10. It is estimated that there are 27 million slaves in the world. The new slavery is a consequence of extreme poverty, resulting in debt bondage and the sale of people to slaveholders.

11. The world economy is controlled by transnational corporations, the majority of which are based in the United States. Their power in the

underdeveloped nations perpetuates the dependency of many developing-world nations on the United States.

12. Transnationals add to the tensions in developing-world countries through arms sales, corporate dumping of products known to be dangerous, and intervention in the domestic affairs of host countries.

13. The developed nations must work to alleviate the problems faced by the developing nations by increasing their financial commitment, by providing debt relief, and by working with international agencies to promote education and health programs. To do so is in our national interest.

■ KEY TERMS

Differential fertility. Differences in the average number of children born to a woman by social category.

Fertility rate. The average number of children born to each woman.

Modern demographic transition. A three-stage pattern of population change occurring as societies industrialize and urbanize, resulting ultimately in a low and stable population growth rate.

Absolute poverty. A condition of life so degraded by disease, illiteracy, malnutrition, and squalor as to deny its victims the basic necessities. Statistically, those making less than $1 a day are in this category.

Life chances. The chances throughout one's life cycle to live and experience the good things in life.

Pandemic. A worldwide epidemic.

New slavery. The new slavery differs from traditional slavery in that it is, for the most part, not a lifelong condition and sometimes individuals and families become slaves by choice—a choice forced by extreme poverty.

Colony. A territory controlled by a powerful country that exploits the land and the people for its own benefit.

Transnational corporation. A profit-oriented company engaged in business activities in more than one nation.

Corporate dumping. The exporting of goods that have either been banned or not approved for sale in the United States because they are dangerous.

■ SUCCEED WITH mysoclab PEARSON www.mysoclab.com

Experience, Discover, Observe, Evaluate
MySocLab is designed just for you. This chapter features a pre-test and post-test to help you learn and review key concepts and terms.

Experience sociology in action with dynamic visual activities, videos, and readings to enhance your learning experience. Complete the following activities at www.mysoclab.com.

Social Explorer is an interactive application that allows you to explore Census data through interactive maps.

- Explore the Social Explorer Map: *Burgess' Concentric Zone Model*

The Core Concepts in Sociology video clips offer a real-world perspective on sociological concepts.

- Watch *Population Growth and Decline*

MySocLibrary includes primary source readings from classic and contemporary sociologists.

- Read Ehrenreich & Hochschild, *Global Woman;* Eglitis, *The Uses of Global Poverty: How Economic Inequality Benefits the West*

Threats to the Environment

From Chapter 4 of *Social Problems, Census Update*, Twelfth Edition. D. Stanley Eitzen, Maxine Baca Zinn, Kelly Eitzen Smith. Copyright © 2012 by Pearson Education, Inc. Published by Allyn & Bacon. All rights reserved.

Threats to the Environment

The threat from climate change is serious, it is urgent, and it is growing. Our generation's response to this challenge will be judged by history, for if we fail to meet it—boldly, swiftly, and together—we risk consigning future generations to an irreversible catastrophe.

—President Barack Obama (2009)

Human societies have always altered their physical environments. They have used fire, cleared forests, tilled the soil, terraced hillsides, mined for mineral deposits, dammed rivers, polluted streams, and overgrazed grasslands. Since 1950 the pace and magnitude of the negative environmental impacts of human activities have increased and intensified. Especially significant are the extraordinary use of fossil fuels, the deforestation of the rain forests, the pumping of billions of tons of greenhouse gases into the air, the pollution of water by fertilizers, pesticides, and animal wastes, emission of toxic chemicals, and the rapid erosion of topsoil. In effect, we human beings are fundamentally changing the planet in ways that are diminishing the planet's ability to sustain life.

The Worldwatch Institute concluded its annual State of the World report in 2000 saying: Species are disappearing, temperatures are rising, reefs are dying, forests are shrinking, storms are raging, water tables are falling: Almost every ecological indicator shows a world in decline. And with the global population expected to hit 9 billion in the next 50 years, those indicators are likely to worsen. (quoted in Braile 2000:16a)

As environmental problems are examined in this chapter, the discussion is guided by three facts. First, while some environmental problems are beyond human control (volcanoes, earthquakes, solar flares), *most are social in origin*. As Paul and Anne Ehrlich summarize it,

Our species' negative impact on our own life-support systems can be approximated by the equation I = PAT. In that equation, the size of the population (P) is multiplied by the average affluence or consumption per individual (A), and that in turn is multiplied by some measure of the technology (T) that services and drives the consumption. Thus commuting in automobiles powered by subsidized fossil fuels on proliferating freeways creates a much greater T factor than commuting on bikes using simple paths or working at home on a computer network. The product of P, A, and T is Impact (I), a rough estimate of how much humanity is degrading the ecosystem services it depends upon. (2008:1)

Second, the magnitude of environmental problems has become so great that the ultimate survival of the human species is in question (see the "Looking Toward the Future" panel). Third, although environmental problems may originate within a nation's borders, they usually have global consequences. Thus, this chapter examines human-made environmental problems at both the domestic and international levels. The first section describes the nature of these problems and their consequences. The second focuses on the United States. The third section examines the social sources of these problems and alternative solutions. The final section describes the long-range international implications of environmental problems.

WORLDWIDE ENVIRONMENTAL PROBLEMS

Earth's biosphere (the surface layer of the planet and the surrounding atmosphere) provides the land, air, water, and energy necessary to sustain life. This life-support system is a complex, interdependent one in which energy from the sun is converted into food:

The goods and services that ecosystems provide us with form the foundation of our economies. Agriculture, forestry, and fishing are responsible for 50% of all jobs worldwide and 70% of the jobs in sub-Saharan Africa, East Asia, and the Pacific. In 25% of the world's nations, crops, timber, and fish still contribute more to the economy than do industrial goods. Ecosystems also purify our air and water, help to control our climate, and produce soil-services that can't be replaced at any reasonable cost. (PBS 2010:1)

Three social forces are disturbing these ecosystems profoundly. First, the tremendous increase in population increases the demand for food, energy, minerals, and other products. With the world's population (approximately 6.8 billion in 2009) increasing by 76 million a year (in effect, adding the population of Sweden every month), the stresses on the environment mount (see Figure 1: World Population Estimates).

LOOKING TOWARD THE FUTURE

ENVIRONMENTAL COLLAPSES

Geographer Jared Diamond, in his book *Collapse: How Societies Choose to Fail or Succeed,* describes a number of past civilizations (e.g., Easter Island, the Anasazi of the Southwest United States, the Maya, and the Norse in Greenland) that disappeared, leaving behind great ruins and a mystery as to why they collapsed. Diamond argues that the mystery is explained, at least in part, by "ecological suicide." That theory has obvious implications for humanity today.

It has long been suspected that many of those mysterious abandonments were at least partly triggered by ecological problems: people inadvertently destroying the environmental resources on which their societies depended. This suspicion of unintended

ecological suicide—ecocide—has been confirmed by discoveries made in recent decades by archaeologists, climatologists, historians, paleontologists, and palynologists (pollen scientists). The processes through which past societies have undermined themselves by damaging their environments fall into eight categories, whose relative importance differs from case to case: deforestation and habitat destruction, soil problems (erosion, salinization, and soil fertility losses), water management problems, overhunting, overfishing, effects of introduced species on native species, human population growth, and increased per capita impact of people.

Those past collapses tended to follow somewhat similar courses

constituting variations on a theme. Population growth forced people to adopt intensified means of agricultural production (such as irrigation, double-cropping, or terracing), and to expand farming from the prime lands first chosen onto more marginal land, in order to feed the growing number of hungry mouths. Unsustainable practices led to environmental damage of one or more of the eight types just listed, resulting in agriculturally marginal lands having to be abandoned again. Consequences for society included food shortages, starvation, wars among too many people fighting for too few resources, and overthrows of governing elites by disillusioned masses. Eventually, population decreased through starvation, war, or disease, and society lost some of the political, economic, and cultural complexity that it had developed at its peak.

FIGURE 1

World Population Estimates 1950–2050

Source: U.S. Census Bureau, International Data Base, December 2010 update.

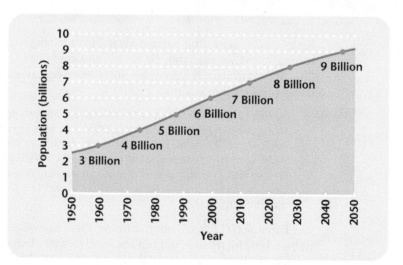

Writers find it tempting to draw analogies between those trajectories of human societies and the trajectories of individual human lives—to talk of a society's birth, growth, peak, senescence, and death—and to assume that the long period of senescence that most of us traverse between our peak years and our deaths also applies to societies. But that metaphor proves erroneous for many past societies (and for the modern Soviet Union): they declined rapidly after reaching peak numbers and power, and those rapid declines must have come as a surprise and shock to their citizens. In the worst cases of complete collapse, everybody in the society emigrated or died. Obviously, though, this grim trajectory is not one that all past societies followed unvaryingly to completion: different societies collapsed to different degrees and in somewhat different ways, whereas many societies didn't collapse at all.

The risk of such collapses today is now a matter of increasing concern; indeed, collapses have already materialized for Somalia, Rwanda, and some other Third World countries. Many people fear that ecocide has now come to overshadow nuclear war and emerging diseases as a threat to global civilization. The environmental problems facing us today include the same eight that undermined past societies, plus four new ones: human-caused climate change, buildup of toxic chemicals in the environment, energy shortages, and full human utilization of the Earth's photosynthetic capacity. Most of these 12 threats, it is claimed, will become globally critical within the next few decades: either we solve the problems by then, or the problems will undermine not just Somalia but also First World societies. Much more likely than a doomsday scenario involving human extinction or an apocalyptic collapse of industrial civilization would be "just" a future of significantly lower living standards, chronically higher risks, and the undermining of what we now consider some of our key values. Such a collapse could assume various forms, such as the worldwide spread of diseases or else of wars, triggered ultimately by scarcity of environmental resources. If this reasoning is correct, then our efforts today will determine the state of the world in which the current generation of children and young adults lives out their middle and late years.

Source: From *Collapse: How Societies Choose to Fail or Succeed* by Jared Diamond, copyright © 2005 by Jared Diamond. Used by permission of Viking Penguin, a division of Penguin Group (USA) Inc.

The second driving force contributing to the pressures on Earth's natural systems is growing inequality in income between the rich and poor. In 2005, the richest 20 percent of the world's population accounted for 76.6 percent of total private consumption, whereas the poorest 20 percent accounted for just 1.5 percent (Shah, 2008). This inequality is a major source of environmental decline. Those at the top overconsume energy, raw materials, and manufactured goods, and for survival the poor must cut down trees, grow crops, fish, or graze livestock, often in ways that are harmful to the planet.

These consumption patterns apply to nations as well. Consider the consumption patterns in the United States, with but 4.5 percent of the world's population:

- The United States consumes 25 percent of the world's fossil fuel, 20 percent of its metals, and 33 percent of its paper, and produces about three-fourths of the world's hazardous waste.
- Americans waste more food than most people eat in sub-Saharan Africa. Forty-eight million tons of food suitable for human consumption is wasted each year in the United States (*Harper's* 2001).
- There are three automobiles for every four people in the United States. These cars guzzle about 11 percent of the world's daily oil output (Zuckerman 2006a).

- On average, a person in India uses only 5 percent of the primary energy (e.g., oil, coal) that an American does, and a person in China uses 10 percent of that used by the average American (Zuckerman 2006a).
- The United States produces 30.3 percent of the greenhouse gases that cause global warming (more than the combined contributions of South America, Africa, the Middle East, Australia, Japan, and all of Asia) (Gore 2006:250).
- For every dollar's worth of goods and services the United States produces, it consumes 40 percent more energy than other industrialized nations (Walter 2001:1).

Although the U.S. population increases by roughly 3 million a year compared to India's nearly 16 million, the additional Americans have greater environmental impact. They are responsible for 15.7 million tons of additional carbon to the atmosphere, compared with only 4.9 million tons in India (Gardner, Assadourian, and Sarin 2004:5).

The third driving force behind the environmental degradation of the planet is economic growth. Since 1950, the global economy has expanded fivefold. This expansion, although important for the jobs created and the products produced, has an environmental downside. Economic growth is powered by the accelerated extraction and consumption of fossil fuels, minerals, water, and timber. In turn, environmental damage increases proportionately.

Degradation of the Land

Across the planet, a thin, three-foot layer of topsoil provides food crops for 6.8 billion people and grazing for about 4 billion domesticated animals. This nutrient-rich topsoil, the source of food, fiber, and wood, is eroding at a faster rate than it can form. In fact, researchers estimate that we are losing about 1 percent of our topsoil every year (Paulson 2008). This topsoil is being depleted or lost because of careless husbandry and urbanization. Farmland is lost because of plowing marginal lands, leading to wind and water erosion. The fertility of farmland is lost because it is exhausted by overuse. It is also lost because of irrigation practices that poison the land with salt, a process called salinization. The overuse of irrigation also drains rivers and depletes aquifers faster than they can be replenished. The use of chemical fertilizers and pesticides kills helpful creatures, taints groundwater, and creates dead zones in the oceans (e.g., where the Mississippi River drains into the Gulf of Mexico). In a special issue on the "State of the Planet," *Time* summarized the United Nations' assessment of Earth's ecosystems. With respect to the situation for agricultural lands:

> One-third of global land has been converted to food production, but three-quarters of this area has poor soil. So far, harvests outpace population growth, but the future is clouded by the loss of land to urban development, soil degradation, and water scarcity. . . . More than 40 percent of agricultural land has been badly degraded [through] erosion, nutrient depletion and water stress. (Linden 2000:20)

In addition to the degradation and loss of topsoil, productive land is lost through the growth of cities and urban sprawl, the building of roads, and the damming of rivers. Consider these facts for the United States (Knickerbocker 2006):

- More area than the entire state of Georgia is now under pavement.
- Nearly 3,000 acres of farmland are converted to nonagricultural uses daily.

- Land is being converted for development at about twice the rate of population growth.
- When housing, shopping, schools, roads, and other uses are added up, each American occupies 20 percent more developed land than he or she did 20 years ago.

Environmental Pollution and Degradation

The following description of the various forms of pollution present in industrial societies, especially the United States, presents a glimpse of how humanity is fouling its nest.

- **Chemical Pollution.** More than 75,000 chemicals have been released into the environment. These chemicals are found in food. They are used in detergents, fertilizers, pesticides, plastics, clothing, insulation, and almost everything else. People are exposed to the often toxic substances in the products they use and to the chemicals that seep into ground water, are carried in the air, and contaminate food. Some 202 of these chemicals, such as lead and mercury, harm children's brains and may be responsible for many developmental disabilities such as autism and attention deficit disorder (Laurance 2006).

   More than 20,000 pesticide products are used in the United States. Agricultural workers use about 1.2 billion pounds of pesticides annually, adversely affecting themselves and their families with disproportionate levels of leukemia and stomach, uterine, and brain cancer (Feagin, Feagin, and Baker 2006:411).

   The manufacture of chemicals requires disposing of the waste. Waste disposal, especially safe disposal of toxic chemicals, is a huge problem. These toxic chemicals are released into the air, water, land, underground, and public sewage either by accident or deliberately. Over 4 billion pounds of toxic chemicals are released by industry in the United States each year, including 72 million pounds of recognized carcinogens (*Scorecard* 2010). Typically, corporations choose the cheapest means of disposal, which is to release the waste products into the air

A crop duster sprays pesticides on a local farm. This is one source of chemical food contamination.

photo by Spencer Tirey/ZUMA Press, © copyright 2001 by Spencer Tirey, via Newscom

and waterways and to bury the materials in dump sites. In one infamous instance, the Hooker Chemical and Plastics Corporation over a number of years dumped 43.6 million pounds of 82 different chemical substances into Love Canal, New York, near Niagara Falls. Among the chemicals dumped were 200 tons of trichlorophenol, which contained an estimated 130 pounds of one of the most toxic and carcinogenic substances known—dioxin. Three ounces of this substance can kill more than a million people. (A variant of dioxin—Agent Orange—was used in the Vietnam War with extremely adverse results to vegetation and human life.) As a result of exposure to the various chemicals dumped at Love Canal, nearby residents had an unusual number of serious illnesses, a high incidence of miscarriages, and an unusual number of children born with birth defects.

The Love Canal dump site is only one of many dangerous locations in the United States. The federal government estimates there are over 400,000 hazardous waste sites. The Environmental Protection Agency (EPA) places sites that pose the greatest risk to public health and the environment on the Superfund National Priorities List. Hurricane Katrina flooded three Superfund toxic waste sites in and around New Orleans, and this poses serious threats if any of their protective shields have been degraded (Eilperin 2005).

A movement known as environmental justice works to improve environments for communities and is especially alert to the injustices that occur when a particular segment of the population, such as the poor or minority groups, bears a disproportionate share of exposure to environmental hazards (Pellow 2000). This movement is a reaction against the overwhelming likelihood that toxic-producing plants and toxic waste dumps are located where poor people, especially people of color, live (when this pattern occurs, it is called environmental racism). In Mississippi, for example, people of color represent 64 percent of residents near toxic facilities—but just 37 percent of the state population (Dervarics 2000). "In Los Angeles more than 71 percent of African Americans live in highly polluted areas, compared to 24 percent of whites. Across the United States, black children are three times more likely to have hazardous levels of lead in their blood as a result of living near hazardous waste sites" (Oliver 2008:2). Robert Bullard, an expert on environmental racism, says that "Blacks and other economically disadvantaged groups are often concentrated in areas that expose them to high levels of toxic pollution: namely, urban industrial communities with elevated air and water pollution problems or rural areas with high levels of exposure to farm pesticides" (Bullard 2000:6–7). For example, the toxic pesticide methyl bromide is permitted on agricultural fields because the growers say that there are no affordable alternatives. As a result, workers in the fields, mostly poor and Latino, risk being poisoned (Lewis 2004).

U.S. corporations are also involved in global chemical pollution. They not only dump wastes into the oceans and the air, which of course can affect the people in other countries, but they also sell to other countries chemicals (such as pesticides) that are illegal to sell here because they are toxic. In addition, U.S. corporations have used other countries as dump sites for their hazardous substances because the U.S. government outlawed indiscriminate dumping of toxic wastes in this country in 1975.

The nations of Western Europe and North America have relatively strict environmental laws, which is good for their inhabitants. These countries, however, transport roughly 2 million tons of toxic waste annually to poor nations that desperately need the cash.

Toxic wastes are also exported when U.S. multinational corporations move operations to countries with less stringent environmental laws. For example, the 2,000 foreign-owned (mostly by the United States) factories along the United States–Mexico border in Mexico (*maquiladoras*) have created environmental hazards on both sides of the border.

Another problem with toxic wastes is accidental spills from tankers, trucks, and trains as the wastes are transported. These spills number about 400 a year in the United States alone. When these incidents occur, the air is polluted, as is the groundwater and the oceans. Fires sometimes occur along with explosions. The result is that people, animals, and plant life are endangered.

- **Solid Waste Pollution.**   The United States discards 30 percent of the world's resources (Rogers 2005). As such, it is the largest producer of solid waste among the industrialized nations, both in absolute and per capita terms. Americans throw away approximately 250 million tons of old food, glass, clothing, electronics, plastics, metals, textiles, rubber, wood, and paper. On average, each American produces 4.5 pounds of solid trash a day (up from 2.7 pounds in 1960). Approximately 33 percent of this trash is recycled, and the rest is incinerated or buried in landfills (see Figure 2).

The problem of what to do with solid waste is compounded by the increased amounts of waste that are contaminated with compounds and chemicals that do not appear in nature. These wastes pose new and unknown threats to human, animal, and plant life. One such health hazard is toxic sludge, a mix of human and industrial waste produced by wastewater treatment plants. About 4 million tons of sludge are dumped on farmland, golf courses, and parks as a form of fertilizer. Unless sludge is carefully treated and monitored, it can be tainted with *E. coli,* bacteria, viruses, heavy metals, solvents, and any combination of the thousands of chemicals used in U.S. industries (Orlando 2001). Exposure to tainted sludge increases the risk of serious infections, illness, and death (Fackelmann 2002).

All landfills leak seeping toxic residues into the groundwater. Many communities have contaminated drinking water and crops as a result. With the problem clearly becoming serious, some experimentation is now being

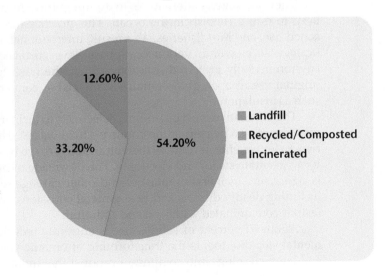

Figure 2

Municipal Solid Waste Disposal in the United States

Source: U.S. Environmental Protection Agency, "Municipal Solid Waste Generation, Recycling, and Disposal in the U.S.: Facts and Figures for 2008." http://www.epa.gov/waste/nonhaz/municipal/pubs/msw2008rpt.pdf

12.60%

33.20%

54.20%

- Landfill
- Recycled/Composted
- Incinerated

A CLOSER LOOK

THE NEW TECHNOLOGY AND TOXIC WASTE

The new technology found in most households in the developed world—personal computers, cell phones, televisions, and other electronic equipment—is laden with toxins that when thrown away will leach into groundwater or produce dioxins and other carcinogens when burned. Let us consider computers.

The computer revolution changes quickly, with each new generation having much more memory and being infinitely faster, yet available at a cheaper price than the original. As a result, millions of computers become obsolete every year. Thus, personal computers and consumer electronics ("e-waste") "compose one of the fastest growing and highly toxic waste streams in the industrialized world" (Grassroots Recycling Network [GRRN]

2005). Following are some facts regarding computers:

- On average, U.S. consumers toss an estimated 2.6 million tons of e-waste each year (Green 2007).
- Printed circuit boards and semiconductors contain cadmium. In 2005, more than 2 million pounds of cadmium were discarded along with computers.
- The batteries and switches contain mercury; 400,000 pounds of mercury were discarded nationwide in 2005.
- Chromium is used as corrosion protection in computers. In 2005, there were an estimated 1.2 million pounds of chromium in landfills.
- PVC (polyvinyl chloride) plastics are used on cables and housings, creating a potential

waste of 250 million pounds per year.
- With the increased use of flat-panel monitors, it is estimated that 500 million defunct monitors were discarded by 2007, each of which contains phosphorous and 4 to 8 pounds of lead.
- Santa Clara County, California, the home of the semiconductor industry, contains more toxic waste sites than any other county in the United States (Worldwatch Institute n.d.).

The problem is that only 10 percent of computers are recycled. The rest threaten the environment—here and abroad. Chances are that most of the obsolete computers will end up in the developing world—Africa, India, and China—where the poor, with little or no protection, are hired to extract items of value (*USA Today* 2002a).

conducted with landfills that have impermeable linings to prevent such pollution. (See "A Closer Look" panel on personal computers and toxic waste.)

There are several alternatives to dumping trash in landfills. One option has been to dump rubbish in the ocean. This practice has polluted beaches, poisoned fish, and hurt fisheries. As a result, international agreements and domestic legislation within various countries have curtailed this alternative. The environmentally preferred solutions are for the trash to be reprocessed to its original uses (paper, glass containers, metals) or converted into new products such as insulation.

The alternative most commonly selected is to incinerate the garbage (which disposes of 12.6 percent of the country's total waste). The burning of trash has two major benefits. It reduces the volume of garbage by almost 90 percent, and it can generate steam and electricity. The downside of burning trash, however, is significant. Incinerating plastics and other garbage releases toxic chemicals, including deadly dioxins and heavy-metal emissions, into the air. The residue (ash) is contaminated with lead and cadmium.

About 33 percent of solid waste is currently recycled, a positive environmental step. So, too, is the transforming of organic waste-paper, food scraps, and lawn clippings into compost, a product that invigorates agricultural soils.

European countries are leading the way with composting. If we could sort trash into recyclables, compostables, and disposables, we could "keep 60 to 70 percent of what was trash out of our landfills and incinerators" (Gavzer 1999:6).

- **Water Pollution.** The major sources of water pollution are: (1) industries, which pour into rivers, lakes, and oceans a vast array of contaminants such as lead, asbestos, detergents, solvents, acid, and ammonia; (2) farmers, whose pesticides, herbicides, fertilizers, and animal wastes drain into streams and lakes; (3) cities, which dispose of their wastes, including sewage, into rivers to end up downstream in another city's drinking water; and (4) oil spills, caused by tanker accidents and leaks in offshore drilling. These are problems throughout the world.

Water pollution is a most immediate problem in the less developed countries. Contaminated water in poor countries results in high death rates from cholera, typhoid, dysentery, and diarrhea. About 1.2 billion people do not have enough safe drinking water. Nearly 3 billion people are at risk of contaminated water because of improper sanitation. More than 5 million die each year of easily preventable waterborne diseases such as diarrhea, dysentery, and cholera (Leslie 2000).

> *The world is facing a water crisis due to pollution, climate change, and surging population growth of unprecedented magnitude. Unless we change our ways, by the year 2025 two-thirds of the world's population will face water scarcity. The global population tripled in the 20th century, but water consumption went up sevenfold. By 2050, after we add another 3 billion to the population, humans will need an 80 percent increase in water supplies just to feed ourselves. No one knows where this water is going to come from. (Barlow 2008:A3)*

In the United States, the Mississippi River provides an example of the seriousness of water pollution. Greenpeace USA, an environmental organization, surveyed pollution in the Mississippi River and found that industries and municipalities along the river discharged billions of pounds of heavy metals and toxic chemicals into it. This dumping occurs along the 2,300 miles of the river; the worst pollution is concentrated along 150 miles in Louisiana, where 25 percent of the nation's chemical industry is located. More than a hundred heavy industrial facilities there release poison into the air, land, and water at a rate of almost half a billion pounds per year (*Witness to the Future* n.d.).

A serious threat to drinking water comes from the chemicals that farmers put on their fields to increase yields (fertilizers), kill pests (pesticides), and destroy weeds (herbicides). The chemicals applied seep into wells and drain into streams and rivers. As a result, about 40 percent of U.S. rivers and lakes are too polluted for fishing or swimming (Kelly 2004).

The EPA has a list of large toxic sites to be cleaned up with funds supplied by Congress. The largest of these Superfund sites is a 200-mile stretch of the upper Hudson River, where General Electric dumped 1.3 million pounds of polychlorinated biphenyls (PCBs) into the river over a 30-year period. PCBs cause cancer in laboratory animals, and they are linked to premature births and developmental disorders. General Electric stopped the practice in 1977 when the federal government banned PCB use. More than three decades later, the New York State Health Department continues to advise women of childbearing age and children under age 15 not to eat any fish from the Hudson River and urges that no one eat any fish from the upper Hudson, where the cancer risk from such consumption is 700 times the EPA protection level. Between May and

October of 2009, Phase 1 of the Hudson River Dredging Project was completed, and 10 percent of the contaminated sediment was removed. The problem is that thousands of pounds of PCBs remain in the sediment of the Hudson and continue to poison fish, wildlife, and humans.

The ocean, the cornerstone of the Earth's life-support system, is also in serious danger because of human activity.

> We are altering the nature of the ocean by what we put in and by what we take out. Tons of toxic substances flowing from the land have altered the ocean's chemistry. More than 50 "dead zones" blight coastal areas. Gigantic swaths of toxic algae are fueled by high levels of nitrates and phosphates in runoff from over-fertilized fields, farms, and lawns. Coral reefs, the "rain forests of the sea," have declined about 30 percent in 30 years, largely because of overfishing, coastal development, and global warming. Mercury levels are so high in some top-of-the-food-chain predators such as swordfish, sharks, and tuna that people are advised to strictly limit their consumption. Swimmers, surfers, and sunbathers are finding many of their favorite beaches contaminated—and closed. (Earle 2003:1)

● **Radiation Pollution.** Human beings cannot escape radiation from natural sources such as cosmic rays and radioactive substances in Earth's crust. Technology has added greatly to these natural sources through the extensive use of x-rays for medical and dental uses, fallout from nuclear weapons testing and from nuclear accidents, and the use of nuclear energy as a source of energy.

The dangers of radiation are evidenced to the extreme in the physical effects on the survivors of the atomic bombs at the end of World War II. These victims experienced physical disfigurement, stillbirths, infertility, and extremely high rates of cancer. A government study estimated that the radioactive fallout from Cold War nuclear weapons tests across the Earth probably caused at least 15,000 cancer deaths and 20,000 nonfatal cancers in U.S. residents born after 1951 (reported in Eisler 2002). In 1986, the most serious nuclear accident to date occurred at Chernobyl in the Soviet Union. The full consequences of this accident will not be known for years, but so far there have been numerous deaths in Russia, a large-scale increase in cancers and other illnesses, and widespread contamination of food and livestock as far away as Scandinavia and Western Europe. The most serious nuclear accident in the United States occurred with the near meltdown in Pennsylvania at Three Mile Island in 1979.

Less dramatic than nuclear accidents but lethal just the same have been the exposures to radiation by workers in nuclear plants and those living nearby. The Hanford nuclear weapons plant in Washington State provides an example. For more than 40 years, the U.S. government ran this facility, monitoring nuclear emissions but not notifying the workers or the 270,000 residents in the surrounding area of the dangers:

> From 1944 to 1947 alone, the Hanford plant spewed 400,000 curies of radioactive iodine into the atmosphere. The bodily absorption of 50 millionths of a single curie is sufficient to raise the risk of thyroid cancer. For years thereafter, Hanford poured radioactive water into the Columbia River and leaked millions of gallons of radioactive waste from damaged tanks into the groundwater. . . . Some 13,700 persons absorbed an estimated dose of 33 rads to their thyroid glands [equivalent to about 1,650 chest x-rays] some time during the last 40 years. . . . There was no diagnostic or therapeutic purpose. No one told them; there was no informed consent. Some have called this situation a "creeping Chernobyl" but there is a difference. Chernobyl was an accident. Hanford was deliberate. Chernobyl was a singular event, the product of faulty reactor

© Dan Lamont/Corbis

Hanford was the world's first full-scale nuclear reactor, built to produce plutonium for an atomic bomb during World War II.

design and human error. Hanford was a chronic event, the product of obsessive secrecy and callous indifference to public health. (Geiger 1990:E19)

Similar situations occurred at the weapons factories at Rocky Flats near Denver, Fernald near Cincinnati, and Savannah River in South Carolina, and at the testing sites for weapons in Nevada and other areas in the Southwest.

Utility companies in thirty-one states operate 103 commercial nuclear reactors, providing about 20 percent of the nation's electricity (second only to coal). Unlike coal, the electricity generated by nuclear energy does not produce carbon dioxide and other greenhouse gases. The problem involves the safe storage of nuclear waste. The generation of nuclear power creates radioactive by-products such as uranium mill tailings, used reactors, and the atomic waste itself. The safe storage of these materials is an enormous and perhaps impossible task because some remain radioactive for as long as 250,000 years. Neither the nuclear industry nor the government has a long-term technology for safe nuclear waste disposal.

- **Air Pollution.** According to the World Health Organization, air pollution causes 70,000 premature deaths a year in the United States (cited in Kelly 2004). It is a major source of health problems such as respiratory ailments (asthma, bronchitis, and emphysema), cancer, impaired central nervous functioning, and cirrhosis of the liver. These problems are especially acute among people who work in or live near industrial plants in which waste chemicals are released into the air and among people who live in metropolitan areas where conditions such as temperature and topography tend to trap the pollutants near the ground (e.g., cities such as Mexico City, Los Angeles, and Denver). The EPA estimates that more than 133 million Americans live in areas where air quality is unhealthy at times because of high levels of at least one pollutant (cited in Kelly 2004). The pollutants emitted into the air have extremely serious consequences for the environment; the greenhouse effect and the loss of ozone protection are topics discussed later in this chapter.

The two major sources of air pollution are emissions from automobiles and from industrial plants (lesser but nonetheless serious sources are toxic waste dumps, burning trash, wood burning, and aerosols). Automobiles emit five gases implicated in global warming: carbon monoxide, carbon dioxide, nitrous oxide, chlorofluorocarbons, and ozone smog. Currently, automobile-generated air pollution is a problem of the wealthier nations.

Simply put, "cars have bad breath," as one environmental biologist observed. The airborne emissions are deadly. Charles Levy of Boston University goes on to say, "The agencies looking at studies of toxins, many on animals, cite acute toxicities—lungs, respiratory, eyes, nasal passages." Such chronic poisons ingested through the lungs and penetrating into the body through the respiratory system, or even through the skin, hit the stomach and bloodstream. Together, they interact, increasing the probability of disease years down the road—cancer, lung diseases like asthma and bronchitis, and possible cardiovascular conditions (Kay 1997:111).

Industrial emissions are the second major source of air pollution in the United States. Industrial plants and factories release several billion pounds of poisonous chemicals annually, and the EPA cites hundreds of industrial plants annually as posing the greatest risks to human health.

GLOBAL ENVIRONMENTAL CRISES

Each form of pollution just described threatens human life. This section focuses on environmental threats to Earth itself. The discussion is limited to three inter-related threats: dependence on fossil fuels for energy, destruction of the tropical rain forests, and global warming.

Fossil Fuel Dependence, Waste, and Environmental Degradation

The Industrial Revolution involved, most fundamentally, the replacement of human and animal muscle by engines driven by fossil fuels. These fuels (coal, oil, natural gas) are also used for heating, cooking, and lighting. Considering just oil, the world consumes 85 million barrels of oil a day. The United States is the greatest consumer of oil products, using approximately 21 million barrels of oil a day (25 percent of the world's daily consumption). China is second at 7.6 million barrels, followed by Japan, Russia, and India (NationMaster 2010). Carbon dioxide emissions from fossil fuels, the main villain among the greenhouse gases, have gone from almost nothing a hundred years ago to more than a ton of carbon per person each year. Each person in the United States, by the way, produces twenty times that much. The United States, for example, with 4.5 percent of the world's population, has one-third of the world's cars and drives 50 percent of the total world mileage. To provide for this extravagance, the United States imports 60 percent of the 21 million barrels used daily. (See the "Social Policy" panel on automobiles and fossil fuels.)

The worldwide demand for energy will rise sharply as the developing nations, where 99 percent of the world's population growth is taking place, industrialize and urbanize. In China, for example, car sales are increasing rapidly (from a private vehicle fleet of 5 million in 2000 to about 20 million in 2005). By 2020, China could have 120 million (Samuelson 2005). In 2000, 71 percent of

© Glow Images/Alamy

The United States is the world's greatest consumer of oil products, using 25 percent of the world's daily consumption.

motor vehicles were in the more developed countries. In 2020, it is projected that this proportion will be reduced to 55 percent (De Souza, Williams, and Meyerson 2003:18). People in the developing countries will be replacing traditional fuels such as wood and other organic wastes with electricity, coal, and oil. This likely trend has important consequences for the world and its inhabitants. First, the demand for fossil fuels has given extraordinary wealth to the elites in the nations of the Persian Gulf area, where two-thirds of the world's estimated petroleum reserves are located. Stability in this region is vital to U.S. interests because interruption in the flow of Persian Gulf oil (primarily Saudi oil, which supplies 15 percent of the world's total oil) would cause shortages and the price of other oil imports to rise dramatically, devastating the U.S. economy (Tepperman 2004)—thus, our involvement in the 1991 Gulf War to stop Iraq's attempts to control Kuwait and other oil-rich nations, as well as the 2003 invasion and control of Iraq. In short, the maldistribution of the world's energy supply heightens world tensions.

Second, because most nations need to import oil, vast amounts are carried across the world's oceans in about 2,600 tankers. Along with offshore drilling, these voyages increase the probability of accidents that damage aquatic life, birds, and coastal habitats. Four examples of large-scale spills are the wreck of the *Amoco Cadiz* off the coast of France in 1978, spilling 68 million gallons of crude oil; the blowout of the Ixtoc I oil well, which poured 140 million gallons of oil into the Gulf of Mexico in 1979; the grounding of the *Exxon Valdez* in Alaska's Prince William Sound in 1989, which released 11 million gallons of crude oil into an ecologically sensitive region, contaminating 1,000 miles of coastline and destroying extraordinary amounts of fish and wildlife; and the April 2010 explosion of the Deepwater Horizon oil rig, operated by British Petroleum [BP]. The BP oil spill killed eleven workers, and at the time of this writing, had leaked 5,000 barrels (i.e., millions of gallons) of oil into the Gulf of Mexico per day. The oil slick is as big as Maryland and Delaware combined, and threatens marine life, the coastal lands of Louisiana, and the livelihoods of people who fish and shrimp in the Gulf.

SOCIAL POLICY

U.S. DEPENDENCE ON THE AUTOMOBILE AND FOSSIL FUELS

Our nation's fleet of automobiles (230 million) smother communities in pollution and contribute 30 percent of the emissions that cause climate change through global warming (Gore 2006). Other forms of environmental degradation from automobiles are the 20 million cars and the 250 million tires discarded each year, the millions of tons of corrosive salt and other chemicals spread on highways to combat icy road conditions, and the almost 40 million acres of roads and parking lots that are covered with asphalt or concrete. The United States in 2006 used about 21 million barrels of oil a day to provide fuel for its cars (and other uses such as heating oil and natural gas), about 60 percent of which is imported (12 million barrels a day). Most of our oil imports go to

> finance both sides of the war on terrorism. We are financing the U.S. armed forces with our tax dollars, and, through our profligate use of energy, we are generating huge windfall profits for Saudi Arabia, Iran and Sudan, where the cash is used to insulate regimes from any pressure to open up their economies, liberate their women or modernize their schools, and where it ends up instead financing madrassas, mosques and militants fundamentally opposed to the progressive, pluralistic agenda America is trying to promote. (Friedman 2005:15)

Moreover, the United States spends hundreds of billions of dollars on a military presence to protect this Middle East energy source (Zuckerman 2005b).

Our insatiable appetite for oil has other negative consequences: degrading local environments by drilling for oil, oozings from pipelines, leaking underground tanks, oil spills from shipping accidents, the routine flushing of tankers, and leaks and accidents from deep-sea drilling.

What can be done to reduce oil consumption? There are several strategies, none of which is currently in political favor: (1) High taxes, such as a tax that would keep prices at $4 a gallon (the average in Europe is about $6 a gallon), could reduce usage. (2) The automobile industry could increase the fuel efficiency of vehicles. Existing technology could bring automobile fuel economy to an average of 45 miles per gallon, but under current federal laws, a passenger car must average 27.5 miles per gallon (the automobile industry lobbies against the higher gas mileage because it would add $2,000 or so to the cost of a vehicle). Moreover, the automobile manufacturers were successful in achieving legislation that creates a loophole for sport utility vehicles (SUVs) and light trucks (52 percent of new vehicles purchased in the United States are SUVs and light trucks), which are held to a lower miles-per-gallon standard (originally 20.7, and increased to 22.2 miles per gallon in 2007). (3) The automobile industry and the government could make a greater effort to produce and market electric and hybrid-electric automobiles.

(4) Instead of subsidizing federal highways, which led to the development of urban sprawl and suburbs where people must drive to work, play, and shop, mass transit in urban areas and train travel between cities could be subsidized to a much greater degree. West Europeans use public transit for 10 percent of all urban trips compared with Americans at only 2 percent. "This is significant because for every kilometer people drive by private vehicle, they consume two to three times as much fuel as they would by public transit" (Sawin 2004:30). (5) Alternative and affordable sources of energy need to be developed for transportation, heating, cooling, and the like. Included among these possibilities are fuel cell, solar, wind, tidal, and geothermal sources. There is a huge roadblock to these needed changes, however, in the form of powerful corporations who profit from the current technologies.

Ultimately, transforming transportation to meet twenty-first-century environmental goals means moving beyond the internal combustion engine and beyond petroleum. Doing so requires major changes in the country's largest business; half of the top ten *Fortune* 500 companies are either automobile or oil companies. Such concentrated economic power leads to great political clout.

Meanwhile, the number of cars grows. Worldwide, there are about 800 million automobiles. It is estimated that by 2050 there will be 3.25 billion—"an unimaginable threat to our environment and a surefire guarantee of global warming" (Zuckerman 2005:72).

Finally, and most important, the combustion of fossil fuels results in the emission of carbon dioxide, which appears to be related to climate change. The consequences of the present level of carbon dioxide emissions, plus the expected increase in the near future, may have disastrous consequences for Earth in the form of global warming, as discussed later in this section.

Destruction of the Tropical Rain Forests and Other Forms of Deforestation

Tropical rain forests cover about 7 percent of Earth's dry land surface (about the same area as the 48 contiguous United States) and house about half of all species on Earth. About 1.9 billion acres of these forests remain in equatorial countries in the Caribbean, West Africa, Southeast Asia, and Latin America. These rich forests are losing an area about half the size of Florida each year (Wilson 2000). For example, it is estimated that the island nation of Comoros (north of Madagascar) lost nearly 60 percent of its forests between 1990 and 2005. In this same period, Brazil led the world in losing 163,543 square miles of forest, which is roughly the size of California (Lindsey 2007). This massive destruction continues to occur because of economics, from the greed of developers to the desperation of poor peasants.

Lumber, petroleum, and mining companies build roads into the jungles to extract their products and transport them to markets. Governments encourage the poor people to settle in these regions by building roads and offering land to settlers, who must clear it for farming. Cattle ranchers require vast expanses for their herds (five acres of pasture for each head). Land speculators clear huge areas for expected profits. The recovered land, however, is fragile, which leads to a cycle of further deforestation.

The sources of deforestation are not just local. The poverty of these nations (often the result of their colonial heritage), their indebtedness to wealthy nations, and the products needed by the wealthy nations are also responsible for the destruction of the tropical forests.

The world's tropical rain forest is losing an area about half the size of Florida each year.

© Chad Ehlers/Alamy

U.S. corporations are directly and indirectly involved in various aspects of rain forest destruction. These involve the timber companies such as Georgia-Pacific and Weyerhaeuser; mining companies such as Alcoa and Freeport McMoRan; oil companies such as Amoco, Arco, Chevron, Exxon-Mobil, Occidental, Conoco Phillips, and Unocal; paper companies such as Kimberly-Clark; and agricultural companies such as Castle & Cooke and Chiquita.

The two major environmental consequences of this deforestation are climate change and the vanishing of species. The climate is affected in several related ways. As hundreds of thousands of forest acres are destroyed, rain patterns change. Huge areas once covered with plants, which give off moisture, are replaced by exposed, sandy soils. Also, the massive burning required to clear the land creates clouds of smoke that block the sun and lead to weather change. Thus, lush, green areas often become near deserts. The tropical forest in Brazil (the world's largest) has so much rainfall that it provides 20 percent of Earth's freshwater supply. What will be the long-range effects as this water supply dwindles? Just as important, forests absorb huge quantities of carbon dioxide through photosynthesis. Consequently, as forests are diminished so, too, is Earth's capacity to absorb the gas most responsible for global warming. This diminished capacity to process carbon dioxide, changing it into oxygen, leads to changes in the climate and to desertification.

The second critical environmental consequence of deforestation is the loss of animal and plant species. The eminent expert on biodiversity, E. O. Wilson, describes the contemporary threat:

> [Biologists] generally agree that the rate of species extinction is now 100 to 1,000 times as great as it was before the coming of humanity. Throughout most of geological time, individual species and their immediate descendants lived an average of about 1 million years. They disappeared naturally at the rate of about one species per million per year, and newly evolved species replaced them at the same rate, maintaining a rough equilibrium. No longer. Not only has the extinction rate soared, but also the birthrate of new species has declined as the natural environment is destroyed. (Wilson 2000:30)

Wherever humans destroy their habitat, species are eliminated. Although these tropical forests cover only 7 percent of Earth's dry land surface, they are Earth's richest factory of life, containing more than half of the world's species of plants, insects, birds, and other animals. As the forests are cleared and burned, species become extinct.

Humanity benefits from nature's diversity in many ways. One important aspect is that exotic plants and animals are major sources of pharmaceuticals. For example, Squibb used the venom of the Brazilian pit viper to develop Capoten, a drug to lower high blood pressure. The yew, which grows in the Pacific Northwest, produces a potent chemical, taxol, which shows promise for curing certain forms of lung, breast, and ovarian cancer. Biotechnology provides the potential to improve agricultural crops by transferring genes from wild plants to domestic crops so that they can be drought resistant, repel insects, or create their own fertilizers naturally. By destroying the forests, we may be eliminating future solutions to disease and famine.

Global Warming

As noted, the burning of fossil fuels and the destruction of the tropical forests contribute to the greenhouse effect. The greenhouse effect occurs when harmful

"Is this a bad time to talk about global warming?"

gases (carbon dioxide, nitrous oxide, chlorofluorocarbons, and methane)—all products of diverse human activities—accumulate in the atmosphere and act like the glass roof of a greenhouse. Sunlight reaches Earth's surface, and the gases trap the heat radiating from the ground. The results, according to the theory, are a warming of Earth, the melting of the polar ice caps, a significant changing of climate, droughts and megastorms, and the rapid spread of tropical diseases such as malaria, dengue fever, cholera, and encephalitis.

Before the Industrial Revolution, forest fires, plant decomposition, and ordinary evaporation released carbon dioxide into the atmosphere, but in small enough amounts to be absorbed by growing plants and by the oceans without noticeable environmental effect. But in the past century or so, human activities—especially the reliance on fossil fuels for internal combustion engines and in smokestack industries, and the use of chlorofluorocarbons to make plastic foam and as coolants in refrigerators and air conditioners, coupled with the destruction of the tropical rain forests—have increased the prevalence of dangerous gases beyond Earth's capacity to absorb them; hence, a gradual warming. The preindustrial concentration of carbon dioxide was 280 parts per million. In 2005, that level was 381 parts per million (Gore 2006:37). This level is expected to rise to 560 parts per million by 2050 (Dybas 2005). This potential doubling (from 280 to 560 parts per million) will increase global temperatures from three and a half to seven degrees. "A global temperature rise of just three degrees would render the earth hotter than it has been at any point in the past two million years" (Kolbert 2006:34).

China and the United States currently emit almost 40 percent of the world's greenhouse gases. China's emissions are the highest in the world, but the United States still leads in carbon dioxide emissions per person. The average American is responsible for 19.4 tons, while the average Chinese is responsible for 5.1 tons (Rosenthal 2008).

Earth is now the warmest it has been in the past 6,000 years or so. The decade of the 1990s was very likely the hottest of the last millennium. The first nine years of the twentieth century have been hotter still. The average global temperature rose 2 degrees over the past 50 years. As a result, mountain glaciers are retreating, polar ice is melting, ocean levels are rising and becoming more acidic, ocean currents are altered, storms are more intense, weather patterns are shifting, pests and diseases are spreading, and the future prospects for the Earth and its inhabitants are grim.

Scientists do not debate that Earth is warmer or that carbon dioxide is emitted into the air in ever-increasing amounts, but they do differ on the relationship between the two facts. Some scientists are cautious, arguing that recent warming and dramatic climatic events are random and part of the natural year-to-year variations in weather. Their skepticism is fueled by a recent scandal in the scientific community. In late 2009, an anonymous computer hacker made public e-mails sent between climate scientists that seemed to indicate that data regarding global warming had been fabricated. Dubbed "Climategate" by the media, it fueled the debate over the extent and cause of global warming. See "A Closer Look" panel for more information on Climategate.

On the other side of the debate, the majority of scientists are convinced that the magnitude of the greenhouse effect is great and accelerating and the cause is human behavior.

> Global warming has become perhaps the most complicated issue facing world leaders. On the one hand, warnings from the scientific community are becoming louder, as an increasing body of science points to rising dangers from the ongoing buildup of human-related greenhouse gases—produced mainly by the burning of fossil fuels and forests. On the other, the technological, economic and political issues that have to be resolved before a concerted worldwide effort to reduce emissions can begin to have gotten no simpler, particularly in the face of a global economic slowdown. (Revkin 2009:1)

SOURCES OF U.S. ENVIRONMENTAL PROBLEMS

The United States has been blessed with an abundance of rich and varied resources (land, minerals, and water). Until recently, people in the United States were unconcerned with conservation because there seemed to be so vast a storehouse of resources that waste was not considered a problem. And as a result, Americans have disproportionately consumed the world's resources. For example, although they constitute 4.5 percent of the world's population, people in the United States use 25 percent of the world's oil output each year. This is because we own 230 million cars and trucks (29 percent of the world's supply) and drive some 1.7 trillion miles annually, almost as much as all the rest of the world.

Although the perception of abundance may explain a tendency to be wasteful, it is only a partial and superficial answer. The underlying sources of our present environmental problems can be located in the culture and structure of U.S. society.

Cultural Sources

Culture refers to the knowledge that the members of a social organization—in this case, a society—share. Shared ideas, values, beliefs, and understandings

A CLOSER LOOK

CLIMATEGATE

In 2007, the Intergovernmental Panel on Climate Change produced a report that claimed:

- Eleven of the previous twelve years (1995–2006) rank among the twelve warmest years on record since 1850.
- Sea levels are rising.
- Snow and ice are decreasing.
- Over the past 50 years, cold days, cold nights, and frosts have become less frequent.

Using data from a number of sources, the IPCC concluded that warming of the climate system is "unequivocal."

The issue of global warming has many critics, however. For example, meteorologist Mark Johnson writes, "I talk about the fallacy of man-made global warming to whomever will listen. I talk to many groups, large and small about how AGW [Anthropogenic Global Warming] is just bad science. I tell them that study results are hand-picked and modified to fit a pre-determined conclusion" (2009:1). Critics of global warming theory have become even more outspoken

since the incident in October 2009 dubbed "Climategate." A computer hacker posted more than a thousand e-mails from scientists at the Hadley Climatic Research Unit at Britain's University of East Anglia. The e-mails contain details regarding data gathering, and sceptics claim they are evidence of scientific fraud and misconduct. One particular e-mail cited most often refers to using a statistical "trick" to "hide the decline" in global temperatures. Although all of this is currently under investigation, a few items are clear. According to Jess Henig at Factcheck.org (2009:1):

- The messages, which span 13 years, show a few scientists in a bad light, being rude or dismissive. An investigation is underway, but there is still plenty of evidence that the earth is getting warmer and that humans are largely responsible.
- Some critics say the e-mails negate the conclusions of the 2007 report by the

Intergovernmental Panel on Climate Change, but the IPCC report relied on data from a large number of sources, of which CRU was only one.

- E-mails being cited as "smoking guns" have been misrepresented. For instance, one e-mail that refers to "hiding the decline" isn't talking about a decline in actual temperature as measured at weather stations. These have continued to rise, and 2009 may turn out to be the fifth warmest year ever recorded. The "decline" actually refers to a problem with recent data from tree rings.

Climategate seems to have had little influence on the world's understanding of global warming, as the U.N. Climate Change Conference proceeded as planned in December 2009. In advance of the conference "the national academies of 13 nations issued a joint statement of their recommendations for combating climate change, in which they discussed the 'human forcing' of global warming and said that the need for action was 'indisputable'" (Henig 2009:4).

shape the behaviors, perceptions, and interpretations of the members of society. Although the United States is a multicultural society filled with diversity, some of the dominant ideologies of U.S. society have tended to legitimize or at least account for the wastefulness of Americans and their acceptance of pollution.

- **Cornucopia View of Nature.** Many Americans conceive of nature as a vast storehouse waiting only to be used by people. They regard the natural world as a bountiful preserve available to serve human needs. In this view, nature is something to be conquered and used; it is free and inexhaustible. This cornucopia view of nature is widespread and will likely persist as a justification for continuing abuse of the environment, even in an age of ecological consciousness. This view is complemented by an abundant faith in science and technology.

● **Faith in Technology.** There are three basic ways in which human beings can relate to nature. They can view it as a controlling force and thereby submit to the environment in a fatalistic manner. They can strive to attain harmony with it: people need nature and nature needs people. Finally, they can try to attain mastery over nature.

Many Americans regard human beings as having mastery over nature. Rather than accepting the environment as given, they have sought to change and conquer it. Damming rivers, cutting down timber, digging tunnels, plowing prairie land, conquering space, and seeding clouds with silver nitrate are a few examples of this orientation to overcoming nature's obstacles rather than acquiescing to them.

From this logic proceeds a faith in technology; a proper application of scientific knowledge can meet any challenge. If the air and water are polluted and if we are rapidly running out of petroleum, science will save us. We will find a substitute for the internal combustion engine, create plants that will "scrub" the air by using carbon dioxide as food, find new sources of energy, develop new methods of extracting minerals, or create new synthetics. Although this faith may yet be vindicated, we are beginning to realize that technology may not be the solution and may even be the source of the problem.

Scientific breakthroughs and new technology have solved some problems and do aid in saving labor. But often, new technology creates unanticipated problems. Automobiles, for example, provide numerous benefits but they also pollute the air and kill about 50,000 Americans each year. It is difficult to imagine life without electricity, but the generation of electricity pollutes the air (over half of the carbon emissions in the United States come from coal-burning electrical plants) and causes the thermal pollution of rivers. Air-conditioning accounts for 16 percent of the average U.S. household's electricity consumption, and it adds 3,400 pounds of global-warming carbon dioxide annually for each household (Cox 2006). Insecticides and chemical fertilizers have performed miracles in agriculture but have polluted food and streams (and even "killed" some lakes). Obviously, the slogan of the DuPont Corporation—"Better living through chemistry"—is not entirely correct. Jet planes, while helping us in many ways, cause air pollution (one jet taking off emits the same amount of hydrocarbon as the exhausts from 10,000 automobiles) and noise pollution near busy airports.

● **Growth Ethic.** Many Americans place a premium on progress and believe that something better is always attainable. This desire (which is encouraged by corporations and their advertisers) causes people to discard items that are still usable and to purchase new things. Thus, industry continues to turn out more products and to use up natural resources.

The presumed value of progress has had a negative effect on contemporary U.S. life. Progress is typically defined to mean either growth or new technology. Community leaders typically want their cities to grow. Chambers of commerce want more industry and more people (and, incidentally, more consumers). The logic of capitalism is that every company needs to increase its profits from year to year. Thus, we all benefit if the gross national product increases each year. For all these things to grow as people wish, there must be a concomitant increase in population, products (and use of natural resources), electricity, highways, and waste. Continued growth will inevitably throw the tight ecological system out of balance, for there are limited supplies of air, water, and places to dump waste materials, and these supplies diminish as the population increases.

- **Materialism.** The U.S. belief in progress is translated at the individual level into consumption of material things as evidence of one's success. The U.S. economic system is predicated on the growth of private enterprises, which depend on increased demand for their products. If the population is more or less stable, then individuals can accomplish growth only through increased consumption. The function of the advertising industry is to create a need in individuals to buy a product that they would not buy otherwise. Consumption is also increased if products must be thrown away (such as nonreturnable bottles) or if they do not last very long. The policy of planned obsolescence (manufacturing and selling goods designed to wear out or to become out of fashion) by many U.S. companies accomplishes this goal of consumption very well, but it overlooks the problems of disposal as well as the unnecessary waste of materials.

- **Belief in Individualism.** Most people in the United States place great stress on personal achievement. They believe that hard work and initiative will bring success. There is a tendency to sacrifice present gains for future rewards (*deferred gratification*). Many people sacrifice by working days and going to school at night to get a better job. Parents may make great sacrifices so that their children have the opportunity for a college education or other advantages the parents never received. In this manner, success is accomplished vicariously through the achievements of one's children.

  This self-orientation (as opposed to a collective orientation) forms the basis for a number of the value configurations of work, activity, and success mentioned previously. The individual is successful through his or her own initiative and hard work. The stress on individualism is, of course, related to capitalism. Through personal efforts, business acumen, and luck, the individual can (if successful) own property and see multiplying profits. Most Americans share this goal of great monetary success—the "American dream"—and believe that anyone can make it if he or she works hard enough. Curiously, people who are not successful commonly do not reject capitalism. Instead, they wait in the hope that their lot will improve or that their children will prosper under the system.

  The belief that private property and capitalism should not be restricted has led to several social problems: (1) unfair competition (monopolies, interlocking directorates, price fixing); (2) an entrepreneurial philosophy of caveat emptor ("let the buyer beware"), whose aim is profit with total disregard for the welfare of the consumer; and (3) the current environmental crisis, which is due in great measure to the standard policy of many people and most corporations to do whatever is profitable while ignoring conservation of natural resources. Industrial pollution of air and water with refuse and agricultural spraying with pesticides that harm animal and human life are two examples of how individuals and corporations look out for themselves with little or no regard for the short- and long-range effects of their actions on life.

  As long as people hold a narrow self-orientation rather than a group orientation, this crisis will steadily worsen. The use people make of their land, the water running through it, and the air above it has traditionally been theirs to decide because of the belief in the sanctity of private property. This belief has meant, in effect, that individuals have had the right to pave a pasture for a parking lot, to tear up a lemon grove for a housing development, to put down artificial turf for a football field, and to dump waste products into the ground, air, and water. Consequently, individual decisions have had the collective effect of taking millions of acres of arable land out of production permanently, polluting the air and water, and covering land where vegetation once grew with asphalt, concrete buildings, and Astroturf, even though green plants are the only source of oxygen.

In summary, traditional values of U.S. citizens lie at the heart of environmental problems. Americans want to conquer nature. They want to use nature for the good life, and this endeavor is never satisfied. Moreover, they want the freedom to do as they please.

Our individualistic and acquisitive values lead us to resist group-centered programs and humanitarian concerns. Will an energy crisis or continued global warming change our values? Will we vote for politicians who argue for societal planning and sacrifice to reduce environmental perils, or will we opt for politicians who favor the traditional values?

Structural Sources

The structural arrangements in U.S. society buttress the belief system that reinforces the misuse of resources and abuses the ecosystem.

- **Capitalist Economy.** The U.S. economic system of capitalism depends on profits. The quest for profits is never satisfied: companies must grow; more assets and more sales translate into more profits. To maximize profits, owners must minimize costs. Among other things, this search for profits results in abusing the environment (such as strip mining and the disposal of harmful wastes into the air or waterways), resisting government efforts to curb such abuse, and using corporate and advertising skills to increase the consumption of products, including built-in obsolescence, and to even denigrate the notion of global warming. For instance, the Union of Concerned Scientists asserted that Exxon-Mobil, the world's largest oil company, funded forty-three ideological organizations between 1998 and 2005 in an effort to mislead the public by discrediting the science behind global warming (reported in the *Hutchinson News* 2007; see also Mooney 2006).

This last point needs elaboration. Profits require consumers; growing profits require overconsumption. Corporations use several mechanisms to generate the desire to purchase unnecessary products. Advertising generates hyperconsumerism by creating demand for products that potential consumers did not know they needed. Innovative packaging designs also help to sell products; the size, shape, and colors of the package and its display affect choices. Another common tactic is product differentiation whereby existing products (such as an automobile) are given cosmetic changes and presented to consumers as new. This planned obsolescence creates consumer demand as purchasers trade or throw away the "old" product for the "new."

The increased production that results from greater levels of consumption has three detrimental consequences for the environment: more pollution of air and water, depletion of resources, and a swelling of waste products (sewage, scrap, and junk).

Because the profit motive supersedes the concern for the environment, corporations are unwilling to comply with government regulations and to pay damages for ecological disasters such as oil spills. In addition, the possibility of solving environmental problems is further minimized under a capitalist system because jobs depend on business profits. Economic prosperity and growth mean jobs. Thus, most observers see only a narrow alternative between a safe environment and relatively full employment. The fate of many workers depends on whether companies are profitable. Solving environmental problems appears to be incompatible with capitalism unless ecological disasters occur.

- **Polity.** Powerful interest groups fundamentally influence political decisions. This bias of the political system is readily seen in what has been government's relatively cozy relationship with large polluters: corporations. Typically, government intervention has had the effect of administering a symbolic slap on the wrist, and pollution of the environment has continued virtually unabated. The government has been ineffective in pushing the largest and most powerful corporations to do something unprofitable. Not only are these corporations the largest polluters, but they also have a vested interest in the status quo. General Motors and Ford, for example, resist congressional attempts to legislate stricter standards for reducing pollution because the necessary devices add to the cost of automobiles and might curb sales. The government has achieved gradual change, but the powerful automobile industry has consistently responded more slowly than the environmental lobby wanted.

  Since Barack Obama became president, there has been a shift toward greater regulation. For example, in October 2009 the Environmental Protection Agency (EPA) proposed a groundbreaking rule that would hold big polluters accountable for their greenhouse gas emissions. In the proposal, large emitters would have to obtain construction and operating permits and prove that they are using the best control technologies and energy efficient measures available. Under the Bush White House, the EPA was loath to regulate greenhouse gas emissions (Bradbury 2009). While a step in the right direction, it remains to be seen whether the rule will be followed and enforced.

- **Demographic Patterns.** The population of the United States is generally concentrated in large metropolitan areas. Wherever people are concentrated, the problems of pollution are increased through the concentration of wastes. Where people are centralized, so too will be the emission of automobile exhausts, the effluence of factories, and the dumps for garbage and other human refuse.

  The location of cities is another source of environmental problems. Typically, cities have evolved where commerce would benefit the most. Because industry needs plentiful water for production and waste disposal, cities tend to be located along lakes, rivers, and ocean bays. Industry's long-established pattern of using available water to dispose of its waste materials has caused rivers, such as the Missouri, Mississippi, and Ohio; lakes, such as Erie and Michigan; and bays like Chesapeake and New York to be badly polluted.

  The ready availability of the automobile and the interstate highway system resulted in the development of suburbs. The growth of suburbs not only strained already burdened sewage facilities but also increased air pollution through increased use of the automobile. The greater the urban sprawl, the greater the smog is.

- **System of Stratification.** One major focus of this text is how U.S. society victimizes the poor. Because of where they live and work, poor people and racial minorities are more susceptible than are the well-to-do to the dangers of

Newscom

The polluted condition of a section of the Hudson River in New York before sewage treatment plants were built to serve towns along the river. Raw sewage had starved the river of dissolved oxygen, harmed fish and rendered the water unsightly and malodorous.

pollution, whether it takes the form of excessive noise, foul air, or toxic chemicals such as lead poisoning. These probabilities are called environmental classism and environmental racism. Another inequity is that the poor will have to pay disproportionately for efforts to eliminate pollution. That is, their jobs may be eliminated, their neighborhoods abandoned, and a greater proportion of their taxes required (through regressive taxes) to pay for environmental cleanups.

The bitter irony of the poor having to sacrifice the most to abate environmental problems is that it is the affluent that drive excessively, travel in jet planes, have air-conditioned, large homes, consume large quantities of resources (conspicuous consumption), and have the most waste to dispose. Their demand increases economic demand and, concomitantly, industrial pollution.

This system of stratification extends globally to the differences between countries, with the world's poorest people having the lowest carbon footprint, but suffering the most from climate change.

> *Comparing the average annual per capita carbon footprints of the rich and poor certainly makes for unsettling reading: The average American's annual carbon footprint—20.4 tons—is around 2,000 times that of someone living in the African nation of Chad. And the average Briton will emit as much carbon dioxide in one day as a Kenyan will in an entire year. Overall, the United Nations estimates that the carbon footprint of the world's 1 billion poorest people (those living on less than $1 a day) represents just 3 percent of the global total. (Oliver 2008)*

In summary, the United States is a wasteful, inefficient, and vulnerable energy-centered economy. The natural environment is being destroyed by pollution and waste, for several reasons. First, the economic system exploits people and resources. The emphasis on profit requires growth and consumption.

Thus, meeting short-term goals supersedes planning to prevent detrimental long-term consequences. Second, we depend on technology that is wasteful. Third, most people believe in capitalism, growth, and consumption. Finally, population growth increases the demand for products, energy, and other resources.

SOLUTIONS TO THE ENVIRONMENTAL CRISES

Probusiness Voluntaristic Approach

The solution advocated by conservatives is based on the premise that if left alone, mechanisms in the marketplace will operate to solve environmental problems. When cleaning up pollution becomes profitable enough, entrepreneurs will provide the services to clean the air, treat the water, and recycle waste. There is a contradiction here, though: the free market approach will not eliminate pollution; pollution controls reduce profits, and the goal of companies is to maximize profits. A possible compromise is for the government to provide incentives to industries to curb their polluting activities. These incentives could take the form of tax breaks for the purchase and use of pollution controls or outright grants for the use of effective controls.

The probusiness approach, exemplified by the George W. Bush administration, sought to unleash the energy industry to produce more by drilling aggressively for more oil and gas, even in marginal areas (Alaska, offshore), burning more coal (of which there is an abundance), and building more nuclear plants. At the same time, efforts at conservation, to quote Vice President Cheney, "may be a sign of personal virtue but not the basis for a sound, comprehensive energy policy" (quoted in Moberg 2001:14). The oil and gas industry during the 2000 and 2004 election cycles gave Bush and Republican politicians considerably more in contributions than it did to Democratic candidates. Moreover, former President Bush and former Vice President Cheney were both executives in the oil industry before their stint in politics.

Egalitarian/Authoritarian Plan

According to its opponents, the business-oriented plan just described has a basic flaw: it lacks overall provision for the whole society. To allow individuals and companies free choice in what to consume, how much to consume, what to produce, and in what quantities is a luxury that society cannot afford in a time of scarcity and ecological crises. Let us look at the two main authoritarian alternatives to solving the problem of pollution.

The current Obama administration has pledged to crack down on polluters and close the "carbon loophole." This approach entails the enactment of comprehensive laws carrying severe criminal and civil penalties for harming the environment. At the corporate level, it means rigorous inspections of companies and prosecution of violators. Moreover, if penalized, these companies must not be allowed to pass the fines on to consumers through higher prices. At the individual level, it means inspection of vehicles and homes to enforce compliance with accepted standards.

One obstacle to a comprehensive plan to curb pollution is our federal system of government, in which states and communities are free to set their own standards. In principle, this system makes sense because the people in an area should be the most knowledgeable about their situation. However, mining operations along Lake Superior cannot be allowed to dump tailings in the lake on the rationale that having to pay for recycling would reduce local employment levels. Similarly, air pollution is never limited to one locality; wind currents carry the pollutants beyond local borders and add to the cumulative effect on an entire region. Therefore, it seems imperative that the federal government establish and enforce minimum standards for the entire country. Localities could make the standards stricter if they wish. For example, because of its high altitude, Denver has special problems with air pollution. Denver is susceptible to temperature inversions that trap pollutants near the land surface, and automobiles at high altitude emit more pollutants than they do at lower elevations. The city of Denver may therefore want to impose very strict automobile emission standards, just as California has to meet the unusual conditions of its geography.

But although it is easy to list what the government should do, it is also easy to see that the implementation of a centralized, authoritarian plan will meet many obstacles and considerable opposition. Industries, corporations, and communities will resist what will be commonly interpreted as arbitrary and heavy-handed tactics by bureaucrats who do not understand the necessity of profits for maintaining employment and a good local tax base. More fundamentally, the concept of free enterprise means, for many, the freedom to use one's property as one wishes. Will Congress, faced with these pressures, institute a national antipollution program with the necessary clout to be effective? Unless people and their representatives take a more realistic view of the ecological dangers that now exist, Congress will not act.

Control of Resource Use

To start any effective system of resource use, the government must begin by gathering correct information about the extent of natural resource reserves. Currently, government data depend largely on information provided by private firms. Data must also be gathered about the use of the various resources. How much actual waste is there? Can the waste be recycled? What is the turnaround time for renewable resources? Are there alternatives to existing resources? Once authoritative answers to these questions are determined, the government can plan rationally to eliminate waste, develop alternatives, and limit use to appropriate levels.

A rational plan to conserve energy, for example, could include government insistence on new-car fuel economy averaging 40 miles per gallon (which would reduce U.S. oil consumption by 2.8 million barrels a day); universal daylight saving time (it could even be extended to a 2-hour difference, rather than one); strict enforcement of a relatively low speed limit (the 55 mph speed limit in 1983 saved an estimated 2.5 billion gallons of gasoline and diesel fuel [Mouawad and Romero 2005]); the use of governors on automobiles and thermostats; banning neon signs and other energy used in advertising; minimal use of outdoor lighting; and a reversal of the current policy that reduces rates for electricity and natural gas as the volume increases. These steps are important, but the key ingredient to conservation is mandatory rationing, which would reduce consumption in an equitable fashion.

Regardless of the plan that is eventually chosen, most people would agree that the waste of energy must be curtailed. Conserving energy will require not only individual alterations of lifestyles but also changes in the economic system.

Under the current private enterprise system based on profits, corporations seek the profitable alternative rather than the conserving one. In the search for greater profits, we have shifted from railroads and mass transit (the most energy-efficient means of moving people and freight on land) to energy-inefficient cars, trucks, and planes. Instead of using energy-sparing and renewable resources such as wood, cotton, wool, and soap, companies have switched to synthetic fibers, plastics, and detergents made from petroleum.

On the positive side, some U.S. corporations are leading the way in promoting conservation efforts. Thanks to "green" ideology becoming mainstream in the media (Davis Guggenheim's documentary of Al Gore's *An Inconvenient Truth* won an Academy Award and was one of the highest grossing documentaries of all time), numerous companies are making a concentrated effort to "go green." In 2009, *Newsweek* magazine ranked the 500 largest U.S. companies based on their environmental impact, their green policies, and their reputation among their peers and environmental experts. Hewlett-Packard earned the title of the "greenest company in America" thanks to its strong program to reduce greenhouse gas emissions and its efforts to use renewable energy (McGinn 2009).

Can the United States continue to operate on an economic system that allows decisions about what to produce and how to produce it to be governed by profit rather than the common good? The heart of the capitalists' argument, going back to Adam Smith more than 200 years ago, is that decisions made on the basis of the entrepreneur's self-interest will also accomplish the needs of society most efficiently. This fundamental precept of capitalism is now challenged by the environmental crisis, the energy crisis, and the problems related to them. Can capitalism be amended to incorporate central planning regarding societal needs of a safe environment and plentiful resources? Perhaps it can. In the case of Hewlett-Packard, the company's recycling program has allowed HP to reclaim 1.7 billion pounds of e-waste over the past decade, including gold and copper, which it resells. In addition, reducing packaging material has paid off in reduced shipping costs (McGinn 2009). This shows that going green can result in company benefits.

The exact form that the economy should take in an energy-short and polluted world is a source of controversy. At one extreme are people who believe that capitalism is the solution, not the problem. Others would demand a socialistic system with its emphasis on the common good as the only answer. At a minimum, it would seem that (1) there must be central planning; (2) pollution must be controlled and such control tightly enforced; (3) the monopoly structure of the energy industry must be broken up (currently, the largest oil companies control the production, refining, transportation, and retail distribution of oil and are the largest owners of coal, uranium, and geothermal energy); (4) there must be mandatory conservation measures; and (5) the government must subsidize efforts to obtain alternative, nonpolluting sources of energy, and the resulting structures should be publicly owned so that the public good, not profit, is the primary aim.

A final problem is that an energy-short world will not continue to tolerate America's disproportionate use of energy and other resources. The possibility of war increases with the growing resentment of have-not nations toward the haves.

At the international level, the United States along with other developed nations must seek solutions to the environmental crises facing the planet. This means mandating that the developed countries reduce the production of materials that pollute the air, water, and land. The United States must also develop for itself and for other countries environmentally appropriate technologies that will sustain economic progress and be substituted for the ecologically destructive technologies currently in use. As the United States makes trade agreements such as the ones encouraging free trade with Mexico and Canada, agreements must include standard environmental protections. Similarly, loan agreements must contain environmental protections as a condition to receive monies. Finally, the wealthy nations can help themselves and help the debtor nations by engaging in "debt-for-nature" exchanges. Many of the poor nations are hopelessly in debt to the rich nations. Presently, many pay the interest (rarely the principal) by cutting down their forests or by farming marginal lands. The creditor nations could reduce debt in exchange for enforceable agreements by the debtor nation to protect vulnerable parts of their environment.

INTERNATIONAL IMPLICATIONS OF ENVIRONMENTAL PROBLEMS

Environmental problems are not confined within political borders. The world's inhabitants share the oceans, rivers, lakes, and air. If a corporation or a nation pollutes, the world's citizens are the victims. If the tropical forests are destroyed, we are all affected. If a country wastes finite resources or uses more than its proportionate share, the other nations are short-changed.

What will the world be like in 50 years or so? In all likelihood, its population will have levelled off at about 9 billion. The planet will be crowded; the production of enough food and its fair distribution will be extremely problematic. Fresh water will be scarce. Oil will have been replaced by some other energy source. Unless dramatic changes are instituted, the quality of air and water, especially in the less developed, rapidly growing nations, will have deteriorated greatly, and the climate will have been altered. Global warming will have altered climates and flooded low-lying regions.

What should the nations of the world do about environmental crises? In December 2009, world leaders met in Copenhagen, Denmark, for the United Nations Climate Change Conference (called COP 15). Eleven days of heated debates ensued, with a dominant theme of rich countries versus poor countries. In the end, leaders from the United States, China, Brazil, India, and South Africa met and drafted what is known as the Copenhagen Accord. The Accord, which lays the foundation for international action to combat climate change, asks for countries to pledge to reduce their greenhouse gas emissions and to work to hold the increase in global temperature below 2 degrees Celsius. (See the Looking Toward the Future panel for some selections from the Accord). It remains to be seen how many countries will agree to sign it.

The safe prediction about the future is that nations that are now affluent will undergo dramatic changes. Expanding technology will have to be limited because of its demands on precious resources, its generation of harmful heat, and other negative ecological effects. People's freedom to order life as they please—to pave a vacant lot, to irrigate land, to have as many children as they want, to acquire things, to consume fuel on a pleasure trip—will be controlled. The needs of the group, community, society, and perhaps even the world will take precedence over those of the individual. Other values people in the United States hold dear—such as growth and progress, capitalism, individualism, and

LOOKING TOWARD THE FUTURE

SELECTIONS FROM THE COPENHAGEN ACCORD

1. We underline that climate change is one of the greatest challenges of our time. We emphasize our strong political will to urgently combat climate change in accordance with the principle of common but differentiated responsibilities and respective capabilities. To achieve the ultimate objective of the Convention to stabilize greenhouse gas concentration in the atmosphere at a level that would prevent dangerous anthropogenic interference with the climate system, we shall, recognizing the scientific view that the increase in global temperature should be below 2 degrees Celsius, on the basis of equity and in the context of sustainable development, enhance our long-term cooperative action to combat climate change. We recognize the critical impacts of climate change and the potential impacts of response measures on countries particularly vulnerable to its adverse effects and stress the need to establish a comprehensive adaptation programme including inter-national support.

2. We agree that deep cuts in global emissions are required according to science, and as documented by the IPCC Fourth Assessment Report with a view to reduce global emissions so as to hold the increase in global temperature below 2 degrees Celsius, and take action to meet this objective consistent with science and on the basis of equity. We should cooperate in achieving the peaking of global and national emissions as soon as possible, recognizing that the time frame for peaking will be longer in developing countries and bearing in mind that social and economic development and poverty eradication are the first and overriding priorities of developing countries and that a low-emission development strategy is indispensable to sustainable development.

3. Adaptation to the adverse effects of climate change and the potential impacts of response measures is a challenge faced by all countries. Enhanced action and international cooperation on adaptation is urgently required to ensure the implementation of the Convention by enabling and supporting the implementation of adaptation actions aimed at reducing vulnerability and building resilience in developing countries, especially in those that are particularly vulnerable, especially least developed countries, small island developing states and Africa. We agree that developed countries shall provide adequate, predictable and sustainable financial resources, technology and capacity building to support the implementation of adaptation action in developing countries.

4. We recognize the crucial role of reducing emission from deforestation and forest degradation and the need to enhance removals of greenhouse gas emission by forests and agree on the need to provide positive incentives to such actions through the immediate establishment of a mechanism including REDD-plus, to enable the mobilization of financial resources from developed countries.

5. We call for an assessment of the implementation of this Accord to be completed by 2015, including in light of the Convention's ultimate objective. This would include consideration of strengthening the long-term goal referencing various matters presented by the science, including in relation to temperature rises of 1.5 degrees Celsius.

Source: http://www.denmark.dk/NR/rdonlyres/C41B62AB-4688-4ACE-BB7B-F6D2C8AAEC20/0/copenhagen_accord.pdf

Note: There are twelve total points in the Accord.

the conquest of nature—will no longer be salient in a world of less space, endangered ecology, energy shortages, and hunger. These values will die hard, especially the choice of individual freedom. No doubt there will be a great deal of social upheaval during the period of transition from growth to stability, from affluence to subsistence. But these changes must occur or we will perish.

The dangers posed by the future require solutions at two levels. At the physical level, efforts must be directed to finding, for instance, new sources of energy (e.g., fuel cells, solar, wind, biomass), methods to increase the amount of arable land, new types of food, better contraceptives, and relatively inexpensive ways to desalt seawater. At the social level, there must be changes in the structural conditions responsible for poverty, wasted resources, pollution, and the like. One such target would be to determine ways of overcoming the cultural habits (customs, values, beliefs) that reinforce high fertility, people's refusal to eat certain foods or to accept central planning, and the dependence on growth and technology. New forms of social organization, such as regional councils and world bodies, may be required to deal with social upheavals, economic dislocations, resource allocation, and pollution on a global scale. These new organizations will require great innovative thinking, for it is likely that the dominant modes of the present age not only are unworkable for the demands of an over-populated planet but also are in large measure responsible for many of our present and future difficulties.

One complicating factor is that, currently, nations tend to focus on national problems rather than on transnational cooperative efforts. Moreover, they direct their efforts to physical rather than social solutions. They seek answers in technological and developmental wizardry. These solutions are important and should not be neglected, but massive efforts should also be directed to finding ethical, legal, religious, and social solutions.

■ CHAPTER REVIEW

1. Three social forces disturb Earth's biosphere profoundly: population growth, the concentration of people in urban areas, and modern technology.

2. Although population growth (which occurs mostly in the developing countries) has adverse effects on the environment, the populations of rich countries are much more wasteful of Earth's resources and generate much more pollution.

3. Chemicals, solid waste disposal, and radiation pollute the land, water, and air.

4. The Earth faces three major interrelated environmental crises: the burning of fossil fuels, the destruction of the tropical forests, and global warming.

5. The United States, although only 4.5 percent of the world's population, consumes roughly one-fourth of the world's resources. China and the United States emit more greenhouses gases than any other countries.

6. The cultural bases of the wasteful and environmentally destructive U.S. society are the dominant ideologies of (a) the cornucopia view of nature, (b) faith in technology, (c) the growth ethic, (d) materialism, and (e) the belief in individualism.

7. The structural bases for the misuse and abuse of the U.S. environment and resources are (a) urbanization, (b) the system of stratification, (c) capitalism, and (d) the bias of the political system.

8. The probusiness voluntaristic solution to the environmental crisis is based on the premise that if left alone, mechanisms in the marketplace will operate to solve environmental problems. When cleaning up pollution becomes profitable enough, entrepreneurs will provide the services to clean the air, treat the water, and recycle waste.

9. The egalitarian/authoritarian solution is based on government planning and control to reduce problems and promote conservation. This solution shares the burdens throughout the social strata. Moreover, it controls consumption to meet societal goals.

10. If world leaders cannot come to an agreement regarding climate change, the worldwide problems of pollution and resource depletion will become more acute in the future because of population growth, urbanization, expanding technology, and the lack of planning by nations individually and collectively.

11. The dangers posed by these critical problems require solutions at two levels: (a) at the physical level, we need discoveries and inventions of non-polluting technologies and renewable resources; and (b) at the social level, we need changes in the structural conditions responsible for these problems and the creation of new forms of transnational social organizations.

■ KEY TERMS

Biosphere. The surface layer of the planet and the surrounding atmosphere.

Ecosystems. The mechanisms (plants, animals, and microorganisms) that supply people with the essentials of life.

Environmental justice. A movement to improve community environments by eliminating toxic hazards.

Environmental racism. The overwhelming likelihood that toxic-producing plants and toxic waste dumps are located where poor people, especially people of color, live.

Greenhouse effect. When gases accumulate in Earth's atmosphere and act like the glass roof of a greenhouse, allowing sunlight in but trapping the heat that is generated.

Culture. The knowledge (ideas, values, beliefs) that the members of a social organization share.

Cornucopia view of nature. The belief that nature is a vast and bountiful storehouse to be used by human beings.

Planned obsolescence. The manufacture of consumer goods designed to wear out. Or existing products are given superficial changes and marketed as new, making the previous products out of date.

Environmental classism. The poor, because of dangerous jobs and residential segregation, are more exposed than the more well-to-do to environmental dangers.

■ SUCCEED WITH ^{PEARSON} mysoclab ⊕ www.mysoclab.com

Experience, Discover, Observe, Evaluate
MySocLab is designed just for you. This chapter features a pre-test and post-test to help you learn and review key concepts and terms.

Experience sociology in action with dynamic visual activities, videos, and readings to enhance your learning experience. Complete the following activities at www.mysoclab.com.

Social Explorer is an interactive application that allows you to explore Census data through interactive maps.

- Explore the Social Explorer Map: *Carbon Emissions and the Effects of Global Warming on the Environment*

The Core Concepts in Sociology video clips offer a real-world perspective on sociological concepts.

- Watch *World Climate Change*

MySocLibrary includes primary source readings from classic and contemporary sociologists.

- Read Scanlan, Jenkins, & Peterson, *The Scarcity Fallacy*; Krauss, *Women of Color on the Front Line*; Brown, *Sixteen Impacts of Population Growth*

Education

From Chapter 16 of *Social Problems, Census Update*, Twelfth Edition. D. Stanley Eitzen, Maxine Baca Zinn, Kelly Eitzen Smith. Copyright © 2012 by Pearson Education, Inc. Published by Allyn & Bacon. All rights reserved.

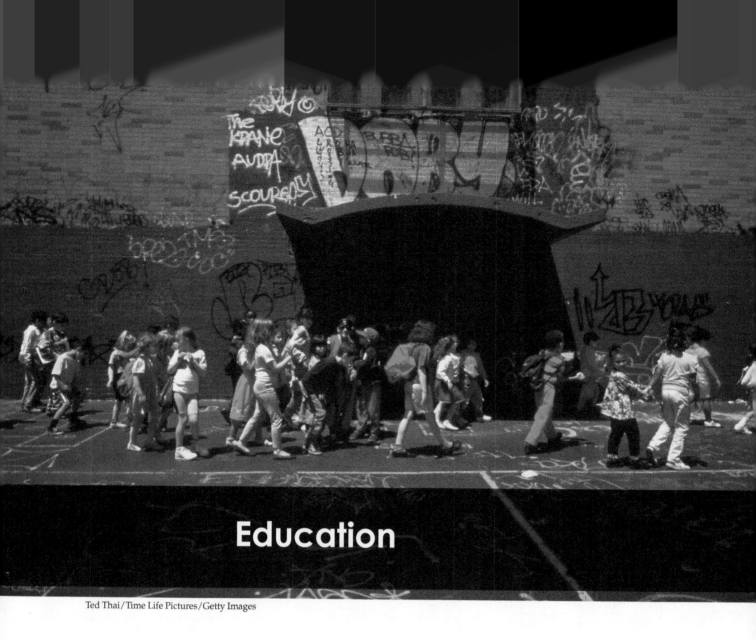

Ted Thai/Time Life Pictures/Getty Images

Education

If you look at the history of public education in our country, it's supposed to be the great equalizer. The dividing line in our country, between the have and have nots, is often around educational opportunity. You can come from real poverty, but if you have a great early childhood program, a great K to 12 education and you have access to college, you'll do great. Yet in far too many places in this country, educational opportunity is tied to race, neighborhood, and zip code. There's something wrong with that picture.

—United States Education Secretary Arne Duncan, 2010

This chapter examines one of society's basic institutions—education. The organization of education in society is both a source of and a potential solution to some of our most vexing social problems. The chapter is divided into three main sections. The first describes the characteristics of U.S. education. The second section describes the current role of education in perpetuating inequality in society. The concluding section describes alternatives to eliminate the race and class biases in education.

CHARACTERISTICS OF EDUCATION IN THE UNITED STATES

Education as a Conserving Force

The formal system of education in U.S. society (and in all societies) is conservative because the avowed function of the schools is to teach newcomers the attitudes, values, roles, specialties, information, skills, and training necessary for the maintenance of society. In other words, the special task of the schools is to preserve the culture, not to transform it. Thus, the schools indoctrinate their pupils in the culturally prescribed ways. Children are taught to be patriotic. They learn the myths of the superiority of their nation's heritage; they learn who the heroes are and who the villains are. As Terry Everton notes,

> *Compulsory schooling defines good citizens as those who play by the rules, stay in line, and do as they're told. Learning is defined by how well we memorize and regurgitate what someone else has deemed we need to know. Creativity is permitted within the parameters of the guidance of licensed professionals whose duty it is to make sure we don't get too wacky with our ideas or stray very far from the boundaries of normalcy. (2004:55)*

There is always an explicit or implicit assumption in U.S. schools that the American way is the only really right way. When this assumption is violated on the primary and secondary school level by the rare teacher who asks students to consider the viability of world government or who proposes a class on the teachings of Karl Marx or about world religions, then strong enough pressures usually occur from within the school (administrators, school board) or from without (parents, the American Legion, Daughters of the American Revolution, the Christian right) to quell the disturbance. As a consequence, creativity and a questioning attitude are often curtailed in school.

Mass Education

People in the United States have a basic faith in education. This faith is based on the assumption that a democratic society requires an educated citizenry so that

Children are taught to be patriotic as part of their cultural indoctrination.

123

individuals can participate in the decisions of public policy. For this reason they not only provide education for all citizens but also compel children to remain in school at least until the eighth grade or until age 16 (although the law varies somewhat from state to state).

Who can quarrel with the belief that all children should be compelled to attend school because it should be for their own good? After all, the greater the educational attainment, the greater the likelihood of larger economic rewards and upward social mobility. However, to compel a child to attend school for 6 hours a day, 5 days a week, 40 weeks a year, for at least 10 years, is quite a demand. The result is that many students are in school for the wrong reason. The motivation is compulsion, not interest in acquiring skills or curiosity about their world. This involuntary feature of U.S. schools is unfortunate because so many school problems are related to the lack of student interest. It is no surprise that despite two decades of intense educational reform, approximately 30 percent of public high school students will drop out before graduation (Thornburgh 2006a).

On the positive side, as a result of the goal of and commitment to mass education, an increasing proportion of people have received a formal education. Between 2005 and 2009, 84.6 percent of Americans over the age of 25 were high school graduates, and another 27.5 percent had a bachelor's degree or higher (Social Explorer Tables: ACS 2005 to 2009 (5-Year Estimates) (SE), ACS 2005–2009 (5-Year Estimates), Social Explorer; U.S. Census Bureau).

Preoccupation with Order and Control

Most administrators and teachers share a fundamental assumption that school is a collective experience requiring subordination of individual needs to those of the school. U.S. schools are characterized, then, by constraints on individual freedom. The school day is regimented by the dictates of the clock. Activities begin and cease on a timetable, not in accordance with the degree of interest shown or whether students have mastered the subject. Another indicator of order is the preoccupation with discipline (i.e., absence of unwarranted noise and movement and concern with the following of orders).

In their quest for order, some schools also demand conformity in clothing and hairstyles. Dress codes are constraints on the freedom to dress as one pleases. School athletic teams also restrict freedom, and the school authorities condone these restrictions. Conformity is also demanded in what to read and how to give the answers the teacher wants.

The many rules and regulations found in schools meet a number of expressed and implicit goals, but many of those goals may be outdated. Zuckerman writes:

> *We are on the threshold of the most radical change in American education in over a century as schools leave the industrial age to join the information age. For most of the past century, our schools were designed to prepare children for jobs on factory lines. Kids lived by the bell, moved through schools as if on conveyor belts, and learned to follow instructions. But today many of these factories are overseas, leaving behind a factory-based school system for an information age. (2005a:68)*

A Fragmented Education System

Certain trends indicate that the educational system in the United States is moving toward greater fragmentation rather than less. According to the National Center for Education Statistics (2009), more and more parents are opting to send their children to private schools (about 11 percent in 2007) or to school them at home (about 2.9 percent). The number of children homeschooled, for example, increased 29 percent from 1999 to 2003. In 2007, roughly 1.5 million children were homeschooled.

Taxpayer-funded charter schools are also growing rapidly. These schools are based on a hybrid "free-market" system in which educators, students, and parents choose a curriculum and educational philosophy free from the dictates of school boards and educational bureaucracies but are financed publicly. In 2006, there were some 3,500 charter schools with more than 1 million students.

Vouchers are another plan that splinters the educational system. This plan gives parents a stipulated amount of money per child that can be used to finance that child's education in any school, public or private. This plan sets up an educational "free market" in which schools have to compete for students. This competition will, theoretically, improve schools because they must provide what parents want for their children, whether that be better discipline, emphasis on learning the fundamentals, religious instruction, focus on the arts, vocational training, or college preparation.

Each of these educational reforms that are underway has strengths and weaknesses. Most important, they represent a trend that is rapidly dividing and subdividing the educational system. For many, this is viewed as a strength, representing the core American values of individualism and competition. Others see this trend as fragmenting further an already disaggregated educational system. Moreover, they see private schools, charter schools, and voucher systems as working against inclusiveness through segregation. For example, 70 percent of Black charter students attend schools where at least 90 percent of students are minorities (Blume 2010). This segregation serves to increase the gap between racial-ethnic groups and social classes in U.S. society.

Local Control of Education

Although the state and federal governments finance and control education in part, the bulk of the money and control for education comes from local communities. There is a general fear of centralization of education under federal control. Local school boards (and the communities themselves) jealously guard their autonomy. Because, as is commonly argued, local people know best the special needs of their children, local boards control allocation of monies, curricular content, and the rules for running the schools, as well as the hiring and firing of personnel.

There are several problems with this emphasis on local control. First, tax money from the local area traditionally finances the schools. Whether the tax base is strong or weak has a pronounced effect on the quality of education received (a point we return to later in this chapter).

Second, local taxes are almost the only outlet for a taxpayers' revolt. Dissatisfaction with high taxes (federal, state, and local) on income, property, and purchases is often expressed at the local level in defeated school bonds and school tax levies. A current population trend—families with school-age children declining while the number of elderly Americans is rising—increases the ever-greater likelihood of the defeat of school issues.

Third, because the democratic ideal requires that schools be locally controlled, the ruling body (school board) should represent all segments of that community. Typically, however, the composition of school boards has overrepresented the business and professional sectors and overwhelmingly underrepresented blue-collar workers, the poor, and various minority groups. The result is a governing body that is typically conservative in outlook and unresponsive to the wishes of people unlike themselves.

Fourth, local control of education may mean that the religious views of the majority (or, at least, the majority of the school board) may intrude in public education. An explicit goal of the Christian Coalition, a conservative religious organization founded by Pat Robertson, is to win control of local school boards. Its agenda opposes globalism, restricts sex education to abstinence from sexual intercourse, promotes school prayer and the teaching of biblical creationism in science classes, and censors books that denigrate Christian values (favorite targets are, for example, *Catcher in the Rye* by J. D. Salinger and John Steinbeck's *The Grapes of Wrath*).

The following are some examples of attempts by states and cities to install religious values in schools:

- In 2002, the Cobb County Board of Education in Georgia voted to insert a sticker in school biology textbooks that reads: "This textbook contains material on evolution. Evolution is a theory, not a fact, regarding the origin of living things. The material should be approached with an open mind, studied carefully, and critically considered" (Slevin 2005). Eleven parents filed suit against the school board, challenging the constitutionality of the textbook warning sticker. On December 19, 2006, a settlement was announced

Some groups have protested the Pledge of Allegiance in schools because of the phrase "one nation under God." Here, students show their support for reciting the pledge in their schools.

Newscom

in which the school board agreed not to restore the warning sticker or take any actions that would prevent or hinder the teaching of evolution (National Center for Science Education 2006).

- In 2005, the Kansas State Board of Education adopted standards of teaching science whereby evolution was to be represented as scientifically controversial. In February 2007, the board overturned that decision, ruling that evolution should be treated in a scientifically appropriate and responsible way (National Center for Science Education 2007).
- Although the U.S. Supreme Court outlawed the posting of the Ten Commandments in public schools, numerous local school boards believe they can survive legal challenges if the commandments are posted in a display with other historical documents, such as the Magna Carta and the Declaration of Independence (Johnson 2000).
- In 2002, the Texas Board of Education objected to a sixth-grade social studies book that read, "Glaciers formed the Great Lakes millions of years ago," because this statement was counter to the creation timeline of religious conservatives. The book was changed to read, "Glaciers formed the Great Lakes in the distant past" (Russell 2003).

As illustrated by these and a number of other lawsuits in recent years, the separation of church and state remains a volatile subject in the United States.

A Lack of Curriculum Standardization

The local control of education results in another much-debated characteristic of U.S. education—the lack of curriculum standardization across more than 14,000 school districts and fifty states. Arguing for a common curriculum, the late Albert Shanker, then president of the American Federation of Teachers, stated,

A common curriculum means that there is agreement about what students ought to know and be able to do and, often, about the age and grade at which they should be able to accomplish these goals. . . . In most countries with a common curriculum, linkage of curriculum, assessment and teacher education is tight. . . . In the U.S., we have no such agreement about curriculum—and there is little connection between what students are supposed to learn, the knowledge on which they are assessed, and what we expect our teachers to know. (Shanker 1991:E7)

Since Shanker wrote this in 1991, there has been a national push for education based on common standards while at the same time preserving local control. This idea is embodied in the 2001 No Child Left Behind Act. Signed by George W. Bush in 2002, the goal of this legislation was to close the gaps that plague education in the United States and make schools accountable for success or failure. For example, according to National Assessment of Educational Progress data, only 29 percent of the nation's eighth graders are proficient in mathematics and just 32 percent read at their level (reported in Symonds 2004). Compared with other industrialized nations, which have prescribed national curricula or highly specified national standards, U.S. students rank near the bottom in achievement. To improve performance, this legislation required states to develop academic standards in reading, math, and science. States, districts, and schools would then be responsible to ensure that all children achieve these state standards by 2013–2014. Adequate yearly progress is measured by a single, statewide assessment system given annually to all students from third to eighth grade. On the basis of these tests, schools are given a grade of "passing" or "failing." In the 2004 to 2005 school year, 24,470 public schools (over one-quarter of the national total) were labeled as "failing to make adequate yearly progress." In 2007, more than 1,000 of California's 9,500 schools were branded as "chronic failures," and state officials predict that all 6,063 public schools serving poor students will be declared in need of restructuring by 2014 (Schemo 2007). Despite these statistics, the U.S. Department of Education argues that No Child Left Behind is working. They argue that multiple studies show that student achievement in reading and math is rising across the nation and that those schools that have been identified as failing are receiving extra help and resources in order to improve (2006).

Although this legislation has been heralded as the most ambitious federal overhaul of public schools since the 1960s, there are a number of problems. First and foremost, instead of one system, we have fifty. Each state was permitted to set its own proficiency benchmarks, with some setting a high and others setting a low standard. Because the federal government rewards those who meet the standards, the ones with high standards are punished, while the ones with low standards are unfairly rewarded. In their 2007 report "The Proficiency Illusion" (Cronin et al., 2007), researchers from the Thomas B. Fordham Institute examine No Child Left Behind in detail. In their comprehensive review, they found:

- State tests vary greatly in their difficulty, with Colorado, Wisconsin, and Michigan having the lowest proficiency standards in reading and math.
- Improvements in the passing rates on state tests can largely be explained by declines in the difficulty on those tests, rather than true growth in student learning.
- The tests in eighth grade are consistently and dramatically more difficult than those in earlier grades. Many states set the bar much lower in elementary school, giving false impressions to parents and teachers that students are doing well.

Critics of No Child Left Behind argue that there is no attempt to address the funding inequities among rich and poor districts within a state that help perpetuate the achievement gaps, the chronic underfunding of poorer schools, or child poverty itself (Metcalf 2002). To rectify this, in March 2010 President Obama announced that an allocation of $900 million in grants would be awarded to help turn around the nation's lowest-performing schools. Unfortunately, the 2007 to 2009 economic recession has left states in fiscal crisis, and budget cuts to education are rampant, resulting in teacher layoffs and the reduction in school programs and supplies. It remains to be seen what effect this will have on state standards and educational outcomes.

In sum, the lack of a common national curriculum has several negative consequences. First, there is a wide variation in the preparation of students, as

Mathematics (2006)		Science (2006)		Reading (2003)		Problem Solving (2003)	
Rank	Score	Rank	Score	Rank	Score	Rank	Score
1 Finland	548	1 Finland	563	1 Finland	543	1 Korea	550
2 Korea	547	2 Canada	534	2 Korea	534	2 Finland	548
3 Netherlands	531	3 Japan	531	3 Canada	528	3 Japan	547
4 Switzerland	530	4 New Zealand	530	4 Australia	525	4 New Zealand	533
5 Canada	527	5 Australia	527	5 New Zealand	522	5 Australia	530
6 Japan	523	6 Netherlands	525	6 Ireland	515	6 Canada	529
7 New Zealand	522	7 Korea	522	7 Sweden	514	7 Belgium	525
8 Belgium	520	8 Germany	516	8 Netherlands	513	8 Switzerland	521
9 Australia	520	9 United Kingdom	515	9 Belgium	507	9 Netherlands	520
10 Denmark	513	10 Czech Republic	513	10 Norway	500	10 France	519
11 Czech Republic	510	11 Switzerland	512	11 Switzerland	499	11 Denmark	517
12 Iceland	506	12 Austria	511	12 Japan	498	12 Czech Republic	516
13 Austria	506	13 Belgium	510	13 Poland	497	13 Germany	513
14 Germany	504	14 Ireland	508	14 France	496	14 Sweden	509
15 Sweden	502	15 Hungary	504	15 United States	495	15 Austria	506
16 Ireland	501	16 Sweden	503	16 Denmark	492	16 Iceland	505
17 France	496	17 Poland	498	17 Iceland	492	17 Hungary	501
18 United Kingdom	495	18 Denmark	496	18 Germany	491	18 Ireland	498
19 Poland	495	19 France	495	19 Austria	491	19 Luxembourg	494
20 Slovak Republic	492	20 Iceland	491	20 Czech Republic	489	20 Slovak Republic	492
21 Hungary	491	21 United States	489	21 Hungary	482	21 Norway	490
22 Luxembourg	490	22 Slovak Republic	488	22 Spain	481	22 Poland	487
23 Norway	490	23 Spain	488	23 Luxembourg	479	23 Spain	482
24 Spain	480	24 Norway	487	24 Portugal	478	24 United States	477
25 United States	474	25 Luxembourg	486	25 Italy	476	25 Portugal	470
26 Portugal	466	26 Italy	475	26 Greece	472	26 Italy	469
27 Italy	462	27 Portugal	474	27 Slovak Republic	469	27 Greece	448
28 Greece	459	28 Greece	473	28 Turkey	441	28 Turkey	408
29 Turkey	424	29 Turkey	424	29 Mexico	400	29 Mexico	384
30 Mexico	406	30 Mexico	410				
OECD average	498	OECD average	500	OECD average	494	OECD average	500

FIGURE 1

U.S. 15-Year-Old Performance Compared with Other Countries

This figure can be found at: http://www.corestandardards.org. Report: "Benchmarking for Success: Ensuring U.S. Students Receive a World-Class Education," p. 13, Figure 1.

129

states have the ability to raise or lower their standards. Second, because families move on the average of once every 5 years (and the rate is probably higher for families with school-age children), there are large numbers of children each year who find the requirements of their new schools different, sometimes very different, from their previous schools. Finally, not only are many American students graduating without the skills necessary to compete in an information economy, but they also appear to be ill poised to compete in a *global* economy (see Figure 1).

In a push for a common national curriculum, the National Governors Association Center for Best Practices has joined with others to form the Common Core State Standards Initiative, an initiative to develop international benchmarks for all states so that all students are prepared to be competitive in a globalized market. Hoping to push the initiative forward in 2010, they write,

> The United States is falling behind other countries in the resource that matters most in the new global economy: human capital. American 15-year-olds ranked 25th in math and 21st in science achievement on the most recent international assessment conducted in 2006. At the same time, the U.S. ranked high in inequity, with the third largest gap in science scores between students from different socioeconomic groups. (2008:5)

"Sifting" and "Sorting" Function of Schools

Schools play a considerable part in choosing the youth who come to occupy the higher-status positions in society. School performance also sorts out those who will occupy the lower rungs in the occupational-prestige ladder. Education is, therefore, a selection process. The sorting is done with respect to two different criteria: a child's ability and his or her social class background. Although the goal of education is to select on ability alone, ascribed social status (the prestige and socioeconomic status of one's family, race, and religion) has a pronounced effect on the degree of success in the educational system. The school is analogous to a conveyor belt, with people of all social classes getting on at the same time but leaving the belt in accordance with social class—the lower the class, the shorter the ride.

EDUCATION AND INEQUALITY

Education is presumed by many people to be the great equalizer in U.S. society— the process by which the disadvantaged get their chance to be upwardly mobile. The data in Figure 2 show, for example, that the higher the educational attainment, the higher the income. But these data do not in any way demonstrate equality of opportunity through education. They show clearly that African Americans and Latinos with the same educational attainment as Whites receive lower economic rewards at every educational level. These differences reflect discrimination in society, not just in schools. This section examines the ways that the schools help to perpetuate class and race inequities.

The evidence that educational performance is linked to socioeconomic background is clear and irrefutable (we include race/ethnicity along with economic status since they are highly correlated).

- Children in the poorest families are six times as likely as children in more affluent families to drop out of school (Children's Defense Fund 2004a:88).

FIGURE 2

Median Annual Earnings of Full-Time Salary Workers Ages 25–34 by Educational Attainment and Race/Ethnicity, 2008

Source: U.S. Department of Commerce, Census Bureau, Current Population Survey (CPS), March and Annual Social and Economic Supplement, selected years, 1981–2009.

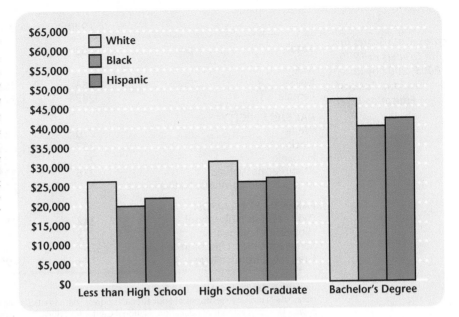

- Researchers at Cornell University have found that the longer children live in poverty, the lower they tend to score on working-memory tests. In fact, those who spent their entire childhood in poverty scored about 20 percent lower on working memory than those who were never poor. They conclude that the chronic stress of poverty impairs the cognitive development of children (Stein 2009).
- In 2005, fourth-grade students in the highest poverty public schools had an average math assessment score of 221, compared with an average score of 255 for students in the lowest poverty schools (National Center for Education Statistics 2010).
- Achievement gaps in reading, writing, and mathematics persist between minority and White students. In the 2009 Condition of Education, researchers note that in reading, gaps between White and minority students remain relatively unchanged since 1992 (National Center for Education Statistics 2010). Table 1 shows the difference in average math scores of eighth graders in 1990, 2005, and 2007. With the exception of Asian students (who scored higher than all other groups), the average score for White students was higher than the scores for Black, Hispanic, and Native American/Alaska Native students in all three years.
- African American, Latino, and Native American students lag behind their White peers in graduation rates and most other measures of student performance. In 2003, the graduation rate from public high school was 78 percent for White students, 72 percent for Asian students, 55 percent for African American students, and 53 percent for Hispanic students (Greene and Winters 2006). A recent study by UCLA indicates that, in the twelve states studied, less than half of American Indian and Alaska Native students graduate from high school each year (Faircloth and Tippeconnie 2010). It is important to note that graduation rates in all racial-ethnic groups also vary greatly by gender. For a closer look at gender and education, see the panel, "Leaving Boys Behind?"
- The high dropout rate for Hispanics and African Americans translates into a lifetime of poor outcomes. According to Thornburgh, "Dropping out of high school today is to your societal health what smoking is to your

TABLE 1

Average Math Scores for 8th Graders in 1990, 2005, 2007 by Race, Sex, and Parents' Education Level

	1990	2005	2007
Total	263	279	281
SEX			
Male	263	280	282
Female	262	278	280
RACE/ETHNICITY			
White	270	289	291
Black	237	255	260
Hispanic	246	262	265
Asian/Pacific Islander	275	295	297
American Indian/Alaska Native	*	264	264
PARENTS' EDUCATION			
Did not finish high school	242	259	263
High school graduate	255	267	270
Some education after high school	267	280	283
Graduated from college	274	290	292

*Reporting standards not met (too few cases).
Note: The National Assessment of Educational Progress mathematics scale ranges from 0 to 500.
Source: U.S. Department of Education, National Center for Education Statistics, National Assessment of Educational Progress (NAEP), 1990–2007 Mathematics Assessments, NAEP Data Explorer.

physical health, an indicator of a host of poor outcomes to follow, from low lifetime earnings to high incarceration rates to a high likelihood that your children will drop out of high school and start the cycle anew" (2006a:32).

- Black, Latino, and Native American students are suspended or expelled in numbers disproportionate to those of Whites. Data from the 2004 to 2005 school year indicate that in every state but Idaho, Black students are being suspended in numbers greater than would be expected from their proportion of the student population. In fact, in twenty-one states the percentage of Black suspensions is more than double their percentage of the student body (Witt 2007).

These social class and racial gaps in academic achievement are found in almost every school and district in the United States. On the surface, these patterns reinforce the social Darwinist assumptions that the affluent are successful because they are intelligent, and, conversely, the poor and minorities are at society's bottom because they do not have the requisite abilities to be successful. Similarly, dysfunctional families, unmotivated students, and the culture of poverty are believed by some to explain the academic achievement gap. We argue, to the contrary, that structural factors explain why the poor and minorities are disadvantaged in our supposedly meritocratic educational system. In effect, the educational system is stacked in favor of middle- and upper-class children and against children from the lowest classes.* Many interrelated factors explain

---

*We have phrased the sentence to focus on the system, not the victims. This focus is contrary to the typical response, which is to focus on the cultural deprivation of the poor. That approach attacks the home and culture of poor people and assumes that poor people perform inadequately because they are handicapped by their culture. Observers cannot, however, make the value judgment that a culture is deprived. They can note only that their milieu does not prepare children to perform in schools geared for the middle class. In other words, children of the poor and/or minority groups are not nonverbal; they are very verbal, but not in the language of the middle class.

A CLOSER LOOK

LEAVING BOYS BEHIND?

In the 1990s, researchers and popular writers started writing about the "girl crisis" in America. According to books like *Reviving Ophelia: Saving the Selves of Adolescent Girls* (Pipher 1994) and *Failing at Fairness: How Our Schools Cheat Girls* (Sadker and Sadker 1994), girls were believed to be suffering when they hit adolescence. In 1992, the American Association of University Women (AAUW) published "How Schools Shortchange Girls," a study conducted by the Wellesley College Center for Research on Women. The report claimed that girls across the country were victims of a pervasive bias in schools. Teachers paid more attention to male students, gave them more time and feedback on their work, and did not encourage girls, especially in the areas of math and science. As a result, millions of dollars in grants were awarded to study the plight of girls in education (Sommers 2000).

More recently, writers have been focusing on a different crisis in education, that of boys, not girls. Christina Hoff Sommers writes,

> The research commonly cited to support the claims of male privilege and sinfulness is riddled with errors. Almost none of it has been published in peer-reviewed journals. Some of the data are mysteriously missing. Yet the false picture remains and is dutifully passed along in schools of education, in "gender equity" workshops, and increasingly to children themselves. . . . A review of the facts shows boys, not girls, on the weak side of an educational gender gap. (2000:14)

According to Garibaldi, boys are increasingly disengaged in the "feminized" classroom (2006). Through movies, television, and rap music, pop culture teaches young boys it is not "cool" to like or do well in school and that to be masculine is to be disengaged and anti-authority (Wenzl 2007). Those who propose that it is boys who are in crisis offer the following arguments:

- Boys are less likely to graduate from high school (65 percent versus 72 percent of girls; Greene and Winters 2006).
- Boys are, on average, a year and a half behind girls in reading and writing (Sommers 2000).
- Each year women receive more bachelor's and master's degrees than men (Mead 2006).
- Boys are more likely to be held back a grade, drop out, and be suspended from school (Sommers 2000).
- Girls continue to score higher on the Scholastic Aptitude test in the area of writing. On the newly revamped SAT in 2006, girls scored an average of 11 points higher in writing (College Board 2006).

So what is the truth concerning the gender gap in education? In a 2006 report by the Education Sector, Mead argued that "the real story is not bad news about boys doing worse; it's good news about girls doing better" (2006:1). In the report, using data from the National Assessment of Education Progress, Mead argued that American boys are scoring higher and achieving more than they have in the past, but girls have improved their performance on some measures even faster, which makes it appear as though boys are doing "worse." The data seem to indicate that younger boys are doing quite well, but older boys are starting to slip when they reach twelfth grade. Mead argued that twelfth-grade girls are sliding as well. She argued, "The fact that achievement for older students is stagnant or declining for both boys and girls, to about the same degree, points to another important element of the boy crisis. The problem is most likely not that high schools need to be fixed to meet the needs of boys but rather that they need to be fixed to meet the needs of *all* students, male and female" (2006:4).

In the battle over who is in crisis and more disadvantaged, two very important ideas seem to get left out. First of all, regardless of the statistics that more boys are dropping out of school and are less likely to go to college, women still, on average, earn less than men at every level of education. Furthermore, women continue to attain a small percentage of high-level jobs in corporations, politics, and other occupations, and they continue to be responsible for the majority of domestic work. In her criticism of the "boy crisis" literature, Douglas writes,

> In 1999, one year before Sommers' book came out, the top five jobs for women did not include attorney, surgeon, or CEO. They were, in order, secretaries, retail and personal

(Cont.)

sales workers (including cashiers), managers and administrators, elementary school teachers and registered nurses. In 2007, when presumably some of the privileged, pampered girls whose advantages over boys Sommers had kvetched about had entered the workforce, the top five jobs for women were, still secretaries in first place, followed by registered nurses, elementary and middle school teachers, cashiers, and retail salespersons.

Farther down the line? Maids, child care workers, office clerks and hairdressers. Not a CEO or hedge fund manager in sight. And, in the end, no president or vice president in 2008. But what about all those career-driven girls going to college and leaving the guys in the dust? A year out of college, they earn 80 percent of what men make. And 10 years out? A staggering 69 percent. (2010:1–2)

Second, for every statistic that indicates a gender gap, there is an even larger gap by social class and race. Mead argues that "the gaps between students of different races and classes are much larger than those for students of different genders—anywhere from two to five times as big, depending on the grade. . . . Overall, poor, Black, and Hispanic boys would benefit far more from closing racial and economic achievement gaps than they would from closing gender gaps" (2006:5).

why the education system tends to reinforce the socioeconomic and racial differences in the United States. We examine a few of these in the following sections.

Financing Public Education

Schools in the United States reflect the economic divide that exists in society:

> In America, the type of education provided, the way it's funded and the content of the curriculum are local matters directed by local authorities. The result is easy to see. Across America one sees the extremes: from schools that resemble shining mansions on a hill to ramshackle, dilapidated structures. (Kamau 2001:81)

Approximately 50 million U.S. children attend public schools (6 million attend private schools and about 1.5 million are homeschooled). These schools receive funds from three governmental sources—about 9 percent from the federal government; about 47 percent from the state, depending on the allocation within each state; and 44 percent from local taxes in each district within the state Villano 2009). The result of this distribution is that schools are funded unequally in the United States, with public schools being more successful in educating children in middle-class communities but often failing children in poor neighborhoods.

Equal opportunity in education (at least as measured by equal finances) has not been accomplished nationwide because wealthier states are able to pay much more per pupil than are poorer states. The top-spending states, for example, invest more than double the amount per pupil than those states spending the least. Because the federal government provides only about 9 percent of the money for public schools, equalization from state to state is impossible as long as education is funded primarily by state and local governments because both entities vary in wealth and commitment to public education.

The disparities in per-pupil expenditures within a given state are also great, largely because of the tradition of funding public schools through local property taxes. This procedure is discriminatory because rich school districts can spend more money than poor ones on each student—and at a lower taxing rate. Thus, suburban students are more advantaged than are students from the inner city; districts with business enterprises are favored over agricultural districts; and districts with natural resources are better able to provide for their children than are districts with few resources. In some states, the disparity in spending for each pupil may be as much as three times more in affluent districts than in poor areas. Some examples:

- In Illinois, the children of all-Black East St. Louis receive an education worth $8,000 yearly, while the children of Lake Forest, a predominantly White suburb of Chicago, receive one worth $18,000 (Kozol 2004).
- Including all the costs of operating a public school, a third-grade class of twenty-five children in the schools of Great Neck, New York, receives at least $200,000 more per year than does a class the same size in Mott Haven, New York, where 99.8 percent of children are Black or Latino (Kozol 2002).
- In the Los Angeles area, the students in McKittrick School in the Central Valley receive $17,000 each, more than twice as much as Laguna Beach schools (*Los Angeles Times* 2003).

Data from the U.S. Census Bureau show that in 2008, per-pupil spending ranged from a high of $17,173 in New York to a low of $5,765 in Utah (see Figure 3). This gap is even greater when one considers the monies raised in each district from fundraisers, soda machine contracts, and foundation contributions.

There have been a number of court challenges to unequal funding within states, and systems in several states have been judged unconstitutional. Various schemes have been proposed to meet the objections of the courts, but inequities remain even in the more progressive states. Progressive plans to address financial inequities are fought by the affluent districts and their constituents because, they argue, their taxes should be spent on their children, not the children of others.

Overall, research shows that poor students and the schools serving them have fewer computers and other supplies; have teachers who are underpaid and have less teaching experience; are more likely to attend schools in need of repairs, renovations, and modernization (Filardo et al., 2006); and have higher pupil–teacher ratios. See the Speaking to Students panel, "In-School Marketing," for a look at what some schools are doing to generate more funds.

FIGURE 3

States with the Highest and Lowest Spending Per Student, 2008

Source: U.S. Census Bureau, Public Education Finances 2008.

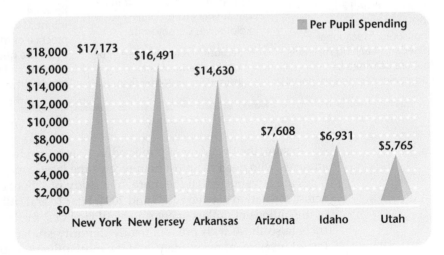

Speaking to Students

In-School Marketing

We live in an advertising age. Through television, radio, billboards, movies, and the Internet, Americans are bombarded with advertisements. Research shows that the average American is exposed to 61 minutes of on-screen ads and promotions per day (Stelter 2009), and the average American living in a big city sees up to 5,000 advertisements per day (Story 2007).

In an effort to make up for declining school revenues, many school districts allow companies to market their products within the school environment in exchange for cash or computers and other supplies. Teenagers provide a target audience for marketers who want to catch consumers early and create brand loyalty. Smart companies understand that teenagers have enormous spending power, and they are ready and willing to capitalize on this through in-school marketing. In elementary, middle, and high schools direct advertising can be found on:

- Book covers and educational posters in hallways.
- Sponsored educational materials. Teaching materials that are provided by companies can be very popular with teachers. "The problem is that the primary goal of the creators is to sell their product; not to educate kids. Content can easily be altered to fit the 'message' that the company wants kids to receive" (Carney, 2007:1).
- Channel One (a division of Alloy Media and Marketing) broadcasts daily to nearly six million teens in approximately 8,000 schools.
- School buses: Some school districts have sold advertising space on the side of their buses, and others broadcast radio programs with advertisements.
- Vending machines: Schools can have exclusive product sponsorships, and can even receive bonuses if certain sales quotas are met (Carney 2007).
- Athletics fields, scoreboards, and gymnasium walls.
- Fundraising items such as cookie dough, magazines, and other branded products.

Critics of this arrangement argue that advertising within an educational institution is exploitative. Carney writes,

Because kids are required to be in school, educational institutions who offer them to advertisers in exchange for money or other incentives are essentially providing companies with a captive audience. In addition, because the products are being presented in a school environment, kids are more likely to believe the advertising promises and take messages at face value. (2007:2)

In this way, marketing to students is dangerous because it seems as though the school endorses the product. A superintendent in Manassas Park says, "To me, it kind of cheapens the education mission, and it takes a captive audience and shoves advertising down their throats" (quoted in Birnbaum 2009:1).

Others argue that in tight economic times schools are forced to do whatever it takes to bring in resources. Furthermore, in a culture saturated with advertising, students will be exposed to ads whether they are presented within the school environment or presented outside of school. Because this is the case, schools might as well benefit from the practice of marketing to students.

So the question for students, parents, and educators is, should education be "commercial-free"?

In sum, the financing of public education is upside down. The schools and students who need the most help receive the least, whereas those with advantages are advantaged all the more. In a study of school construction spending across the nation between 1995 and 2004, Filardo and colleagues found that out of the billions of dollars spent on school facilities, the least-affluent school districts (also those with predominantly minority student enrollment) made the lowest investment per student, and the most affluent districts made the highest investment (2006). Further, the money spent on schools serving low-income students was more likely used to fund basic repairs, but schools in more affluent districts were more likely to add science labs, technology, or other new programs. As stated by President Barack Obama, "For low-income students, the schools are made less decrepit; for wealthier students, they are made more enriching. . . . For all students to achieve, all must be provided adequate resources: effective teachers, inspiring school leaders, and enriching classroom environments" (2006:1).

Family Economic Resources

The average SAT (Scholastic Aptitude Test) scores for youth from families whose annual income was $200,000 or more was 381 points higher than for youth from families whose income is $20,000 or less (1702 versus 1321). By race, Whites scored about 300 points higher than African Americans on average (Marklein 2009). How are we to explain these differences on the SATs by income and race? One factor highly correlated with income is parents' education level. For SAT takers in the class of 2004, scores were approximately 50 points higher than the national average for those whose parents had a graduate degree and 39 points lower than the national average if their parents had only a high school diploma (Carnahan and Coletti 2006).

Many benefits come from economic privilege. Poor parents (disproportionately people of color), most without health insurance, are unable to afford prenatal care, which increases the risk of babies being born at low birth weight, a condition that may lead to learning disabilities. As these poor children age, they are less likely to receive adequate nutrition, decent medical care, and a safe and secure environment. These deficiencies increase the probability of their being less alert, less curious, and less able to interact effectively with their environment than are healthy children.

Poor children are more likely than the children of the affluent to attend schools with poor resources, which, as we have seen, means that they are less likely to receive an enriched educational experience. In their analysis of a nationally representative sample of kindergarten children, Lee and Burkam argues,

> Low-SES [socioeconomic status] children begin school in kindergarten in systematically lower-quality elementary schools than their more advantaged counterparts. However school quality is defined—in terms of higher student achievement, more school resources, more qualified teachers, more positive teacher attitudes, better neighborhood or school conditions, private vs. public schools—the least advantaged U.S. children begin their formal schooling in consistently lower-quality schools. This reinforces the inequalities that develop even before children reach school age. (2002:3)

Similarly, most poor young people live in communities that have few opportunities to apply academic skills and build new ones because such opportunities are either not available or not accessible (libraries, planetariums, summer camps, zoos, nature preserves, museums). The lack of community resources is especially destructive during the summer months, the time when children doing least well in school (a group that is disproportionately poor) slide backward the furthest.

Children from poor families cannot afford private early development programs, which prepare children for school. They can be in Head Start, but these government programs have funding for only about 60 percent of those eligible. As Jonathan Kozol notes,

> The most exclusive of the private preschools in New York, which are known to those who can afford them as "Baby Ivies," cost as much as $24,000 for a full-day program. Competition for admission to these pre-K schools is so extreme that private counselors are frequently retained, at fees as high as $300 an hour, to guide the parents through the application process. At the opposite extreme along the economic spectrum in New York are the thousands of children who receive no preschool opportunity at all. (2005:46)

The level of affluence also affects how long children will stay in school because schools, even public schools, are costly. There are school fees (many school districts, e.g., charge fees for participation in music, athletics, and drama), supplies, meals, transportation, and other costs of education. These financial demands pressure youngsters from poorer families to drop out of school prematurely to go to work. The children from the middle and upper classes, not constrained by financial difficulties, tend to stay in school longer, which means better jobs and pay in the long run.

The affluent also give their children educational advantages such as home computers; travel experiences abroad and throughout the United States; visits to zoos, libraries, and various cultural activities; and summer camps to hone their skills and enrich their experiences in such activities as sports, music, writing, and computers. Another advantage available to the affluent is the hiring of tutors to help children having difficulty in school or to transform good students into outstanding ones.

The well-to-do often send their children to private schools (about 11 percent of U.S. children attend these schools). Parents offer several rationales for sending their children to private schools. Some do so for religious reasons. Another reason is that private schools, unlike public schools, are selective in whom they accept. Thus, parents can ensure that their children will interact with children similar to

© Susan Van Etten/PhotoEdit

America's elite prep schools have a distinguished list of alumni, from former presidents to U.S. ambassadors.

theirs in race (some private schools were expressly created so that White children could avoid attending integrated public schools) and social class. Similarly, private schools are much more likely than public schools to get rid of troublesome students (e.g., behavioral problems and low achievers), thereby providing an educational environment more conducive to learning and achievement. A final reason for attending private schools is that the most elite of them provide a demanding education and entry to the most elite universities, which, in turn, lead to placement in top positions in the professional and corporate occupational worlds.

The preceding arguments show that a family's economic resources are correlated to their child's educational success. From test scores to dropout rates, some students are more advantaged than others.

Higher Education and Stratification

As noted earlier, obtaining a college degree is an important avenue to later success. Because the payoff in jobs and pay is directly related to the prestige of the college or university attended, colleges play an important role in maintaining the stratified structure of society. From those who receive no college education to those who attend private, elite universities, each tier in the hierarchy results in different life chances.

On the lowest tier of the hierarchy are those who cannot afford to attend college. Although economic success is possible without a college degree, for most individuals, no college education translates into a lifetime of lower earnings and low-mobility jobs. Throughout the 1980s and 1990s, the cost of college rose at a rate more than twice the inflation rate. In 2009–2010, on average, the total annual expenses to attend a four-year private school as a resident were $26,273 compared to $7,020 for a four-year public school for in-state students and $11,528 for out-of-state students (College Board 2010). The cost of room, board, fees, and tuition at the nation's most exclusive schools is $35,000 or more for a single school year. The high costs, coupled with declining scholarship monies, prohibit college attendance not only for the able poor but also increasingly for children of the working and lower middle classes. A comparison of students from different income groups shows that 14 percent of those from the lowest income group will enroll in college, compared to 64 percent of those from the highest income group (Symonds 2006).

Because racial minorities are much more likely than Whites to be poor or near poor, they are underrepresented in colleges and among college graduates. The percentages of all racial groups who have completed a bachelor's degree or higher have increased since 1971, but the gaps between Whites and Blacks and Whites and Hispanics remain (U.S. Department of Education, National Center for Education Statistics 2006; see Table 2). The disproportionately low number of college degrees earned by minorities is reflected in the relatively low number of students who attend and graduate from graduate school. This, of course, results in a low proportion of minorities in the various professions in the near future. Of special significance is the low minority representation among full-time faculty in higher education now and projected for the future.

For students who do attend college, money stratifies. The poorest, even those who are talented, are most likely to attend community colleges, which are the least expensive; these schools emphasize technical careers and are therefore limiting in terms of later success (around 44 percent of the nation's college students attend community colleges).

Students with greater resources are likely to attend public universities. State schools are subsidized by their legislators according to their level of prestige. Similar to the funding of public education from kindergarten through high school, the funding of public higher education benefits the already advantaged and neglects the already neglected. In Colorado, for instance, Colorado State University in 2002 received from the state $5,394 for each student enrolled, compared to the $2,582 that the Community College of Aurora received per student (Greenberg 2002). This means, in effect, that all taxpayers, including those of modest means, support this elitist system.

Finally, on the highest tier of the hierarchy are the students with the greatest financial backing who are the most likely to attend elite and prestigious private institutions. The most prestigious schools have the most resources, which means they can hire the most prestigious professors, maintain the most complete libraries and research facilities, and equip state-of-the-art classrooms. Despite falling endowments due to the economic recession, in 2009 Harvard had an endowment valued at $36.5 billion, Yale had an endowment worth $3 billion, and Stanford had an endowment worth $12.6 billion (National Association of College and University Business Officers [NACUBO] 2010).

Although talent is an important variable, it is money—not ability—that places college students in this stratified system. For example, admission committees at elite universities give students from upper-class families favorable ratings if they are children of alumni or children of big contributors to the university's fundraising campaigns (this is a reverse form of affirmative action, benefiting the children of the affluent, the most notable example being George W. Bush's acceptance into Yale). Reporter Daniel Golden argued that these children of celebrities, politicians, and wealthy executives, called "development cases," are often admitted to elite colleges with SAT scores sometimes 300 or 400 points lower than those of some rejected applicants (Golden 2006). Peter Schmidt writes:

Conservatives often complain that because of affirmative action, colleges are no longer meritocracies. But the reality is that it's not lesser-qualified black and Hispanic

TABLE 2

Educational Attainment by Race/Ethnicity for U.S. Population 25 Years and Older, 2006–2009

Highest Level Reached	All Races	Asian American/ Pacific Islander	White	Black	Hispanic/ Latino	American Indian/ Alaskan Native
Some High School	15.4%	14.7%	13.1%	20.0%	39.6%	24.0%
High School Graduate	29.3%	16.0%	29.7%	32.9%	27.0%	32.1%
Some College or Associate's Degree	27.7%	19.6%	28.2%	30.0%	20.9%	31.2%
Bachelor's Degree	17.4%	29.7%	18.3%	11.4%	8.7%	8.5%
Graduate or Professional Degree	10.1%	19.7%	10.7%	5.9%	4.0%	4.3%

Source: Social Explorer Tables: ACS 2005 to 2009 (5-Year Estimates) (SE), ACS 2005–2009 (5-Year Estimates), Social Explorer; U.S. Census Bureau; American Community Survey Tables: 2005–2009 (5-Year Estimates) (ACS09_5yr), ACS 2005–2009 (5-Year Estimates), U.S. Census Bureau.

students who elbow most of the worthier applicants aside. It's rich white kids with cash and connections. A five-year study of 146 top colleges by the Educational Testing Service found that white students with subpar qualifications were nearly twice as prevalent on such campuses as black and Hispanic students who received an admissions break based on their ethnicity or race. Some of those white students were jocks, recruited to win ballgames. But most had connections to people the institution wanted to keep happy, such as alumni, donors, and politicians. (2007:14)

A degree from a prestigious school opens doors of opportunity rarely available to graduates of the less-prestigious schools, yet entry goes disproportionately to the already advantaged. A study of the most selective universities found that "just 3 percent of the students admitted were from families of modest social and economic backgrounds. Fully 74 percent of the students came from the top quarter of the nation's social and economic strata" (reported in Sacks 2003:B7).

Segregation

Schools in the United States tend to be segregated by social class and race, both by neighborhood and, within schools, by ability grouping. Schools are based in neighborhoods that tend to be relatively homogeneous by socioeconomic status. Racial and economic segregation is especially prevalent at the elementary school level, carrying over to a lesser degree in the secondary schools. Colleges and universities, as we have seen, are peopled by a middle- and upper-class clientele. Thus, at every level, children tend to attend a school with children like themselves in socioeconomic status and race. A study by Harvard University found that public schools are highly segregated and becoming more so: "Although minority enrollment now approaches 40 percent nationwide, the average White student attends a public school that is 80 percent White. At the same time, one-sixth of Black students—the figure is one-quarter in the Northeast and Midwest—attend schools that are nearly 100 percent non-White" (reported in the *New York Times* 2003a:1). According to Fuentes (2007), Latinos living in New York attend schools that are 80 percent non-White. These figures are the same in the West, which has seen a swell in the Latino population overall. In short, the progress toward desegregation peaked in the late 1980s and has retreated because of racially segregated neighborhoods and school districts across the country challenging integration policies.

Two recent cases illustrate this challenge to integration: Louisville and Seattle. In both cases, officials have worked to ensure that the student bodies of their public schools reflect their city's ethnic composition. Based on the belief that students learn best in a diverse environment, students are assigned by race to some kindergarten to twelfth-grade public schools. White parents have challenged these policies in court, and the Bush administration came forward in siding with these opponents, saying that race-conscious admissions policies violate the Constitution (Lane 2006).

At the college level, some universities have also addressed the issue of segregation through the use of race-conscious admissions. At the University of Michigan, for example, the admissions committee uses a point scale whereby students need 100 points to be accepted to the university. Prior to 2003, underrepresented ethnic minorities received an automatic 20-point bonus toward admission. A 2003 Supreme Court decision (*Gratz v. Bollinger*) found this system to be unconstitutional and too close to a quota system. At the same time, however, another

Supreme Court decision (*Grutter v. Bollinger*) upheld that race could still be considered in the admission process, but minorities could not be awarded a fixed quantity of extra points. This decision has come under fire from the public. In 2006, Michigan residents voted overwhelmingly in favor of barring the state from granting preferences based on skin color or gender in public contracting, employment, and education (Brown 2006).

Tracking and Teachers' Expectations

In 1954, the Supreme Court declared segregated schools unconstitutional. As we have seen, many schools remain at least partially segregated by social class and race because schools draw students from residential areas that are more or less homogeneous by class and race. Segregation is reinforced further by the tracking system within the schools. Tracking (also known as ability grouping) sorts students into different groups or classes according to their perceived intellectual ability and performance. The decision is based on grades and teachers' judgments but primarily through standardized tests. The result is that children from poor families and from ethnic minorities are overrepresented in the slow track, whereas children from advantaged backgrounds are disproportionately in the middle and upper tracks. The rationale for tracking is that it provides a better fit between the needs and capabilities of the student and the demands and opportunities of the curriculum. Slower students do not retard the progress of brighter ones, but teachers can adapt their teaching more efficiently to the level of the class if the students are relatively homogeneous in ability. The special problems of the different ability groups, from gifted to challenged, can be dealt with more easily when groups of students share the same or similar problems. The arguments are persuasive.

Although these benefits may be real, tracking is open to serious criticisms. First, students in lower tracks are given low-level work that increases the gap between them and students in the higher tracks, thereby reinforcing the U.S. stratification system. As noted by McLaren and Farahmandpur,

> As the standardized curriculum and standardized testing widen the achievement gap between poor and wealthy school districts, working class students and students of color continue to be tracked into vocational programs and classes that teach life-skills or offer basic training that prepares them for jobs in the retail and service industry. Even more disturbing perhaps is the placement of high school female students in sewing and cosmetology classes. As we know by now, these classes do little for students who must compete with advanced placement and college-tracked students. It is painfully ironic that just as we are witnessing the factory model of schooling returning with a vengeance, the factories of yesteryear in which working-class students traditionally sought employment after graduation are moving out of the country, escaping the unions and depriving workers of medical benefits. (2006:97)

Thus the tracking system is closely linked to the stratification system—that is, students from low-income families are disproportionately placed in the lowest track, resulting in a reinforcement of the social class structure.

Second, students in the upper track develop feelings of superiority, while those in the lower track tend to define themselves as inferior. As early as the second grade, students know where they stand on the smart-to-dumb continuum, and this knowledge profoundly affects their self-esteem. These psychological wounds can have devastating effects.

Third, the low-track students are tracked to fail. The negative labels, low teacher expectations, poor education resources (e.g., the highest track is much more likely to have access to computers and to have the most talented teachers), and reluctance of teachers to teach these classes (there is a subtle labeling among teachers regarding who gets to teach what level) all lead to a high probability of failure among students assigned to the lowest track. Given all these negatives, it is not surprising that students who are discipline problems or who eventually drop out come disproportionately from the low track. To summarize, Datnow and Cooper argues,

Because of tracking practices, educational institutions, like the communities in which they are embedded, sort individuals by race, social class, language, and ability. Tracking serves as the major vehicle to sort and institutionalize the division between the "haves" and "have-nots," resulting in racially identifiable groups of students, with African American, Latino, and low-income students receiving an unequal distribution of educational access and opportunity. (2002:690)

The tracking system is powerful in its negative effects. There are four principal reasons this system stunts the success of students who are negatively labeled: stigma, self-fulfilling prophesies, beliefs about future payoffs to education, and the creation of negative student subcultures.

- **Stigma.** Assignment to a lower track carries a strong stigma (a label of social disgrace). Such students are labeled as intellectual inferiors. Their self-esteem wanes as they see how other people perceive them and behave toward them. Thus, individuals assigned to a track other than college prep perceive themselves as second class, unworthy, stupid, and in the way. Clearly, assignment to a low track is destructive to a student's self-concept.

- **Self-Fulfilling Prophecy.** A self-fulfilling prophecy is an event that occurs because it is predicted, and people alter their behavior to conform to the prediction. This effect is closely related to stigma. If placed in the college-prep track, students are likely to receive better instruction, have access to better facilities, and be pushed more nearly to their capacity than are students assigned to other tracks. The reason is clear: teachers and administrators expect great things from the one group and lesser things from the other. Moreover, these expectations are fulfilled. Students in the higher track do better, and those in the lower track do not. These behaviors justify the greater expenditures of time, faculties, and experimental curricula for those in the higher track.

  An example comes from a classic controversial study by Rosenthal and Jacobson (1968). Although this study has been criticized for a number of methodological shortcomings, the findings are consistent with theories of interpersonal influence and with the labeling view of deviant behavior. In the spring of 1964, all students in an elementary school in San Francisco were given an IQ test. The following fall, the teachers were given the names of children identified by the test as potential academic spurters, and five of these children were assigned to each classroom. The spurters were chosen by means of a table of random numbers. The only difference between the experimental group (those labeled as spurters) and the control group (the rest of the class) was in the imaginations of the teachers. At the end of the year, all the children were again tested, and the children from whom the teachers expected greater intellectual gains showed such gains (in IQ scores and grades). Moreover, they were rated by their teachers as being more curious, interesting, happy, and more likely to succeed than were the children in the control group.

The implications of this example are clear. Teachers' expectations have a profound effect on students' performance. When students are overrated, they tend to overproduce; when they are underrated, they underachieve. The tracking system is a labeling process that affects the expectations of teachers (and fellow students and parents). The limits of these expectations are crucial in the educational process. Yet the self-fulfilling prophecy can work in a positive direction if teachers have an unshakable conviction that their students can learn. Concomitant with this belief, teachers should hold themselves, not the students, accountable if the latter should fail. Used in this manner, the self-fulfilling prophecy can work to the benefit of all students.

- **Future Payoff.** School is perceived as relevant for students going to college. Grades are a means of qualifying for college. For the non-college-bound student, however, school and grades are much less important for entry into a job. At most, students need a high school diploma, and grades really do not matter as long as one does not flunk out. Thus, non-college-bound students often develop negative attitudes toward school, grades, and teachers. This is reflected in the statistic that students from the lowest income quarter are more than six times as likely to drop out of high school as students from the highest income quarter (U.S. Department of Education, National Center for Educational Statistics 2006).

  As we have seen, being on the lower track has negative consequences. Lower-track students are more rebellious, both in school and out, and do not participate as much in school activities. Finally, what is being taught is often not relevant to their world. Thus, we are led to conclude that many of these students tend to feel that they are not only second-class citizens but perhaps also even pariahs. What other interpretation is plausible in a system that disadvantages them, shuns them, and makes demands of them that are irrelevant?

- **Student Subculture.** The reasons given previously suggest that a natural reaction of people in the lower track would be to band together in a student subculture that is antagonistic toward school. This subculture would quite naturally develop its own system of rewards because those of the school are inaccessible.

  These factors (stigma, negative self-fulfilling prophecy, low future payoff, and a contrary student subculture) show how the tracking system is at least partly responsible for the fact that students in the lower tracks tend to be low achievers, unmotivated, uninvolved in school activities, and more prone to break school rules and drop out of school. To segregate students either by ability or by future plans is detrimental to the students labeled as inferior. It is an elitist system that for the most part takes the children of the elite and educates them to take the elite positions in society. Conversely, children of the nonelite are trained to recapitulate the experiences of their parents.

  The conclusion is inescapable: Inequality in the educational system causes many people to fail in U.S. schools. This phenomenon is the fault of the schools, not of the children who fail. To focus on these victims is to divert attention from the real problem—the inadequacies of the school system.

POSSIBILITIES FOR PROMOTING EQUALITY OF OPPORTUNITY

A fundamental tenet of U.S. society is that each individual, regardless of sex, race, ethnicity, religion, sexuality, age, and social class, has the opportunity to be equal on her or his own merits. In other words, the system must not impede individuals from reaching their potential and from gaining the unequal rewards of an unequal society. The data presented in this chapter show that U.S. schools tend to block the chances of minority and poor children in their quest to be successful in society. This section outlines several programs that schools and society could adopt to promote equality of opportunity for all children.

We must realize at the start that if the situation for poor and minority children is difficult now, it will worsen significantly if changes are not made. This assertion is based on three societal trends. The first, is that the gap between the affluent and the poor is widening. Also, as the demographic mix of the nation continues to change, increasing numbers of children of color from relatively poor families will attend schools. Today about 22 percent of schoolchildren have a foreign-born parent (mostly Latino and Asian), a proportion that will likely increase. The poor and children of immigrants are disproportionately found in inner cities in increasingly segregated neighborhoods. With the poor and people of color clustered in cities, these local governments, faced with a declining tax base, will be less and less able to provide the services required of their citizens, including education. Similarly, certain regions—the Pacific Coast, the Southwest, and Florida—are especially affected by immigration, placing an extraordinary financial burden on those states and localities.

The second trend that will negatively affect the educational opportunities of minorities unless changes are made is that the number of minority students is increasing and will in the next decades make Whites the numerical minority (as they are today in many school districts). Moreover, racial and ethnic minorities are concentrated in poor states (the South and Southwest), in poor geographical regions (Appalachia, the Ozarks, along the Rio Grande, and in the Mississippi delta), and in poor sections of cities. This is significant because racial/ethnic minorities have higher rates of poverty, more unemployment, and lower educational attainment than do the more fortunate majority. In effect, under current policies, children from minorities are disadvantaged economically and are at greater risk of educational failure. So, wherever these children are overrepresented, there will be disproportionately less local money to meet their educational needs (because of the lower tax base). Ironically, the poor require more money than the affluent to catch up, such as enriched preschool, after-school programs, summer reading programs, and small classes, yet the richest school districts spend more per student.

In addition to the rise in the proportion of racial minority students, several demographic trends make reform difficult. One demographic trend negatively affecting education is the aging of society. As a greater proportion of the population no longer has children in school, there will be a greater reluctance on their part to vote for tax increases directed at education. Another population trend is for increased enrollments from the baby boom echo—that is, the children of children of the disproportionately large baby boom generation are in school or soon will be, swelling the numbers significantly. This means that more classrooms and teachers are needed at a time when many states are making cuts to education due to the economic recession.

All the previously mentioned demographic changes point to a society that is at risk for increasing the gap between rich and poor students. The next sections discuss several programs that schools and society could adopt to promote equality of opportunity for all children.

Provide Universal Preschool Programs

The most important variable affecting school performance is not race but socio-economic status. Regardless of race, children from poor families tend to do less well in school than do children from families who are better off. Long-term studies are beginning to show that the United States needs to invest in preschool-age children from disadvantaged families to counter some of these poor outcomes. In fact, the earlier the investment, the better. For example, in a 40-year study of 123 low-income children, intensive preschool attention resulted in higher academic achievement, higher earnings, and lower rates of criminal activity compared to a control group (reported in Farrell 2006). Although the program was expensive ($10,600 investment per pupil), researchers estimated that the benefit-to-cost ratio comes to $17 for every $1 invested. The Economic Policy Institute argues,

> Our failure to invest in the healthy development of young children leads to enormous problems and enormous costs to society. Poor children overwhelmingly suffer from society's neglect as they go through school, and then enter the workforce (or, too often, the criminal justice system) unprepared to be productive workers and citizens. And the costs to taxpayers and society are enormous because funds not spent on early childhood programs are spent later on remedial and special education, criminal justice programs and welfare benefits. (Reported in Hickey 2004:12)

Compensatory programs such as Head Start and Follow Through are predicated on the assumption that if children from lower-class homes are to succeed in middle-class schools, they must have special help to equalize their chances. The Bill and Melinda Gates Foundation plans to invest up to $90 million on early intervention programs and is currently backing several experiments to find out what works (Farrell 2006).

Offer Free Education

Beginning with preschool, there must be a commitment to a free education for all students. Presumably, public education at the elementary and secondary levels is free, but this assumption is a fallacy, as discussed earlier. Although circumstances vary by district, typically children must pay for their supplies, textbooks, laboratory fees, locker rental, admission to plays and athletic events, meals, and participation in extracurricular activities. Some districts waive these costs for poor families. But waivers do not occur uniformly across school districts, and the procedures for granting these waivers are often degrading (i.e., done in such a way that other people know who receives the handouts). These costs are regressive because they take a larger proportion of the poor family's budget, thereby increasing the pressure to withdraw the child from school, where he or she drains the family resources.

By making education absolutely free to all children, communities could reduce dropout rates among the poor. A program of greater scope would also provide a living allowance for each child from a poor family who stayed in school beyond the eighth grade. This program would be analogous to the GI Bill, which provided similar benefits to soldiers returning after World War II. Special care must be given to provide these benefits, as did the GI Bill, without making their acceptance degrading.

An important way to produce equal opportunity is to provide a free college education to all students who qualify. This means the elimination of tuition and fees and an allowance for books for everyone, plus grants and loans for students in need to pay for living expenses while attending college. Students could then "give back" through community service or working on campus.

Set National Education Standards

The government should provide national education standards, a national curriculum, and national tests. As noted before, the No Child Left Behind Act is a step in this direction, but it allows each of the fifty states to set its own standards. There are more than 14,000 school districts and 83,000 schools in the United States. We must require that each school district and school, rather than acting on its own, meet specific standards for school achievement agreed to by a national consensus among educational leaders. The minimum result of this requirement would be that students, whether growing up in Nebraska or New York, would learn the same basic materials at about the same time. It would also mean that as students move with their families from one locality to another, they would not be at a disadvantage because of the esoteric schooling they had received.

Reduce Funding Disparities across States and Districts

Another reform at the federal level would be to spend the federal monies unequally to equalize differences among the states. In effect, the federal government must take the money it receives in taxes, taking disproportionately from the wealthy states, and redistribute it to the poor states. Otherwise, the gap between the rich and poor states will be maintained.

Nationwide, the traditional property tax system of raising money for education locally is under assault. The supreme courts in various states are ruling in case after case that the states are failing the children in the poorer districts. States should be encouraged to distribute their funds to eliminate or minimize disparities between rich and poor districts. This could be done by the federal government's withholding funds from states with discrepancies between their poor and rich districts that exceed federal guidelines. In such cases, the federal government could channel its monies directly to the poorer districts within the offending states.

Reduce Class and School Size

Schools can be restructured to better meet the needs of students. A beginning would be to reduce class size. A Tennessee study (Project Star) found that students in smaller classes tended to achieve higher grades, had better high school graduation rates, and were more likely to attend college, and the gap between Black–White academic achievement narrowed by 38 percent (Herbert 2001b). Not only small classes but smaller schools are also beneficial, generating higher graduation rates, more participation, less alienation, and less violence. Results from the National Longitudinal Study of Adolescent Health, a federally funded survey of 72,000 junior high and high school students, found that when the number of students in a school exceeded 1,200, students became more isolated from one another. Isolation contributes to the greater likelihood of engaging in risky behavior such as drug use, violence, and early sexual activity (reported in Fletcher 2002). Smaller schools and smaller classes create an intimacy that can improve performance. A study of Chicago's experiment with small schools in some of its poorest neighborhoods found that student attendance rose and dropout rates fell with reduced class sizes (reported in Symonds 2001).

Attract and Retain Excellent Teachers

Schools need to attract and retain excellent teachers. This means higher salaries, mentoring of new teachers, and paying teachers a bonus for teaching in difficult school situations. This is especially challenging when states are inclined to make large cuts to education as they attempt to balance their budgets. In 2009, President Obama announced a national grant competition entitled "Race to the Top." State governors will apply for $4.35 billion in grants to improve educational quality and results in their state. In their application they must include a plan to recruit, develop, reward, and retain effective teachers and principals.

Extend the School Day and Year

The United States devotes the shortest amount of time to teaching its children of any advanced nation (see Figure 4). The 6-hour day and the 9-month calendar instituted to accommodate farm life have not changed since the nineteenth century. Pushing for an extended school year, President Obama said,

> We can no longer afford an academic calendar designed when America was a nation of farmers who needed their children at home plowing the land at the end of the day. That calendar may have once made sense, but today, it puts us at a competitive disadvantage. Our children spend over a month less in school than children in South Korea. That is no way to prepare them for a 21st century economy. (quoted in Thomma 2009:1)

FIGURE 4

Average Number of School Days in Global Perspective

Country	Days of School
Japan	243
South Korea	220
Israel	216
Luxembourg	216
The Netherlands	200
Scotland	200
Thailand	200
Hong Kong	195
England	192
Hungary	192
Swaziland	191
Finland	190
New Zealand	190
Nigeria	190
France	185
United States	180

Hold Educators Accountable

Virtually every state has instituted statewide examinations in the past decade, linking the results to such things as grade promotion, high school graduation, and teacher and principal salaries. The cornerstone of the No Child Left Behind legislation is to have nationwide testing, mandating annual tests in grades 3 through 8, plus one in high school, with penalties for those schools that fail. There are difficulties with this assessment of schools, as noted earlier. Do you punish schools from economically disadvantaged districts with children who are more proficient in a language other than English? When a school fails, do you punish, or do you invest in more resources (tutoring, after-school programs, summer school, smaller class size, modern-schools wired for the future)?

The pressure on teachers and administrators that their schools score well may lead to cheating or to manipulating their rankings by exempting special education students and slow learners from taking the tests, or through the subtle encouragement of slow learners to drop out of school.

A final criticism of high-stakes testing is that research at the state level finds that tests attached to grade promotion and high school graduation lead to increased dropout rates, especially for minority students (Orfield and Wald 2000).

These criticisms are valid and important, but to criticize them does not invalidate the need for standards and evaluation. The key is to heavily invest in poor children, beginning in preschool, and to enrich their school with meaningful experiences and talented, caring teachers. With such a commitment, over time all children can be held to the same standards and their schools held accountable.

Reform the Educational Philosophy of Schools

The reforms listed earlier do not question the structure and philosophy of the educational system, which opponents argue stifles children in attaining their potential. In the view of the critics, the system itself is wrong and the generator of many profound problems. These critics want to reconstruct the entire educational enterprise along very different lines. This demand for change is based on three related assumptions. The first is that the school is a microcosm of the larger society. Because society is too competitive, repressive, inhumane, materialistic, racist, and imperialist, so, too, are the schools. Changing society entails changing the schools.

The second assumption of the radical critics of education is that the process of public education as it currently exists damages, thwarts, and stifles children. The schools somehow manage to suppress the natural curiosity of children. They begin with inquisitive children and mold them into acquisitive children with little desire to learn.

Third, the educational system is a product of society and hence shapes its products to meet the requirements of society. The present system is predicated on the needs of an industrial society in which citizens must follow orders, do assigned tasks in the appropriate order and time span, and not challenge the status quo. According to Everton, "This is why school sucks. Rather than do what it pretends to—educate, foster curiosity, expand our intellects, and promote diversity—compulsory schooling segregates people on the basis of how well they're willing to do what they're told. . . . Compulsory schooling is at its best when diluting intellects in preparation for lifetimes of subservience to corporate masters" (2004:55).

The demands of the 21st century require students to work cooperatively, to be knowledgeable about technology, and to think outside the box.

But these behaviors will not be appropriate for life in the twenty-first century. The future will likely require people who can cope with rapid turnover—changes in occupations, human relationships, and community ties. Moreover, the citizens of the future must be able to cope with myriad choices. Does an educational system built on order, a rigid time schedule, and the lecture method adequately prepare youngsters for life as it is and will be? The proponents of these and other alternatives are critical of U.S. education. They conclude that schools are failing not only children from the ghettos of large cities but also suburban and small-town youngsters. Wallis and Steptoe write,

> For the past five years, the national conversation on education has focused on reading scores, math tests and closing the "achievement gap" between social classes. This is not a story about that conversation. This is a story about the big public conversation the nation is not having about education, the one that will ultimately determine not merely whether some fraction of our children get "left behind" but also whether an entire generation of kids will fail to make the grade in the global economy because they can't think their way through abstract problems, work in teams, distinguish good information from bad or speak a language other than English. (2006:52)

Today's economy demands that schools rethink their educational philosophy and focus more on twenty-first-century skills. Those skills include (1) knowing more about the world as global citizens, (2) thinking outside the box, (3) becoming smarter about new sources of information, and (4) developing good people skills (Wallis and Steptoe 2006).

Restructure Society

The approaches to equality described previously focus on changing either individual students or the schools. But if equality of opportunity is truly the goal, education cannot accomplish it alone. Closing the achievement gap between advantaged and disadvantaged students cannot be accomplished without a societywide assault on racism and poverty. Poverty can be eliminated only through fundamental revisions in the economic and familial institutions. This is not to say that reform of the schools should be ignored. Efforts to improve our schools should parallel attempts to restructure the other institutions of society.

■ CHAPTER REVIEW

1. The system of education in the United States is characterized by (a) conservatism—the preservation of culture, roles, values, and training necessary for the maintenance of society; (b) a belief in compulsory mass education; (c) a preoccupation with order and control; (d) fragmentation; (e) local control, which results in (f) a lack of curriculum standardization across the country; and (g) reinforcement of the stratification system through the sifting and sorting of students.

2. The belief that our society is a meritocracy, with the most intelligent and talented at the top, is a myth. Education, instead of being the great equalizer, reinforces social inequality.

3. Educational outcomes are strongly linked to social class, race, and ethnicity.

4. The schools are structured to aid in the perpetuation of social and economic differences in several ways: (a) by being financed principally through property taxes so that rich school districts spend more per student; (b) by offering private schools that the poor cannot afford; (c) by increasing the cost of attending college; (d) by segregating students by race and social class; and (e) by tracking according to presumed level of ability.

5. The tracking system is closely correlated with social class; students from low-income families are disproportionately placed in the lowest track. Tracking thwarts the equality of educational opportunity for the poor by generating four effects: (a) a stigma, which lowers self-esteem; (b) the self-fulfilling prophecy; (c) a perception of school as having no future payoff; and (d) a negative student subculture.

6. Demographic changes such as the increasing number of minority students and students with a foreign-born parent are widening the gap between poor and rich students.

7. The government needs to invest in preschool programs to improve the life chances of disadvantaged youth.

8. Beginning with preschool and continuing through college, there must be a societal commitment to free education.

9. The federal government could promote equality of opportunity by providing national educational standards, a national curriculum, and national tests.

10. The federal government must level the playing field by distributing money unequally to the states according to need and encouraging states to minimize economic disparities among their school districts.

11. Promoting equality of opportunity and excellence in the public schools requires (a) reducing class and school size; (b) attracting and retaining excellent teachers; (c) extending the school year; (d) holding educators responsible for their students' outcomes; and (e) changing the philosophy of schools to meet the needs of the twenty-first century and global economy.

12. The restructuring of schools will not meet the goal of equality of educational opportunity, radical critics argue, unless the society is also restructured. This change requires a societywide assault on racism and poverty and a redistribution of wealth to reduce the inequalities that result from economic advantage.

■ KEY TERMS

Cultural deprivation. Erroneous assumption that some groups (e.g., the poor) are handicapped by a so-called inferior culture.

No Child Left Behind Act. Federal legislation requiring states to develop academic standards in reading, math, and science. All children must reach these standards by 2013–2014.

Tracking. Ability grouping in schools.

Stigma. Powerful negative social label that affects a person's social identity and self-concept.

Student subculture. Members of the disadvantaged band together in a group with values and behaviors antagonistic toward school.

■ SUCCEED WITH PEARSON mysoclab www.mysoclab.com

Experience, Discover, Observe, Evaluate

MySocLab is designed just for you. This chapter features a pre-test and post-test to help you learn and review key concepts and terms.

Experience sociology in action with dynamic visual activities, videos, and readings to enhance your learning experience. Complete the following activities at www.mysoclab.com.

Social Explorer is an interactive application that allows you to explore Census data through interactive maps.

- Explore the Social Explorer Map: *Patterns of Privilege in Public and Private Schools*

The Core Concepts in Sociology video clips offer a real-world perspective on sociological concepts.

- Watch *ABC Nightline: Recipe for Success*

MySocLibrary includes primary source readings from classic and contemporary sociologists.

- Read Bersani & Chapple, *School Failure as an Adolescent Turning Point*; Rosser, *Too Many Women in College?*; Kozol, *Savage Inequalities: Children in America's Schools*

Racial and Ethnic Inequality

Racial and Ethnic Inequality

Yuri Gripsas/AFP/Getty Images

Racial oppression makes the United States very distinctive, for it is the only major Western country that was explicitly founded on racial oppression. Today, as in the past, this oppression is not a minor addition to U.S. society's structure but rather is systemic across all major institutions. Oppression of non-European groups is part of the deep social structure.

—Joe R. Feagin

ince its beginning, the United States has been a nation with a "race problem." Today, racial divisions are changing, but they are not disappearing. One in three U.S. residents is a minority. Instead of fading into an integrated social order, new color lines prevent equal opportunities for all. This society is moving from being predominantly White to being a global society of diverse racial and ethnic peoples. As this occurs, blatant forms of racism that existed in the past have given way to new, more subtle practices (Lewis et al., 2004). As the proportion of racially defined minority groups in the United States increases, the problems they face become more and more the problems of the entire society. This chapter focuses on how structured racial inequality produces social problems.

HOW TO THINK ABOUT RACIAL AND ETHNIC INEQUALITY

Why are some groups dominant and others subordinate? The basic reason is power—power derived from superior numbers, technology, weapons, property, or economic resources. Those holding superior power in a society—the dominant group—establish a system of inequality by dominating less powerful groups. This system of inequality is then maintained by power. The terms *dominant group* and *minority group* describe power differences regardless of the size of the groups.

Racial inequalities produce opportunities for some and oppression for others. The word *oppression* comes from a Latin word meaning "to crush," and thus racial oppression means keeping people of color down—that is, crushing them physically and in many other ways (Feagin 2006:8). Racial oppression reaches far back into the past of the United States. The racial hierarchy with White groups of European origin at the top and people of color at the bottom serves important functions for society and for certain categories of people. It ensures, for example, that some people are available to do society's dirty work at low wages. The racial hierarchy reinforces the status quo. It enables the powerful to retain their control and their advantages.

Racial stratification offers better occupational opportunities, income, and education to White people. These patterns are found throughout the world even as societies become more racially and ethnically diverse. Today, many racially defined people are becoming even more marginalized by global restructuring, which includes sweatshops that employ people of color, new fiscal policies imposed on developing countries, and disruptions of national and local economies that force people to migrate in search of better jobs and better lives. Racial inequalities shape social relations around the world.

This chapter examines racial inequality from several vantage points. First, we outline the important features of racial and ethnic groups. We then profile four racial minority groups: African Americans, Latinos, Asian Americans, and Native Americans. Next, we examine explanations of racial inequality, followed by a look at its effect on Blacks and Hispanics in terms of income, jobs, education, and health. Finally, the chapter turns to contemporary trends in racial and ethnic relations.

The theme of the chapter is that racial problems have structural foundations. This framework challenges myths about race and "the race problem." Many people think that the United States is now a "color blind" society where race no longer matters. They claim that the election of the first African American president in U.S. history reflects a postracial society. But despite the tremendous significance of President Obama's electoral victory, and despite the changing character of racism, our society remains structured by racial inequality. In this chapter we show that racial divides persist and that minority groups lack the same opportunities as everyone else. Keep in mind that minorities are not to blame for the race problem. Instead, the cause lies in our race-based system of social rights and resources. Keep in mind that our emphasis on persistent racial domination does not mean that minorities are passive victims of oppression. Their histories are filled with human agency and for centuries, racial minorities in the United States have fought against oppression, both as individuals and in groups.

RACIAL AND ETHNIC MINORITIES

Racial categories are a basis of power relations and group position. Because race relations are power relations, conflict (or at least the potential for conflict) is always present. Overt conflict is most likely when minority groups attempt to change the distribution of power. Size is not crucial in determining whether a group is the most powerful. A numerical minority may in fact have more political representation than the majority, as is the case in South Africa. Thus, the most important characteristic of a minority group is that it is dominated by a more powerful group.

Determining who is a minority is largely a matter of history, politics, and judgment—both social and political. Population characteristics other than race and ethnicity—such as age, gender, or religious preference—are sometimes used to designate minority status. However, race and ethnicity are the characteristics used most often to define the minority and majority populations in contemporary U.S. society (O'Hare 1992:5).

Sociologists agree that race is socially constructed. This means that some groups are racially defined, even though races per se, do not exist. What does exist is the *idea* that races are distinct biological categories. Races are thought to be physically distinguishable populations that share a common ancestry. But despite the common belief, social scientists now reject the biological concept of race. Scientific examination of the human genome finds no genetic differences between the so-called races. Fossil and DNA evidence show that humans are all one race, evolved in the last 100,000 years from the same small number of tribes that migrated from Africa and colonized the world (Angier 2000; American Sociological Association 2003; Mukhopadhyay and Henze 2003; Bean, et al., 2004). Although there is no such thing as biological race, races are real insofar as they are *socially defined*. In other words, racial categories *operate* as if they are real. Racial categories are a mechanism for sorting people in society. They structure and segregate our neighborhoods, our schools, our churches, and our relationships (Higginbotham and Andersen 2009).

Racial classification in the United States is based on a Black–White dichotomy—that is, the construction of two opposing categories into which all people fit. However, social definitions of race have changed throughout the nation's history. At different points in the past, "race has taken on different meanings. Many of the people considered White and thought of as the majority group are descendants of immigrants who at one time were believed to be racially distinct from native-born White Americans, the majority of whom were Protestants" (Higginbotham and Andersen 2009:41). Racial categories vary in different parts of the country and around the world. Someone classified as "Black" in the United States might be considered "White" in Brazil and "Colored" (a category distinguished from both Black and White) in South Africa (Bamshad and Olson 2003:80). In the United States, a Black–White color line has always been complicated by regional racial divides. Today, the rapidly growing presence of Latino and Asian immigrants and the resurgence of Native American identification have changed the meaning and boundaries of racial categories (Lewis, Kryson, and Harris 2004:5). Their non-White racial status marks them as "other" and denies them many opportunities (Pyke 2004:55). Global events also complicate the color lines. Since the terrorist attacks on the World Trade Center and the Pentagon, Arab Americans, Muslims, and people of Middle-Eastern descent (viewed by many as a single entity) are stereotyped as different and possibly dangerous.

Racial Categories

Consider current immigration patterns that are reshaping the U.S. racial landscape. Immigration from Asia, Latin America, and the Caribbean is changing the character of race and ethnic relations. Sociologists Michael Omi and Howard Winant use the term racial formation to mean that society is continually creating and transforming racial categories (1994:55). For example, groups once self-defined by their ethnic backgrounds such as Mexican Americans and Japanese Americans are racialized as "Hispanics" and "Asian Americans." Middle Easterners coming from such countries as Syria, Lebanon, Egypt, and Iran are commonly grouped together and called "Arabs."

The U.S. government has changed its racial categories over time. The U.S. Census Bureau, which measures race on the basis of self-identification, revised its racial categories for the 2000 Census. In 2000, for the first time, people were allowed to record themselves in two or more racial categories. Of the U.S. population, 2.4 percent, or 7 million people, identified themselves as multiracial, reporting that they were of two races. The option of choosing more than one race provides a more accurate and visible portrait of the multiracial population in the United States. The 2010 Census provides, for the first time, a glimpse at the evolution of racial identification. Of all racial categories, the Two or More Races population was one of the fastest-growing, increasing approximately one-third between 2000 and 2010 Census. "Those who were children in 2000 and were identified as one race by their parents may respond differently as adults today, and select more than one race" (El Nasser 2010:1A–2A). In addition, marrying across racial lines is on the increase, as attitudes toward interracial unions become more tolerant. Already, children are much more likely than adults to identify themselves as multiracial. Four percent of the population under age 18 were identified in more than one racial category in the 2000 Census, twice the percentage for adults (Kent et al., 2001:6; Prewitt 2003:39).

Although the 2000 Census began to capture the complex mix of racial groups present in the United States, it used a confusing classification for Hispanics. According to the 2000 U.S. Census guidelines, Hispanics were considered to be an ethnic group, not a race. People who identified their ethnicity as Hispanic could also indicate a racial background by choosing "some other race." The Census Bureau acknowledged that the distinction between race and ethnicity is flawed and even tested options for adding "Hispanic" to the list of racial categories for the 2010 Census (Lewis 2006). In reality, Hispanics *are racialized* in the United States. Although classified as an ethnic group, "Hispanic" encompasses a range of ethnic groups. At the same time, although Hispanics are not officially defined as a race, they are *socially defined* in racial terms. In other words, the dominant society treats them as racially inferior. When any

Speaking to Students

Got Privilege? Studying What It Means to Be White

What does it mean to be "white"? Surprisingly, the answer to this question is not as simple as it may seem. Whiteness is not biological, nor is it determined solely by skin color or other physical attributes. Instead, whiteness is socially constructed, a product of micro and macro social forces and interactions across time. These forces work together to create the boundaries for the unique racial location we call white. Although all of those who identify or are identified as white live within the boundaries of this racial location, the concept of whiteness does not imply that everyone who is white will have identical experiences. Historical and demographic location, class, gender and sexuality amongst other things shape what it means to be white.

Over the past thirty years, a new field has begun to emerge that studies the social constructions and boundaries of whiteness, which is called "Critical Whiteness Studies (CWS)." This field has begun to piece together historical and contemporary data and narratives to determine who was considered to be "white" at different historical periods and why. In addition, CWS examines how these racial determinations granted individuals privilege based on whether or not they were perceived to be white.

One of clearest texts in showing how white privilege operates is Peggy McIntosh's "Unpacking the Invisible Knapsack" (1988). By privilege, she means "an invisible package of unearned assets that [whites] can count on cashing in each day, but about which [whites were] "meant," to remain oblivious. White privilege is like an invisible weightless knapsack."*

At the heart of her argument is a focus on whiteness as a system, not an individual identification. What this means is that white people reap certain benefits based on the fact that the system is set up to accommodate them, whether or not they themselves directly support racist practices or ideologies. These privileges allow whites as a whole greater access to society's resources than people of color and leave less than an equal share of resources for those who are not similarly privileged.

As a student, you may be asking yourself "What, if anything does this have to do with me?" If you are white, you may feel that you did not receive any special treatment just because of your skin color. You may have had to overcome obstacles that were placed in your path due to your class, gender or sexuality. It may be especially difficult for you to accept your privilege in comparison with other people of color who you perceive as not having had to overcome such obstacles. Recognizing white privilege does not mean that across the board, in every

group comes to be thought of as a race, this means the group has become racialized (Taylor 2009:4). Hispanics are treated as a racial group, and many identify themselves as belonging to a distinctive racial category.

Despite the past and present racialization of people of color, common thinking about race is flawed. We tend to see race through a Black and White lens, thereby neglecting other rapidly growing racial groups. At the same time, we think of Whites, the dominant group, as raceless, or having no race at all (McIntosh 1992:79). In this view, Whiteness is the natural or normal condition. It is racially unmarked and immune to investigation. This is a false picture of race. In reality, the racial order shapes the lives of all people, even Whites who are advantaged by the system. (See the Speaking to the Students Panel titled "Got Privilege? Studying What It Means to Be White.") Just as social classes exist in relation to each other, "races" are labeled and judged *in relation to other races*. The categories "Black" and "Hispanic" are meaningful only insofar as they are

scenario, whites always have it better than people of color. Just as there is white privilege, there are also privileges that come with being from the upper class, or possessing masculinity and/or heterosexuality. What it does mean is that you have been privileged in the area of race.

David Roediger's *Wages of Whiteness: Race and the Making of the American Working Class* (1991) is a great example of how white working class men, although not having access to the privileges of the upper class, utilized white privilege to their benefit. In this work, Roediger argues that constructions of whiteness were at the heart of the establishment of the working class. White workers used race to separate themselves from workers of color and to rally other white workers, including white ethnics. This gave them enough power to receive certain benefits as a group, including higher wages and better jobs that were not accessible to other workers.

Another book that highlights the interplay between different categories of social location is Ruth Frankenburg's *White Women,*

Race Matters: The Social Construction of Whiteness (1993). The primary focus of this text is to show how whiteness is constructed via gender and sexuality. Frankenburg provides numerous examples to detail how white women's experience of race differs from white men's, especially within sexual relationships. For example, she shows how white women who were in relationships with men of color were often seen as "supersexual" beings in ways they would not have been if they were a white man choosing to date a woman of color. Although white women have to overcome barriers created by their gender and sexuality, Frankenburg notes it is still important to recognize the fact that they are at the same time able to maintain their racial privilege.

Fortunately, there is a growing movement to examine white privilege. There are small steps we all can take to assist in this process. Becoming aware of the different ways "whiteness" affects you and those around you is the first step toward fighting against white privilege and for racial

equality. If you are white, another step you can take is to attempt to forego the benefits reaped upon you by whiteness. This will be difficult, especially in the beginning since you may be unaware of many of these benefits. Tim Wise, in his book *White Like Me: Reflections on Race from a Privileged Son,* outlines a number of practical strategies that can be used to help tear down white privilege. These include "refus[ing] to shop at institutions with a pattern or history of discrimination," and "refer[ing] to white people with a racial designation when discussing them so as to stop normalizing whites as synonymous with human beings, people, or Americans."[**]

[*]Working Paper 189, "White Privilege and Male Privilege: A Personal Account of Coming to See Correspondences through Work in Women's Studies" (1988), by Peggy McIntosh.
[**]Wise, Tim (2008). *White Like Me: Reflections on Race from a Privileged Son.* Soft Skull Press. Brooklyn, NY. Page 118.

Source: Paula Miller, Department of Sociology, Michigan State University, 2010. This essay was written expressly for *Social Problems, 12th Edition.*

set apart from, and in distinction to, "White." This point is particularly obvious when people are referred to as "non-White," a word that ignores the differences in experiences among people of color (Lucal 1996:246). Race is not simply a matter of two opposite categories but of power relations between dominant and subordinate groups (Weber 2010).

How is race different from ethnicity? Whereas race is used for socially marking groups on the basis of presumed physical differences, ethnicity allows for a broader range of affiliation. Ethnic groups are distinctive on the basis of national origin, language, religion, and culture. Today's world is replete with examples of socially constructed ethnicities. At the same time that the world is becoming thoroughly globalized, it is also becoming transformed by new ethnic diversities. As European countries struggle with political and economic integration, people may no longer identify as Italian, but as Lombardians, Sicilians, or Romans (Wali 1992:6). "The arrival of large numbers of people from the Middle

East, East Asia, and Africa—many European countries now have minority ethnic populations of around 10 percent—is pushing aside old concepts of what it means to be French, or German, or Swedish" (Richburg 2004:17). Expanding communications networks and the increased social interaction that has resulted from immigration have not suppressed ethnic conflicts. In the last decade of the twentieth century, ethnic and religious differences led to massacres of ethnic Tutsis by Hutus in Rwanda; full-scale war involving Serb, Bosnian, Albanian, and other ethnic groups in the Balkans; and violence against ethnic Chinese in Indonesia (Pollard and O'Hare 1999:5). Across Europe today, anti-immigrant racism is on the rise. Growing fears of a mounting foreign influx are fueling political movements to stop immigration.

In the United States, race and ethnicity both serve to mark groups as different. Groups *labeled as races* by the wider society are bound together by their common social and economic conditions. As a result, they develop distinctive cultural or ethnic characteristics. Today, we often refer to them as **racial-ethnic groups** (or racially defined ethnic groups). The term *racial-ethnic group* refers to groups that are socially subordinated and remain culturally distinct within U.S. society. It is meant to include (1) the systematic discrimination of socially constructed racial groups and (2) their distinctive cultural arrangements. The categories of *African American, Latino, Asian American,* and *Native American* have been constructed as both racially and culturally distinct. Each group has a distinctive culture, shares a common heritage, and has developed a common identity within a larger society that subordinates it. The racial characteristics of these groups have become meaningful in a society that continues to change (Baca Zinn and Dill 1994).

Terms of reference are also changing, and the changes are contested both within groups as well as between them. For example, *Blacks* continue to debate the merits of the term *African American*, whereas *Latinos* disagree on the label *Hispanic*. In this chapter, we use such terms interchangeably because they are currently used in both popular and scholarly discourse.

Differences among Ethnic Groups

Both race and ethnicity are historical bases for inequality in that they are constructed in a hierarchy from "superior" to "inferior." In the United States, some immigrants were viewed as belonging to an inferior race. For example, Jews were once racialized and later reconstructed as White (Brodkin 2009). Nevertheless, race and ethnicity have differed in how they incorporated groups into society. Race was the social construction setting people of color apart from European immigrant groups (Takaki 1993:10). Groups identified as races came into contact with the dominant majority through force and state-sanctioned discrimination in work that was unfree and offered little opportunity for upward mobility. In contrast, European ethnics migrated to the United States voluntarily to enhance their status or to market their skills in a land of opportunity. They came with hope and sometimes with resources to provide a foundation for their upward mobility. Unlike racial groups, most had the option of returning if they found the conditions here unsatisfactory. The voluntary immigrants came to the United States and suffered discrimination in employment, housing, and other areas. Clashes between Germans, Irish, Italians, Poles, and other European groups during the nineteenth and early twentieth centuries are well documented. But most European immigrants and their descendants—who accounted for four-fifths of the U.S. population in 1900—eventually achieved full participation in U.S. society (Pollard and O'Hare 1999:5).

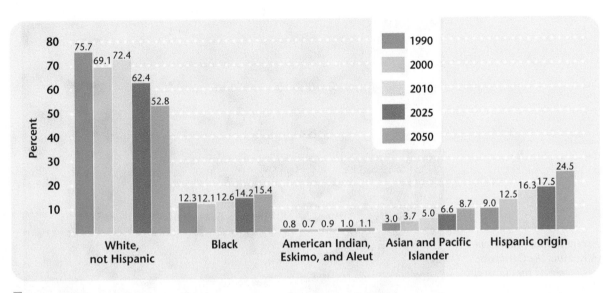

FIGURE 1

Percent of the Population, by Race and Hispanic Origin, 1990, 2000, 2025, and 2050 (middle-series projection)

Sources: U.S. Bureau of the Census, 1997. "Population of the United States: 1997." *Current Population Reports.* Series P23-194. Washington, DC: U.S. Government Printing Office, p. 9. U.S. Bureau of the Census accessed online: www.census.govb/population/www/cen2000; U.S. Census Bureau, *Census 2000 Redistricting Data (Public Law 94-171) Summary File*, Tables PL1 and PL2; and *2010 Census Redistricting Data (Public Law 94-171) Summary File*, Tables P1 and P2.

Although European ethnics have moved into the mainstream of society, racially defined peoples have remained in a subordinate status. Native Americans, African Americans, Latinos, and Asians have not been assimilated. Continuing racial discrimination sets them apart from others. (See Figure 1 for the percentage of the U.S. population by race in selected years.)

- **African Americans.** By 2010, African Americans (38.9 million) were 12.6 percent of the total population (U.S. Census Bureau, Census *2000 Redistricting Data (Public Law 94-171) Summary File*, Tables PL1 and PL2; and *2010 Census Redistricting Data (Public Law 94-171) Summary File*, Tables P1 and P2). Before 1990, virtually all African Americans descended from people who were brought involuntarily to the United States before the slave trade ended in the nineteenth century. They entered the southern states to provide free labor to plantations, and as late as 1890, 90 percent of all Blacks lived in the South, 80 percent as rural dwellers. In the South, they endured harsh and violent conditions under slavery, an institution that would have consequences for centuries to come. During the nineteenth century, the political storm over slavery almost destroyed the nation. Although Blacks left the South in large numbers after 1890, within northern cities they also encountered prejudice, discrimination, and segregation that exposed them to unusually high concentrations of poverty and other social problems (Massey 1993:7; Takaki 1993:7). African Americans have a distinctive history of slavery and oppression.

  In the past two decades, the Black population in the United States has changed due to immigration from Africa and the Caribbean. In fact, more Blacks are coming from Africa than during the slave trade. About 50,000 legal immigrants arrive annually, and more have migrated here than in nearly the entire preceding centuries (Roberts 2005:A1). The increase in Black immigration from Africa and the Caribbean is making the population more diverse and posing unique challenges to today's Black immigrants (Shaw-Taylor 2009). The

Recent immigration from Africa and the Caribbean has increased the cultural diversity of "African Americans."

© Melanie Stetson Freeman/The Christian Science Monitor/Getty Images

demographic shift is also changing what it means to be Black. It has sparked a new debate about the "African American." It ignores the enormous linguistic, physical, and cultural diversity of the peoples of Africa. The term *Black* is also problematic in that it risks conflating people of African descent who were brought here as slaves with recent immigrants from Africa and the Caribbean (Mukhopadhyay and Henze 2003:675). In fact, the experiences of today's immigrants are markedly different from those who have descended as slaves.

- **Latinos.** The U.S. Latino population has now surpassed the African American population to become the nation's largest minority. In many respects, the Latino population is the driving force of this society's racial and ethnic transformation (Saenz 2004:29). In 2010, Hispanics or Latinos numbered 50.5 million, or 16.3 percent of the total U.S. population (U.S. Census Bureau, Overview of Race and Hispanic Origin: 2010, 2010 Census Briefs, March 2011). Although Hispanics are the largest minority, they are a varied collection of ethnic groups. Two-thirds (65 percent) of all Hispanic Americans are Chicanos or Mexican Americans, 9.2 percent are Puerto Ricans, 3.5 percent are Cubans, and 6.6 percent are "other Hispanic or Latino" (Social Explorer Tables: ACS 2005 to 2009 (5-Year Estimates) (SE), ACS 2005–2009 (5-Year Estimates), Social Explorer; U.S. Census Bureau).

  The *Hispanic* category was created by federal statisticians to provide data on people of Mexican, Cuban, Puerto Rican, and other Hispanic origins in the United States. The term was chosen as a label that could be applied to all people from the Spanish-speaking countries of Latin America and from Spain. Because the population is so heterogeneous, there is no precise definition of group membership. Even the term *Latino,* which many prefer, is a new invention.

  Immigration is a thread that unifies much of the Latino experience in the United States. The vast majority of Latinos are immigrants or children of immigrants (Suarez-Orozco and Paez 2002). However, the national origins of Latinos are diverse, and so is the timing of their arrival in the United States. As a result, Mexicans, Puerto Ricans, Cubans, and other Latino groups have distinctive histories that set them apart from each other. Cubans arrived largely in the period between 1960 and 1980; Mexicans indigenous to the Southwest were forcibly annexed into the United States in 1848, whereas others have been migrating continuously since 1890. Puerto Ricans came under U.S. control in 1898 and obtained citizenship in 1917; Salvadorans and Guatemalans have been migrating to the United States in substantial numbers during the past two decades.

As a result of these different histories, Hispanics are found in many legal and social statuses—from fifth-generation Americans to new immigrants, from affluent and well-educated to poor and unschooled. Such diversity means that there is no "Hispanic" population in the sense that there is a Black population. Hispanics neither have a common history nor compose a single, coherent community. Rather, they are a collection of national-origin groups with heterogeneous experiences of settlement, immigration, political participation, and economic incorporation into the United States. Saying that someone is Hispanic or Latino reveals little about attitudes, behaviors, beliefs, race, religion, class, or legal situation in the United States (Massey 1993).

Despite these differences, Latinos in the United States have a long history of discrimination by governments controlled by non-Hispanic Whites. Mexican Americans in the Southwest lost property and political rights as Anglos moved into the region in the 1800s. As late as the 1940s, local ordinances in some Texas cities blocked Mexican Americans from owning real estate or voting. Also, Mexican Americans were required to attend segregated public schools in many jurisdictions before 1950 (Pollard and O'Hare 1999:6).

- **Asian Americans.** Asian Americans are another rapidly growing minority group in the country. In 2010, Asian Americans numbered 14.7 million, or about 4.8 percent of the U.S. population (Humes, Karen R., Nicholas A. Jones, and Roberto R. Ramirez. 2011. "Overview of Race and Hispanic Origin: 2010." *U.S. Census Briefs*, U.S. Census Bureau and the U.S. Department of Commerce.).

Like the Latino population, the Asian population in the United States is extremely diverse, giving rise to the term *Pan-Asian*, which encompasses immigrants from Asian and Pacific Island countries and native-born citizens descended from those ethnic groups (Lott and Felt 1991:6). Until recently, immigrants who arrived in the United States from Asian countries did not think of themselves as Asians, or even as Chinese, Japanese, Korean, and so forth, but rather as people from Toisan, Hoeping, or some other district in Guangdong Province in China or from Hiroshima, Yamaguchik, or some other locale. It was not until the late 1960s, with the advent of the Asian American movement, that a Pan-Asian consciousness was formed (Espiritu 1996:51).

The largest Asian American groups in the United States are Chinese (23 percent), Filipinos (18 percent), Japanese (6.1 percent), Vietnamese (11 percent), Koreans (10 percent), and Asian Indians (19 percent) (Social Explorer Tables: ACS 2005 to 2009 (5-Year Estimates) (SE), ACS 2005–2009 (5-Year Estimates), Social Explorer; U.S. Census Bureau). There also are Laotians, Kampucheans, Thais, Pakistanis, Indonesians, Hmong, and Samoans (Lee 1998:15).

The characteristics of Asians vary according to their national origins and time of entry into the United States. Most come from recent immigrant families, but many Asian Americans can trace their family's American history back more than 150 years. Much of this period was marked by anti-Asian laws and discrimination. The 1879 California Constitution barred the hiring of Chinese workers, and the federal Chinese Exclusion Act of 1882 halted the entry of most Chinese immigrants until 1943. Americans of Japanese ancestry were interned in camps during

World War II by an executive order signed by President Franklin D. Roosevelt. Not until 1952 were Japanese immigrants granted the right to become naturalized U.S. citizens (Pollard and O'Hare 1999:6–7).

Whereas most of the pre–World War II Asian immigrants were peasants, recent immigrants vary considerably by education and social class. On the one hand, many arrived as educated middle-class professionals with highly valued skills and some knowledge of English. Others, such as the Indochinese, arrived as uneducated, impoverished refugees. These differences are reflected in the differences in income and poverty level by ethnic category. Asian Americans taken together have higher average incomes than do other groups in the United States. Although a large segment of this population is financially well off, many are poor. Asian Americans are commonly seen as "the model minority," a well-educated and upwardly mobile group. But this stereotype is misleading. Not only is it used to blame other racial minorities for their own inequality, but it also ignores both the history of discrimination against Asians and their wide differences. Even the term *Asian American* masks great diversity.

- **Native Americans.** Once thought to be destined for extinction, today the Native American or American Indian population is comprised of 2.9 million individuals (U.S. Census Bureau, 2010 Census Redistricting Data (Public Law 97-171) Summary File, Table P1). Native Americans have more autonomy and are more self-sufficient than at any time since the last century (Snipp 1996:390). Nevertheless, the population remains barred from full participation in U.S. society.

The tribes located in North America were and are extremely heterogeneous, with major differences in physical characteristics, language, and social organization. As many as 7 million indigenous people lived in North America when the Europeans arrived. The conquest made them "Indians." By 1890, they were reduced to less than 250,000 by disease, warfare, and in some cases, genocide. In the first half of the nineteenth century, the U.S. government forced Indians from their homelands. Those forced migrations accelerated after President Andrew Jackson signed the Indian Removal Act of 1830. Many tribes then lived on marginal land that was reserved for them.

The current political and economic status of Native Americans is the result of the process that forced them into U.S. society. Many factors led to the disparities we now observe between Native Americans and others, including the appropriation of Indian land for the gain of White Settlers, the mismanagement by the Bureau of Indian Affairs of resources found on native lands, and the underinvestment of land by the general government in Native American education and health care (Adamson 2009).

Important changes have occurred in the social and economic well-being of the Native American population from 1960 to the present. At the time of the 1970 Census, Native Americans were the poorest group in the United States, with incomes well below those of the Black population. By 1980, despite poverty rates as high as 60 percent on many Indian reservations, poverty among Native Americans had declined. At the end of the twentieth century, Native Americans were better off than they were in the 1900s. Over the past few decades, Native Americans have made important gains in cutting poverty rates and increasing their educational levels. Yet even with these gains, Native Americans are nowhere near parity with White Americans. Today, Native Americans have a poverty rate of almost 24 percent, twice the White poverty rate (Muhammad 2009). Native peoples rank at the bottom of most U.S. socioeconomic indicators, with the lowest levels of life expectancy, per capita income, employment, and education (Harjo 1996; Thornton 1996; Pollard and O'Hare 1999; Muhammad 2009).

Although the conditions prevailing on many reservations resemble conditions in the developing world, a renaissance has occurred in Native American communities. In cities, modern pan-Indian organizations have been successful in making the presence of Native Americans known to the larger community and have mobilized to meet the needs of their people (Snipp 1996:390). A college-educated Native American middle class has emerged, Native American business ownership has increased, and some tribes are creating good jobs for their members (Fost 1991:26).

To summarize this section, the combined population of the four racial minority groups now accounts for 30 percent of the total U.S. population. New waves of immigration from non-European countries, high birthrates among these groups, and a relatively young age structure account for the rapid increase in minorities. By the middle of the twenty-first century, today's minorities will comprise nearly one-half of the U.S. population. (See Figure 1 for population projections through 2050.) African Americans, Latinos, Asian Americans, and Native Americans are different in many respects. Each group encounters different forms of exclusion. Nevertheless, as racial minorities, they remain at the lowest rungs of society.

EXPLANATIONS OF RACIAL AND ETHNIC INEQUALITY

Why have some racial and ethnic groups been consistently disadvantaged? Some ethnic groups, such as the Irish and the Jews, have experienced discrimination but managed to overcome their initial disadvantages. However, African Americans, Latinos, Asian Americans, and Native Americans have not been able to cast off their secondary status. Three types of theories have been used to explain why some groups are treated differently: deficiency theories, bias theories, and structural discrimination theories.

Deficiency Theories

A number of analysts have argued that some groups are disadvantaged because they *are* inferior. That is, when compared with the majority, they are deficient in some important way. There are two variations of deficiency theories.

- **Biological Deficiency.** This classical explanation for racial inferiority maintains that group inferiority is the result of flawed genetic—and therefore hereditary—traits. This is the position of Arthur Jensen, Richard Herrnstein, and Charles Murray. *The Bell Curve* (Herrnstein and Murray 1994) is the latest in a long series of works claiming that Blacks are genetically inferior to Whites and that this inferiority explains differences in the social success of racial groups. Despite the media attention given the work of these and other theorists, there is no definitive evidence for the thesis that racial groups differ in intelligence. Biological deficiency theories are generally not accepted in the scientific community (see *Contemporary Sociology* 1995).

- **Cultural Deficiency.** Many explanations of racial subordination center on group-specific cultural traits handed down from generation to generation. According to this explanation, the cultures and behaviors of minority groups are dysfunctional when compared to those of the dominant group. In addition, these groups remain at the bottom because they fail to take advantage of the opportunities in society (Brown and Wellman 2005:188). From this perspective, minorities are disadvantaged because of their group-specific heritage and customs. Cultural deficiency was the basis of Daniel Patrick Moynihan's famous 1967 report, which charged that the "tangle of pathology" within Black ghettos was rooted in the deterioration of the Negro family (U.S. Department of Labor 1965). High rates of divorce, female-headed households, out-of-wedlock births, and welfare dependency were said to be the residues of slavery and discrimination, a complex web of pathological patterns passed down through the generations. The Moynihan report was widely criticized for being a classic case of "blaming the victim." It finds the problem within Blacks, not in the structure of society.

Cultural deficiency theorists ignore the social opportunities that affect groups in different ways. Many social scientists have long opposed cultural explanations. Nevertheless, this approach is still found in scholarship and popular thought. Today, much of the public discussion about race and poverty rests on false assumptions about deficient minorities (Reed 1990; di Leonardo 1992; Bonilla-Silva 2003). Family "breakdown" is still used to explain African American problems, whereas a backward culture is said to produce Latino problems. Today's immigrant debates use culture to generate fear. For example, in his book, *Who Are We? The Challenges to American Identity* (2004), Samuel, P. Huntington argues that a culture alien to Anglo-Saxon ways makes unchecked Latino immigration a threat to U.S. society.

Bias Theories

The deficiency theories blame minorities for their plight. Bias theories, on the other hand, blame the members of the dominant group. They blame individuals who hold *prejudiced attitudes* toward minorities. Gunnar Myrdal, for example, argued in his classic book, *An American Dilemma*, that prejudiced attitudes toward an entire group of people are the problem (Myrdal 1944). This argument reduces racism to the "prejudiced" acts of individual White Americans (Brown and Wellman 2005:189).

Many sociologists have argued that prejudiced attitudes are not the essence of racism. For example, David Wellman (1977) has challenged the notion that the hostile attitudes of White Americans, especially lower-class Whites, are the major cause of racism. Instead, he shows that many unprejudiced White people defend the traditional social arrangements that negatively affect minorities. Research by Lawrence Bobo (2009) shows that although prejudice has declined, most White Americans are still unwilling to support social practices and policies to address racial inequalities. Unbiased people fight to preserve the status quo by favoring, for example, the seniority system in occupations, or they oppose affirmative action, quota systems, busing to achieve racial balance, and open enrollment in higher education.

Today, we live in an era when laws to protect citizens from racial discrimination are firmly in place. The new conventional wisdom views racism as a remnant of the past, the result of individual White bigotry, which is diminishing (Brown and Wellman 2005). The focus strictly on prejudice is inaccurate because it concentrates on the bigots and ignores the structural foundation of racism. The determining feature of dominant-minority relations is not prejudice but differential systems of privilege and disadvantage. "The subordination of people of color is functional to the operation of American society as we know it and the color of one's skin is a primary determinant of people's position in the social structure" (Wellman 1977:35). Even if active dislike of minorities ceases, "persistent social patterns can endure over time, affecting whom we marry, where we live, what we believe and do, and so forth" (Elliot and Pais 2006:300).

Thus, institutional and individual racism generate privilege for Whites. Discrimination provides the privileged with disproportionate advantages in the social, economic, and political spheres. Racist acts, in this view, not only are based on hatred, stereotyped conceptions, or prejudgment but also are rational responses to the struggle over scarce resources by individuals acting to preserve their own advantage.

Structural Discrimination Theories

Deficiency and bias theories focus, incorrectly, on individuals: the first on minority flaws and the second on the flawed attitudes of the majority. Both kinds of theory ignore the social system that oppresses minorities. Michael Parenti has criticized those who ignore the system as victim blamers: "Focusing on the poor and ignoring the system of power, privilege, and profit which makes them poor is a little like blaming the corpse for the murder" (1978:24). The alternative view is that racial inequality is not fundamentally a matter of what is in people's heads, not a matter of their private individual intentions, but rather a matter of public institutions and practices that create racism or keep it alive. Structural discrimination theories move away from thinking about "racism-in-the-head" toward understanding "racism-in-the-world" (Lichtenberg 1992:5).

Many sociologists have examined race as a structural force that permeates every aspect of life. Those who use this framework make a distinction between individual racism and institutional racism (Carmichael and Hamilton 1967). Individual racism is related to prejudice. It consists of individual behavior that harms other individuals or their property. Institutional racism is structural. It comprises more than attitudes or behavior. It is structural, that is, *a complex pattern of racial advantage built into the structure of society*—a system of power and privilege that advantages some groups over others (Higginbotham and Andersen 2009:78). Because institutional racism views inequality as part of society's structure, individuals and groups discriminate whether they are bigots or not. These individuals and groups operate within a social milieu that ensures racial dominance. The social milieu includes laws, customs, religious beliefs, and the stable arrangements and practices through which things get done in society.

Institutional or structural racism is not about beliefs. It is not only about actions directed at those considered racially different (meaning those not considered White). According to Howard Winant:

> . . . structural racism is about the accretion of inequality and injustice in practice; it's about the way things work, regardless of the reasons why, it's about outcomes, not intentions or beliefs. So, if vast inequalities in wealth persist across racial lines, for example, they may persist not because White people presently intend to impoverish Black or Brown people; they may persist because of years and years of some people doing better than others do. Inequality accumulates; injustice becomes normal; they come to be taken for granted. (Winant 2009:58).

Structural racism operates through social institutions in three ways. First is the importance of history in determining present conditions and affecting resistance to change. Historically, institutions defined and enforced norms and role relationships that were racially distinct. The United States was founded and its institutions established when Blacks were slaves, uneducated, and different culturally from the dominant Whites (Patterson 2007:58). From the beginning, Blacks were considered inferior (the original Constitution, for example, counted a slave as three-fifths of a person). Religious beliefs buttressed this notion of the inferiority of Blacks and justified the differential allocation of privileges and sanctions in society.

Second, discrimination can occur without conscious bigotry. Everyday practices reinforce racial discrimination and deprivation. Although the actions of individual bigots are unmistakably racist, many other actions (choosing to live in a suburban neighborhood, sending one's children to a private school, or opposing government intervention in hiring policies) also maintain racial dominance (Bonilla-Silva 1996:475). With or without malicious intent, racial discrimination is the "normal" outcome of the system. Even if racism-in-the-head disappeared, racism-in-the-world would not, because it is the *system* that disadvantages (Lichtenberg 1992).

Finally, institutional discrimination is reinforced because institutions are interrelated. The exclusion of minorities from the upper levels of education, for example, is likely to affect their opportunities in other institutions (type of job, level of remuneration). Similarly, poor children will probably receive an inferior education, be propertyless, suffer from bad health, and be treated unjustly by the criminal justice system. These inequities are cumulative.

Institutional derogation occurs when minority groups and their members are made to seem inferior or to possess negative stereotypes through legitimate means by the powerful in society. The portrayal of minority group members in the media (movies, television, newspapers, and magazines) is often derogatory. For example, many studies depict Black men disproportionately as drug users, criminals, lower class, and "pathological" (Muwakkil 1998b:18). Such stereotypes are "controlling images" that define perceptions of minorities (Collins 1990). If we based our perceptions of minority populations on media images, we would have considerably skewed views. The media also provide us with explanations and interpretations intended to help us make sense of our society, including its multiracial composition. The ideas that pervade today's mass media obscure pervasive racial inequality. Instead we are bombarded by depictions of race relations that suggest discriminatory racial barriers have been dismantled and that the United States has become a truly color-blind nation (Gallagher 2010; Weber 2010).

Why is U.S. society organized along racial lines? Sociologists have a long-standing debate over the relative importance of race and class in shaping systems of racial inequality. Those emphasizing class contend that the economy and class system are what produce racial inequality (see the discussion of the underclass later in the chapter). Some scholars argue that modern race relations are produced by world capitalism. Using the labor of non-White peoples began as a means for White owners to accumulate profits. This perspective contends that capitalism as a system of class exploitation has shaped race and racism in the United States and the world (Bonacich 1992).

Other structural theories point to race itself as a primary shaper of inequality. For example, racial-formation theory explains the sociohistorical process by which racial categories are created. This theory proposes that the United States is organized along racial lines from top to bottom—a racial state composed of institutions and policies to support and justify racial stratification (Omi and Winant 1986, 1994). Another theory, called *systemic racism,* also argues that race itself explains racial inequality. Systemic racism includes a diverse assortment of racism practices: the unjustly gained economic and political power of Whites, the continuing resource inequalities, and the White-racism ideologies, attitudes, and institutions created to preserve White advantages and power. Systemic racism is both structural and interpersonal. "At the macrolevel, large-scale institutions . . . routinely perpetuate racial subordination and inequalities. These institutions are created and re-created by routine actions at the microlevel by individuals" (Feagin 2000:16) Systemic racism is far more than a matter of individual bigotry, for it has been from the beginning a mental, social, and ideological reality (Feagin 2006: xiii).

Why does the United States have this tremendous degree of racial equality even though most White people are not "racist"? According to sociologist Eduardo Bonilla-Silva (2009:176), racial inequality exists because it benefits members of the dominant race.

DISCRIMINATION AGAINST AFRICAN AMERICANS AND LATINOS: CONTINUITY AND CHANGE

The treatment of Blacks and Hispanics has been disgraceful throughout American history. Through public policies and everyday practices, they have been denied the opportunities that should be open to all people. Since World War II, however, under pressure from civil rights advocates, the government has led the way in breaking down many discriminatory practices. Community organizing, civil rights legislation, landmark court decisions, and rising education have advanced the cause of racial equality. By the close of the twentieth century, many well-educated people of color had climbed into the middle class.

In 2009, 41 percent of African Americans and 42 percent of Latino families had incomes of $50,000 or more (compared with 64.5 percent of White families; U.S. Census Bureau, 2005–2009 American Community Survey (5-Year Estimates). They have taken advantage of fair-housing legislation and moved to the suburbs looking for better schools, safer streets, and better services. Yet having "made it" in the United States does not shield people of color from discrimination. Studies of public accommodation have found that in stores, bars, restaurants, and theaters, middle-class Blacks are ignored or treated with hostility (Feagin and Sikes 1994). No matter how affluent or influential, Blacks and other dark-skinned people are vulnerable to "microinsults" such as being followed around in stores (Muwakkil 1998a; Bonilla-Silva 2003; Feagin 2006).

Substantial growth of the minority middle class has not erased the problem of segregation. A class divide now characterizes minority communities across the country. As some successful people of color have become richer, many more unsuccessful ones have been marginalized. To be sure, much progress is evident in some areas. But in others, "there are clear signs of retrenchment, if not outright worsening. Across a range of institutions, the most consistent pattern is one of both persistence and change" (Lewis et al., 2004:104).

Racism was clearly present in the aftermath of Hurricane Katrina, the costliest natural disaster ever to hit the United States. For days, the world watched as federal officials moved slowly to assist those stranded and dying in flooded houses and overcrowded shelters in New Orleans and the Gulf Coast areas. What was exposed was not just a broken levee but race and class divides both familiar and yet new. Even media commentators raised the reasonable question of whether the fact that a majority of those hardest hit in New Orleans were low-income Black residents had affected the slowness of the federal government response (Feagin 2006:xv; DeParle 2007:163). The most comprehensive survey of Hurricane Katrina survivors found that both race and class played important roles in shaping response to the disaster (Elliot and Pais 2006). The evacuation plan was based on people driving out, yet 35 percent of Black households did not have a car, compared to 15 percent of White households. The Lower Ninth Ward, very poor and almost entirely Black, was one of the most heavily damaged areas of the city, while Whites disproportionately lived in more affluent higher areas less likely to suffer flooding (Feagin 2006:xv; DeParle 2007).

The present segregation of African Americans cannot be dismissed as wrongs committed in the past. U.S. neighborhoods were sharply segregated in the 1990s (Massey and Denton 1993). Today, they are just as segregated. Whites and African Americans tend to live in substantially homogeneous neighborhoods as do many Asians and Hispanics. In recent years, the segregation rates of Blacks have declined slightly while the rates of Asians and Hispanics have increased (Higginbotham and Andersen 2009:34).

Income

The average income for White families and households is greater than the average income for those of Blacks and Hispanics. Racial income disparities have remained unchanged over time. In 2008, the median income of Black households was about $34,000, the median income of White households was about $55,000, and the median income of Hispanic households was about $37,000 (DeNavas-Walt et al., 2009:5). Even though the median household income for Blacks is still below that of Hispanics, per-person income for Hispanics is actually lower because Hispanics tend to have larger households (see Figure 2).

Although the racial income gap is wide, the racial *wealth gap* is even wider. White families are generally wealthier than Black or Latino families (Collins, Leondar-Wright, and Sklar 1999). *Wealth* is the sum of important assets a family owns. It includes home ownership, pension funds, savings accounts, and investments. Many of these resources are inherited across generations. White families generally have greater resources for their children and bequeath them as assets at death. Sociologists call this "the cost of being Black" (Oliver and Shapiro 1995). According to this line of thought, African American disadvantage will persist until the wealth divide is closed (Shapiro 2004).

One important indicator of a family's wealth is home ownership. Paying off a home mortgage is the way most people build net worth over their lifetimes. But because racial minorities encounter discrimination in their efforts to buy, finance, or insure a home, a great race gap remains (Farley and Squires 2009:360). Fewer than half of Blacks and Latinos and fewer than 60 percent of Asian Americans and Native Americans own their own homes, compared to three-quarters of Whites. Rampant racial discrimination prevails in the housing market, even after 40 years of federal housing laws (Crowley 2002:25; Briggs 2005; Leondar-Wright et al., 2005:11).

Poverty rates for all minority groups are higher than for Whites. The percentage of Blacks, Hispanics, and Native Americans in poverty is about three

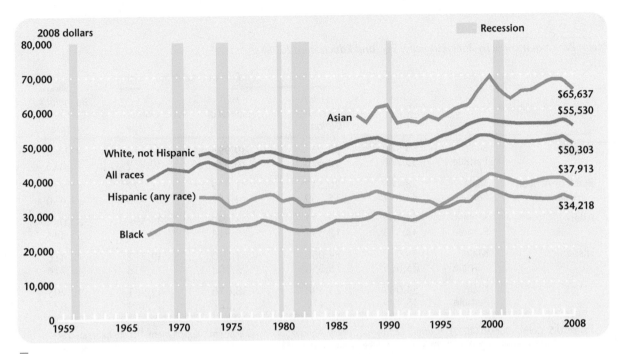

FIGURE 2

Real Median Household Income by Race and Hispanic Origin: 1967–2008

Source: Carmen DeNavas Walt, Bernadette D. Proctor, and Jessica C. Smith, 2009 U.S. Census Bureau, Current Population Reports, P60-236, *Income, Poverty, and Health Insurance Coverage in the United States: 2008.* Washington, DC: U.S. Government Printing Office, p. 7.

times that of Whites. Even Asian Americans, who have a higher average income than Whites, are more likely to live in families with incomes below the poverty line (O'Hare 1992:37). Although most poor people are White, Blacks and Hispanics are disproportionately poor. In 2008, 11 percent of Whites were poor, compared with 11 percent of Asian Americans, 23 percent of Hispanics, and 24 percent of Blacks (DeNavas-Walt et al., 2008:15). Although this is an advance for African Americans in recent decades brought about by the growth of the Black middle class, it is still a shamefully high number. By contrast, immigration has increased poverty among Hispanics (Alter 2007:37).

Many factors explain the difference in White and minority incomes. Racial-ethnic groups are concentrated in the South and Southwest, where incomes are lower for everyone. Another part of the explanation is the differing age structure of minorities. They are younger, on average, than the White population. A group with a higher proportion of young people of working age will have a lower average earning level, higher rates of unemployment, and lower rates of labor force participation.

Looking at racial inequalities by age reveals another disturbing pattern. The degree of inequality increases after the teenage years. Racial disparities become greater in peak earning years. This fact suggests that another part of the explanation for racial inequalities in earnings lies in the lack of education and the skill levels required to move out of poor-paying jobs. All these explanations leave a substantial amount of inequality unexplained. Minorities at all levels of employment and education still earn less than do Whites. (See Table 1 for average earnings by race, sex, and Hispanic origin.)

TABLE 1

Mean Personal Income by Race-Ethnicity, Sex, and Education (2008)

			Educational Attainment			
		All	No High School Diploma	High School or Equivalent	Some College	Bachelor's Degree or Higher
White	Male	55,900	23,961	39,996	47,175	93,765
	Female	35,748	13,676	26,978	30,759	53,816
Black or African American	Male	38,185	20,517	31,909	36,277	64,717
	Female	31,591	15,059	24,752	29,456	51,450
Asian	Male	61,369	22,777	33,699	38,597	83,084
	Female	43,393	18,597	25,416	30,344	58,446
Hispanic	Male	35,032	24,056	31,818	39,772	70,416
	Female	25,805	15,358	22,902	26,936	45,716
Totals	Male	54,063	23,398	38,670	45,561	90,795
	Female	35,429	14,118	26,527	30,484	53,873

Source: U.S. Census Bureau (2009). "Current Population Survey, Annual Social and Economic Supplement," Table generated at url: http://www.census.gov/hhes/www/cpstc/cps_table_creator.html.

Education

In 1954, the Supreme Court outlawed segregation in the schools. Yet the landmark *Brown v. Board of Education* ruling did not end segregation. By 2004, on the fiftieth anniversary of the historic ruling, U.S. racial gaps in education were on the rise, and schools had become increasingly segregated. Today, schools are nearly as segregated as they were fifty years ago. Almost half of Latino and Black students attend school where students of color make up more than 90 percent of the students body. In contrast, the average White student goes to a school that is 80 percent White (Williams 2007; Orfield 2009). Latino students are the most segregated group in today's public schools (Tienda and Simonelli 2001).

Among young adults, Hispanics have the lowest levels of educational completion, whereas Whites and Asians have the highest. The 2009 high school graduation rate for Whites was 87 percent compared with 88 percent for Asian Americans, 84 percent for African Americans, and 62 percent for Hispanics (U.S. Census Bureau, Statistical Abstract of the United States: 2011, Table 225. Educational Attainment by Race and Hispanic Origin: 1970 to 2009). This is a growing problem because most new jobs in the twentieth century require education beyond high school (Pollard and O'Hare 1999c:30).

What explains the minority education gap? Although some educators point to a "culture of opposition" that causes underperformance among Black and Latino students, recent research suggests that school practices and personnel is a better explanation for racial differences. The minority education gap is caused by several factors, including a difference in their social class characteristics, which produce different educational opportunities (Lewis et al., 2004; Rothstein 2007:120).

TABLE 2

Percentage distribution of students enrolled in degree-granting institutions, by race/ethnicity: Selected years, fall 1976 through fall 2007

Race/ethnicity	Institutions of Higher Education			Degree-Granting Institutions						
	1976	*1980*	*1990*	*2000*	*2002*	*2003*	*2004*	*2005*	*2006*	*2007*
Total	**100.0**	**100.0**	**100.0**	**100.0**	**100.0**	**100.0**	**100.0**	**100.0**	**100.0**	**100.0**
White	82.6	81.4	77.6	68.3	67.1	66.7	66.1	65.7	65.2	64.4
Total minority	15.4	16.1	19.6	28.2	29.4	29.8	30.4	30.9	31.5	32.2
Black	9.4	9.2	9.0	11.3	11.9	12.2	12.5	12.7	12.8	13.1
Hispanic	3.5	3.9	5.7	9.5	10.0	10.1	10.5	10.8	11.1	11.4
Asian or Pacific Islander	1.8	2.4	4.1	6.4	6.5	6.4	6.4	6.5	6.6	6.7
American Indian/ Alaskan Native	0.7	0.7	0.7	1.0	1.0	1.0	1.0	1.0	1.0	1.0
Nonresident alien	2.0	2.5	2.8	3.5	3.6	3.5	3.4	3.3	3.4	3.4

Source: U.S. Department of Education, National Center for Education Statistics. (2009). *Digest of Education Statistics, 2008* (NCES 2009-020), Table 226.

Several additional trends are creating problems for minority students. The general movement against increased taxes hurts public schools. Inner-city schools, where minorities are concentrated and which are already understaffed and underfinanced, face even greater financial pressures because of current reduction in federal programs.

Minority participation in high education has risen since the 1960s. College campuses are far more diverse than they were a century ago (Rothstein 2007:129). Nevertheless, there are large racial gaps in college enrollment. Of the total campus population in 2007, 64 percent were White, 13 percent were African American, 11 percent were Latino and 6 percent were Asian (U.S. Department of Education 2008). (See Table 2.) Although many colleges actively recruit students of color, many factors contribute to low retention rates. Even when they reach college, students of color often confront a range of discriminatory barriers. Studies have consistently found that they are more alienated than White students and drop out more often than White students. Discrimination by Whites on and off campus is a recurring problem (Feagin 2000:170).

All these disparities translate into economic inequalities. Yet education alone is not the answer. Even with a college degree, African Americans and Latinos have higher unemployment rates than their White counterparts. This is compounded by the reality that education does not pay equally. Minority membership, regardless of the level of education, is underpaid compared with Whites of similar education. A highly educated White man still makes more money than anyone else (U.S. Bureau of the Census 2009c). (See Table 3.)

TABLE 3

Selected Labor Force Characteristics by Sex, Race, and Ethnicity (2008)

		Total %	Black %	Hispanic %	Asian %	White %
In civilian labor force	Men	73	66.7	80.2	75.3	73.7
	Women	59.5	61.3	56.2	59.4	59.5
Unemployed	Men	6.1	11.4	7.6	4.1	5.5
	Women	5.4	8.9	7.7	3.7	4.9
Occupations						
Management and profession	Men	33.5	23	14.8	50.1	34
	Women	39.5	31.3	23.5	46	40.6
Sales and Service	Men	30.4	38.3	33.5	31.1	29.3
	Women	53.7	60.1	64.2	45.5	53
Skilled and unskilled manual	Men	36.1	38.7	51.7	18.8	36.7
	Women	6.8	8.6	12.3	8.4	6.3

Source: Bureau of Labor Statistics (2009). "Current Population Survey, Household Data Annual Averages," Tables 4, 5, 10. Can be accessed from http://www.bls.gov/cps/tables.htm.

Unemployment

African Americans and Latinos are more likely than Whites to be unemployed. For the last three decades, unemployment among Black workers has been twice that of White workers, with Latinos in between. In 2009, the unemployment rate for Latinos was 5.2 percent, compared with 8.9 percent for African Americans and 4.0 percent for Whites (Bureau of Labor Statistics 2009a). Minority teenagers had an even harder time. The unemployment rate among Black teens was 48 percent; for Latinos, it was 34 percent; and for Whites, it was 23 percent (Bureau of Labor Statistics 2009a).

These government rates are misleading because they count as employed the almost 6 million people who work part time because they cannot find full-time jobs, and these rates also do not count as unemployed the discouraged workers, numbering more than 1 million, who have given up their search for work.

Type of Employment

African Americans and Latinos have always been an important component of the U.S. labor force. However, their job prospects are different from those of other people in the United States. Not only are they twice as likely as Whites to be unemployed, but they are also more likely to work in low-skilled occupations and less likely to work in managerial or professional occupations (see Table 3). Black and Latino workers are more likely to be in jobs with pay too low to lift a family of four above the poverty line (Leondar-Wright et al., 2005:9). Sociological research shows that race is related to workplace recruitment, hiring, firing, job levels, pay scales, promotion, and degree of autonomy on the job. Seemingly neutral practices can advantage some groups and adversely affect others (American Sociological Association 2003; Shulman 2007).

Immigrants generally work in the lowest rungs of the low-wage workforce. They are more likely than natives to be food-preparation workers, sewing machine operators, parking lot attendants, housekeepers, waiters, private household cleaners, food-processing workers, agricultural workers, elevator operators and janitors, operators, fabricators, and laborers (Shulman 2007:101). Although Blacks, Hispanics, and Native Americans are in the least rewarding jobs, and many face discrimination in hiring and promotion, the occupational status of minorities improved slowly during the last decade. Between 1990 and 2009, the percentage of Blacks in managerial and professional occupations increased from 17 to 27 percent, while the percentage increased from 13 to 18 percent for Hispanics (Pollard and O'Hare 1999:33; Bureau of Labor Statistics 2009a). Despite these gains, however, a huge gap remains. As more minorities enter high-status work, they are confronting new discrimination practices in the form of "job ceilings" that keep them out of executive suites and boardrooms (Higginbotham 1994).

Seismic shifts in the U.S. economy have diminished work opportunities across the land. The job crisis in minority communities is linked to globalization and the structural transformation of the economy. This transformation is eliminating jobs for unskilled, poorly educated workers. The Great Recession has affected minority communities much like a depression and has threatened the viability of many Black communities. In 2009, joblessness for 16- to 24-year-old Black men reached Great Depression proportions with a rate of 34 percent—more than three times the rate for the general U.S. population (Ehrenreich and Muhammad 2009; Haynes 2009).

Because African Americans and Latinos established successful niches in civil service, they are also being replaced by government downsizing (American Sociological Association 2003). The new economy will be increasingly made up of people of color. If they continue to be denied equal access to higher-paying jobs, the entire society will be at risk for poverty and other problems associated with economic inequality.

Health

The health of the U.S. population is distributed unevenly across race. Hispanics are the most likely to be without health coverage. Thirty percent of Hispanics, 19 percent of African Americans, 17 percent of Asian Americans, and 12 percent of Whites were not covered by private or government medical insurance in 2007 (DeNavas-Walt et al., 2008; see Figure 3). Hispanics born outside the United States were almost twice as likely to lack health insurance as their U.S.-born counterparts. Many are unfamiliar with the U.S. health care system, and a few are illegal immigrants who are afraid to seek medical assistance (del Pinal and Singer 1997:37; Folbre and Center for Popular Economics 2000).

Racial discrimination affects health in other ways as well. Environmental racism is the disproportionate exposure of some racial groups to environmental toxic substances. Race is the strongest predictor of hazardous waste facility location in the country, even after adjustment for social class. Even before Hurricane Katrina struck in 2005, New Orleans was already struggling with environmental assaults that ranged from floodwaters to toxic debris. People of color were most vulnerable to these assaults. Katrina was among the deadliest and most devastating disasters in U.S. history. Although public attention has

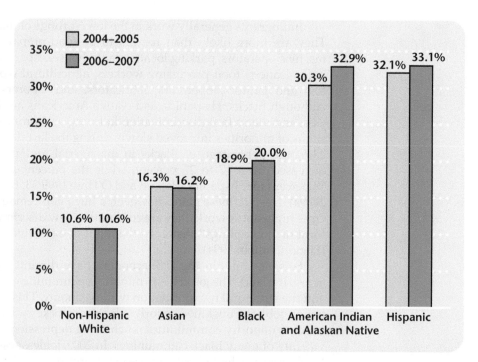

FIGURE 3

Percentage without Health Insurance Based on Two-Year Averages

Source: Dedrick Muhammad. 2009. *Challenges to Native American Advancement: The Recession and Native America.* New York: Institute for Policy Studies, p. 16.

focused on rebuilding the Gulf Coast, a lesser known crisis of lethal debris lingers, left over from hurricane damage (Bullard and Wright 2009). Nationally, three out of five African Americans and Latinos live in communities with abandoned toxic waste sites because of land use, housing patterns, and infrastructure development (Bullard 2007:87).

There are significant racial disparities between racial minorities and Whites in access to health care and in treatment of serious diseases. Minorities receive lower-quality health care than Whites, even when their insurance and income are the same, because of racial prejudice and difference in the quality of health plans (Stolberg 2002; Brown and Wellman 2005:191). On virtually every measure of health, African Americans and Latinos are disadvantaged, as revealed in the following selected facts:

- Compared to the general population, Blacks and Hispanics are less likely to have a consistent source of medical care and more likely to use emergency rooms as a primary source of care. Compared to Whites, Hispanics had a 700 percent higher rate of visits to community health centers but a 35 percent lower rate of visits to physicians' offices. Compared to Whites, Blacks had a 550 percent higher rate of visits to community health centers but a 48 percent lower rate of visits to physicians' offices (Forrest and Whelan 2000).

- Black Medicare patients are more likely than White women to reside in areas where medical procedure rates and the quality of care is low. In addition, a small group of physicians, who are more likely to practice in low-income areas, provide most of the care to Black patients. These providers are less likely than other physicians to be board certified and less able to provide high-quality care and referrals to specialty care (Bach 2004; Baicker

Perceptions that immigrants are taking jobs from Anglos increase racial tensions.

© Steve Rubin/The Image Works

2004). Also, pharmacies in segregated neighborhoods are less likely to have adequate medication supplies, and hospitals in these neighborhoods are more likely to close (Williams and Jackson 2005).

- In 2009, American Indian women were 1.9 times as likely to die from cervical cancer compared to White women, and African Americans were 1.5 times as likely as Whites to have high blood pressure (National Conference of State Legislatures 2009).

- Black babies are nearly twice as likely as White babies to die within their first year. Although the infant mortality rate for Hispanic infants is less than the rate for White infants, within the Puerto Rican subgroup, the rate of infant deaths from sudden infant death syndrome is 1.5 times higher than for Whites (U.S. Department of Health and Human Services 2004b).

- HIV/AIDS has had a devastating impact on minorities in the United States. In 2007, racial-ethnic minorities accounted for almost 68 percent of newly diagnosed cases of AIDS. In 2007, 88 percent of babies born with HIV/AIDS belonged to minority groups (U.S. Department of Health and Human Services 2009b).

CONTEMPORARY TRENDS AND ISSUES IN U.S. RACIAL AND ETHNIC RELATIONS

Racial diversity presents new social conditions that reflect differences in group power and access to social resources. Three major trends reveal old and new forms of racial inequality: racial strife, economic polarization of minorities, and a national shift in U.S. racial policies. These trends are occurring in a global context, closely associated with macrosocial forces around the world.

Ongoing Racial Strife

Although the social dynamics of race are changing, the United States has not transcended racial divisions. The growing immigrant and minority presence together with the economic crisis gripping the nation are adding *new* tensions in society. In the United States and other countries, racial and ethnic diversity is marked by growing conflicts. Some cities are divided societies where minorities seldom meet Whites as neighbors, as classmates in public schools, in church, or in the new ethnic shopping centers now springing up across the country (Harris and Bennett 1995:158).

Racial conflict is often associated with uncertain economic conditions. Lack of jobs, housing, and other resources can add to fear and minority scapegoating on the part of Whites. In Florida and many parts of the West and Southwest, perceptions that Cubans, Mexicans, and other Hispanics are taking jobs from Anglos have touched off racial tensions. Racial tensions often erupt in violence between Whites and minorities and among minorities themselves as individuals compete for a shrinking number of jobs and other opportunities.

We now see new expressions of anti-Muslim/anti-Arab racism. Like old-fashioned forms of bigotry and hate crimes, this racism is also fueled by misbeliefs about minorities (Blauner 2001:191). Anti-Hispanic incidents have increased steadily during the past two decades. Crimes against Hispanics are on the rise. Anti-immigration movements often translate into hate-related activities. One effect of the increasing anti-immigrant sentiment in the nation is the surge in incidents of vigilantism—unauthorized attempts by ordinary citizens to enforce immigration laws. Some private citizens are increasingly taking the law into their own hands to stem the perceived "flood" of illegal immigrants into the country (National Council of La Raza 1999; Southern Poverty Law Center [SPLC] 2006b, 2007, 2009b).

Instead of moving society "beyond race," the historic election of the first African American president has thrust some incidents of racial conflict onto center stage. In 2009, President Obama hosted a "beer summit" at the White House to try to smooth over a controversy he helped fuel with comments at a press conference regarding the arrest of a Black Harvard professor by a White Cambridge policeman. Prominent Democrats such as former President Carter have publicly speculated that race—and by implication racism—is behind some of the attacks on President Obama at venues ranging from town hall meetings to the floor of Congress. And Republicans accuse Democrats of playing the race card to deflect legitimate criticisms of the president's policies (Morin 2009).

More Racially Based Groups and Activities

The Southern Poverty Law Center (SPLC) documented 888 hate groups in forty-eight states and the District of Columbia in 2008, a number that has swelled by 48 percent since 2000 (SPLC 2008). Hate groups include White supremacist groups with such diverse elements as the Ku Klux Klan, neo-Confederate groups (those describing Southern culture as fundamentally White), Nazi-identified parties, and skinheads. Many groups use the Internet to spread their literature to young people. As a result, more than half of all hate crimes are now committed by young people ages 15 to 24. In addition to racist websites, cyber extremism flourishes in e-mail and in discussion groups and chat rooms (*Intelligence Report* 2001:47). Racism is also fueled by the proliferation of cable TV hosts, who

Inner cities are beset with a disproportionate share of social problems.

© Orjan F. Ellingvag/Corbis

spread and legitimize extremist propaganda. In 2009, the SPLC reported a rise in right-wing racial extremism reinvigorated by fears of immigration, the election of President Obama, and the nation's economic woes (SPLC 2009a, 2009b).

- **Profiling and Maltreatment.** Racial discrimination in the criminal justice system has drawn scrutiny in recent years. The past three decades have seen "numerous cases of race-related police brutality and misconduct, and official acknowledgements of systematic racial profiling" (Lewis et al., 2004:95). Blacks and dark-skinned Latinos are disproportionately targeted by police officers. Lower-class communities where minorities reside are often subjected to higher levels of police suspicion, stops, interrogations, and searches (Bonilla-Silva 2003; Warren et al., 2006). *Racial profiling* is the use of race and ethnicity as clues to criminality and potential terrorism. According to the Federal Bureau of Justice Statistics, in 2005 Black drivers were twice as likely to be arrested during traffic stops, whereas Latino drivers were more likely than Black or White drivers to receive a ticket (Robinson 2007). Racial profiling on the highways has become so prevalent that a term has emerged to explain it: "driving while Black" (Bonilla-Silva 2003). Prior to the September 11 terrorist attacks, racial profiling was a state and local law enforcement practice that unfairly targeted Blacks, Native Americans, Asian Americans, and Latinos. Since September 11, Arab Americans, Muslims, and other Middle Easterners have been the targets of threats, gunshots, firebombs, and other forms of vigilante violence (Fahim 2003). Fear of terrorism has provoked a rash of hate crimes and a national debate about the official use of profiling—that is, the use of race and ethnicity as clues to criminality and potential terrorism.

- **Campus Racial Tensions.** Recent headlines about racism on college campuses have surprised many people because educational institutions are formally integrated. Yet campus racism is widespread. Over the past few years, students of color have reported a dramatic increase in acts of racial discrimination, intolerance, hate crimes, and insensitivity among different cultures at institutions of higher education. Hateful and racially insensitive incidents have occurred on some of the most prestigious campuses in the country (NAACP 2009). According to the U.S. Department of Education and watchdog and advocacy groups, every year more than half a million college students are targets of bias-driven slurs or physical assaults. Every day, at least one hate crime occurs on a college campus, and every minute, a college student somewhere sees or hears racist, sexist, homophobic, or otherwise biased words or images. Of all hate crime incidents motivated by racial bias in 2008, 12.5 percent happened at schools or colleges (Federal Bureau of Investigation [FBI] 2008). These problems are not isolated or unusual events. Instead, they reflect what is occurring in the wider society (Sidel 1994; Feagin 2000).

Social and Economic Isolation in U.S. Inner Cities

The notion of a troubled "underclass," locked in U.S. inner cities by a deficient culture, is commonly used to explain racial poverty. According to this reasoning, broken families and bad lifestyles prevent minorities from taking advantage of the opportunities created by antidiscrimination laws. However, like the older cultural deficiency models we discussed earlier, this explanation is wrong on many counts. It relies heavily on behavioral traits to explain poverty. It blames the victims for conditions that are actually rooted in social structure. Social and economic changes have removed jobs and resources from inner-city residents. This reality is a better explanation of poverty among African Americans.

Hurricane Katrina exposed stark levels of racial impoverishment in the northern Gulf Coast. But disparities between Blacks and Whites are not unique to New Orleans. In large cities across the nation, African Americans are much more likely than Whites to live in communities that are geographically and economically isolated from the economic opportunities, services, and institutions that families need to succeed. Of the fifteen U.S. metropolitan areas with the most African Americans in absolute numbers in 2000, New Orleans had the highest Black poverty rate at 33 percent. But racial differences in poverty were stark in each of these metropolitan areas except New York. In Chicago, Newark, Memphis, and St. Louis, African Americans were about five times more likely than Whites to be impoverished. High poverty rates for African Americans are linked to lower levels of education and employment. In 2000, Blacks in these large cities were also far less likely to own a car or a phone (Saenz 2005:1).

Without jobs, cars, or phones, inner-city residents are utterly vulnerable to urban disaster. (See the "Social Policy" panel on reducing the risk of future disasters for African Americans.) This social entrapment can be explained *structurally*. In his classic studies of African American poverty at the end of the twentieth century, sociologist William J. Wilson found that the problems of the inner city are due to transformations of the larger economy and to the class structure of ghetto neighborhoods (1987, 1996). The movement of middle-class Black professionals from the inner city has left behind a concentration of the most disadvantaged segments of the Black urban population. Wilson's research reveals how crime, family dissolution, and welfare are connected to the structural removal of work from the inner city. The Black inner city is not destroying itself by its own culture; rather, it is being destroyed by economic forces.

SOCIAL POLICY

REDUCING THE RISK OF FUTURE DISASTERS FOR URBAN AFRICAN AMERICANS

African Americans not only have the highest levels of poverty in the country, but they are also the group that is most residentially segregated from and least likely to intermarry with Whites. Surveys also continue to reveal that many non-Black Americans express high levels of social distance (the degree to which people desire close or remote social relations with members of other groups) from African Americans. Given their limited social and economic resources, along with their geographic isolation, poor urban African Americans—especially children and the elderly—are disproportionately vulnerable to being left behind during a crisis situation.

What measures need to be taken to improve the social and economic position of African Americans and to avoid future disasters such as the recent one in New Orleans?

- Skills-development, employment, and health-maintenance programs need to be targeted to and strengthened for African Americans.
- Funding and access to education—including Head Start—should be increased for African Americans to bolster their social and economic well-being and competitiveness in the labor market.
- Additional policies, resources, and investment are needed to promote the development and relocation of businesses (and thus jobs) to African American urban neighborhoods.

- Government agencies responsible for responding to natural disasters need to factor into their planning the economic and geographic isolation of African Americans—especially the African American urban poor.

Aggressive actions are needed to erase the marginalization of African Americans that Hurricane Katrina exposed. The failure to take such actions will have enormous economic and social costs—not just for African Americans, but for a society living with a disjuncture between its ideals and the reality of continued stratification along the color line.

Source: Rogelio Saenz, "The Social and Economic Isolation of Urban African Americans." Population Reference Bureau (2007):3–4. Reprinted with permission from the Population Reference Bureau.

Rising poverty rates among Latinos have led many policy makers and media analysts to conclude that Latinos have joined inner-city African Americans to form a hopeless underclass. This view of minority impoverishment is inaccurate. Although changes in the U.S. economy have hit Latinos hard because of their low educational attainment and their labor market position, structural unemployment has different effects on the many diverse Latino barrios across the nation (Moore and Pinderhughes 1994). The loss of jobs in Rust Belt cities has left many Puerto Ricans living in a bleak ghetto economy. Mexicans living in the Southwest, where low-paying jobs remain, have not suffered the same degree of economic dislocation. Despite high levels of poverty, Latino communities do not fit the conventional portrait of the underclass.

A structural analysis of concentrated poverty does not deny that inner cities are beset with a disproportionate share of social problems. As poverty is more concentrated in inner cities, crime and violence proliferate. The poor may adopt violence as a survival strategy, which escalates violence even further (Massey 1996a). A structural analysis, however, focuses on social conditions, not immoral people. Vanishing jobs and many forms of unemployment are related to the worldwide realignment of work that accompanies corporate globalization. According to national Urban League president Hugh Price, "The manufacturing jobs that once enabled blue-collar workers to purchase their own homes and occasional new cars have all but vanished from the inner city"; and although racism is still widespread, "the global realignment of work and wealth is also a culprit" (cited in Brecher, Costello, and Smith 2000).

Racial Policies in the New Century

The 1960s civil rights movement legalized race-specific remedies to end racial bias. Government policies based on race overturned segregation laws, opened voting booths, created new job opportunities, and brought hopes of racial justice for people of color. As long as it appeared that conditions were improving, government policies to end racial injustice remained in place.

But by the 1980s, the United States had become a very different society from the one in which civil rights legislation was enacted. Economic restructuring brought new dislocations to both Whites and minorities. As racial minorities became an ever larger share of the U.S. population, racial matters grew more politicized. Many Whites began to feel uncomfortable with race-conscious policies in schools and the workplace. The social climate fostered an imaginary White disadvantage, said to be caused by affirmative action and multiculturalism. Although there is no empirical evidence for White disadvantage, a powerful conservative movement is producing new debates about the fairness of racial policies.

The United States is becoming a multiracial society. Barack Obama's rise to the presidency galvanized debates about race in the United States. His election marked a transformative moment in U.S. history. But despite these changes, new forms of racism support White privilege. Claims of color blindness only obscure twenty-first-century racism in all arenas of public life. Higginbotham and Andersen (2009) describe race as a building block of society: Race . . . "segregates our neighborhoods, our schools, our churches, and our relationships. Race . . . is often a matter of heated political debate, and the dynamics of race lie at the heart of the systems of justice and social welfare" (7–8).

Despite claims about color blindness, contemporary forms of racism continue in all arenas of public life. Racial equality is being downsized through policies related to affirmative action, school desegregation, and voting rights. Growing racial populations are controlled through many different forms of discrimination, including employment practices, neighborhood and school segregation, and other inequalities discussed in this chapter. In addition, the demise of the welfare state and the retreat from health care and other forms of social responsibility have caused minorities to lose ground. Finally, international systems of dominance (global capitalism and geopolitical relations) are producing still more racial inequalities in the United States (Allen and Chung 2000:802; Barlow 2003).

Dominant groups use their power to marginalize minorities, but racial inequalities are not simply accepted. Although racism is a tool for exclusion, it is also the basis for political mobilization. Since the country was founded, people of color have struggled for social change. All racially defined groups have rich histories of resistance, community building, and social protest. Racial projects, according to Omi and Winant (1994), are organized efforts to distribute social and economic resources along racial lines. Through social movements, groups organize and act to bring about social change (Higginbotham and Andersen 2009:431). Despite the new racial climate, the struggle against racism continues. Multiracial organizations composed of racial ethnic *and* White antiracist activists continue to work at national and local levels to fight and eradicate racist prejudices and institutional racism.

■ CHAPTER REVIEW

1. Racial and ethnic stratification are basic features of U.S. society. They are also found throughout the world and are an important feature of globalization. Patterns of inequality are built into normal practices. They exclude people from full and equal participation in society's institutions. Racial and ethnic stratification exist because they benefit certain segments of society.

2. The concept of race is a social invention. It is not biologically significant. Racial groups are set apart and singled out for unequal treatment.

3. An ethnic group is culturally distinct in race, religion, or national origin. The group has a distinctive culture. Some ethnic groups such as Jews, Poles, and Italians have distinguishing cultural characteristics that stem from religion and national origin. Because racial groups also have distinctive cultural characteristics, they are referred to as *racial-ethnic* groups.

4. Minority racial and ethnic groups are systematically disadvantaged by society's institutions. Both race and ethnicity are traditional bases for social inequality, although there are historical and contemporary differences in the societal placement of racial-ethnic groups and White ethnic groups in this society.

5. Racial-ethnic groups are socially subordinated and remain culturally distinct within U.S. society. African Americans, Latinos, Asian Americans, and Native Americans are constructed as both racially and culturally distinct. Each group has a distinctive culture, shares a common history, and has developed a common identity within a larger society that subordinates it.

6. Deficiency theories view minority group members as unequal because they lack some important feature common among the majority. These deficiencies may be biological (such as low intelligence) or cultural (such as the culture of poverty).

7. Bias theories place the blame for inequality on the prejudiced attitudes of the members of the dominant group. These theories, however, do not explain the discriminatory acts of the unprejudiced, which are aimed at preserving privilege.

8. Structural theories argue that inequality is the result of external constraints in society rather than cultural features of minority groups. There are four main features of institutional discrimination: (a) forces of history shape present conditions; (b) discrimination can occur without conscious bigotry; and (c) institutional discrimination is less visible than are individual acts of discrimination; and (d) discrimination is reinforced by the interrelationships among the institutions of society.

9. Civil rights legislation improved the status of some racial-ethnic groups, yet the overall position of Blacks and Latinos relative to Whites has not improved. Large gaps remain in work, earnings, and education. Global and economic transformations have contributed to the persistent poverty in U.S. urban centers.

10. The racial demography of the United States is changing dramatically. Immigration and high birthrates among minorities are making the United States a multiracial, multicultural society. These trends are also creating racial anxiety and racial conflict.

11. Public policy has shifted from race-conscious remedies to a color-blind climate that is dismantling historic civil rights reforms.

■ KEY TERMS

Dominant group. Group assigning subordinate status to minority groups.

Racial stratification. System of inequality in which race is the major criterion for rank and rewards.

Minority group. Subordinate group in society.

Racial formation. Sociohistorical process by which races are continually being shaped and transformed.

Ethnic groups. Culturally distinctive characteristics based on race, religion, or national origin.

Racial-ethnic group. Group labeled as a "race" by the wider society and bound together by their common social and economic conditions, resulting in distinctive cultural and ethnic characteristics.

Deficiency theories. Explanations that view the secondary status of minorities as the result of their own behaviors and cultural traits.

Bias theories. Explanations that blame the prejudiced attitudes of majority members for the secondary status of minorities.

Structural discrimination theories. Explanations that focus on the institutionalized patterns of discrimination as the sources of the secondary status of minorities.

Individual racism. Overt acts by individuals that harm members of another race.

Institutional racism. Established and customary social arrangements that exclude on the basis of race.

Environmental racism. The disproportionate exposure of some racial groups to toxic substances.

Color blindness. Idea that race no longer matters in explaining inequality or in policymaking because racism has been overcome.

■ SUCCEED WITH mysoclab www.mysoclab.com

Experience, Discover, Observe, Evaluate
MySocLab is designed just for you. This chapter features a pre-test and post-test to help you learn and review key concepts and terms.

Experience sociology in action with dynamic visual activities, videos, and readings to enhance your learning experience. Complete the following activities at www.mysoclab.com.

Social Explorer is an interactive application that allows you to explore Census data through interactive maps.

- Explore the Social Explorer Map: *Racial Income Extremes*

The Core Concepts in Sociology video clips offer a real-world perspective on sociological concepts.

- Watch *Discrimination at Swim Club*

MySocLibrary includes primary source readings from classic and contemporary sociologists.

- Read Lui, *Doubly Divided: The Racial Wealth Gap*; McArdle, *Sociologists on the Color Blind Question*; Ogbu, *Racial Stratification and Education in the United States: Why Inequality Persists*

Gender Inequality

More than ever, it is time to take stock of current experiences with and perceptions of sexism. We are living at a particularly crucial historical moment for examining the problem of sexism.

—Carol Rambo Ronai, Barbara A. Zsembik, and Joe R. Feagin

Every society treats women and men differently. Today, there is no nation where women and men are equals. Worldwide, women perform an estimated 60 percent of the work, yet they earn only 10 percent of the income and own only 10 percent of the land. Two-thirds of the world's illiterate are women. Despite massive political changes and economic progress in countries throughout the world, women continue to be the victims of abuse and discrimination. Even where women have made important strides in politics and the professions, women's overall progress remains uneven.

This chapter examines the social basis of gender inequality. We show how gender disparity and its problems are built into the larger world we inhabit. From the macrolevel of the global economy, through the institutions of society,

From Chapter 9 of *Social Problems, Census Update*, Twelfth Edition. D. Stanley Eitzen, Maxine Baca Zinn, Kelly Eitzen Smith. Copyright © 2012 by Pearson Education, Inc. Published by Allyn & Bacon. All rights reserved.

to interpersonal relations, gender is the basis for dividing labor, assigning roles, and allocating social rewards. Until recently, this kind of differentiation seemed natural. However, new research shows that gender is not natural at all. Instead, "women" and "men" are social creations. To emphasize this point, sociologists distinguish between *sex* and *gender*. Sex refers to the biological differences between females and males. Gender refers to the social and cultural patterns attached to women and men. Both sex and gender organize social life throughout the world.

Gender is not only about women. Men often think of themselves as "genderless," as if gender did not matter in the daily experience of their lives. Yet, from birth through old age, men are also gendered. This "gendering process, the transformation of biological males into socially interacting men, is a central experience for men" (Kimmel and Messner 2007:xvi). In the big picture, gender divisions make women and men unequal. But, we cannot understand the gender system, or women's and men's experiences, by looking at gender alone; gender operates together with other power systems such as race, class, and sexual orientation. These overlapping categories produce different gender experiences for women and men of different races and classes. Nevertheless, the gender system denies women and men the full range of human and social possibilities. Gender inequalities produce social problems. This chapter examines gender stratification in U.S. society at both structural and interpersonal levels of social organization. Taking a feminist approach (one in support of women's equality), the theme of this chapter is that social factors make women unequal to men.

WOMEN AND MEN ARE DIFFERENTIATED AND RANKED

Gender stratification refers to the hierarchical placement of the sexes that gives women unequal power, opportunities, and resources. Although there is worldwide variation in women's and men's roles, gender inequality exists in most parts of the world. Every society has certain ideas about what women and men should be like as well as ways of producing people who are much like these expectations.

Scientists have competing explanations for gender differences. Biological models argue that innate biological differences between males and females program different social behaviors. Anthropological models look at masculinity and femininity cross-culturally, stressing the variations in women's and men's roles. Sociologists treat gender as a feature of social structure.

Is Gender Biological or Social?

We know that there *are* biological differences between the two sexes. Debates about gender differences often fall back on "nature vs. nurture" arguments. The nurture camp argues that most differences are socially constructed. The opposing camp claims that differences between women and men are rooted in evolution. In 2005, Larry Summers, then president of Harvard University, caused a storm by suggesting that innate ability could be a reason there were so few women in the top positions in mathematics, engineering, and the physical sciences. Biological explanations have also become a favorite theme in the media

(Barnett and Rivers 2004). Is the popular biological explanation correct? Are men "hardwired" to dominate women? To answer this question, let us first review the evidence for each position.

- **Biological Bases for Gender Roles.** Males and females are different from the moment of conception. Chromosomal and reproductive differences make males and females physically different. Hormonal differences in the sexes are also significant. The male hormones (androgens) and female hormones (estrogens) direct the process of sex differentiation from about six weeks after conception throughout life. They make males taller, heavier, and more muscular. At puberty, they trigger the production of secondary sexual characteristics. In males, these include body and facial hair, a deeper voice, broader shoulders, and a muscular body. In females, puberty brings pubic hair, menstruation, the ability to lactate, prominent breasts, and relatively broad hips. Actually, males and females have both sets of hormones. The relative proportion of androgens and estrogens gives a person masculine or feminine physical traits.

  These hormonal differences may explain in part why males tend to be more active, aggressive, and dominant than females. However, there are only slight differences in the levels of hormones between girls and boys in childhood. Yet, researchers find differences in aggression between young girls and boys (Fausto-Sterling 1992).

  Biological differences between women and men are only averages. They are often influenced by other factors. For example, although men are on the average larger than women, body size is influenced by diet and physical activity, which in turn may be influenced by culture, class, and race. The all-or-none categorizing of gender traits is misleading because there is considerable overlap in the distribution of traits possessed by women and men. Although most men are stronger than most women, many women are stronger than many men. And although males are on the average more aggressive than females, the differences among males and among females are greater than the differences between males and females (Basow 1996:81; Barnett and Rivers 2004). Furthermore, gender is constantly changing. Femininity and masculinity are not uniformly shaped from genetic makeup. Instead, they are molded differently (1) from one culture to another, (2) within any one culture over time, (3) over the course of all women's and men's lives, and (4) between and among different groups of women and men, depending on class, race, ethnicity, and sexuality (Kimmel 1992:166).

- **The Social Bases for Gender Roles.** Cross-cultural evidence shows a wide variation of behaviors for the sexes. Table 1 provides some interesting cross-cultural data from 224 societies on the division of labor by sex. This table shows that for the majority of activities, societies are not uniform in their gendered division of labor. Even activities requiring strength, presumably a male trait, are not strictly apportioned to males. In fact, activities such as burden bearing and water carrying are done by females more than by males. Even an activity such as house building is not exclusively male. Although there is a wide variety in the social roles assigned to women and men, their roles seldom vary "randomly" (O'Kelly 1980:41). Despite the widespread cultural variation in women's and men's activities, every known society makes gender a major category for organizing social life. This is the social construction of gender. It is a sociological perspective that calls on social rather than biological differences to show how

TABLE 1

Gender Allocation in Selected Technological Activities in 224 Societies

Activity	Number of Societies in Which the Activitiy Is Performed by:					
	Males Exclusively	Males Usually	Both Sexes Equally	Females Usually	Females Exclusively	Percent Male
Smelting of ores	37	0	0	0	0	100.0
Hunting	139	5	0	0	0	99.3
Boat building	84	3	3	0	1	96.6
Mining and quarrying	31	1	2	0	1	93.7
Land clearing	95	34	6	3	1	90.5
Fishing	83	45	8	5	2	86.7
Herding	54	24	14	3	3	82.4
House building	105	30	14	9	20	77.4
Generation of fire	40	6	16	4	20	62.3
Preparation of skins	39	4	2	5	31	54.6
Crop planting	27	35	33	26	20	54.4
Manufacture of leather products	35	3	2	5	29	53.2
Crop tending	22	23	24	30	32	44.6
Milking	15	2	8	2	21	43.8
Carrying	18	12	46	34	36	39.3
Loom weaving	24	0	6	8	50	32.5
Fuel gathering	25	12	12	23	94	27.2
Manufacture of clothing	16	4	11	13	78	22.4
Pottery making	14	5	6	6	74	21.1
Dairy production	4	0	0	0	24	14.3
Cooking	0	2	2	63	117	8.3
Preparation of vegetables	3	1	4	21	145	5.7

Source: Adapted from George P. Murdock and Caterina Provist. 1973. "Factors in the Division of Labor by Sex. A Cross-cultural Analysis." *Ethnology* 12 (April):2007. Reprinted by permission from *Ethnology*.

all societies transform biological females and males into socially interacting women and men (Andersen 2009).

Gender and Power

Gender differences are social creations that are embedded in society. The term gendered institutions means that entire institutions are patterned by gender (Acker 1992; Lorber 2005). Everywhere we look—the global economy, politics, corporate life, family life—men are in power. But men are not uniformly dominant. Some men have great power over other men. In fact, most men do not feel powerful; most feel powerless, trapped in stifling old roles and unable to changes their lives in ways they want (Kimmel 1992:171). Nevertheless, socially defined differences between women and men legitimate male dominance, which refers to the beliefs, meanings, and placement that value men over women and that institutionalize male control of socially valued resources. Patriarchy is the term used for forms of social organization in which men are dominant over women.

Like race and class, "gender is a multilevel system of differences and disadvantages that includes socioeconomic arrangements and widely held cultural beliefs at the macrolevel, ways of behaving in relation to others and the interactional level, and acquired traits and identities at the individual level" (Ridgeway 1997:219). Gender inequality is tied to other inequalities such as race, class, and sexuality to sort women and men differently. These inequalities also work together to produce differences *among women* and differences *among men*. Some women derive benefits from their race, their class, or their sexuality while they are simultaneously restricted by gender. Such women are subordinated by patriarchy, yet race, class, and sexuality intersect to create for them privileged opportunities and ways of living (Baca Zinn, Hondagneu-Sotelo, and Messner 2005). For example, men are encouraged to behave in "masculine" fashion to prove that they are not gay (Connell 1992). In defining masculinity as the negation of homosexuality, compulsory heterosexuality is an important component of the gender system. Compulsory heterosexuality inflicts negative sanctions on those who are homosexual or bisexual. This system of sexuality shapes the gender system by discouraging attachment with members of the same sex. This enforces the dichotomy of "opposite" sexes. Sexuality is also a form of inequality in its own right because it grants privileges to those in heterosexual relationships. Like race, class, and gender, sexual identities are socially constructed categories. Sexuality is a way of organizing the social world on the basis of sexual identity and is a key linking process in the matrix of domination structured along the lines of race, class, and gender (Messner 1996:223).

Gender scholars have debated the question of universal male dominance, that is, whether it is found in all societies across time and space. Many scholars once claimed that all societies exhibit some forms of patriarchy in marriage and family forms, in division of labor, and in society at large (Ortner 1974; Rosaldo 1974). Other scholars have challenged universal patriarchy with cases that serve as counterexamples (Shapiro 1981). Current thought follows the latter course. Sexual differentiation, it seems, is found in all societies, but it does not always indicate low female status (Rogers 1978). Male dominance is not homogeneous. Instead, it varies from society to society.

We should keep in mind that although gender stratification makes women subordinate to men, they are not simply the passive victims of patriarchy. Like other oppressed groups, women find ways to resist domination. Through personal and political struggles, they act in their own behalf, often changing the social conditions that subordinate them.

What Causes Gender Inequality?

To explain gender and power, sociologists turn to social conditions. Structural thinking treats gender inequality as the outcome of male control over socially valued resources and opportunities. There are several models of gender inequality. Most of them focus on the divisions of labor and power between women and men and the different value placed on their work. This idea originated in the work of Friedrich Engels and Karl Marx. They wrote that industrialism and the shift to a capitalist economy widened the gap between the power and value of men and women. As production moved out of the home, the gendered division of labor left men with the greater share of economic and other forms of power (Chafetz 1997; Sapiro 1999:67).

Macrostructural theories explain gender inequality as an outcome of how women and men are tied to the economic structure of society (Neilson 1990:215).

These theories say that women's economic role in society is a primary determinant of their overall status (Dunn 1996). The division between domestic and public spheres of activity gives men and women different positions of advantage and disadvantage. Their roles in the labor force and in the family are interdependent. Whether or not they work outside the home, women do the vast majority of child care and household labor. Men are freed from these responsibilities. Women's reproductive roles and their responsibilities for domestic labor limit their association with the resources that are highly valued (Rosaldo 1980; Ridgeway 1997). Men's economic obligations in the public sphere ensure them control of highly valued resources and give rise to male privilege.

In capitalist societies, the domestic–public split is even more significant because highly valued goods and services are exchanged in the public, not the domestic, sphere. Women's domestic labor, although important for survival, ranks low in prestige and power because it does not produce exchangeable commodities (Sacks 1974). Because of the connections between the class relations of production (capitalism) and the hierarchical gender relations of its society (patriarchy; Eisenstein 1979), the United States is a capitalist patriarchy where male supremacy keeps women in subordinate roles at work and in the home.

Socialization versus Structure: Two Approaches to Gender Inequality

To understand gender inequality, we must distinguish between (1) a gender roles approach and (2) a gender structure approach. The gender roles approach emphasizes traits that individuals acquire during the course of socialization, such as independent or dependent behaviors and ways of relating. The gender structure approach emphasizes factors that are external to individuals, such as the social structures and social interactions that reward women and men differently. These approaches differ in how they view the sexes, in how they explain the causes and effects of sexism, and in the solutions they suggest for ending inequality. Understanding sexism requires both the individual and the structural approaches. Although gender roles are learned by individuals, and produce differences in the personalities, behaviors, and motivations of women and men, gender stratification is essentially maintained by societal forces. This chapter places primary emphasis on social structure as the cause of inequality.

LEARNING GENDER

The most complex, demanding, and all-involving role that a member of society must learn to play is that of female or male. "Casting" for one's gender role takes place immediately at birth, after a quick biological inspection; and the role of "female" or "male" is assigned. It is an assignment that will last one's entire lifetime and affect virtually everything one ever does. A large part of the next 20 years or so will be spent gradually learning and perfecting one's assigned sex role (David and Brannon 1980:117).

Sociologists use the term *gender socialization* to describe how gender is learned. Understanding socialization is important not only to explaining gender, but to the construction of gender inequality (Martin 2005:457). From infancy through early childhood and beyond, children learn what is expected of boys and girls, and they learn to behave according to those expectations.

The traits associated with conventional gender roles are those valued by the dominant society. Keep in mind that gender is not the same in all classes and races. However, most research on gender socialization reflects primarily the experience of White middle-class people—those who are most often the research subjects of these studies. How gender is learned depends on a variety of social conditions affecting the socialization practices of girls and boys. Still, society molds boys and girls along different lines.

Children at Home

Girls and boys are perceived and treated differently from the moment of birth. Their access to clothes, toys, books, playmates, and expressions of emotion are severely limited by gender (Martin 2005:457). Parents' and "congratulations" greeting cards describe newborn daughters as "sweet," whereas boys are immediately described as "strong" and "hardy." Cards sent to parents depict ribbons, hearts, and flowers for girls, but mobiles, sports equipment, and vehicles for boys. Newborn greeting cards thus project an early gender scheme that introduces two "classes" of babies: one decorative, the other physically active and bringing greater joy (Valian 1998:19–20).

Children learn at a very early age what it means to be a boy or girl in our society. One of the strongest influences on gender role development in children occurs within the family setting, with parents passing on both overtly and covertly their own beliefs about gender (Witt 1997:254). From the time their children are babies, parents treat sons and daughters differently, dressing infants in gender-specific colors and giving them gender-differentiated toys. Color-coded differences reveal a relentless gender segregation with "little girls becoming adamantly attached to pink" (Sandler 2009). Parents expect different behaviors from boys and girls (Thorne 1993; Witt 1997). Although both mothers and fathers contribute to the gender stereotyping of their children, fathers have been found to reinforce gender stereotyping more often than mothers (Idle, Wood, and Desmarias 1993; Witt 1997; Valian 1998; Campenni 1999).

In addition to the parents' active role in reinforcing society's gender demands, a subtler message is emitted from picture books for preschool children. A classic sociological study of award-winning children's books conducted 40 years ago found the following characteristics (Weitzman et al., 1972):

- Females were virtually invisible. The ratio of male pictures to female pictures was 11:1. The ratio of male to female animals was 95:1.
- The activities of boys and girls varied greatly. Boys were active in outdoor activities, whereas girls were passive and most often found indoors. The activity of the girls typically was that of some service for boys.
- Adult men and women (role models) were very different. Men led, women followed. Females were passive and males active. Not one woman in these books had a job or profession; they were always mothers and wives.

We have seen improvements in how girls and women are portrayed. Females are no longer invisible, they are as likely as males to be included in the books, and they have roles beyond their family roles. In many respects, however, gendered messages in children's books still exist (Crabb and Bielawski 1994). An update of the classic Weitzman study found that although the majority of female characters were portrayed as dependent and submissive, male characters were commonly portrayed as being independent and creative (Oskamp, Kaufman, and Wolterbeek 1996). A subsequent study, which focused on the representation of gender and physical activity level in award-winning books from 1940 through 1999, found that female characters are much less likely than male characters to be depicted in active roles and that this depiction has not changed significantly over this vast time period (Nilges and Spencer 2002).

Gendered socialization is found even where gender roles are changing and socialization is becoming more flexible or androgynous. Androgyny refers to the combination of feminine and masculine characteristics in the same individual. Are girls more androgynous than boys? If so, what explains the difference? And what difference does androgyny make in an individual's overall well-being? Research has found that fathers who display the most traditional attitudes about gender transmit their ideas onto their sons more so than onto their daughters, whereas mothers who tend to have more liberal attitudes do not transmit their attitudes onto their daughters more than their sons. Consequently, "when the sons establish their own families, they will be more likely than the daughters to transmit traditional attitudes to their own sons" (Kulik 2002:456). Other researchers have also found that whereas adolescent girls tend to be more supportive of egalitarian gender roles than their parents (especially their fathers), adolescent boys follow their fathers' resistance to changes in traditional male roles. Therefore, it is predictable that males would be less likely than females to develop androgynous characteristics (Burt and Scott 2002). In a study of child care books and parenting websites, sociologist Karen Martin found some evidence of gender-neutral child rearing. But she also found that children's nonconformity to gender roles is still viewed as problematic because it is linked with homosexuality (Martin 2005).

Gender identities affect individuals' well-being in various ways. Witt (1997) found that parents who foster androgynous attitudes and behaviors in their children ultimately cause their girls and boys to have high self-esteem and self-worth. Androgynous individuals appear to be able to more effectively manage stress and practice good health (Edwards and Hamilton 2004), and androgynous college students report having better relationships with their parents (Guastello and Guastello 2003:664).

Children at Play

Children teach each other to behave according to cultural expectations. Same-sex peers exert a profound influence on how gender is learned. In a classic study of children's play groups, Janet Lever (1976) discovered how children stress particular social skills and capabilities for boys and others for girls. Her research among fifth-graders (most of whom were White and middle class) found that boys, more than girls, (1) played outdoors, (2) played in larger groups, (3) played in age-heterogeneous groups, (4) were less likely to play in games dominated by the opposite sex, (5) played more competitive games, and (6) played in games that lasted longer.

Barrie Thorne's (1993) study of gender play in multiracial school settings found that boys control more space, more often violate girls' activities, and treat girls as contaminating. According to Thorne, these common ritualized interactions reflect larger structures of male dominance. In reality, the fun and games of everyday schoolchildren are *power play*, a complex social process involving both gender separation and togetherness. Children's power play changes with age, ethnicity, race, class, and social context. In her analysis of how children themselves construct gender in their daily play, Thorne shifted the focus from individual to *social relations*:

> *The social construction of gender is an active and ongoing process. . . . Gender categories, gender identities, gender divisions, and gender-based groups, gender meanings—all are produced actively and collaboratively, in everyday life. When kids maneuver to form same-gender groups on the playground or organize a kickball game as "boys-against-the-girls," they produce a sense of gender as dichotomy and opposition. And when girls and boys work cooperatively on a classroom project, they actively undermine a sense of gender as opposition. This emphasis on action and activity, and on everyday social interactions that are sometimes contradictory, provides an antidote to the view of children as passively socialized. Gender is not something one passively "is" or "has." (Thorne 1993:4–5)*

New research on fourth-grade children in schoolyards supports Thorne's conclusions about gendered interaction in schoolyards. Boyle and her colleagues (Boyle, Marshall, and Robeson 2003) found a great deal of intragender variation in the schoolyard, with girls in particular engaging in many different activities. They also found that boys are more easily accepted into play with girls than is the case when girls try to play with a group of boys, and that boys tend to use more space in the schoolyard and are more likely to violate girls' space and games than the reverse.

Toys play a major part in gender socialization. Toys entertain children; they also teach them particular skills and encourage them to explore a variety of roles they may one day occupy as adults. Like clothing, kids' toy stores and departments are sharply divided into girls' and boys' sections. Toys for boys tend to encourage exploration, manipulation, invention, construction, competition, and aggression. In contrast, girls' toys typically rate high on manipulability, creativity, nurturance, and attractiveness. Playing with gendered toys may encourage different skills in girls and boys (Renzetti and Curran 2003:89–92).

In a study of parents and children in a day care setting, children eagerly accepted most of the toys presented to them by their parents and discarded other available toys in favor of their parents' choices (Idle et al., 1993). When parents discouraged their sons from playing with cross-gender toys, their sons learned and adopted this behavior. Campenni (1999) found that adults were most likely to choose gender-specific toys for their children. Toys that adults deemed most appropriate for girls included items pertaining to domestic tasks (such as a vacuum cleaner or kitchen center), child rearing (dollhouse, cradle stroller), or beauty enhancement (makeup kits, jewelry items). Toys rated "appropriate" for boys included sports gear, male action figures, building items, plastic bugs, and attire for traditional male occupations. Like other researchers, the Campenni study found that girls are often involved in cross-gender or neutral toy behavior. Girls are encouraged by both parents to branch out and play with neutral toys some of the time, but boys tend not to be given this same encouragement (Campenni 1999). Although we may be seeing some breakdown of traditional play patterns and socialization of girls, the same does not appear true for boys. Studies have also found that messages transmitted to children from advertisements affect their toy use and that the effects are different for boys and girls. Research finds that the messages in commercials have stronger effects on boys than on girls (Pike and Jennings 2005).

Although girls are now encouraged to engage in activities such as playing video games, traditional gender stereotypes still underlie this pastime. Research finds that girls tend to become less stereotypical in their play as they age—choosing more neutral toys, sports, and computer games (while boys remain masculine in their play) (Orenstein 2008).

Dichotomous gender experiences may be more characteristic of White middle-class children than of children of other races. An important study on Black adolescent girls by Joyce Ladner has shown that Black girls develop in a more independent fashion (Ladner 1971). Other research has also found that among African Americans, both girls and boys are expected to be nurturant and expressive emotionally as well as independent, confident, and assertive (McAdoo 1988; Stack 1990). Recent studies examining whether or not the socialization of Black children is more gender-neutral than that in other groups is inconsistent. Most scholars now say there is too much variation in any group to make generalizations (Hill and Sprague 1999; M. Smith 2001).

Formal Education

In 1972, Congress outlawed gender discrimination in public schools through Title IX of the Educational Amendments Act. More than three decades later, girls and boys in the United States are still not receiving the same education. Reports by the American Association of University Women (AAUW 1992, 1999) have offered compelling evidence that two decades after the passage of Title IX, discrimination remained pervasive.

Research contradicts the media myth of the "boy crisis," which portrays young men as marginalized, while girls are taking over the schools. Studies find that "over the past three decades, boys' test scores are mostly up, more boys are going to college, and more are getting bachelor's degrees" (Matthews 2006:A01; Von Drehle 2007). Although males do drop out of school more often than females, the trend is most pronounced among minorities and boys from low-income homes (Barnett and Rivers 2004; Matthews 2006). The "boy crisis" is an issue of race and class disadvantage, not one of gender difference.

Schools shortchange girls in every dimension of education. Let us examine the following areas: course offerings, textbooks, teacher–student interactions, sports, female role models, and counseling.

- **Curriculum.** Schools are charged with the responsibility of equipping students to study subjects (e.g., reading, writing, mathematics, and history) known collectively as the formal curriculum. But schools also teach students particular social, political, and economic values that constitute the so-called hidden curriculum operating alongside the more formal one. Both formal and informal curricula are powerful shapers of gender (Renzetti and Curran 2003:109, Booher-Jennings 2008).

  The courses that high school girls enroll in are increasingly similar to those of boys. Still, there are noticeable gaps. Female enrollment in science and mathematics courses increased dramatically in recent years. Girls are more likely to take biology and chemistry as well as trigonometry and algebra II. But in general, girls are more oriented toward the life sciences and boys toward preparation in the physical sciences (Adamuti-Trache and Andres 2007; Sadker 2002:238).

Although girls on the average receive higher grades in high school than boys, they tend to score lower on some standardized tests, which are particularly important because such tests scores are used to make decisions on the awarding of scholarships and admissions. Schools ignore topics that matter in students' lives. The "evaded curriculum" is a term coined in the AAUW Report to refer to matters central to the lives of students that are touched on only briefly, if at all, in most schools. Students receive inadequate education on sexuality, teen pregnancy, the AIDS crisis, and the increase of sexually transmitted diseases among adolescents. According to the AAUW report, gender bias also affects males. Three out of four boys currently report that they were the targets of sexual harassment in schools—usually of taunts challenging their masculinity. In addition, although girls receive lower test grades, boys often receive lower overall course grades.

- **Textbooks.** The content of textbooks transmits messages to readers about society, about children, and about what adults are supposed to do. For this reason, individuals and groups concerned about gender bias in schools have looked carefully at how males and females are portrayed in textbooks assigned to students. Their findings provide a consistent message: Textbooks commonly used in U.S. schools are both overtly and covertly sexist. Sexism has become a recent concern of publishers, and a number have instituted guidelines for creating inclusive images in educational materials.

  No doubt these efforts have produced better textbooks. Reading lists are more inclusive and textbooks are more balanced than they used to be. But notable disparities still exist. Girls, for instance, tend to be in needy positions, whereas males are more likely to be portrayed as offering help. Furthermore, girls are pictured less often, but if included, they typically maintain supportive rather than lead roles in the stories or pictures. Also, girls are more likely to be the spectators rather than the participants in textbook pictures (Bauer 2000:23). "Males are more likely to be discussed in the context of their occupational roles, whereas when females are discussed, it is their personality characteristics that get the most attention" (Renzetti and Curan 2003:109).

- **Teacher–Student Interactions.** Even when girls and boys are in the same classrooms, boys are given preferential treatment. Girls receive less attention and different types of attention from classroom teachers.

  Teachers are now advised to encourage cooperative cross-sex learning, to monitor their own (teacher) behavior, to be sure that they reward male and female students equally, and to actively familiarize students with gender-atypical roles by assigning them specific duties as leaders, recording secretary, and so on (Lockheed 1985; cited in Giele 1988).

  Despite the fact that many teachers are trying to interact with their students in nongendered ways, they nonetheless continue to do so. In her study of third-grade classes, Garrahy (2001) found that although the teachers were claiming to be gender neutral, they often interacted differently with boys in the classroom. Spencer and Toleman (2003) found that the teachers spent more time with the male students when they were working independently and in small groups; perhaps most troubling, the students normalized and naturalized these gender differences. Unfortunately, despite the increasing awareness of gender inequality within schools, new teachers are not adequately being taught about gender equity issues.

© Mary Kate Denny/PhotoEdit

Many forms of gender bias exist in education. For example, girls receive less attention and different types of attention from classroom teachers.

- **Sports.** Sports in U.S. high schools and colleges have historically been almost exclusively a male preserve (this section is dependent on Eitzen and Sage 2010). The truth of this observation is clearly evident if one compares by sex the number of participants, facilities, support of school administrations, and financial support.

  Such disparities have been based on the traditional assumptions that competitive sport is basically a masculine activity and that the proper roles of girls and women are as spectators and cheerleaders. What is the impact on a society that encourages its boys and young men to participate in sports while expecting its girls and young women to be spectators and cheerleaders? Sports reinforce societal expectations for males and females. Males are to be dominant and aggressive—the doers—while females are expected to be passive supporters of men, attaining status through the efforts of their menfolk.

  An important consequence of this traditional view is that approximately half of the population has been denied access to all that sport has to offer (physical conditioning, enjoyment, teamwork, goal attainment, ego enhancement, social status, and competitiveness). School administrators, school boards, and citizens of local communities have long assumed that sports participation has general educational value. If so, then girls and women should also be allowed to receive the benefits.

  In 1972, passage of Title IX of the Educational Amendments Act required that schools receiving federal funds must provide equal opportunities for males and females. Despite considerable opposition by school administrators, athletic directors, and school boards, major changes occurred over time because of this federal legislation. More monies were spent on women's sports; better facilities and equipment were provided; and women were gradually accepted as athletes. The most significant result was an increase in female participation. The number of high school girls participating in interscholastic sports increased from 300,000 in 1971 to 3.11 million in 2008. By the 2008 school year, 41.3 percent of all high school participants were female, and the number of sports available to them was more than twice the number available in 1970. Similar growth patterns occurred in colleges and universities.

At the intercollegiate level, on the positive side, budgets for women's sports improved dramatically, from less than 1 percent of the men's budgets and no athletic scholarships in 1970 to 38 percent of the men's budgets and 33 percent of the scholarship budgets in 2008. Despite this marked improvement, women athletes remain underfunded. Although women account for 57 percent of the college student population, female athletes receive only 43 percent of participation opportunities. And male athletes receive $179 million more in athletic scholarships than their female counterparts (Lopiano 2008). This inequality is reinforced by unequal media attention, the scheduling of games (men's games are always the featured games), and the increasing lack of women in positions of power. One ironic consequence of Title IX has been that as opportunities for female athletes increased and programs expanded, the opportunities for women as coaches and administrators diminished. In the early 1970s, most coaches of women's intercollegiate teams were women. By 2008, 46 percent of women's team coaches were women (Lopiano 2008). Females who aspire to coaching and athletic administration have fewer opportunities than males; girls and women see fewer women as role models in such positions. Thus, even with federal legislation mandating gender equality, male dominance is maintained.

- **Female Role Models.** The work that women and men do in the schools supports gender inequality. The pattern is the familiar one found in hospitals, business offices, and throughout the work world: Women occupy the bottom rungs while men have the more powerful positions. Women make up a large percentage of the nation's classroom teachers but a much smaller percentage of school district superintendents. In 2008, women comprised 81 percent of all elementary school teachers, more than half of all secondary school teachers (56 percent), and 65 percent of all school administrators (Bureau of Labor Statistics 2009b).

  As the level of education increases, the proportion of women teachers declines. In the 2007–2008 academic year (more than 20 years after the Office of Civil Rights issued guidelines spelling out the obligations of colleges and universities in the development of affirmative action programs), women represented only 45 percent of full-time faculty. Furthermore, they remained overwhelmingly in the lower faculty ranks, where faculty are much less likely to hold tenure. In 2009, women comprised 26 percent of full professors, 39 percent of associate professors, 47 percent of assistant professors, and 53 percent of instructors/lecturers. Since 1986, the percentage of college presidents has doubled—from 10 percent to 23 percent of the total in 2009 (National Center for Education Statistics 2008). Although women now hold a greater percentage of the top positions at colleges and universities than ever before, women presidents remain underrepresented in comparison to their share of all faculty and senior staff positions (American Council on Education 2000).

- **Counseling.** A fundamental task of school guidance personnel is to aid students in their choice of a career. The guidance that students receive on career choice tends to be biased. High school guidance counselors may channel male and female students into different (i.e., gender-stereotyped) fields and activities. There is evidence that gender stereotyping is common among counselors and that they often steer females away from certain college preparatory courses, especially in mathematics and the sciences (Renzetti and Curran 2003:116).

In the past, aptitude tests have themselves been sex-biased, listing occupations as either female or male. Despite changes in testing, counselors may inadvertently channel students into traditional gendered choices.

Socialization as Blaming the Victim

The discussion so far demonstrates that gender differences are learned. This does not mean that socialization alone explains women's place in society. In fact, a socialization approach can be misused in such a way that it blames women themselves for sex inequality. This is the critique offered by Linda Peterson and Elaine Enarson (1974). Many years ago, they developed the argument that socialization diverts attention from structured inequality: "Misuse of the concept of socialization plays directly into the Blaming the Victim ideology; by focusing on the victim, responsibility for 'the woman problem' rests not in the social system with its sex-structured distribution of inequality, but in socialized sex differences and sex roles" (1974:8).

Not only is the cause of the problem displaced, but also so are the solutions. "Rather than directing efforts toward radical social change, the solution seems to be to change women themselves, perhaps through exhortation ('If we want to be liberated, we'll have to act more aggressive'). . . . Or, for example, changing children's literature and mothers' child-rearing practice" (8).

This issue raises a critical question: If the socialization perspective is limited and perhaps biased, what is a better way of analyzing gender inequality? To answer this question, let us look at how male dominance affects our society.

REINFORCING MALE DOMINANCE

Male dominance is both a force that socializes and a force that structures the social world. It exists at all levels of society, from interpersonal relations to outside institutions. This section describes the interpersonal and institutional reinforcement of gender inequality.

Language

Language perpetuates male dominance by ignoring, trivializing, and sexualizing women. Use of the pronoun *he* when the sex of the person is unspecified and of the generic term *mankind* to refer to humanity in general are obvious examples of how the English language ignores women. Common sayings such as "that's women's work" (as opposed to "that's men's work!"), jokes about female drivers, and phrases such as *women and children first* or *wine, women, and song* are trivializing. Women, more than men, are commonly referred to in terms that have sexual connotations. Terms referring to men (*studs, jocks*) that do have sexual meanings imply power and success, whereas terms applied to women (*broads, bimbos, hos*) imply promiscuity or subordination. In fact, the term *promiscuous* is usually applied only to women, although its literal meaning applies to either sex (Richmond-Abbott 1992:93). Research shows that there are many derogatory terms for women, but there are few for men generically (Sapiro 1999:329). Not only are there fewer derogatory terms that refer to men, but often such terms are considered derogatory because they invoke the images of women.

"Some of the more common derogatory terms applied to men such as *bastard,* *motherfucker,* and *son of a bitch* actually degrade women in their role as mothers" (Romaine 1999:99). (See "A Closer Look" on the use of animal terms to denigrate women.)

Interpersonal Behavior

Gender inequality is different than other forms of inequality because individuals on both sides of the power divide (that is women and men) interact very frequently (in the home, in the workplace, and in other role relations). Consequently, gender inequalities can be reproduced and resisted in everyday interactions (Ridgeway and Smith-Lovin 1999:191).

Sociologists have done extensive research on the ways in which women and men interact, with particular attention being paid to communication styles. This research has found that in mixed-sex groups, men talk more, show more visual dominance, and interrupt more, whereas women display more tentative and polite speech patterns (Ridgeway and Smith-Lovin 1999).

Various forms of nonverbal communication also sustain male dominance. Men take up more space than do women and also touch women without permission more than women touch men. Women, on the other hand, engage in more eye contact, smile more, and generally exhibit behavior associated with low status. These behaviors show how gender is continually being created in various kinds of social interaction. Candace West and Don Zimmerman (1987) call this "doing gender." It involves following the rules and behaviors expected of us as males or females. We "do gender" because if we do not, we are judged incompetent as men and women. Gender is something we create in interaction, not something we are (Risman 1998:6).

Producing gender through interaction is becoming a lively sociological topic. Instead of treating gender only as identity, or a socialization, or stratification, this perspective emphasizes gender as dynamic *practices*—what people say and do as they engage in social interaction (Ridgeway 1997; Martin 2003). In this view, gender is a system of action:

> *Gendered practices are learned and enacted in childhood and in every major site of social behavior over the life course, including in school, intimate relationships, families, workplaces, houses of worship, and social movements. In time, like riding a bicycle, gendering practices become almost automatic.* (Martin 2003:352)

Mass Communications Media

Much of the information we receive about the world around us comes not from direct experience but from the mass media—radio, television, newspapers, magazines, and the Internet. Although media are often blamed for the problems of modern society, they are not monolithic and do not present us with a simple message. The media have tremendous power. They can distort women's images and they can bring about change as well (Sapiro 1999:224). Women are still underrepresented on op-ed pages, on Sunday chat shows, and as experts in news stories (Pollit 2010). Studies show that women journalists' role in newsrooms is shrinking even though women predominate in undergraduate and graduate journalism programs and have for decades (Lauer 2002). In magazines, women's portrayal has become less monolithic since the 1980s. With the

A CLOSER LOOK

"BITCHES," "BUNNIES," AND "BIDDIES"

How Animal Metaphors Degrade, Sexualize, and Denigrate Women

Many of the most derogatory words used to refer to women in our society share something in common: they use animal imagery to degrade women. For instance, women are frequently ridiculed as "bitches" and "shrews." Examining the definitions of these words makes their deeper meanings clear: in *Webster's New World Dictionary,* the word *bitch* is defined as "the female of the dog, wolf, fox, etc." and second as "a lewd, or promiscuous woman" (1991:143), and a *shrew* is defined as "a scolding, nagging, evil-tempered woman" (1991:1243).

Why have such words that originally referred to animals come to be used as common slurs against women? To answer this question, we must address the positioning of animals in our society. In brief, humans are perceived as being distinct from and superior to other animals. This belief has left animals vulnerable to widespread abuse at human hands. This widespread abuse is possible because animals are considered property and are generally treated as commodities. Equating women (and other marginalized groups) with animals through language simultaneously degrades them as "less-than-human" (read as "less-than-men") and reinforces our society's devaluation of their lives.

Animal metaphors are also used to refer to privileged groups of men, but such references are certainly fewer in number (as are derogatory terms toward men in general) and tend to invoke the image of strong, virile, and more revered animals, such as tigers and bulls. In contrast, women are compared to smaller, domesticated/dominated animals (such as cats or "chicks"), or to animals that are hunted as prey (such as foxes; Romaine 1999:101; Weatherall 2002:26). The use of specific animal metaphors therefore both illustrates and reinforces the power differentials between men and women in society. As Lakoff explained,

> English (like other languages) has many words describing women who are interested in power, presupposing the inappropriateness of that attitude. *Shrew* and *bitch* are among the more polite. There are no equivalents for men. There are words presupposing negative connotations for men who do not dominate "their" women, *henpecked* and *pussy-whipped* among them. There is no female equivalent. (2003:162; emphasis in original)

rise of feminism, many magazines devoted attention to women's achievements. Alongside these new magazines, many "ladies" magazines continue to define the lives of women in terms of men—husbands or lovers.

Two of the network news programs are now anchored by women (Katie Couric and Diane Sawyer), while "Rachel Maddow rules on cable" (Pollitt 2010). Still, women are underrepresented in television newsrooms. In 2008, women made up 40 percent of the television news workforce, whereas the percentage of women news directors in television was at 28 (Radio-Television News Directors Association [RTNDA 2008).

Studies have continually demonstrated that highly stereotyped behavior characterizes both children's and adult programming as well as commercials. Male role models are provided in greater numbers than are female, with the exception of daytime soap operas, in which men and women are equally represented. Prime-time television is distorted. Although men represent 49 percent of the U.S. population, they represented 60 percent of prime-time television characters in 2007 (Media Report to Women 2007).

Images of women on entertainment television have changed greatly in recent decades. A report by the National Commission on Working Women found increasing diversity of characters portraying working women as television's most significant improvement. In many serials, women do play strong

Not only are women who seek power commonly vilified as animals, but also the terms used to refer to men who fail to invoke their power against women likewise appeal to images of women as animals. Women are said to "henpeck," "pussywhip," and consequently emasculate and thus dehumanize men.

These animal metaphors not only serve to degrade individuals, but some also objectify and sexualize women: referring to a woman as a "pussy" or a "piece of tail" are clear illustrations. Often this sexualization is intertwined with the imagery of the hunt, whereby the (heterosexual) man is viewed as the predator and the woman/animal his prey. Is it a coincidence that the most infamous corporate symbol of the sexualization of women—the Playboy bunny—is an animal, and a popularly hunted animal at that? The reverse is also true:

hunted animals are frequently referred to in ways that conjure up sexualized images of women. For instance, a study of sport hunting magazines details instances where bird decoys were referred to as "Barbie hens," deer antlers were referred to as "big 'uns," and the use of the feminine pronoun "she" to refer to hunted animals was commonplace (Kalof, Fitzgerald, and Baralt forthcoming).

In addition to the use of animal metaphors to degrade and sexualize women, animals and women who do not conform to society's demands and standards are also referred to using the same terms. For instance, the term *maiden* refers to a horse who has not won a race, but it is also used to refer to an unmarried woman (Romaine 1999:92). Animals and women who are perceived as being "past their prime" and whose bodies no longer neatly

conform to the needs of society are referred to using the same terms, such as "biddy": "The hen ('biddy') who offers neither desirable flesh nor continued profitable egg production is regarded as 'spent'—and discarded. No longer sexually attractive or able to reproduce, the human 'old biddy' too has outlived her usefulness" (Dunayer 1995:13).

At first glance these linguistic metaphors may appear to be harmless. However, they not only reflect the current place of women and animals in society relative to men, but they also serve to subtly reinforce it. Therefore, these metaphors, and what they represent, warrant further examination and critique.

Source: Amy Fitzgerald, Department of Sociology, Michigan State University, 2004. This essay was written expressly for *Social Problems*, 10th edition.

and intelligent roles, but in just as many shows, men are still the major characters and women are cast as glamorous objects, scheming villains, or servants. And for every contemporary show that includes positive images of women, there are numerous other shows in which women are sidekicks to men, sexual objects, or helpless imbeciles (Andersen 2009:62). In response to the imbalances in prime-time television, the National Organization for Women states, "If you are a middle-aged woman, a lesbian, a Latina, a woman with a disability, a woman of size, a low-income mom struggling to get by . . . good luck finding programming that even pretends to reflect your life" (National Organization for Women 2002).

Television commercials have long presented the sexes in stereotyped ways. Women appear less frequently in ads than men, are much more likely to be seen in the home than in work settings, and are much more likely to appear in ads for food, home, and beauty/clothing products (Andersen 2009:61). In the past decade, however, the potential buying power of working women has caused the advertising industry to modify women's image. Working women have become targets of advertising campaigns. But most advertising aimed at career women sends the message that they should be superwomen—managing multiple roles of wife, mother, and career woman, and being glamorous as well. Such multifarious expectations are not imposed on men.

The advertising aimed at "the new woman" places additional stresses on women and at the same time upholds male privilege. Television commercials that show women breezing in from their jobs to sort the laundry or pop dinner in the oven reinforce the notion that it is all right for a woman to pursue a career as long as she can still handle the housework.

Religion

Most U.S. religions follow a typical pattern. The clergy is male, while the vast majority of worshipers are women (Paulson 2000). Despite important differences in religious doctrines, there are common views about gender. Among these are the beliefs that (1) women and men have different missions and different standards of behavior, and (2) although women and men are equal in the eyes of the deity, women are to some degree subordinated to men (Sapiro 1999:219; Thomas, 2007). Limiting discussion to the Judeo-Christian heritage, let us examine some teachings from the Old and New Testaments regarding the place of women. The Old Testament established male supremacy in many ways. Images of God are male. Females were second to males because Eve was created from Adam's rib. According to the scriptures, only a male could divorce a spouse. A woman who was not a virgin at marriage could be stoned to death. Girls could be purchased for marriage. Employers were enjoined to pay women only three-fifths the wages of men: "If a male from 20 to 60 years of age, the equivalent is 50 shekels of silver by the sanctuary weight; if it is a female, the equivalent is 30 shekels" (Leviticus 27:3–4). As Gilman (1971) notes:

> The Old Testament devotes inordinate space to the listing of long lines of male descent to the point where it would seem that for centuries women "begat" nothing but male offspring. Although there are heroines in the Old Testament—Judith, Esther and the like—it's clear that they functioned like the heroines of Greek drama and later of French: as counterweights in the imaginations of certain sensitive men to the degraded position of women in actual life. The true spirit of the tradition was unabashedly revealed in the prayer men recited every day in the synagogue: "Blessed art Thou, O Lord . . . for not making me a woman." (51)

The New Testament retained the tradition of male dominance. Jesus was the son of a male God, not of Mary, who remained a virgin. All the disciples were male. The great leader of the early church, the Apostle Paul, was especially adamant in arguing for the primacy of males over females. According to Paul, "the husband is supreme over his wife," "woman was created for man's sake," and "women should not teach nor usurp authority over the man, but to be silent." Contemporary religious thought reflects this heritage. In 1998, the Southern Baptist Convention, the nation's biggest Protestant denomination, amended its statement of beliefs to include a declaration that "a woman shall submit herself graciously to her husband's leadership and a husband should provide for, protect and lead his family." Some denominations limit or even forbid women from decision making. Others allow women to vote but limit their participation in leadership roles.

There are, however, many indications of change. Throughout the West, women are more involved in churches and religious life (Paulson 2000; Van Biema 2004; Thomas 2007). The National Council of Churches seeks to end sexist language and to use "inclusive language" in the Revised Standard Version of the Bible. Terms such as *man, mankind, brothers, sons, churchmen,* and *laymen* would be replaced by neutral terms that include reference to female gender. But these terms, although helpful, do not address a fundamental theological cause: "When God is perceived as a male, then expecting a male voice interpreting the word of God naturally follows" (Zelizer 2004:11A).

The percentage of female seminary students has exploded in the past few decades. Yet women made up only 14.8 percent of the nation's clergy in 2008 (Bureau of Labor Statistics 2009b). Across the United States, women clergy are struggling for equal rights, bumping up against what many call a "stained glass ceiling." Today, half of all religious denominations in the United States ordain women. At the same time, the formal rules and practices discriminate against women. In denominations that ordain women and those that do not, women often fill the same jobs: leading small churches, directing special church programs, preaching, and evangelizing (Van Biema 2004). Despite the opposition of organized religion, many women are making advances within established churches and leaving their mark on the ministerial profession.

The Law

That the law has been discriminatory against women is beyond dispute. We need only recall that women were denied the right to vote prior to the passage of the Nineteenth Amendment.

During the past four decades, legal reforms and public policy changes have attempted to place women and men on more equal footing. Some laws that focus on employment include the 1963 Equal Pay Act, Title VII of the 1964 Civil Rights Act, and the 1978 Pregnancy Discrimination Act. The 1972 Educational Amendments Act calls for gender equality in education. Other reforms have provided the framework for important institutional changes. For example, sexist discrimination in the granting of credit has been ruled illegal, and discrimination against pregnant women in the workforce is now prohibited by the law. Affirmative action (which is now under assault) remedied some kinds of gender discrimination in employment. Sexist discrimination in housing is prohibited, and the gendered requirements in the airline industry have been eliminated. Such laws now provide a basis for the equal treatment of women and men. But the force of these new laws depends on how well they are enforced and how they are interpreted in the courts when they are disputed.

Legal discrimination remains in a number of areas. There are still hundreds of sections of the U.S. legal code and of state laws that are riddled with sex bias or sex-based terminology, in conflict with the ideal of equal rights for women (Benokraitis and Feagin 1995:24). State laws vary considerably concerning property ownership by spouses, welfare benefits, and the legal status of homemakers.

Today, many legal reforms are threatened by recent Supreme Court decisions in the areas of abortion and affirmative action. In 1989 and 1992, the Supreme Court narrowed its 1973 landmark *Roe v. Wade* decision, which established the right to abortion. *Roe v. Wade* was a major breakthrough for women, giving them the choice to control their bodies. The 1989 and 1992 decisions made it easier for the states to restrict women's reproductive freedoms at any stage of pregnancy, including the first three months. These decisions have steadily chipped away at a woman's right to abortion.

Roe v. Wade is still on the books, but the Supreme Court has returned the nation to a pre-Roe patchwork of laws and conditions by moving the battleground to state legislatures. State restrictions that now make it more difficult for women to obtain abortions include parental notification rules and mandatory waiting periods. In 2005, the House passed a teen endangerment bill, restricting the ability of young women to obtain an abortion outside their home state. The bill makes no exception for a medical emergency unless the young woman has complied with her home state's parental involvement laws (National Organization for Women 2005). Since 1995, more than 4,000 antichoice measures have been enacted. In the congressional heath care reform debate of 2010, antichoice legislators removed abortion coverage from the health care bill (National Organization of Women 2010).

Politics

Women's political participation has always been different from that of men. Women received the right to vote in 1920, when the Nineteenth Amendment was ratified. Although women make up a very small percentage of officeholders, 1992 was a turning point for women in politics. Controversies such as Anita Hill's harassment allegations, the abortion rights battle, and the lack of representation at all levels of politics propelled women into the political arena. In 1992, Congress experienced its biggest influx of women (and minorities) in history. Subsequent elections have increased the number of women in our national legislature. As of 2009, 17 U.S. senators are women, and 73 women are in the House of Representatives (Center for American Women and Politics 2009). (See Table 2 for the percentages of U.S. women in elective office.) If Congress were representative of the nation, the Senate would have 51 women and the House 222 (Sklar 2004c).

The gender gap in our nation's capital is scandalous. In Washington, D.C.'s less visible workforce of professional staff employees, women hold 60 percent of the jobs, but they are nowhere equal to men. Congress has two classes of personal staff employees: highly paid men who hold most of the power and lower-paid women who are relegated to clerical and support staff. Many answer the phones and write letters to constituents—invisible labor that is crucial to their boss's reelection.

The United States lags behind other countries in the number of women elected officials. (Pictured is Nancy Pelosi, Speaker of the U.S. House of Representatives)

AP Images/Dennis Cook

TABLE 2

Percentages of Women in Elective Offices

Year	U.S. Congress	Statewide Elective	State Legislatures	Year	U.S. Congress	Statewide Elective	State Legislatures
1979	3%	11%	10%	1999	12.1%	27.6%	22.4%
1981	4%	11%	12%	2001	13.6%	27.6%	22.4%
1983	4%	11%	13%	2003	13.6%	26.0%	22.4%
1985	5%	14%	15%	2004	13.8%	26.0%	22.5%
1987	5%	14%	16%	2005	15.0%	25.7%	22.7%
1989	5%	14%	17%	2006	15.0%	25.1%	22.8%
1991	6%	18%	18%	2007	16.1%	24.1%	23.5%
1993	10.1%	22.2%	20.5%	2008	16.5%	23.2%	23.7%
1995	10.3%	25.9%	20.6%	2009	16.8%	22.6%	24.3%
1997	11.0%	25.4%	21.6%				

[1] According to data from the U.S. Bureau of the Census.

[2] Information was compiled using the United States Conference of Mayors' 2009 website directory, www.usmayors.org/uscm/meet_mayors, as the primary reference

Source: Center for Women in Politics (CWAP). "Women in Elective Office 2009." Eagleton Institute of Politics, Rutgers. The State University of New Jersey. p. 2. http://www.rci.rutgers.edu/~cwap/Officeholders/elective.pdf; "Women Officeholders Fact Sheets and Summaries, 2008."

Women had a major place in the 2008 presidential election, with Hillary Clinton in the Democratic primary and Sarah Palin as the Republican nominee for vice president. Although neither candidate was elected to office, their campaigns sparked a national debate about women's access to political power. Globally, women are making substantial gains in politics. The United States has just over 16 percent female lawmakers in Congress. Although many facets of the gender gap appear to be narrowing, as Nancy Pelosi was sworn in as the first female speaker of the House of Representatives, sixty-five countries do better than the United States when it comes to women serving in national legislatures. For example, in Norway, 37 percent of lawmakers are women. In Sweden it is 45 percent (Wheatcroft 2007). Furthermore, women have served as heads of state in nations such as Canada, France, Germany, United Kingdom, Turkey, Pakistan, Chile, South Korea, and Liberia (Falk 2008). In the 200-year history of the United States, there has never been a female president or vice president. With the appointment of Justice Sonia Sotomayor to the highest court in the land, there are now two female justices on the U.S. Supreme Court.

The gender gap refers to measurable differences in the way women and men vote and view political issues. Voting studies of national elections since 1980 demonstrate that women often vote differently from men, especially on issues of economics, social welfare, and war and peace (Renzetti and Curran 2003:229).

STRUCTURED GENDER INEQUALITY

In this section of the chapter, we focus on the contemporary workplace because its patterns of segregation are among "the most tenacious problems in U.S. society" (Williams 1992:235). In fact, the United States has one of the highest levels of workplace gender inequality in the industrial world (Kimmel 2004:186). The workplace distributes women and men in different settings, assigns them different duties, and rewards them unequally.

Occupational Distribution

The new economy has changed both women's and men's employment rates. Increasingly, it is viewed as "normal" for adult women and men, regardless of parental status, to be employed (Bianchi 1995:110). The increase in women's participation in the U.S. labor force is one of the most important social, economic, and cultural trends of the past century. Yet men's labor force participation rates have decreased slightly while women's have increased dramatically. (See the labor force participation rates for men and women, 1950 through 2009, in Figure 1.)

Women's labor force participation has grown at a faster pace than men's in recent decades. Between 1970 and the early 1990s, women's number in the labor force increased twice as fast as those of men. At present, women's rate of labor force participation is holding steadily, while men's is declining slightly. Today, as in the past, the proportions of employed women vary by race. African American women have had a long history of high workforce participation rates. In 2004, they edged ahead of other women. By 2008, they participated in the labor force at a rate of 61 percent; 59 percent of White women were in the labor force in 2008, compared with 56 percent of Hispanic women (Bureau of Labor Statistics 2008). (See the projected labor force participation rates for women by race in Table 3.)

Today's working woman may be any age. She may be any race. She may be a nurse or a secretary or a factory worker or a department store clerk or a public school teacher. Or she may be—though it is much less common—a physician or the president of a corporation or the head of a school system. Hers may be the familiar face seen daily behind the counter at the neighborhood coffee shop, or she may work virtually unseen, mopping floors at midnight in an empty office building. The typical female worker is a wage earner in clerical, service, manufacturing, or some technical jobs that pay poorly, give her little possibility for advancement, and often little control over her work. More women work as sales workers, secretaries, and cashiers than in any other line of work. The largest share of women (54 percent), however, works in "service" and "sales and office" jobs (Bureau of Labor Statistics 2006c).

FIGURE 1

Labor Force Participation Rate by Sex, 1950–2009, and Projected, 2009–2016

Sources: Occupational Outlook Quarterly, Winter 2001–2002. Washington DC: U.S. Department of Labor, Bureau of Labor Statistics, p. 39; "Employment Projections." U.S. Department of Labor, 2007. Online: http://www.bls.gov/emp/emplab05.htm

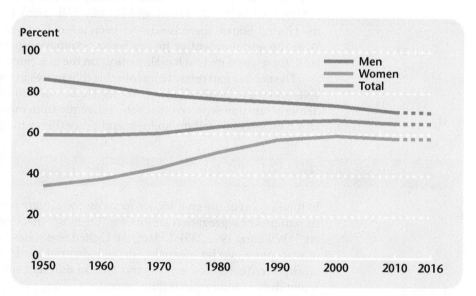

TABLE 3

Labor Force Participation Rates for Women, by Race, Selected Years and Projected 2016

Year	Black	White	Hispanic	Asian
1975	48.8	45.9	n.a.	n.a.
1986	56.9	55.4	50.1	57.0
1996	60.4	59.8	53.4	58.8
2006	61.5	59.3	56.1	57.6
2016	63.1	58.8	57.8	58.7

Source: "Employment Projections," U.S. Department of Labor, 2007, Table 3. Online http://www.bls.gov/emp/emplab05.htm

Economic restructuring has fundamentally altered the gender distribution of the labor force. Since 1980, women have taken 80 percent of the new jobs created in the economy. This gender shift in the U.S. workforce has accelerated in the current economic downturn, which has affected men and women differently. The current recession has disproportionately laid off men, who are more likely to work in cyclically sensitive industries like manufacturing and construction. Women, on the other hand, are overrepresented in economic sectors that are growing, like education and health care. As a result, for the first time in history, women are coming close to representing the majority of the national workforce. As of June 2009, women held 49.83 percent of jobs, compared to men, who held 50.17 percent of jobs (Cauchon 2009; Rampell 2009). Although this marks a historic shift in the national workforce, it does not mean that women have achieved equality in the workforce. Women still lag behind on many measures. In this chapter we examine gender segregation and earnings.

Gender segregation refers to the pattern whereby women and men are situated in different jobs throughout the labor force (Andersen 2009:124). The overall degree of gender stratification has not changed much since 1900. Women and men are still concentrated in different occupations (Dubeck and Dunn 2002). Overall, just 15 percent of women work in jobs typically held by men (engineer, stockbroker, judge), whereas fewer than 8 percent of men hold female-dominated jobs such as nurse, teacher, or sales clerk (Bernstein 2004).

In 2009, the six most prevalent occupations for women in order of magnitude were: (1) secretary and administrative assistant, (2) registered nurse, (3) elementary and middle school teacher, (4) cashier, (5) retail sales, and (6) nursing, psychiatric, and home health aide (Bureau of Labor Statistics 2009b; see Table 4).

Media reports of women's gains in traditionally male jobs are often misleading. In blue-collar work, for example, gains look dramatic at first glance, with the number of women in blue-collar jobs rising by 80 percent in the 1970s. But the increase was so high because women had been virtually excluded from these occupations until then. Women's entry into skilled blue-collar work such as construction and automaking was limited by the very slow growth in those jobs (Amott 1993:76). In 2008, only 1.6 percent of automotive service technicians and mechanics, 3 percent of construction workers, and 1 percent of tool and die makers were women (Bureau of Labor Statistics 2009b). The years from 1970 to

TABLE 4

Twenty Leading Occupations of Employed Women 2008 Annual Averages (employment in thousands)

Occupation	Total Employed Women	Total Employed (Men and Women)	Percent Women	Women's Median Weekly Earnings
Total, 16 years and older (all employed women)	67,876	145,362	46.7	$638
Secretaries and administrative assistants	3,168	3,296	96.1	614
Registered nurses	2,548	2,778	91.7	1,011
Elementary and middle school teachers	2,403	2,958	81.2	871
Cashiers	2,287	3,031	75.5	349
Retail salespersons	1,783	3,416	52.2	440
Nursing, psychiatric, and home health aides	1,675	1,889	88.7	424
First-line supervisors/managers of retail sales workers	1,505	3,471	43.3	556
Waiters and waitresses	1,471	2,010	73.2	367
Receptionists and information clerks	1,323	1,413	93.6	502
Bookkeeping, accounting, and auditing clerks	1,311	1,434	91.4	603
Customer service representatives	1,302	1,908	68.3	568
Maids and housekeeping cleaners	1,287	1,434	89.7	371
Child care workers	1,256	1,314	95.6	393
Managers, all others	1,244	3,473	35.8	1,010
First-line supervisors/managers of office and administrative support	1,169	1,641	71.2	688
Accountants and auditors	1,077	1,762	61.1	908
Office clerks, general	993	1,176	84.4	582
Teacher assistants	936	1,020	91.8	413
Cooks	801	1,997	40.1	363
Personal and home care aides	744	871	85.4	404

Source: U.S. Department of Labor, Bureau of Labor Statistics, Women's Bureau, 2008. "20 Leading Occupations of Employed Women 2008 Annual Averages (employment in thousands)," http://www.dol.gov/wb/factsheets/20lead2008.htm

1990 found more women in the fields of law, medicine, journalism, and higher education. Today, women fill 37 percent of all management positions (up from 19 percent in 1972). Still, there are fewer women than men in prestige jobs. In 2008, only 30 percent of lawyers, and 35 percent of physicians and surgeons were women (Bureau of Labor Statistics 2009b).

Although women have made inroads in the high-paying and high-prestige professions, not all have fared equally. White women were the major beneficiaries of the new opportunities. There has been an occupational "trickle down" effect, as White women improved their occupational status by moving into male-dominated professions such as law and medicine, and African American women moved into the female-dominated jobs, such as social work and teaching, vacated by White women. This improvement for White women was related to federal civil rights legislation, particularly the requirement that firms receiving federal contracts comply with affirmative action guidelines (Amott 1993:76).

The Earnings Gap

Although women's labor force participation rates have risen, the gap between women's and men's earnings has remained relatively constant for three decades. Women workers earn less than men even when they work in similar occupations and have the same levels of education.

The pay gap between women and men has narrowed. It hovered between 70 and 74 percent throughout the 1990s. In 2009, women earned 78.2 cents for every dollar men earned. Closing the wage gap has been slow, amounting to less than half a cent per year! "At this rate, 87 more years could go by before women and men reach parity" (Sklar 2004c).

For women of color, earning discrimination is even greater. Women's incomes are lower than men's in every racial group. Among women and men working year-round and full-time in 2008, White women earned 80 percent of White men's earnings; Black women earned 89 percent of Black men's earnings; Hispanic women earned 89 percent of Hispanic men's earnings (Bureau of Labor Statistics, 2009b; see Figure 2). The earnings gap affects the well-being of women and their families. If women earned the same as men, their annual family incomes would rise by $4,000. and poverty rates would be cut in half. Their lost earnings could have bought a home, educated their children, and been set aside for retirement (Greim 1998; Love 1998; The Wage Gap 2003).

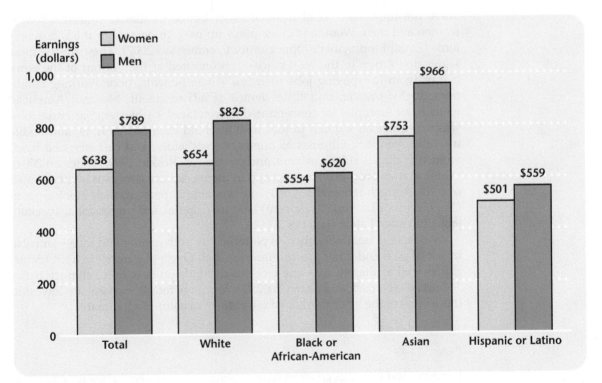

Figure 2

Median Weekly Earnings of Full-Time Wage and Salary Workers, by Sex, Race, and Hispanic or Latino Ethnicity, 2008 Annual Averages

Source: U.S. Department of Labor, Bureau of Labor Statistics, "Highlights of Women's Earnings in 2008" (July 2009), p. 4.
http://www.dol.gov/wbls.gov/opub

The earnings gap persists for several reasons:

- Women are concentrated in lower-paying occupations.
- Women enter the labor force at different and lower-paying levels than men.
- Women as a group have less education and experience than men; therefore, they are paid less than men.
- Women tend to work less overtime than men.

These conditions explain only part of the earnings gap between women and men. They do not explain why female workers earn less than male workers with the same educational level, work histories, skills, and work experience. Men with professional degrees may expect to earn almost $2 million more than their female counterparts (Sklar 2004c). Study after study finds that if women were men with the same credentials, they would earn substantially more. Research on the income gap has found that women's and men's credentials explain some differences, but experience accounts for only one-third of the wage gap. The largest part of the wage gap is caused by sex discrimination in the labor market that blocks women's access to the better-paying jobs through hiring, promotion, and simply paying women less than men in any job (*ISR Newsletter* 1982; Dunn 1996; Leinwand 1999).

Intersection of Race and Gender in the Workplace

There are important racial differences in the occupational concentration of women and men. Women of color make up over 16 percent of the U.S. workforce (Equal Employment Opportunity Commission 2007). They are the most segregated group in the workplace—concentrated at the bottom of the work hierarchy, in low-paying jobs with few fringe benefits, poor working conditions, high turnover, and little chance of advancement. Mexican American women, for example, are concentrated in secretarial, cashier, and janitorial jobs; Central American women in jobs as household cleaners, janitors, and textile machine operators; Filipinas as nurses, nurses' aides, and cashiers; and Black women as nurses aides, cashiers, and secretaries (Reskin 1999; Andersen 2009). White women are a privileged group in the workplace compared with women of color. A much larger share of White women (38 percent) than Black women (31 percent) or Latinas (23 percent) held managerial and professional specialty jobs (Bureau of Labor Statistics 2009b).

Workplace inequality, then, is patterned by both gender and race—and also by social class and other group characteristics. One's placement in a job hierarchy as well as the rewards one receives depends on how these characteristics "combine" (Dubeck and Dunn 2002:48). Earnings for all workers are lowest in those areas of the labor market where women of color predominate.

Pay Equity

Women's low earnings create serious problems for women themselves, for their families, and for their children. Increasingly, families need the incomes of both spouses, and many working women are the sole providers for their children. Given these trends, equal pay is a top social concern.

The Equal Pay Act, passed in 1963, made it illegal to pay women less for doing the same work as men. However, the law is difficult to enforce because women and men are located in different occupations. For example, to be a secretary (usually a woman) requires as much education and takes as much responsibility as being a carpenter (usually a man), but the secretarial job pays far less (Folbre, Heintz, and Center for Popular Economics 2000). Pay equity in jobs that are dominated by women (where women comprise 70 percent or more of the workforce) would result in an 18 percent increase in wages for women (National Organization for Women 2005).

In the early 1980s, a number of state and local governments began addressing the pay-gap issue by instituting policies for pay equity in the public sector. Pay-equity policies are a means to eliminating sex and race discrimination in the wage-setting system. Pay equity means that the criteria employers use to set wages must be gender and race neutral. Today, the National Committee on Pay Equity supports legislation in the U.S. Senate aimed at curbing wage discrimination (National Committee on Pay Equity 2007a). In 2009, the Lilly Ledbetter Fair Pay Act became a crucial step forward in the battle to close the wage gap. The law reverses a 2007 Supreme Court ruling and restores the right of workers to go to court to hold their employers accountable for pay discrimination (National Committee on Pay Equity 2009; Samuels 2009).

Since 1980, more than twenty states have implemented pay-equity programs that reduced the gender wage gap. Minnesota, Oregon, and Washington were among the most successful (Folbre et al., 2000). Pay-equity struggles are difficult. Yet, in recent years, women willing to fight for their rights have won multimillion-dollar pay-equity settlements from corporations such as Home Depot, Eastman Kodak, Merrill Lynch, and Texaco.

How Workplace Inequality Operates

Why are women unequal in the workplace? Several theories are used to explain job segregation and ongoing wage inequality. Some focus on individuals, others focus on structural conditions, and others call on interactional processes to explain women's disadvantages in the workplace.

Popular explanations for gender differentials point to women themselves. They claim that women's socialization, their education, and the "choices" they make to take time out of the workforce to have children produce different work experiences for men and women. *Human capital theory*, for example, rests on the individual characteristics that workers bring to their jobs. Of course, time in the workplace, education, and experience all play a part. But the reality is far more complex. Research finds that woman's individual characteristics, or their human capital, explains only a small part of employment inequality (Ridgeway 1997:224). Research shows that ideas and practices about gender are embedded in workplace structures. This means that the workplace itself produces gender disparities (Acker 1990; Williams 1995; Martin 2003). Let us examine the organization of the labor force that disadvantage women and advantage men.

Dual labor market theory centers on the labor market itself. The labor market is divided into two separate segments, with different characteristics, different roles, and different rewards. The primary segment is characterized by stability, high wages, promotion ladders, opportunities for advancement, good working conditions, and provisions for job security. The secondary market is characterized by low wages, fewer or no promotion ladders, poor working conditions, and little provision for job security. Women's work tends to fall in the secondary segment. For example, clerical work, the largest single occupation for women, has many of the characteristics associated with the secondary segment.

To understand women's disadvantages, we must look at structural arrangements that women confront in the workplace. A classic study by Rosabeth Kanter (1977), *Men and Women of the Corporation,* found that organizational location is more important than gender in shaping workers' behavior. Although women and men behave differently at work, Kanter demonstrated that the differences were created by organizational locations. Workers in low-mobility or blocked situations (regardless of their sex) tended to limit their aspirations, seek satisfaction in activities outside work, dream of escape, and create sociable peer groups in which interpersonal relationships take over other aspects of work. Kanter argued that "when women seem to be less motivated or committed, it is probably because their jobs carry less opportunity" (Kanter 1977:159).

Many features of work itself block women's advancement. For example, some structural explanations call on gender segregation, per se, in which women and men are concentrated in occupational categories based on gender. Much research in this tradition has explained why job segregation and wage inequality persist even as women have flooded the workforce and moved into "male" jobs. Sociologists Barbara Reskin and Patricia Roos (1990) studied eleven once-male-dominated fields that had become integrated between 1979 and 1988: book editing, pharmacy, public relations, bank management, systems analysis, insurance sales, real-estate sales, insurance adjusting and examining, bartending, baking, and typesetting and composition. Reskin and Roos found that women gained entry into these fields only *after* earnings and upward mobility in each of these fields declined; that is, salaries had gone down, prestige had diminished, or the work had become more like "women's work" (Kroeger 1994:50). Furthermore, in each of these occupations, women specialized in lower-status specialties, in different and less desirable work settings, and in lower-paid industries. Reskin and Roos call this process *ghettoization.* Some occupations changed their sex-typing completely, whereas some became resegregated by race as well as gender (Reskin and Roos 1990; Amott 1993:80).

Many fields that have opened up to women no longer have the economic or social status they once possessed. Their structures now have two tiers: (1) higher-paying, higher-ranking jobs with more authority and (2) lower-paying, more routinized jobs with less authority. Women are concentrated in the new, more routinized sectors of professional employment, but the upper tier of relatively autonomous work continues to be male dominated, with only token increases in female employment (Carter and Carter 1981). For example, women's entry into three prestige professions—medicine, college teaching, and law—has been accompanied by organizational changes. In medicine, hospital-based practice has grown as more women have entered the profession. Women doctors are more likely than men to be found in hospital-based practice, which provides less autonomy than the more traditional office-based practice. In college teaching, many women are employed in two-year colleges, where heavy teaching loads leave little time or energy for writing and publishing—the keys to academic career advancement. And in law, women's advancement to prestigious positions is being eroded by the growth of the legal clinic, where much legal work is routinized.

Many organizational features block women's advancement. In the white-collar workforce, the well-documented phenomenon of women going just so far—and no further—in their occupations and professions is called the glass ceiling. This refers to the invisible barriers that limit women's mobility despite their motivation and capacity for positions of power and prestige (Lorber 1994:227). In contrast, men who enter female-dominated professions generally encounter *structural advantages,* a "glass escalator," which tends to enhance their careers (Williams 1992).

Many of the old discriminatory patterns are difficult to change. In the professions, for example, sponsor–protégé systems and informal interactions among colleagues limit women's mobility. Sponsorship is important in training personnel and ensuring leadership continuity. Women are less likely to be acceptable as protégés. Furthermore, their sex status limits or excludes their involvement in the buddy system or the old-boy network (Epstein 1970). Such informal interactions continually re-create gender inequality. *Interactional theories* also explain why gender is such a major force in the labor process. Taken-for-granted interactions block women's progress:

> *Interactional processes contribute to the sex-labeling of jobs, to the devaluation of women's jobs, to forms of sex-discrimination, . . . to differences between men's and women's reward expectations, and to the processes by which women's entrance into male occupations sometimes leads to feminization or resegregation by specialty. (Ridgeway 1997:231)*

Individual, structural, and interactional explanations of women's workplace inequality rest on *social processes* rather than outright discrimination. But it is important to recognize that outright discrimination can be found in the workplace. For example, sexual harassment affects women in all types of jobs. Sexual harassment can include unwanted leers, comments, suggestions, or physical contact of a sexual nature as well as unwelcome requests for sexual favors. Some research finds that sexual harassment is prevalent in male-dominated jobs in which women are new hires because it is a way for male workers to dominate and control women who should be their equals. The problem is one outcome of gender segregation, with serious and harmful consequences for many women (Renzetti and Curan 2003:226–227).

Gender in the Global Economy

Gender relations in the United States and the world reflect the larger changes of economic globalization. Private businesses make investment decisions that have a major impact on the work, community, and family lives of women and men all around the world. In their search for profit, transnational corporations have turned to developing nations and the work of women and children. The demand for less expensive labor has produced a global system of production with a strong gendered component. The international division of labor affects both men and women. As manufacturing jobs switch to low-wage economies, men are often displaced. The global assembly line uses the labor of women, many of them young, single, and from poor rural areas. Women workers of particular classes/castes and races from poor countries provide a cheap labor supply for the manufacture of commodities distributed in the richer industrial nations.

Economic globalization is altering gender relations around the world by bringing women into the public sphere (Walby 2000). Although this development presents new opportunities for women, the disruption of male dominance can also result in the reaffirmation of local gender hierarchies through right-wing militia movements, religious revivalism, and other forms of masculine fundamentalism (Connell 1998). In addition, old forms of women's exploitation and abuse are being remade on a massive scale. For example, the commodification of women in the sex industry is now seen as an important part of globalization. The worldwide expansion of the sex club industry is closely linked to organized crime and the trafficking of women and girls across national boundaries (Jeffries 2008).

THE COSTS AND CONSEQUENCES OF SEXISM

Who Benefits?

Clearly, gender inequality enters all aspects of social life in the United States and globally. This inequality is profitable to certain segments of the economy, and it also gives privileges to individual men.

Transnational corporations derive extra profits from paying women less than men. Women's segregation in low-paying jobs produces higher profits for some economic sectors—namely, those where most workers are women. Women who are sole breadwinners and those who are in the workforce on a temporary basis have always been a source of exploitable labor. These women provide a significant proportion of the marginal labor force capitalists need to draw on during upswings in the business cycle and to release during downswings (Edwards, Reich, and Weisskopf 1978:333).

Gender inequality is suited to the needs of the economy in other ways as well. The U.S. economy must accumulate capital and maintain labor power. This requires that all workers be physically and emotionally maintained. Who provides the daily maintenance that enable workers to be a part of the labor force? Women! They maintain workers through the unpaid work they do caring for home, children, and elders. Their caregiving keeps the economy going, and it also provides privileges for individual men at women's expense.

The Social and Individual Costs

Gender inequality benefits certain segments of society. Nevertheless, society at large and individual women and men pay a high price for inequality. Sexism diminishes the quality of life for all people. Our society is deprived of half of its resources when women are denied full and equal participation in its institutions. If women are systematically kept from jobs requiring leadership, creativity, and productivity, the economy suffers. The pool of talent consisting of half the population will continue to be underutilized.

Women's inequality also produces suffering for millions. We have seen that individual women pay a heavy price for economic discrimination. Their children pay as well. The poverty caused by gender inequality is one of the most pressing social problems facing the United States in the new century. Adult women's chances of living in poverty are still higher than men's at every age. This phenomenon is called the *feminization of poverty* (Pearce 1978). Economist Nancy Folbre points out that the highest risk of poverty comes from being female and having children—which helps explain the high rates of both female and child poverty in the United States. Folbre calls this trend the "pauperization of motherhood" (Folbre 1985; cited in Albelda and

214

Tilly 1997:23). Of course, sexism produces suffering around the world. Some women are persecuted simply because they are women.

Sexism also denies *men* the potential for full human development because gender segregation denies employment opportunities to men who wish to enter such fields as nursing, grade-school teaching, or secretarial work. Eradicating sexism would benefit such males. It would benefit all males who have been forced into stereotypic male behaviors. In learning to be men, boys express their masculinity through physical courage, toughness, competitiveness, and aggression. Expressions typically associated with femininity, such as gentleness, expressiveness, and responsiveness, are seen as undesirable for males. Rigid gender norms make men pay a price for their masculinity.

Male inexpressiveness can hinder communication between husbands and wives, between fathers and children; it has been called "a tragedy of American society" (Balswick and Peck 1971). Certainly, it is a tragedy for the man himself, crippled by an inability to show the best part of a human being—his warm and tender feelings for other people (Balswick and Collier 1976:59).

FIGHTING THE SYSTEM

Feminist Movements in the United States

Gender inequality in this society has led to feminist social movements. Three stages of feminism have been aimed at overcoming sex discrimination. The first stage grew from the abolition movement of the 1830s. Working to abolish slavery, women found that they could not function as equals with their male abolitionist friends. They became convinced that women's freedom was as important as freedom from slavery. In July 1848, the first convention in history devoted to issues of women's position and rights was held at Seneca Falls, New York. Participants in the Seneca Falls convention approved a declaration of independence, asserting that men and women are created equal and that they are endowed with certain inalienable rights.

During the Civil War, feminists for the most part turned their attention to the emancipation of Blacks. After the war and the ratification of the Thirteenth Amendment abolishing slavery, feminists were divided between those seeking far-ranging economic, religious, and social reforms and those seeking voting rights for women. The second stage of feminism gave priority to women's suffrage. The women's suffrage amendment, introduced into every session of Congress from 1878 on, was ratified on August 26, 1920—nearly three-quarters of a century after the demand for women's suffrage had been made at the Seneca Falls convention. From 1920 until the 1960s, feminism was dormant. "So much energy had been expended in achieving the right to vote that the women's movement virtually collapsed from exhaustion" (Hole and Levine 1979:554).

Feminism was reawakened in the 1960s. Social movements aimed at inequalities gave rise to an important branch of contemporary feminism. The civil rights movement and other protest movements of the 1960s spread the ideology of equality. But like the early feminists, women involved in political protest movements found that male dominance characterized even movements seeking social equality. Finding injustice in freedom movements, they broadened their protest to such far-reaching concerns as health care, family life, and relationships between the sexes. Another strand of contemporary feminism emerged among

UPI Photo/Landov

Surrounded by members of Congress, President Barack Obama signs the Lilly Ledbetter bill with Lilly Ledbetter, at center, behind Obama.

professional women who discovered sex discrimination in earnings and advancement. Formal organizations such as the National Organization for Women evolved, seeking legislation to overcome sex discrimination (Freeman 1979).

These two branches of contemporary feminism gave rise to a feminist consciousness among millions of U.S. women. As a consequence, during the 1960s and early 1970s, many changes occurred in the roles of women and men. However, periods of recession, high unemployment, and inflation in the late 1970s fed a backlash against feminism. The contemporary women's movement may be the first in U.S. history to face the opposition of an organized antifeminist social movement. From the mid-1970s, a coalition of groups calling themselves profamily and prolife emerged. These groups, drawn from right-wing political organizations and religious organizations, oppose feminist gains in reproductive, family, and antidiscrimination policies. In addition, many gains have been set back by opposition to affirmative action programs and other equal rights policies. Political, legal, and media opposition to feminism continues to undermine women's equality (Faludi 1991).

Women's Struggles in the Twenty-First Century

The women's movement is not over. Quite the contrary, the women's movement remains one of the most influential sources of social change, even though there is not a unified organization that represents feminism (Andersen 2009:351). Not only do mainstream feminist organizations persist, but also the struggles for women's rights continue. Today, many feminist activities occur at the grassroots level, where issues of race, class, and sexuality are important. In communities across the country women and men fight

> *against the abuse of women, against corporate poisoning of their neighborhoods, against homophobia and racism, and for people-centered economic development, immigrants' rights, educational equity, and adequate wages. Many have been engaged in such struggles for most of their lives and continue despite the decline in the wider society's support for a progressive social agenda. (Naples 1998:1)*

Whether or not they call themselves feminists, activists across the country and around the world are using their community-based organizing to fight for social justice. Instead of responding passively to the outside world, women are forging new agendas and strategies to benefit women.

■ CHAPTER REVIEW

1. U.S. society, like other societies, ranks and rewards women and men unequally.
2. Gender differences are not natural. They are social inventions. Although gender divisions make women unequal to men, different groups of men exhibit varying degrees of power, and different groups of women exhibit varying levels of inequality.
3. Men as well as women are gendered beings.
4. Gender works with the inequalities of race, class, and sexuality to produce different experiences for all women and men.
5. Many sociologists have viewed gender inequality as the consequences of learned behavior. More recently, sociologists have moved from studying gender as the individual traits of women and men to studying gender as social structure and social interaction.
6. Gender inequality is reinforced through language, interpersonal behavior, mass communication, religion, the law, and politics.
7. The segregation of women in a few gendered occupations contrasts with that of men, who are distributed throughout the occupational hierarchy; and women, even with the same amount of education and when doing the same work, earn less than men in all occupations.
8. Gender segregation is the basic source of women's inequality in the workforce. Work opportunities for women tend to concentrate in a secondary market that has few advancement opportunities, fewer job benefits, and lower pay.
9. The combined effects of gender and racial segregation in the labor force keep women of color at the bottom of the work hierarchy, where working conditions are harsh and earnings are low.
10. The global economy is strongly gendered. Around the world, women's labor is the key to global development strategies.
11. Gender inequality deprives society of the potential contributions of half its members, creates poverty among families headed by women, and limits the capacities of all women and men.
12. Feminist movements aimed at eliminating inequality have created significant changes at all levels of society. Despite a backlash against feminism, women and men across the country and around the world continue to work for women's rights.

■ KEY TERMS

Sex. Biological fact of femaleness and maleness.

Gender. Cultural and social definition of feminine and masculine.

Gendered. Differentiation of women's and men's behaviors, activities, and worth.

Feminist approach. View that supports equal relations between women and men.

Gender stratification. Differential ranking and rewarding of women's and men's roles.

Gendered institutions. All social institutions are organized by gender.

Male dominance. Beliefs, meanings, and placement that value men over women and that institutionalize male control of socially valued resources.

Patriarchy. Forms of social organization in which men are dominant over women.

Compulsory heterosexuality. The system of sexuality that imposes negative sanctions on those who are homosexual or bisexual.

Sexuality. A way of organizing the social world on the basis of sexual identity.

Capitalist patriarchy. Condition of capitalism in which male supremacy keeps women in subordinate roles at work and in the home.

Gender roles approach. Males and females differ because of socialization. The assumption is that males and females learn to be different.

Gender structure approach. Males and females differ because of factors external to them.

Androgyny. The integration of traditional feminine and masculine characteristics.

Gender segregation. Pattern whereby women and men are situated in different jobs throughout the labor force.

Pay equity. Raising pay scales according to the worth of the job instead of the personal characteristics of the workers.

Glass ceiling. An invisible barrier that limits women's upward occupational mobility.

■ **SUCCEED WITH** PEARSON mysoclab **www.mysoclab.com**

Experience, Discover, Observe, Evaluate
MySocLab is designed just for you. This chapter features a pre-test and post-test to help you learn and review key concepts and terms.

Experience sociology in action with dynamic visual activities, videos, and readings to enhance your learning experience. Complete the following activities at www.mysoclab.com.

Social Explorer is an interactive application that allows you to explore Census data through interactive maps.

- Explore the Social Explorer Map: *Gender Stratification in Wealth, Power, and Privilege*

The Core Concepts in Sociology video clips offer a real-world perspective on sociological concepts.

- Watch *Gender Socialization*

MySocLibrary includes primary source readings from classic and contemporary sociologists.

- Read Jacobs, *Detours on the Road to Equality: Women, Work and Higher Education*; Espiritu, *All Men Are Not Created Equal: Asian Men in U.S. History*; Lorber, *Night to His Day: The Social Construction of Gender*

Drugs

From Chapter 13 of *Social Problems, Census Update*, Twelfth Edition. D. Stanley Eitzen, Maxine Baca Zinn, Kelly Eitzen Smith. Copyright © 2012 by Pearson Education, Inc. Published by Allyn & Bacon. All rights reserved.

Drugs

Nothing so needs reforming as other people's habits.

—Mark Twain

Throughout history, people have sought to alter their consciousness through the use of both legal and illegal substances. A **drug** is any substance that affects the structure or function of the body when ingested. This broad definition includes such substances as aspirin, caffeine, nicotine, heroin, and alcohol. Every society accepts some drugs as appropriate and regards others as unacceptable. Some drugs are considered dangerous, and others are harmless. But the definitions vary from society to society, and within U.S. society, they are inconsistent and often ambiguous.

Many people in the United States are concerned about the drug problem. But what is meant by "the drug problem"? Is drug use equated with abuse? Why are alcohol and tobacco legal drugs when they are addictive, physically harmful, and socially disruptive? Put another way, why is the use of alcohol accepted by U.S. society, whereas the use of marijuana is not? Is drug use a medical or a criminal problem?

> *In considering issues related to drug use and drug policies in the United States, it is useful to begin by noting some rather strange paradoxes. To take just one example, it is estimated that several million Americans use the antidepressant drug Prozac, and several million more use other antidepressants. These drugs are widely advertised and marketed, and the individuals who consume them experience no legal penalties for their consumption of these substances. At the same time, over half a million individuals, the majority of whom are members of minority groups, languish in American jails and prisons for possession and trafficking in consciousness-altering substances that the United States has deemed to be illegal. In fact, the increasing stringency of drug laws has been one of the primary factors associated with unprecedented levels of incarceration in the United States over the past 25 years. (Mosher and Akins 2007:x)*

Three points should be made at the outset of this discussion. First, definitions concerning drugs and drug-related behaviors are socially constructed. That is, definitions about drugs are not based on some universal standard but rather on meanings that people in groups have imputed to certain substances and behaviors. Second, as is true with all social problems, members of different societies or groups (e.g., religious and political) within societies often differ in their beliefs about this phenomenon. Third, the definition of drugs by the most powerful interest groups in a society will become part of the law and be enforced on others. Thus, the labeling of some drugs as licit and others as illicit involves politics. Therefore, in examining such topics as the history of drug laws, the extent of drug use and abuse, types of drugs, and the consequences of official drug policies, this chapter continually refers to the politics of drugs.

THE POLITICS OF DRUGS

Drugs are a social problem in U.S. society. Yet not all drugs are considered problems, nor are all people who take drugs. Some drugs are legal, and others are not. Some drugs caused problems once but are now considered safe; some that were not considered problems now are. Some drug use is labeled "abuse," whereas other use is not. Ironically, the drugs most objected to and most strictly controlled are not those most dangerous to users and society. Marijuana and heroin, though illegal, are less dangerous than are barbiturates, alcohol, and nicotine, which can be legally obtained and used indiscriminately. To explain such irrationality, we must understand how drugs and their use came to be considered safe or illicit.

Historical Legality of Drugs

The definition of drug use and abuse is complicated in U.S. society because different patterns of use are acceptable for different people. Some religious groups forbid the use of any drugs, even for medicinal purposes. Others accept medicines but reject all forms of drugs, including caffeine, for recreational use. At the other extreme are groups that may use drugs in their religious rituals to expand the mind. Time also changes interpretation. Early in the twentieth century, for example, it was socially acceptable for men to smoke tobacco, but not for women to do so. Then around 1950 or so, it became socially acceptable for women to smoke tobacco, and smoking was regularly seen in movies and on television. Now, increasingly, smokers of both sexes find their smoking unacceptable in public places.

Not only is there variance from group to group within society and from time to time, but there has also been virtually no consistency concerning the legality of drugs historically. The history of the acceptance or rejection of opiates (such as opium, morphine, and heroin) in the United States affords a useful example, for it parallels what happened to public attitudes toward other drugs.

Opiates were legal in the nineteenth-century United States and were widely used as painkillers in the Civil War, with many soldiers becoming addicted. Morphine was legally manufactured from imported opium, and opium poppies were legally grown in the United States. Opium was widely dispensed in countless pharmaceutical preparations.

The only nineteenth-century context in which opiates were declared illegal was one created by anti-Chinese sentiment. The Chinese, who were imported to the West Coast to provide cheap labor to build the railroads, brought opium with them. At first, their opium dens were tolerated. But as the cheap Chinese labor began to threaten the White labor market, there was agitation to punish the Chinese for their "evil" ways. San Francisco and several other West Coast cities passed ordinances around 1875 prohibiting opium dens. These laws were, as some analysts have noted, aimed at the Chinese, not the drug.

The early 1900s were characterized as a period of reform. A number of individuals and groups wanted to legislate morals; the Eighteenth Amendment, which prohibited the sale and use of alcohol, was passed in 1919 as a result of pressure from these reform forces. These groups rallied against **psychoactive drugs** because they believed them to be sinful. They fought against "demon rum" and "demon weed," as well as other moral evils such as gambling and prostitution. They believed that they were doing God's will and that, if successful, they would provide a better way of life for everyone. Therefore, they lobbied vigorously to achieve appropriate legislation and enforcement of the laws to rid the country of these immoral influences.

As a result of these reform efforts, Congress passed the Harrison Narcotics Act of 1914. This act was basically a tax law requiring people who dispensed opium products to pay a fee and keep records. The law was relatively mild. It did not prohibit the use of opium in patent medicines or even control its use. It did, however, establish a Narcotics Division in the Treasury Department (which eventually became the Bureau of Narcotics). This department assumed the task (which was not specified in the formal law) of eliminating drug addiction. Treasury agents harassed users, physicians, and pharmacists. The bureau launched a propaganda campaign to convince the public that there was a link between drug use and crime. Finally, the bureau took a number of carefully selected cases to court to broaden its powers. In all these endeavors, the bureau was successful. The net result was that a medical problem became a legal problem.

This point cannot be overemphasized: Prior to the Harrison Act, drug addicts were thought (by the public and government officials) to be sick and in need of individual help. They were believed to be enslaved and in need of being salvaged through the humanitarian efforts of others. But with various government actions (laws, court decisions, and propaganda) and the efforts of reformers, this image of addicts changed from a "medical" to a "criminal" problem. Once defined as a criminal problem, the solution became incarceration.

Factors Influencing Drug Laws and Enforcement

The previous section shows how differently a drug can be viewed over time. Clearly, current policies regarding opium (most common in the form of heroin) are repressive, but alcohol and tobacco continue to be socially acceptable drugs. These differences, especially because the laws do not reflect the drugs' relative dangers to users, demonstrate that official drug policies are arbitrary and problematic. What, then, are the factors that affect the focus of our drug laws? We examine two factors: cultural reasons and interest groups.

- **Cultural Reasons.** Drug laws and policies tend to reflect how people typically perceive drug use. Certain drugs have negative stereotypes, and others do not. Government may have orchestrated these stereotypes or they may be the result of faulty research, propaganda of reformers, negative portrayals in the media, religious ideology, and so on. In the 1940s, for example, most people in the United States shared the assumption that marijuana smokers were "dope fiends." They believed that marijuana users were criminals, immoral, violent, and out of control. Until about 1965, public consensus supported the strict enforcement of marijuana laws. Marijuana was believed to be a dangerous drug associated with other forms of deviance, such as sexual promiscuity and crime. Even college students were virtually unanimous in their condemnation of marijuana smokers as deviants of the worst sort. But the social upheavals of the 1960s included experimentation with drugs and the questioning of society's mores. Rapid changes in attitudes and behavior occurred, especially among the young and college educated. Most significantly, the use of marijuana skyrocketed. In 1965, 18,815 people were arrested for violations of state and local marijuana laws, and these numbers continue to increase each year. Between 1980 and 2002, several million people were arrested for marijuana offenses in the United States (Mosher and Akins 2007).

  Public opinion polls reveal that Americans are divided over the legalization of marijuana. A 2009 Gallup poll found that 44 percent of Americans were in favor of legalizing marijuana, and 54 percent were opposed (Saad 2009). Those opposed believe that marijuana is physically addictive and that its use leads to the use of hard drugs (in other words, they believe it is a "gateway drug"). Research has shown both notions to be false. Marijuana is not physically addictive; it does not cause people to use heroin or other harder drugs. Despite the facts, however, the public generally accepts the negative stereotypes and thus fears the drug and supports strict enforcement.

  Some drug use has been interpreted as a symbolic rejection of mainstream values, and in this situation those supporting the status quo condemn the drug. Drugs such as alcohol and nicotine do not have this connotation. Because marijuana use was closely associated with the youth protest of the 1960s, many construed it as a symbol of an alternative lifestyle, a rejection of the traditional values of hard work, success through competition, initiative, and materialism and as support for socialism, unpatriotic behavior, sexual promiscuity, and rejection of authority. As long as this view prevailed, punitive measures against marijuana users seemed justified to many if not most citizens.

- **Interest Groups.** The approaches for controlling drug use have more to do with the power and social class structure of society than with the inherent characteristics of the substance being controlled. Just as the early anti-opium laws were aimed at Chinese workers, not at opium itself, so the reform movements aimed at prohibition of alcohol represented retaliation by the old middle class—rural, Protestant, native born—against the largely Catholic urban workers and immigrants who threatened their privileged status. Jenkins examines the relationship between power and drug laws and finds,

> Historical examples are not hard to find. Joseph Gusfield's book Symbolic Crusade explained the temperance movement in nineteenth-century America in terms of underlying conflicts between old-established elite groups, who were mainly Anglo-Saxon and Protestant, and newer Catholic populations, who were German and Irish. As Catholics viewed alcohol consumption more tolerantly than did Protestants, temperance laws became a symbolic means of reasserting WASP power and values. Other writers have suggested ethnic agendas for the campaigns to prohibit opium in the 1880s (as part of an anti-Chinese movement) and marijuana in the 1930s (which stigmatized a drug associated with African Americans and Mexicans). Repeatedly, African Americans have been the primary targets of such movements, whether the drug in question was cocaine in the progressive era, heroin in mid-century, or crack in the 1980s. During the drug war launched by Presidents Reagan and Bush, for example, the crack cocaine favored by black users attracted savage penalties in the form of severe mandatory sentences for dealing and possession, while lesser sanctions were inflicted upon the mainly white users of cocaine in its powdered form.
> (Jenkins 1999:13)

A final example of the relation between social class use and drug policy can be found in the current drive to liberalize marijuana laws. When marijuana was used primarily by the lower working class (such as Mexican Americans), the law against its use was extremely punitive. In the 1960s, this changed when middle-class, White, affluent college youth became the primary users. However much parents may have disagreed with their children's use of marijuana, they did not want them treated as criminals and stigmatized as drug users. The ludicrousness of the gap between the punishments for marijuana use and for alcohol use became readily apparent to the educated. As a result, White, affluent, and powerful people in most communities and states mounted a push to liberalize the laws.

Mosher and Akins (2007) argued that by demonizing certain drugs and not others, the government, the criminal justice system, and the media all serve their own interests. For example, a significant part of U.S. agriculture and consumer industry is engaged (with government support) in the production and marketing of nicotine and alcohol products. Even though it is well known that tobacco is harmful to users, the government will not ban its use because of the probable outcry from farmers, the states where tobacco is a major crop, and the tobacco manufacturers, wholesalers, retailers, transporters, and advertisers. Marijuana, on the other hand, is merchandised and sold illegally, so there is no legitimate economic interest pushing for its legalization.

Similarly, the pharmaceutical industry works diligently to dissuade Congress from further restricting amphetamines and other pills. In 1970, pushed by President Nixon, Congress passed the Comprehensive Drug Abuse Prevention and Control Act. Some forces tried to include amphetamines in the dangerous-drug category in that bill, but without success. The law declared marijuana possession a serious crime but did not do the same for amphetamines, despite irrefutable evidence that they are more dangerous to the user.

The illegal status of some drugs enables illicit economic interests to flourish. Underworld suppliers of drugs oppose changes in the law because legalization would seriously reduce their profits. They therefore promote restrictive legislation. The result is often a strange alliance between underworld economic interests and religious/moral interests seeking the same end—prohibition of the drug—but for opposite reasons. Thus, a member of Congress could safely satisfy religious zealots and organized crime alike by voting for stricter drug laws.

The law enforcement profession is another interest group that may use its influence to affect drug policy. If drugs and drug users are considered threats, then budgets to seize them will be increased. More arrests will be made, proving the necessity of enforcement and, not incidentally, the need for higher pay and more officers. Perhaps the best example of this syndrome is provided by the activity of the Narcotics Bureau, created by the Harrison Act of 1914. As mentioned earlier, the bureau was instrumental in changing the definition of opiate use from a "medical" activity to a "criminal" one. The bureau used a number of tactics to "prove" that its existence was necessary: It won court cases favorable to its antidrug stance; it vigorously used the media to propagate the "dope fiend" mythology; and it used statistics to incite the public or to prove its own effectiveness.

In effect, the Narcotics Bureau created a moral panic. Moral panics occur when a social problem is defined as a threat to societal values and interests. Moral panics often involve the exaggeration of social phenomena and can result in changes in social policy. Some examples include the media's portrayal of crack cocaine and "crack babies" in the 1980s; the "dope fiend" mythology promoted by the United States government in the early 1900s and again in the 1960s; and more recently, the media portrayal of methamphetamine, "meth babies," and methamphetamine-related crime. Robinson and Scherlen notes,

> The danger of moral panics is that they often lead to unnecessary changes in existing public policies or entirely new policies that are based on exaggerated threats. Misguided drug policies result from at least three factors: political opportunism; media profit maximization; and desire among criminal justice professionals to increase their spheres of influence. Following this logic, politicians create concern about drug use in order to gain personally from such claims in the form of election and reelection; they achieve this largely by using the media as their own mouthpiece. After media coverage of drugs increases, so does public concern. Indeed, research shows that public concern about drugs increases after drug threats have been hyped in the mass media. Finally, criminal justice professionals and government institutions . . . agree to fight the war not only because they see drug-related behaviors (such as use, possession, manufacturing, sales) as crimes but also because it assures them continued resources, clients, and thus bureaucratic survival. (2007:11)

Although *all* drugs are associated with certain harms to individuals and to society, the current drug laws are illogical. They reflect successful political lobbying by a variety of powerful interest groups, with the less powerful suffering the consequences. Despite the drug laws and shifting definitions of certain drugs, an examination of the extent of drug use in U.S. society demonstrates the prevalence of this social problem among all social groups.

DRUG USE IN U.S. SOCIETY

Drugs are used worldwide for pleasure and medicinal purposes. The average U.S. family has about thirty different drugs in its medicine cabinet and numerous alcoholic beverages in its liquor cabinet. Approximately 90 percent of the people in the United States are daily caffeine users, and roughly 59.8 million

Americans currently smoke cigarettes. One of the most comprehensive studies on drug use is the annual National Household Survey on Drug Use and Health conducted by SAMHSA (Substance Abuse and Mental Health Services Administration 2009). According to the most recent reports for 2008, 51.6 percent of the population over age 12 (~129 million people) reported being a current user of alcohol, 28.4 percent (70.9 million people) used tobacco in the past month, and 8.0 percent (20.1 million people) used an illicit drug in the past month (see Figure 1). A 2009 University of Michigan survey (Monitoring the Future) found that 36.5 percent of twelfth-graders had used some illicit drug and 66.2 percent had used alcohol in the last year (Johnston et al., 2009). In 2007, there were over 1.8 million state and local arrests for drug abuse violations (Bureau of Justice Statistics 2010). In short, psychoactive drugs, both legal and illegal, are important to a significant portion of Americans.

Commonly Abused Illegal Drugs

- **Marijuana.** Very much like alcohol, marijuana is a social drug. Marijuana comes from the hemp plant *Cannabis sativa*, a plant cultivated for at least 5,000 years and found throughout the world. It is the world's fourth most widely used psychoactive drug (following caffeine, nicotine, and alcohol) and, by far, the most widely used illicit drug in the United States. In 2008, the federal government seized over 1.4 million pounds of marijuana (Drug Enforcement Administration [DEA] 2009). In 2008, approximately 15.2 million Americans used marijuana at least once in the month prior to being surveyed, and an estimated 3.9 million Americans use marijuana on a daily or almost daily basis (SAMHSA 2009). Although it is often thought that marijuana is a relatively harmless drug, in 2006, marijuana was a factor in 290,563 hospital emergency room visits in the United States (SAMHSA 2008).

  The main active chemical in marijuana is tetrahydrocannabinol (THC), which stimulates the brain cells to release the chemical dopamine. Dopamine

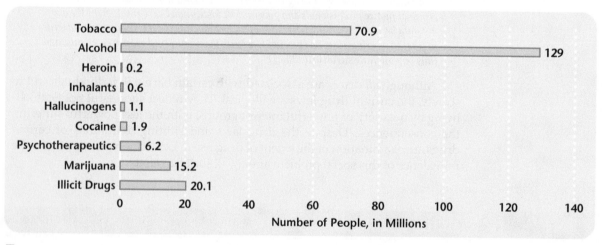

Past Month Drug Use among Persons Aged 12 and Older: 2008

Source: SAMHSA, Substance Abuse and Mental Health Services Administration. (2009). Results from the 2008 National Survey on Drug Use and Health: National Findings (Office of Applied Studies, NSDUH Series H-36, HHS Publication No. SMA 09-4434). Rockville, MO.

produces a relaxing effect, increases the intensity of sense impressions, and provides a "high" akin to one produced by alcohol.

Marijuana is a widely misunderstood drug. Under the Controlled Substances Act, the Drug Enforcement Administration classifies marijuana as a Schedule 1 drug. That is, it has high potential for abuse and no currently accepted medical use in treatment in the United States. Many consider marijuana addictive, asserting that it creates psychological dependence. Some researchers have argued that it causes lower levels of sex hormones to be produced in males and breaks up chromosomes, causing genetic problems for future generations. The current data on marijuana are inconsistent, however, on these and other alleged problems. For example, five research studies done in the 1970s reported that marijuana caused a loss of motivation and the ability to think straight; another five studies reported no such effect.

Although much remains to be learned about the effects of marijuana, some dangers are evident. Marijuana has a negative effect on the lungs (smokers get about four times as much tar in their lungs per puff as tobacco smokers). As a result, smoking marijuana increases the likelihood of developing cancer of the neck or head, as well as increasing the risk of chronic cough, bronchitis, and emphysema. Its use also increases dangers for people with damaged hearts. A 2001 study indicated that a user's risk of heart attack more than quadruples in the first hour after smoking marijuana (Mittleman et al., 2001). According to the National Institute on Drug Abuse, heavy marijuana use is also associated with depression, anxiety, job-related problems and higher job turnover, lower high school graduation rates, and lower grades (2004). A final danger is arrest and a criminal record, the consequence of its use being officially defined as criminal. On the positive side, we know that marijuana is not physiologically addictive; there is no evidence of a lethal dose; and it has been found to have positive effects for certain medical problems, such as migraine headaches, muscle spasms associated with epilepsy and multiple sclerosis, glaucoma, and asthma. Of special note is the successful use of marijuana to reduce or eliminate the nausea that accompanies chemotherapy treatments for cancer. It can also stimulate appetite in the chronically ill. Currently, Alaska, California, Colorado, Washington, D.C., Hawaii, Maine, Maryland, Michigan, Montana, Nevada, New Jersey, New Mexico, Oregon, Rhode Island, Vermont, and Washington have laws that remove the state-level criminal penalties for growing or possessing medical marijuana, something that the U.S. Drug Enforcement Administration is openly against (DEA 2007). In these states, individuals who use marijuana for medical purposes are not exempt from the federal laws, however.

- **Hallucinogens.** Also called psychedelics, hallucinogens produce sensory experiences that represent a different reality to the user. The person may react to trivial everyday objects as if they had great meaning. Emotions may be greatly intensified. Among the perceptual phenomena experienced by some is the feeling that one is looking at oneself from the outside. Hallucinogens occur naturally in the peyote cactus, some mushrooms, and certain fungi and other plants. Bad experiences with psychedelics include panic associated with loss of control, the common hallucination that spiders are crawling over the body, paranoia and delusions, and occasionally suicide. The psychedelic drug phencyclidine (PCP), also known as angel dust, is perhaps most dangerous. This drug, which is relatively easy to manufacture, can cause psychotic reactions (hallucinations, combative or self-destructive impulses), loss of bowel and bladder control, slurred speech, and inability to walk. Taken in large quantities, it can induce seizures, coma, and death. There is no evidence that physical dependence develops for any of the hallucinogenic drugs. For some people, though, psychological dependence occurs. In 2008, 1.1 million people reported using a hallucinogen in the previous month (SAMHSA 2009).

The drug ecstasy is a synthetic drug with stimulant and hallucinogenic effects. Users say that ecstasy produces a high for up to 6 hours with feelings of euphoria, empathy, and heightened senses. Ecstasy is one of several popular drugs known as "club drugs," used by youth at all-night dance parties, dance clubs, and bars. In 2008, 555,000 Americans reported using ecstasy in the previous month (SAMHSA 2009). According to research by the University of Michigan, ecstasy use has declined among eighth, tenth, and twelfth graders since it peaked in 2001, but rates are currently holding steady. Researchers are concerned that this may change, however, as the proportion of young people who see "great risk" associated with trying ecstasy has fallen appreciably and steadily since 2004 (Johnston et al., 2009). Regular use can produce blurred vision, confusion, sleeplessness, depression, muscle cramping, fever, chills, hallucinations, and anxiety. Used in combination with alcohol, the effects can be dangerous. The most serious effect of ecstasy is that the drug interferes with the body's ability to regulate temperature. The sharp increase in body temperature can result in severe dehydration, or, on the opposite extreme, an individual will drink too much water and can suffer from water poisoning of their bloodstream.

- **GHB (Gamma Hydroxybutyrate).** GHB is a central nervous system depressant. It is a colorless, odorless liquid that is mixed with alcoholic drinks or fruit juices. It relaxes or sedates the body, slowing breathing and the heart rate. Users feel euphoric, then sleepy. Overdose results in nausea, vomiting, drowsiness, and headache and can escalate to loss of consciousness, seizures, and a comatose state. GHB has two qualities that make it a favorite date-rape drug: (1) it knocks out users and their short-term memory, and (2) it clears quickly from the body, so laboratory tests might not detect it (Leinwand 2001). Hospital emergency room episodes involving GHB rose from 55 in 1994 to a peak of 3,340 in 2001 but decreased to 1,861 in 2005 (Drug Abuse Warning Network [DAWN] 2005).

- **Narcotics (Opiates).** Narcotics are powerful depressants that have a pronounced effect on the respiratory and central nervous systems. Medically, they are used very effectively to relieve pain, treat diarrhea (paregoric), and stop coughing (codeine). These drugs, which include opium and its derivatives, morphine and heroin, also produce a feeling of euphoria. Many users describe the first "rush" as similar to sexual orgasm, followed by feelings of warmth, peacefulness, and increased self-esteem.

Opiates are highly addictive. Prolonged users experience severe withdrawal symptoms. It is dangerous for four reasons—each a result of the drug's illegal status, not of the drug itself. First, because the drug is not regulated, it can include harmful impurities and be of varying potency. As a result, between 3,000 and 4,000 users die annually of heroin overdoses. In 2006, 189,780 emergency room visits involved heroin abuse (SAMSHA 2006). Second, the sharing of needles is a major cause of hepatitis and, in recent years, HIV infection (the precursor of AIDS). Efforts to supply clean needles to the addict population are resisted by government officials because that would appear to condone, even promote, an illegal activity. The third danger associated with heroin is the high cost of purchasing the illegal drug (maintaining a heroin addiction can cost hundreds of dollars per day). The users must spend much of their time finding funds to supply their habit. For men, finding funds to purchase heroin typically means theft, and for women, shoplifting or prostitution—all hazardous occupations. Fourth, possession of heroin is a criminal offense, leading to incarceration. Taken together, then, the criminal activities an addict turns to plus the complications of poor-quality drugs and infection lead to a relatively high rate of deaths.

The annual prevalence of heroin use has remained fairly constant among teenagers, fluctuating between .7 percent and .9 percent from 2005 to 2008 (Johnston et al., 2009). More disturbing are trends for other opiate-based painkillers such as Vicodin and OxyContin. The potential for addiction to painkillers and other prescription drugs was made public when Rush Limbaugh, a well-known conservative radio host, admitted to being addicted to prescription painkillers in 2003, as well as the drug-related deaths of popular stars Anna Nicole Smith, Brittany Murphy, and Michael Jackson. The authors of the Monitoring the Future study note that "these prescription-type drugs have become more important in the nation's larger drug abuse problem, reflecting their gradual increase in popularity over an extended period of time while the use of a number of illegal drugs (e.g., LSD, ecstasy, and heroin) has receded considerably" (Johnston et al., 2007:14). According to the Centers for Disease Control and Prevention (CDC 2010), prescription drugs have now surpassed heroin and cocaine as the leading cause of fatal overdoses.

- **Cocaine.** Cocaine is a strong central nervous system stimulant. It stimulates an area in the brain that regulates the sensation of pleasure, intensifying sexual highs and producing euphoria, alertness, and feelings of confidence. Two studies conducted in 2004 used rats to demonstrate the addictive nature of cocaine. In a French study, rats were given cocaine for three months, and then the scientists cut the rats' drug supply. They found that a certain percentage of the rats were very persistent in trying to get their cocaine, even if it meant getting shocked electrically. In the British study, they also found that rats were willing to experience shocks on their feet to get their fix of cocaine, but only those rats that had been taking cocaine for a long time. The rats that had been taking cocaine for only a short time gave up after their first electric shock (reported in *Medical News Today* 2004).

In 2008, there were 1.9 million current cocaine users (SAMHSA 2009). Repeated use of cocaine can produce paranoia, hallucinations, sleeplessness, tremors, weight loss, and depression. Snorting cocaine (the typical procedure) draws the cocaine powder through the nasal passages, leading to permanent damage to the mucous membranes and serious breathing difficulties. Moreover, snorting allows the cocaine to be absorbed rapidly into the bloodstream and subsequently the brain. If the user desires a more potent dosage, cocaine can be injected in solution directly into the veins or chemically converted and smoked in the process called *freebasing*. Another variation is to mix cocaine with heroin, which combines a powerful stimulant with a potent depressant.

Crack is a smokable form of cocaine, created by mixing cocaine, baking soda, and water and heating them. This potent drug provides an almost instant rush, reaching the brain within eight seconds, with peak effects within a few minutes. Because crack's effects are more short-lived and more intense than powder cocaine, there is a greater urge toward repeated use. Crack, compared with powder cocaine, is cheaper and provides a quicker high.

- **Methamphetamine.** Also known as speed, crystal, crank, chalk, or ice, methamphetamine is part of a subclass of amphetamines. It is a powerful addictive stimulant that affects the central nervous system. It can be injected, smoked, snorted, and ingested orally or anally. Methamphetamine use decreases appetite, heightens energy levels, enables people to be physically active for long periods, and provides a sense of euphoria similar to that of cocaine (Covey 2007).

  Methamphetamine use is associated with a number of negative effects, both short- and long-term. Short-term effects include higher pulse rate, higher blood pressure, increased body temperature, convulsions, irritability, and nervousness. During the coming-down period, the user may become agitated and potentially violent (Covey 2007). Long-term effects include severe psychological and physical dependence, violent behavior and paranoia, chronic fatigue, depression, open sores and infections on the skin from picking and scratching at imaginary bugs, tooth decay and dental deterioration, and severe weight loss. Methamphetamine acts as a corrosive on the gums and teeth and softens the teeth so that they literally melt away.

  Methamphetamine use and addiction has become a frequent topic in the mass media. Much as it did during the "crack epidemic" of the 1980s and 1990s, the media is again using the word *epidemic* to describe the problem. The government has turned its attention to methamphetamine as well. Congress passed the Comprehensive Methamphetamine Control Act of 1996, the Methamphetamine Anti-Proliferation Act of 2000, and the Combat Methamphetamine Epidemic Act (CMEA) of 2005. The first of these acts doubled the maximum penalties for possession of the drug and possession of equipment used to manufacture the drug from four to ten years. All three acts also focus on limiting the sale of ingredients that can be used to manufacture methamphetamine. The CMEA of 2005 regulates the retail over-the-counter sales of ephedrine, pseudoephedrine, and phenylpropanolamine, which are common ingredients in cough, cold, and allergy products. Those drugs are now placed out of customer reach, customers must show identification and sign a log book, and customers are limited to no more than 9 grams of ephedrine per month. In March 2007, the first arrest was made in New York when log books showed that a customer had purchased over 29 grams of ephedrine from several pharmacies in a one-month period (DEA 2007).

  Studies on the amount of methamphetamine use are mixed. Many substance abuse authorities believe that use and distribution are on the rise, thus resulting in an "epidemic" (for a review of these studies, see Covey 2007). On the other hand, the U.S. DEA claims that the number of meth labs has decreased as a result of the Combat Methamphetamine Epidemic Act, and prominent research studies show a decline in use. The Monitoring the Future study indicates that methamphetamine use is low among youth and is declining. In 1999, 4.7 percent of high school seniors had used methamphetamine in the past year compared to 1.2 percent in 2008 (Johnston et al.,

DON'T LET DRUG DEALERS CHANGE THE FACE OF YOUR NEIGHBOURHOOD.
Call Crimestoppers anonymously on 0800 555 111.

Reuters/HO/Landov

Regular methamphetamine use can cause dramatic physiological damage both inside and outside the body.

2009). Similarly, the National Survey on Drug Use and Health shows that numbers of past-month users have declined from 731,000 in 2006 to 314,000 in 2008 (SAMHSA 2009). Despite these declining numbers, the spread of methamphetamine use has been "likened to an epidemic moving from the West and Southwest to the rest of the country" (Covey 2007:23).

Legal but Dangerous Drugs

At the beginning of this chapter, we pointed out that the definitions concerning drugs and drug-related behaviors are socially constructed; that is, these definitions shift and change over time. Nothing illustrates this more poignantly than looking at the legality of certain drugs and the age at which the consumption of such drugs becomes *defined* as legal. For example, in 1992, Congress directed all states to establish 18 as the minimum age to purchase and smoke cigarettes. In Alaska, the minimum age is 19. That a person can simply step over a state line and their behavior will be defined as criminal or not demonstrates this social construction.

- **Nicotine.** Nicotine is the active ingredient of tobacco. Because the vast majority of smokers smoke fifteen or more cigarettes a day, they are averaging at least one cigarette for each hour they are awake. Cigarette smoking remains the leading preventable cause of death in the United States—accounting for one of every five deaths (443,000 people) each year (CDC 2010). Nicotine is a stimulant that raises blood pressure, increases the heart rate, dulls the appetite, and provides the user with a sense of alertness. As a stimulant, nicotine is responsible for a relatively high probability of heart disease and strokes among cigarette smokers. In addition to the nicotine, smokers inhale various coal tars, nitrogen dioxide, formaldehyde, and other ingredients that increase the chances of contracting lung cancer, throat cancer, emphysema, and bronchitis. Former Surgeon General Richard Carmona has reported that smoking causes no fewer than twenty-six diseases, including cancers of the stomach, uterus, cervix, pancreas, and kidneys (*Arizona Daily Star* 2004). Moreover, inhaling secondary tobacco smoke contributes to respiratory infections in babies, triggers new cases of asthma in previously unaffected children, and exacerbates symptoms in asthmatic children. Because of all the health problems associated with smoking, the CDC estimates that the cost of smoking to the nation for the years 2000 to 2004 was approximately $193 billion in medical costs and lost worker productivity (CDC 2010).

Current estimates indicate that approximately 59.8 million Americans smoke cigarettes. Looking at patterns of smoking behavior, several points are clear (SAMHSA 2009): (1) more adult men smoke than women (34.5 percent versus 22.5 percent); (2) smoking and education are inversely related. That is, as education level goes up, the incidence of smoking goes down (see Figure 2); and (3) cigarette smoking is more common among unemployed adults than among adults who work full or part time (43.0 percent versus 27.2 and 23.8 percent, respectively). Thus, the poor and uneducated are more likely to smoke.

Although the tobacco industry is enormous, it is faced with declining sales due to public smoking bans, increased tobacco taxes, and public antismoking campaigns. The tobacco companies have responded in three ways. First, the tobacco companies have invested heavily in the federal, state, and local campaigns of politicians in the hope of favorable legislation (regarding such issues

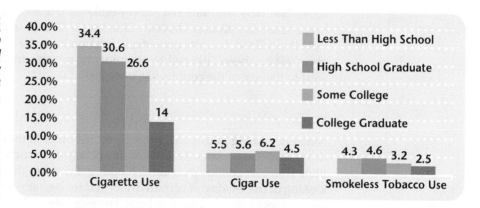

FIGURE 2

Past Month Tobacco Use among Adults Aged 18 and Over, by Education: 2008

Source: SAMHSA, Substance Abuse and Mental Health Services Administration. (2009). Results from the 2008 National Survey on Drug Use and Health: National Findings (Office of Applied Studies, NSDUH Series H-36, HHS Publication No. SMA 09-4434). Rockville, MO.

as public smoking, selling through vending machines, reining in the Federal Drug Administration, and the extent of liability in impending lawsuits). The tobacco industry gave more than $2 million in contributions to federal candidates, political parties, and other political action committees in the 2007 to 2008 election cycle (Common Cause and Tobacco-Free Kids Action Fund 2010).

The second strategy of the tobacco companies is to increase their advertising in the United States and attempt to hook new users. According to the CDC (2007b), in 2005, tobacco companies spent $13.1 billion on advertisements and promotions. This amounts to $36 million per day, or annually more than $45 for every person in the United States and more than $290 for each adult U.S. smoker. This advertising is aimed primarily at minorities, women, and youth. Consider the following:

- Studies have found a high density of tobacco billboards in racial and ethnic minority communities. A study by the University of Pittsburgh School of Medicine found that there are 2.6 times as many ads per person in predominantly black neighborhoods as there are in predominantly white neighborhoods (Toland 2007).
- In 2007, R.J. Reynolds unveiled a new product called "Camel No. 9," a cigarette with a decorative pink band, a tiny pink camel, and an ebony box with hot-pink and teal accents. With the slogan "light and luscious," it is clearly a product targeting women and young girls (Quindlen 2007).
- Smoking is featured in many video games targeting youth. For example, the game "The Chronicles of Riddick: Escape from Butcher Bay" has players win packs of cigarettes, and the game makes fun of the warning labels on the packs (Perry 2010).
- In 2007, a report by the Harvard School of Public Health showed that cigarette companies increased the amount of nicotine in their cigarettes by an average of 11 percent from 1998 to 2005 (reported in Siegel 2007). Although tobacco companies deny claims of a deliberate increase in nicotine, anti-smoking groups argue that this was a calculated move to hook new smokers on their product.

A third strategy of the tobacco companies is to increase advertising and sales overseas to compensate for declining domestic sales. According to Kluger (2009),

This year tobacco companies will produce more than 5 trillion cigarettes—or about 830 for every person on the planet. In China, 350 million people are currently hooked on

tobacco, which means the country has more smokers than the U.S. has people.
(Kluger 2009: 50)

In 2007 a federal judge ruled that tobacco companies are prohibited from marketing their cigarettes overseas as "low tar" and "light" and otherwise giving the impression that their cigarettes are less dangerous.

- **Alcohol.** Alcohol is a relatively safe drug when used in moderation but one of the most dangerous when abused. According to the National Household Survey on Drug Use and Health, 51.6 percent of the population over age 12 consumed alcohol in the past month (SAMHSA 2009). Although alcohol is not legal for those under age 21, the University of Michigan found that 43 percent of twelfth graders, 29 percent of tenth graders, and 16 percent of eighth graders had consumed alcohol in the past month (Johnston et al., 2009). Alcohol is a depressant that directly affects the central nervous system, slowing brain activity and muscle reactions. Thus, it is a leading cause of accidents:

  - Approximately 12.4 percent of persons drove while under the influence of alcohol in 2008 (SAMHSA 2009).
  - In 2003, 40 percent of all fatalities from car accidents were alcohol related (National Highway Traffic Safety Administration 2004). Automobile accidents involving intoxicated drivers are a leading cause of death among teenagers.
  - Approximately seven out of ten drowning victims had been drinking prior to their deaths.

  Alcohol consumption is related to other problems as well:

  - Underage drinking costs Americans $62 billion per year in injuries, deaths, and lost work time (reported in Portillo 2006).
  - There are intangible and unmeasurable expenses due to disrupted families, spouse and child abuse, desertion, and countless emotional problems that arise from drinking. Most significant, two-thirds of victims who suffered violence from an intimate (a current or former spouse, boyfriend, or girlfriend) reported that alcohol had been a factor (Bureau of Justice Statistics 2007).
  - Among youth (high school and college), excessive drinking is related to risky sexual behavior, vandalism, racist acts, homophobic violence, and sexual assault.
  - One of the strongest risk factors for attempted suicide in both adults and youth is alcohol use.

  Continued use of large quantities of alcohol can result in indigestion, ulcers, degeneration of the brain, and cirrhosis of the liver; over 20,000 Americans die of cirrhosis of the liver each year. Malnutrition is often associated with prolonged use of alcohol; a pint of whiskey provides about half of a person's daily calorie requirements but without the necessary nutrients. Heavy consumption also reduces the production of white blood cells, so alcoholics have a low resistance to bacteria. Alcoholics, in addition, run the danger of permanent destruction of brain cells, resulting in memory loss and sometimes psychotic behavior. Chronic use also results in physiological addiction. Withdrawal can be very dangerous, with the individual experiencing convulsions and delirium. The conclusion is inescapable, then, that alcohol is the most dangerous legal drug physically for the individual and socially for society.

Drug Use Patterns by Class, Race, and Gender

Drug use and abuse is most often discussed as an individual's choice, an individual's behavior, and an individual's problem. However, examining drug use from a sociological standpoint reveals interesting patterns by class, race, and gender. These patterns demonstrate that a person's place in the social structure can increase or decrease the odds that he or she will use drugs and alcohol. Drug use is not uniform throughout society. For example, men of all ages and races are more likely than women to use illicit drugs. Even marital status matters—married women are less likely to use tobacco, engage in binge alcohol use, or use an illicit drug compared to divorced, separated, never married, or cohabiting women. In terms of social class, intravenous drug users continue to be found predominantly among the inner-city poor. This practice places them at great risk of exposure to the AIDS virus from the sharing of needles. The CDC estimates that 36 percent of the women who are living with AIDS in the United States contracted the disease through intravenous drug use, compared to 23 percent of the men with the disease (2004).

The disproportionate use of drugs by the poor is not limited to illicit drugs. As indicated previously in Figure 2, cigarette smoking is inversely related to education level. The lower the education level, the greater the incidence of cigarette smoking. The CDC estimates that nearly 31.5 percent of people living below the poverty line smoke. Statistics also reveal interesting differences by race/ethnicity and smoking. Native Americans have the highest rates of smoking (48.7 percent), and Asians have the lowest rates of smoking (13.9 percent; SAMHSA 2009).

Alcohol use also varies greatly by race, social class, and age. Whites are more likely to report current use (defined as consuming any alcohol in the past month) than any other racial group (56.2 percent compared to 41.9 percent for Blacks and 37 percent for Asians). Youth in general are more likely to report binge and heavy use, with the highest prevalence among 18- to 25-year-olds. Gender, too, is relevant, as Black women are much more likely than White women to be abstainers. Recall that the incidence of smoking decreases with higher levels of education. The opposite is true for drinking. The rates of current alcohol use increase with increasing levels of education. A study by the CDC found this pattern to hold true for women who drink during pregnancy. The study found that women who were White, older, more educated, and had higher income were more likely to drink during their pregnancy than women in other demographic categories (Fong 2004).

To examine further the relationship between social class and alcohol use, consider drinking by college students. College students, mostly from relatively privileged backgrounds, often are heavy binge drinkers during their college years. In fact, research indicates that around 61 percent of college students drink alcohol, and 40.5 percent binge drink (defined as five or more drinks in a row; SAMHSA 2009). At many colleges and universities, there is a very significant drinking subculture. At the University of Virginia, one of the finest public universities in the United States, there is a tradition for seniors to consume a fifth of liquor at the last home football game (a practice known as the "fourth-year fifth"). This tradition resulted in the deaths of eighteen students between 1990 and 1999.

Although Whites report a higher incidence of current alcohol use, illicit drug use reveals a different pattern. Individuals of two or more races report the highest rates of illicit drug use, followed by Native Americans (see Figure 3). Illicit drug use is also higher in large metro areas than in nonmetro areas (SAMHSA 2009).

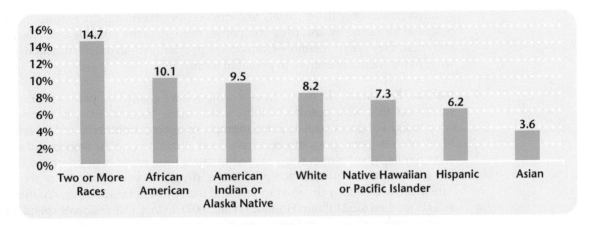

Past Month Illicit Drug Use among Persons Aged 12 or Older, by Race/Ethnicity: 2008

Source: SAMHSA, Substance Abuse and Mental Health Services Administration. (2009). Results from the 2008 National Survey on Drug Use and Health: National Findings (Office of Applied Studies, NSDUH Series H-36, HHS Publication No. SMA 09-4434). Rockville, MO.

In general terms, the poor are more inclined than the rich to use illicit harmful substances. Why? One possibility is the irrelevance of the antidrug campaigns, which are implicitly based on the premise that a young person has a lot to lose by using drugs. The young poor who live in situations where jobs and other opportunities for advancement are scarce or nonexistent have nothing to lose by using drugs—they have already lost. The threat of drug-screening programs now increasingly used by employers may constrain people with a chance for a job, but it has no hold on the hopeless. Some observers have theorized that the urban poor are prone to take drugs as an escape from a harsh and painful reality.

Others argue that tobacco and alcohol companies target minority neighborhoods. They sponsor sports tournaments and music festivals in predominantly Black neighborhoods and purchase considerable advertising in Black publications. In 2004, cigarette companies came out with a new line of flavored cigarettes that antismoking activists claim specifically targets minority teens. The packaging features graffiti artists and other hip-hop imagery that appeals to minority youth (Associated Press 2004).

In looking at the statistics, it is clear that drug use cuts across all class, racial, and gender lines. It is how the drugs (and the persons using those drugs) are defined that determines drug treatment and handling by the authorities. For example, in 2008 an estimated 4.7 million persons used pain relievers nonmedically, and they are often middle- and upper-class Whites (1.8 million used tranquilizers, 904,000 used stimulants, and 234,000 used sedatives; SAMHSA 2009). Unlike the poor—who tend to use illicit drugs and therefore are hassled by the authorities and treated in prisons and public hospitals—the more affluent tend to use legal and prescription drugs and are treated by private physicians. Thus, their addiction is typically protected and hidden from public awareness.

Why Use Drugs?

It is clear that *all* drugs have the potential for harm, even those drugs that seem completely risk free. Aspirin, for example, may seem like a drug with few side effects, but taken in large doses, it can result in ulcers and stomach bleeding.

A person needs only listen closely to commercials advertising drugs to see their potential for harm. By law, drug companies must state the possible side effects, and often they are numerous—from bowel problems to sexual dysfunction. So why do we subject ourselves to potential harm?

- **Medical Pressures.**   In recent times, chemists have created numerous synthetic substances that have positive health consequences. Vaccines have been developed to fight diseases such as polio, mumps, smallpox, diphtheria, and measles. Many of these contagious diseases have been eliminated by the wonders of science. Similarly, antibiotics were created as cures for a number of infectious diseases. The public quickly accepted these drugs as beneficial. As a result, Americans are a highly drugged society, and total prescription drug expenditures in 2005 reached $252 billion (Hoffman et al., 2007). In fact, U.S. residents spend far more on prescription drugs than do people in other developed countries, and rising costs have even driven some to smuggle prescriptions from other countries.

- **Cultural Pressures.**   The United States has become a "quick-fix" society, with individuals seeking instant results and striving to meet cultural ideals about perfection. In seeking mental perfection, physical perfection, and improved physical performance, Americans have increasingly turned to artificial substances and enhancements to meet those ideals. In the early 1950s, chemists made a breakthrough in drugs that treated mental disorders such as depression, insomnia, aggression, hyperactivity, and tension. These drugs (tranquilizers, barbiturates, and stimulants) have since been widely prescribed by doctors for these problems.
    Psychopharmacology, the science of drugs that affect the mind, is on the verge of developing pills that will enrich memory, heighten concentration, enhance intelligence, and eliminate shyness or bad moods:

    We have become so muddle-headed by constant marketing to take these drugs for every emotional malady that we now live in a ridiculous world where we have signs that say "This is a Drug-Free Zone" on the front of a school that is handing out psychotropics

© Peter C. Vey/The New Yorker Collection/www.cartoonbank.com.

to the children for depression, hyperactivity, anxiety, etc. Psychiatric drugs have become a first resort. That is the real nightmare that the FDA should confront. Doctors no longer look for causes of depression, such as thyroid problems, lack of exercise, a bad diet, a guilty conscience, medical problems, allergies—the likely culprits could be many. By using drugs to treat the symptoms, they not only expose patients to the effects of the drugs but they let the real causes go untreated. (Stradford 2004:2)

Recently, there has been much controversy over the use of so-called behavior drugs for children. The CDC estimates that in 2006 ADHD (attention deficit/hyperactivity disorder) diagnoses in children rose to 4.5 million (CDC 2010). From 2001 to 2004, there was a 49 percent rise in the use of ADHD drugs by children under the age of 5 and an astonishing 369 percent increase in spending on such drugs. In fact, this spending exceeded the spending for antibiotics and asthma medication for children (Johnson 2004). The symptoms for ADHD are inattentiveness, fidgeting, not listening, being easily distracted, making careless mistakes, and excessive talking. Stimulants such as Ritalin, Adderall, Concerta, and Dexedrine are prescribed to have the paradoxical effect of calming and focusing children who are chronically inattentive and hyperactive. These drugs stimulate the central nervous system, with many of the same pharmacological effects of cocaine. They affect the brain by enhancing the chemical dopamine, the neurotransmitter that plays a major role in cognition, attention, and inhibition. Their side effects are nervousness, insomnia, and loss of appetite. Although these stimulants for children are often successful, their widespread use raises some important questions:

- The United States consumes 80 percent of the world's methylphenidate (the generic name for Ritalin). "Are American youngsters indeed suffering more behavioral illnesses, or have we as a society become less tolerant of disruptive behavior?" (Shute, Locy, and Pasternak 2000:47).
- Is hyperactivity the inevitable by-product of a societywide addiction to speed—to cellular phones, faxes, e-mail, overnight mail, ever-faster computers? How are children affected by the high-stimulus activities that saturate their lives—video games, interactive television, hundreds of cable channels, and fast-action movies with vivid violence?
- According to the CDC (2010), in 2006, 9.5 percent of boys received a diagnosis of ADHD compared to 5.9 percent of girls. Is the preponderance of boys diagnosed as hyperactive because adults find that boys are more difficult to control than girls?
- What is the role of the pharmaceutical companies in the rapid growth of medications for ADHD? This is a billion-dollar sector of the pharmaceutical market. Brand-name ads for ADHD drugs appear in women's magazines and on cable TV, breaking a longstanding agreement between nations and the pharmaceutical industry not to market controlled substances that have high potential for abuse (K. Thomas 2001).
- What is the role of managed-care companies and insurers in promoting the medication of children for ADHD? These organizations are concerned with costs, and it is much cheaper to prescribe pills, thus avoiding referring children to more expensive mental health specialists (Bloom 2000; Shute, Locy, and Pasternak 2000).
- Ritalin and other stimulants prescribed for ADHD work on the brain much like cocaine does. Children using this drug are "wired" every day, raising concern over its long-term effects. This is not the only way that children are

wired. Companies promote energy drinks (high in caffeine) targeting youth by using names like RockStar, Monster, Red Bull, and Venom. Are we creating an entire generation (called by some the "Rx generation") with a "sweet tooth for cocaine"?

The widespread use of these stimulants leads to their abuse by adolescents and adults seeking pharmacological highs. Taken in larger amounts than prescribed and crushed and snorted, these drugs produce euphoria, greater energyand productivity, increased sexual appetite, and an overall feeling of being a lot smarter (K. Thomas 2000b). As a result, the DEA says that drugs to treat ADHD rank among today's most stolen prescriptions and most abused drugs (K. Thomas 2001). The Monitoring the Future study found that in 2006, 4.4 percent of high school seniors, 3.6 percent of tenth graders, and 2.6 percent of eighth graders had abused Ritalin in the previous year (Johnston et al., 2007).

Not only has U.S. society become increasingly concerned with mental perfection, but also the cultural ideals of physical perfection are overwhelming. Drugs can offer a way to meet these ideals. Consider the following:

- The largest area of growth in plastic surgery is in Botox injections (2,557,068 procedures in 2009). The injected toxin blocks the nerve impulses, temporarily paralyzing the muscles that cause wrinkles (American Society for Aesthetic Plastic Surgery 2010).
- In 2003, the FDA approved Humatrope, a brand of human growth hormone, for healthy children with short stature (defined as height more than 2 standard deviations below the mean for their age and sex).
- Ephedra, found in products to aid weight loss, enhance sports performance, and increase energy, was banned in 2004 after it was linked to deaths and reports of serious health problems.

Mental perfection and physical perfection pave the way for other performance pressures as well. The pressure to succeed in competitive situations may also encourage some people to take drugs. Individuals who want to be especially alert or calm to do well may take a drug to accomplish their goal. Sports present an excellent example of drug use to enhance performance. Athletes use two types of drugs: restorative drugs (to heal a traumatized part of the body) and additive drugs (to improve performance). Amphetamines, human growth hormones, hormones such as androstenedione (the favorite of home-run king Mark McGwire) and Creatine, and anabolic steroids are the additive drugs commonly used by athletes. Amphetamines increase alertness, respiration rate, blood pressure, muscle tension, heart rate, and blood sugar. The user is literally "psyched up" by amphetamines. Moreover, these drugs have the capacity to abolish a sense of fatigue. Growth hormones increase body size and strength. Anabolic steroids are male hormones that aid in adding weight and muscle. If an athlete wants to be a world-class weightlifter, shot putter, or discus thrower, the pressures are great to use anabolic steroids: they make the user stronger, and many competitors use such drugs to get the edge on the competition. Prior to the 2010 Winter Olympics, thirty athletes were banned from competition for testing positive for performance-enhancing drugs. Football players, even in high school, also use these drugs to gain weight and strength to be a "star." In 2008, approximately 3.2 percent of high school seniors reported using androstenedione or anabolic steroids in the previous year, and 16 percent of boys reported using Creatine (Johnston et al., 2009).

Performance pressures have also extended into the bedroom, with drugs like Viagra, Cialis, and Levitra available to aid with sexual performance. Viagra, approved by the FDA in 1998, is a $2 billion-per-year seller for Pfizer, Inc.

The pressures to use drugs are unrelenting. They come from doctors, coaches, parents, teachers, peers, and advertising. People may learn to drink in families where social drinking is an integral part of meals, celebrations, and everyday relaxation. In situations such as cocktail parties, guests are expected to drink alcoholic beverages as part of the social ritual. Peer groups are also important for the entry of the individual into the world of illicit drug use. The person learns from others how to use the drug and how to interpret the drug's effects positively. Similarly, the pressures to meet society's ideals of mental and physical perfection and performance can be overwhelming, with drugs offering a "quick-fix" solution.

U.S. OFFICIAL POLICY: A WAR ON DRUGS

The U.S. drug war is fought on two fronts: stopping the flow of drugs into the United States and using the criminal justice system to punish those who sell and use illegal drugs within the United States. The cost of this program is roughly $1 billion per week (Zeese 2006). In fact, the drug war has cost taxpayers more than $1 trillion since 1970 (Cole 2007).

Stopping the supply of drugs into the country (interdiction) involves the use of customs agents at the borders inspecting the baggage of passengers and cargo from planes, trucks, and ships. It involves working with other countries (especially Colombia, Peru, Ecuador, Bolivia, and Mexico) to destroy the places

SOCIAL PROBLEMS IN GLOBAL PERSPECTIVE

MEXICO'S DRUG WAR

There is a war going on in Mexico. In 2006, Mexican President Felipe Calderón declared war on the country's drug cartels. Putting 45,000 army troops on the streets, he pledged to arrest the cartel leaders, confiscate their drugs, and seize the large amounts of cash that they need to operate. Since then, over 10,000 people have died in drug-related violence. The drug cartels have conducted kidnappings, executions, and assaults. In early 2009, the police chief in Ciudad Juarez resigned after drug traffickers began to make good on their promise to kill

police officers in the city until the chief stepped down (Navarrette 2009). The gangs have dumped severed heads in front of town halls and have essentially terrorized the Mexican people to put pressure on the government to back down.

The United States has a large stake in Mexico's war, as it is estimated that 90 percent of all the cocaine flowing into the United States comes from Mexico, and 90 percent of the guns seized in drug-related violence in Mexico come from the United States (Navarrette 2009). In addition, the Mexican drug cartels have

established a presence in approximately 230 U.S. cities (see Figure 4). The United States has stepped in and pledged funds (part of the $1.4 billion Merída Initiative) to help combat the war on drugs in Mexico and Central America. In addition, they have added officers and announced new security measures at the border. But according to some experts, the American demand for illegal drugs plays the most important role in fueling Mexico's drug war. "No matter how much law enforcement or financial help the U.S. government provides Mexico, the basics of supply and demand prevent it from doing much good" (Crary 2009:1).

239

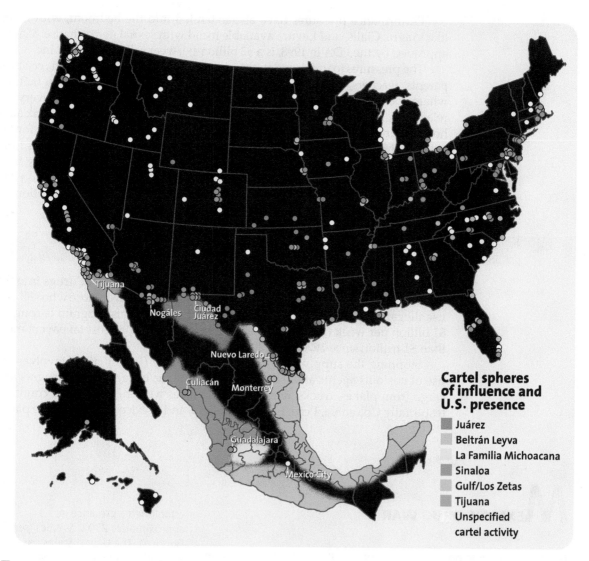

FIGURE 4

There are six dominant drug cartels in Mexico with influence spreading into the United States

where drugs are grown, manufactured, and processed and to destroy the transportation networks to the United States (by sea and air, and by land through Mexico). These efforts involve the State Department, the Treasury Department, the Coast Guard, various branches of the military, and the Central Intelligence Agency (CIA). These agencies train local soldiers and supply them with equipment (helicopters, radar, and surveillance aircraft) and supplies (herbicides, guns, munitions). This means, of course, that the United States is involved in destroying the crops (opium poppy and coca) of local farmers. It means the involvement of the United States (through the CIA) in local politics, siding with pro-U.S. factions against anti-U.S. factions, or involvement in civil wars, where rebels finance their operations with drugs in the fight against the established governments. It encourages violence, threats, and bribery as drug cartels use any means to keep their lucrative businesses flourishing (see the "Social Problems in Global Perspective" panel on the drug war in Mexico).

The policy of interdiction clearly is a failure. Drugs are found by the U.S. Customs, sometimes in large amounts. But massive amounts of drugs cross U.S. borders and enter an intricate distribution system within this country. Despite all our efforts, we have not stopped the supply; we have only dented it and made the drugs that enter the United States more expensive. The drug policy of interdiction also fails because it has led to strained relations with drug-producing nations in South America. By fighting our battles on their soil, the United States is often viewed as the villain.

The second front in the war on drugs occurs within the United States. Beginning in the 1970s, the courts became more punitive toward people selling or possessing illegal drugs. In New York State, for example, a law was passed in 1973 requiring a minimum sentence of 15 years to life for a first-time offender caught selling as little as 2 ounces or possessing 4 ounces of cocaine or heroin. The police, too, became more active in ferreting out buyers and sellers through the use of undercover agents, wiretaps, and sting operations. As a result, the number of adults arrested for drug offenses grew from about 500,000 in 1980 to approximately 1.7 million in 2007 (Bureau of Justice Statistics 2010; see Figure 5). In fact, the United States imprisons a larger fraction of its population for drug offenses than European nations do for all crimes. This has led to tremendous overcrowding of both the courts and the prisons, resulting in a huge and costly growth in the number and size of prisons (each new cell built costs about $80,000, and each new prisoner added costs about $25,000 annually).

Consequences of Official Drug Policies

The drug laws in the United States are irrational, and they do not achieve their intended goals of deterring crime by severely punishing the seller and user. There are three reasons this approach does not work to deter crime. First, by making drugs illegal and therefore dangerous to produce, transport, and sell,

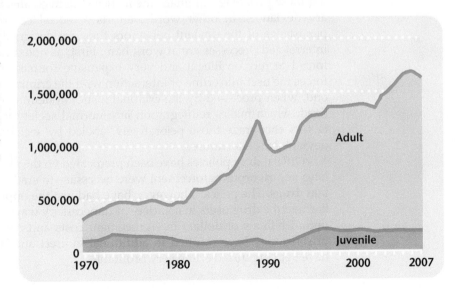

FIGURE 5

Drug Arrests by Age, 1970–2007

This chart can be found on the Bureau of Justice Website, Key Facts at a Glance, on the following page: http://bjs.ojp.usdoj. gov/content/glance/ drug.cfm

society pushes the cost to many times what it would be if they were legally available. Thus, heroin users, for example, are often forced into crime to sustain a high-cost habit. Crimes committed to produce money for drugs are typically nonviolent (pimping, prostitution, shoplifting, selling drugs, and burglary), but their cost is enormous. Suppose, for example, that there are 100,000 addicts in New York City with habits each costing $50 daily. If they each steal $300 worth of goods daily to get the $50 (a 6-to-1 ratio is about the way fencing works), the amount stolen in the city would be $30 million daily, or $10.68 billion a year!

The second reason that punitive drug laws encourage crime is that someone has to supply the illicit goods. Legislation does not dry up demand, as was vividly shown during Prohibition. Organized crime thrives in this climate. Illegal drugs are, for the most part, imported, processed, and distributed by organized crime groups. Drug laws, then, have the indirect effect of providing organized crime with its most lucrative source of income.

A third source of crime caused by drug laws is police corruption. Black market activities by organized crime or other entrepreneurs are difficult without the cooperation of police officials or drug enforcement agents, so their assistance is often bought.

The end result of police corruption and the realization that drug laws are arbitrary (such as the fact that marijuana is illegal but alcohol is legal) causes widespread disrespect for the law and the judicial system. As Garrison Keillor has said, "A marijuana grower can land in prison for life without parole while a murderer might be in for eight years. No rational person can defend this . . ." (2005:26). A final source of irreverence toward the law is the overzealousness of narcotics agents. In their efforts to capture drug law violators, agents have sometimes violated the constitutional rights of individuals (wiretapping, search and seizure without a warrant, entrapment, use of informants who are themselves addicts, and so on). All these abuses have contributed to an attitude of insolence on the part of many people toward agents of the law.

Criminal laws create crime and criminals. If there were no law regulating a behavior, then there would be no criminal. So it is with drug laws. Prior to 1914, heroin users were not criminals, nor were marijuana users before 1937. The drug laws, then, have created large numbers of criminals. By labeling and treating these people as criminals, the justice system creates further crime (secondary deviance). In other words, efforts at social control actually cause the persistence of the deviant behaviors they are designed to eliminate. Several interrelated processes are at work here. First, as noted earlier, the drug user is forced to rely on illegal and very expensive sources. This reliance typically forces the user into crime or interaction with the criminal fringes of society. Second, when processed by the criminal justice system, the individual is stigmatized, which makes reintegration into normal society very difficult. All these factors encourage those pejoratively labeled by society to join together in a deviant drug subculture.

Official drug policies have been predicated on the assumption that punitive laws and rigorous enforcement were necessary to eradicate the menace of certain drugs. The policies, however, have had just the opposite effect. They have harmed the drug users in a variety of unnecessary ways; they have cost society untold billions of dollars in enforcement costs and have clogged courts and prisons; they have resulted in additional indirect and direct crime; and they have kept organized crime very profitable.

Is the Drug War Racist?

The official policy of the federal government is to punish the sellers and users of illicit drugs. The problem is that the laws and the punishment for their violation are unfair to African Americans and other racial minorities. Four facts buttress this allegation. First, recall that the data on past month illicit drug use by race reveals a rate of 10.1 percent for African Americans, and 8.2 percent for Whites. Given their numbers in the general population, this means that overall there are more Whites using illicit drugs than Blacks, yet the data show consistently that *African Americans are more likely to be imprisoned for drug offenses.*

- In every year from 1980 to 2007, Blacks were arrested nationwide on drug charges at rates relative to the population that were 2.8 to 5.5 times higher than White arrest rates (see Figure 6). In some states, Blacks were arrested at rates up to 11.3 times greater than the rate for Whites (Human Rights Watch 2009).
- Of White drug felons, 32 percent are given probation or nonincarceration sentences in state courts, compared to 25 percent of Blacks (U.S. Department of Justice 2000).
- Human Rights Watch reported that Blacks and Latinos are far more likely to be arrested, prosecuted, and given long sentences for drug offenses. Nationally, Latinos comprise almost one-half of those arrested for marijuana offenses (reported by the Drug Policy Alliance 2003).
- Taken together, approximately 22 percent of monthly drug users are Black or Latino, but 80 percent of people in prison for drug offenses are Black or Latino (Glasser 2006).

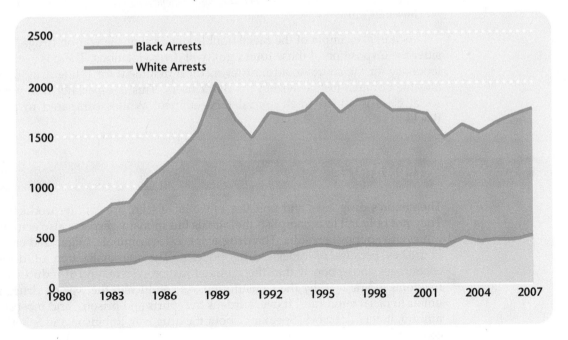

FIGURE 6

U.S. Rates of Adult Drug Arrests by Race, 1980–2007

Source: "Decades of Disparity: Drug Arrests and Race in the United States," March 2009. Human Rights Watch: (Figure 1, page 6).

Second, federal drug enforcement has waged its war against crack cocaine almost exclusively in minority neighborhoods. According to SAMHSA (2003), Whites are more likely than African Americans or Hispanics to report lifetime use of cocaine but are much less likely to be arrested for cocaine use. The issue is one of targeting—studies show that Blacks are more likely to be stopped while driving and searched. As Glasser notes,

> In Florida blacks were seventy-five times more likely than whites to be stopped and searched for drugs while driving. And it turned out that these racially targeted stops were the explicit result of a Drug Enforcement Administration program begun in 1986, called Operation Pipeline, that "trained" 27,000 state troopers in forty-eight states to spot cars that might contain drugs. Most of the cars spotted were driven by blacks. And this happened even though three-quarters of monthly drug users are white! (2006:25)

Third, the laws differ in the severity of punishment if violated. Although powder cocaine and crack cocaine are the same drugs, federal law treats them quite differently. For example, possession of 5 grams of crack (a teaspoon) gets a mandatory 5-year sentence, while it takes 100 times that amount of powder cocaine to get a comparable sentence. This unfair 100-to-1 ratio is racist because the defendants in crack cocaine cases are almost always Black.

> A common illustration of the racial bias in drug laws is crack cocaine. . . . In fiscal year 2001, of all of those sentenced to federal prison for crack cocaine, 83 percent were black, compared to only 7 percent for whites and 9 percent for Latinos. For powder cocaine, the discrepancies are not nearly so stark: half of those sentenced for this drug were Latinos, while only 31 percent were black and 18 percent were white. Put somewhat differently, of all blacks sentenced to federal prison for drugs, 59 percent were convicted for crack cocaine; only 5.5 percent of whites were sentenced for this drug. (Shelden and Brown 2004:3)

As a final example of the racial double standard in the war on drugs, consider the disposition of those found guilty of drug violations. There is a strong tendency for the courts to administer medical treatment for White drug users and the criminal justice system for Black users. This is especially true when social class is added to the racial mix—affluent Whites compared to poor Blacks.

ALTERNATIVES

The nation's drug laws and policies, as we have seen, are counterproductive. They not only fail to accomplish their goals but in many respects also actually achieve the opposite results. The drug war creates criminals. Organized crime flourishes because of official drug policies. The criminalization of drugs encourages corruption within the criminal justice system, and it reduces the freedoms guaranteed by the Constitution. As conducted, the war on drugs is unfair to racial minorities. It overburdens the courts and prisons, and most significant, it does not work. Speaking about the drug war, Robinson and Scherlen concludes,

> Taken together, all the findings suggest the Office of National Drug Control Policy (ONDCP) failed from 1989 to 1998 to achieve its goals of reducing drug use, healing drug users, disrupting drug markets, and reducing health and social costs to the

public. Yet, during this same time period, funding for the drug war grew tremendously and costs of the drug war expanded as well. Further, despite its manifest failure, ONDCP was reauthorized in 1994, 1998, and 2003. (2007:198)

The United States has alternatives concerning drug policy: (1) to continue to wage the war on drugs by enacting and enforcing criminal laws, (2) to legalize drugs and regulate them through licensing and taxation, (3) to take a public health approach, with an emphasis on decriminalization, and (4) to address the social causes of drug use. We have already considered the first option—the criminalization of drug use—so we concentrate here on the other alternatives.

Regulation of Trade or Use through Licensing and Taxation

Legalizing a drug but regulating its use, as is now the case with alcohol, tobacco, and prescription drugs has some obvious benefits:

- It ensures the products' conformity to standards of purity and safety.
- It dries up the need for vast criminal networks that distribute drugs.
- It provides the government with revenues.
- Prison space and police activities would be reserved for the truly dangerous.

Most important, prohibition has not worked:

Law enforcement can't reduce supply or demand. As a Baltimore police officer, I arrested drug dealers. Others took their place. I locked them up, too. Thanks to the drug war, we imprison more people than any other country. And America still leads the world in illegal drug use. We can't arrest and jail our way to a drug-free America. (Moskos 2008:8)

Opponents argue that government regulation would actually condone the use of drugs. This apparent approval, together with the easy availability and relatively low prices, would promote experimentation and use of the drug, perhaps increasing the number of users. Politically, such a policy would be difficult if not impossible to implement. Opinion polls show that the public strongly opposes legalization, and politicians do not want to seem "soft on drugs."

Under this regulation option, the biggest population to deal with would be the heroin addicts. These users are a special problem to themselves and society. Their habits are the most expensive, so of all drug users, they are most likely to turn to crime. Their habit also requires almost full-time diligence in securing the drug; and being "strung out," they do not function normally in society. How, then, should the government deal with them? Hard-liners argue that they should be classified as criminals and incarcerated. Other people suggest that addicts could remain in society and be relatively productive if drugs were supplied to them cheaply, under government regulation and medical supervision.

This can be accomplished through heroin maintenance, which treats addicts as medical problems rather than criminal problems. Methadone or buprenorphine are medications that can be taken orally for the treatment of narcotic withdrawal and dependence. Taken once per day, methadone suppresses withdrawal symptoms for 24 to 36 hours. The drug does not make the user drowsy, it does not impair cognitive functions, and it does not interfere with

SOCIAL POLICY

DUTCH MARIJUANA POLICY

A wave of marijuana law reform is now occurring today in Latin America, Europe and Australia. Paving the way for this reform was the Netherlands in the 1970s. Following the recommendations of two national commissions, the Dutch Parliament decriminalized cannabis possession and retail sale in 1976. Even before this date, the police seldom made arrests for possession or small-volume sales. Although it does not officially legalize marijuana, the 1976 law allowed the Dutch government to create a set of guidelines under which coffee shops could sell marijuana and hashish without fear of criminal prosecution.

Guidelines for the coffee shops have changed somewhat over time and vary slightly from community to community. The basic rules in place today include a ban on advertising, a minimum purchase age of 18, and a 5-gram limit on individual transactions. The sale of any other illicit drug on the premises is strictly prohibited and is grounds for immediate closure. Local government officials may limit the number of coffee shops concentrated in one area, and they can close an establishment if it creates a public nuisance. In the Netherlands, there are over 700 coffee shops where adults can purchase marijuana and hashish to be used there or carried away for use later.

The decision of Dutch legislators to permit the regulated sale and use of cannabis was based on a number of practical considerations. By allowing marijuana to be sold indoors rather than on the streets, the Dutch sought to improve public order. By separating the retail market for marijuana from the retail market for "hard drugs," they sought to reduce the likelihood of marijuana users being exposed to heroin and cocaine. By providing a nondeviant environment in which cannabis could be consumed, they sought to diminish the drug's utility as a symbol of youthful rebellion. Dutch officials have little faith in the capacity of the criminal law to stop people from using marijuana. They fear that arresting and punishing marijuana users—particularly youthful marijuana users—will alienate them from society's mainstream institutions and values.

These principles of normalization also guide the Dutch approach to drug education and prevention. Programs are specifically designed to be low key and minimalist, to avoid provoking young people's interest in drugs. There are no mass media campaigns against drugs, and school-based programs do not use scare tactics or moralistic "just say no" messages. Instead, in the context of general health education, young people in the Netherlands are given information about drugs and cautionary warnings about their potential dangers. In leaflets distributed through the coffee shops, current users of cannabis are advised to be "sensible and responsible."

Starting in the 1990s, the governments of Switzerland, Germany, Spain, Austria, Belgium,

driving a car or operating machinery. Although it is also addictive, the net effect is that a methadone user can continue to be a productive member of society without having to steal for his or her habit.

About 20 percent of the nation's heroin addicts are on methadone maintenance (Office of National Drug Control Policy 2000). Most states control and closely monitor the distribution of the drug. A benefit to this close monitoring is that there is no sharing of needles, a common problem among heroin users. Thus, it helps to control the spread of HIV infection.

In addition, methadone costs about $13 per day, a cheaper alternative to incarceration where the average cost in state prison is approximately $67 per day. Through the methadone maintenance program, addicts are not labeled as criminals. They are considered to have a medical, not a moral, problem. Equally important is that addicts remain participating members of the community.

Luxembourg, and Italy all shifted their laws toward decriminalization of marijuana. In 2001 Portugal decriminalized the use and possession of all drugs, including heroin and cocaine. At the same time, the United States government has moved in the opposite direction toward harsher penalties and increasing arrests for marijuana use and possession (Reinarman and Cohen 2007). Since 1996, in the United States, the number of arrests involving marijuana exceeds arrests for other types of drugs, reaching over 750,000 arrests in 2005 (Bureau of Justice Statistics 2007).

Researchers have found no evidence that the decriminalization of marijuana has led to increased drug use. In fact, a recent study comparing drug use in Amsterdam to drug use in San Francisco found similarities in patterns of marijuana use. The mean age at onset of use was 16.95 years in Amsterdam and 16.43 years in San Francisco (Reinarman and Cohen 2007). A 2010 study found that in comparing 16-year-old boys and girls in the United States and the Netherlands, adolescents in the

United States had a *higher* rate of marijuana use (Simons-Morton et al., 2010).

One argument against the decriminalization of marijuana is that it is a "gateway drug," leading to other illicit drug use. Again comparing Amsterdam and San Francisco, Reinarman and Cohen found that Amsterdam respondents reported significantly lower lifetime use of other illicit drugs than respondents in San Francisco (2007). As shown in the following table, marijuana prevalence rates are actually higher in the United

States than in the Netherlands, despite high arrest rates for marijuana offenses.

Sources: Simons-Morton, Bruce, William Pickett, Will Boyce, Tom F. M. ter Bogt, and Wilma Vollebergh. (2010). "Cross-National Comparison of Adolescent Drinking and Cannabis Use in the United States, Canada, and the Netherlands," *International Journal of Drug Policy* 21:64–69.

Craig Reinarman and Peter Cohen. 2007. "Law, Culture, and Cannabis: Comparing Use Patterns in Amsterdam and San Francisco." In Mitch Earleywine (Ed.), *Pot Politics: Marijuana and the Costs of Prohibition.* New York: Oxford University Press, pp. 113–137.

Drug Use (Age 12+)	United States (2002)	Netherlands (2001)
Lifetime marijuana use	40.4%	17.0%
Past month marijuana use	6.2%	3.0%
Lifetime heroin use	1.6%	0.4%
Past month heroin use	0.1%	0.1%
Lifetime cocaine use	14.4%	2.9%
Past month cocaine use	0.9%	0.4%

Sources: SAMHSA, Office of Applied Studies, National Survey on Drug Use and Health. 2002.

National Drug Monitor, Trimbos Institute. Report to the EMCDDA by the Reitox National Focal Point. "The Netherlands: Drug Situation 2002."

Critics of methadone maintenance argue that such programs encourage wider use of hard drugs. They also assert that these plans will not be acceptable to most citizens, who will continue to label addicts as criminals and sinful. Liberals, although likely to approve of either plan over the current criminal model, foresee a danger in government control over an addict population dependent on it for drugs. Also, such programs attack the problem at the individual level (blaming the victim) and ignore the social and cultural sources of drug use.

Noninterference

Libertarians argue that it is none of the government's business what drugs people put into their bodies. There should be no governmental interference in this private act. This view, however, does not excuse drug users from their behavior. Former Seattle police officer Norm Stampler says,

> *If I choose to inject, inhale, sniff, snort, or for that matter, put a bullet in my brain, that's a choice I should have as an adult. Where the line is drawn for society is if I choose to be irresponsible in committing those acts. Then I need to be held accountable for my behavior. For instance, if I furnish a kid with drugs, or if I abuse a spouse, then I need to be held accountable for my criminal actions. The hypocrisy of keeping the prohibition on these substances going, yet making no moves to ban alcohol as a choice for adults, is staggering. We know there are far greater problems associated with alcohol abuse. Just as with alcohol, though, I think it should be viewed as a basic civil liberty for people to be able to use whatever drugs they want, and second, to treat the abuse of drugs as a medical problem, which is what it is. It is a public health issue, not an issue for the law to deal with. (Quoted in Talvi 2005:27)*

Proponents of total decriminalization of drugs argue that all societies throughout known history have had psychoactive drugs. Legislation and strict enforcement will not curb the tendency among many people to want to alter their consciousness artificially. Such acts should be neither penalized nor encouraged because it is none of the government's business what individuals do to themselves. The United States could follow the example of Latin American countries such as Brazil, Uruguay, Portugal, and Mexico, who have all changed their laws to eliminate jail time for people carrying small amounts of drugs for personal use. (For the way that the Dutch handle marijuana, see the Social Policy panel titled "Dutch Marijuana Policy.")

Critics suggest that decriminalization will encourage the spread of drug use. Drug use will spread because drugs will be readily available and because commercial interests will see potential profits in these formerly illicit drugs and will produce them and promote their use. Finally, and perhaps most significant, some argue that drug use is not an isolated act that affects only the user. In short, although many people believe that drug use is a "victimless vice," there is always a victim. To those who would argue that at the very least, marijuana should be put in the same category as alcohol and tobacco, Sabet argues,

> *Alcohol and tobacco are a favorite reference point for those who wish to legalize drugs. Since those two killers are legal—indeed alcohol contributes to more violent crime than crack cocaine—why not just legalize other dangerous substances (or at least one more) and regulate their sale? Why the difference between alcohol and tobacco on one hand and marijuana on the other, especially when we know that alcohol use has a much greater association with violence than marijuana use?*
>
> *Even a cursory glance at the status of our two legal drugs shows us that to add a third drug to this list would exacerbate an already difficult public health problem. Tobacco kills half a million people every year. Alcohol is worse—not only is it responsible for negative health effects on the drinker but on people around them. If we are to look at these two legal drugs as indicators of behavior associated with legal drug use, we see a pattern: legal drugs are by definition easy to obtain; commercialization glamorizes their use and furthers their social acceptance, their price is low, and high profits make promotion worthwhile for sellers. Subsequently—inevitably—more users occur, more addicts, and the increased use results in more social and health damage, increased deaths, and greater economic burden. When sellers rely on addiction for profit, there is not a strong case that drugs—even just marijuana—should be sold alongside alcohol and tobacco. (Sabet 2007:341)*

What, then, is the answer to drug use? Probably some combination of these alternatives makes the most sense. Clearly, the arguments about the solution will continue to incite passion. There will be those who are concerned with the use of certain drugs and who feel that society must control such deviance. They insist on imposing their morals on others. At the other extreme are those who are more concerned with how the laws and their rigorous enforcement cause social problems. As the various segments of society continue the debate, legislation will be proposed and eventually passed. The astute observer should note the role of interest groups in what is decided and also who benefits and who loses by the decision reached.

Address the Social Causes of Drug Use

When one looks at drug use across the United States, it is clear that drugs are correlated with poverty, education, gender, social location, and race/ethnicity. Elliott Currie, who has written perceptively about drugs in the United States, writes:

> If we are to solve the drug problem, we must attack the conditions that breed it. It is not accidental that the United States has both the developed world's worst drug problem and its worst violence, poverty, and social exclusion, together with its least adequate provision of health care, income support, and social services. Taking on the drug problem in an enduring way means tackling those social deficits head-on. (Currie 1993:280–281)

The United States has spent billions of dollars tackling the supply side of drugs through regulating its borders and other social control efforts, yet an effective drug policy must also focus on reducing the demand for drugs. Addressing social problems such as poverty, violence, and racial-ethnic inequality is a necessary first step in lowering drug use rates in America.

■ CHAPTER REVIEW

1. Whether drugs in U.S. society are defined as legal or illegal is based not on their potential for harm to the users or society but on politics—the exercise of power by interest groups and the majority to legislate their views on others.

2. The acceptability of certain drugs such as marijuana or heroin has varied historically. Opiates, once legal in the United States, became illegal for two reasons: (a) members of the White working class on the West Coast felt threatened by cheap Chinese labor and sought coercive measures against those Chinese; and (b) religious groups interpreting opiate use as a moral evil mounted successful pressure. The result was the Harrison Narcotics Act of 1914, which established a Narcotics Division of the Treasury

Department whose goal was to eliminate drug addiction. Behavior once considered a medical problem became a criminal problem.

3. Laws defining which drugs are legal and which are not reflect negative stereotypes held by the general public and efforts for control by interest groups (such as religious groups, the pharmaceutical industry, and organized crime) and law enforcement professionals. The result is that current drug laws are illogical. They are not related to the danger of the drugs but reflect the political interests of the powerful.

4. Most people in the United States take some drug on a regular basis. Those drugs considered legal are caffeine, alcohol, nicotine, tranquilizers, amphetamines, and barbiturates. Illegal drugs

used by millions in U.S. society are marijuana, cocaine, methamphetamine, inhalants, psychedelics, and heroin.

5. The prevailing culture, group norms, and social pressures strongly affect the patterns of drug use and their behavioral effects. Drug use varies by age, education level, race, gender, and social class. Men of all ages are more likely than women to use illegal drugs.

6. The pressure to use drugs may come from doctors, coaches, pharmaceutical firms, tobacco and alcohol companies, and one's friends and associates. Drugs are used increasingly to meet cultural standards of mental and physical perfection.

7. The U.S. war on drugs costs approximately $1 billion per week. It entails stopping drugs from coming into the country and punishing those who use and sell drugs. In large part, this war has not succeeded.

8. Drug laws promote crime in at least three ways: (a) users often engage in criminal activity because the drugs, being illegal, are so expensive; (b) punitive drug laws encourage organized crime by making importation, processing, and distribution of illegal drugs extremely lucrative; and (c) people selling illicit drugs often corrupt the police.

9. The drug war appears to be racist because of four patterns in the criminal justice system: (a) Blacks and Latinos are overrepresented in the prison population for drug offenses given their numbers in the population and their drug usage statistics; (b) drug enforcement of crack cocaine occurs almost exclusively in minority neighborhoods; (c) although crack cocaine and powder cocaine are basically the same, the government punishes the (primarily Black) users and sellers of crack much more severely; and (d) the courts tend to administer medical treatment for White drug users and the criminal justice system for Black users.

10. Government can adopt alternative policies toward drug use: (a) prohibition of trade and use through enforcement of criminal penalties (the current policy); (b) regulation through licensing and taxation; (c) noninterference (ignoring drugs because what people do to themselves is not the government's business); and (d) address the underlying social causes of drug use to reduce the demand for drugs.

■ KEY TERMS

Drug. Any substance that affects the structure or function of the body when ingested.

Politics of drugs. The labeling of some drugs as licit and others as illicit depends on the definition of drugs by the most powerful interest groups, which are able to get their definitions incorporated into the law.

Psychoactive drug. Chemical that alters the perceptions and/or moods of people who take it.

Gateway drug. The belief that the use of a drug will lead to the use of other hard drugs like heroin and cocaine.

Moral panic. Moral panics occur when a social problem is defined as a threat to societal values and interests. Moral panics typically involve the exaggeration of a social problem; the public response to it is also exaggerated.

Psychopharmacology. Science of drugs that affect the mind.

Restorative drug. Chemical that heals a traumatized part of the body.

Additive drug. Chemical that improves performance.

Interdiction. Public policy of stopping the flow of drugs into the United States by guarding the borders and by curtailing the creation, processing, and distributing of drugs in other countries.

Heroin maintenance. British approach to heroin addiction that treats addicts as sick rather than as criminal; thus, addicts are placed under the jurisdiction of physicians who administer drugs to their patients.

Methadone maintenance. Used for heroin maintenance, this treatment provides a heroin substitute (methadone) to addicts under medical supervision.

Decriminalization of drugs. Legalization of drugs.

■ SUCCEED WITH PEARSON mysoclab www.mysoclab.com

Experience, Discover, Observe, Evaluate
MySocLab is designed just for you. This chapter features a pre-test and post-test to help you learn and review key concepts and terms.

Experience sociology in action with dynamic visual activities, videos, and readings to enhance your learning experience. Complete the following activities at www.mysoclab.com.

Social Explorer is an interactive application that allows you to explore Census data through interactive maps.

- Explore the Social Explorer Map: *Increases in Prison Populations*

The Core Concepts in Sociology video clips offer a real-world perspective on sociological concepts.

- Watch *Opium Addiction*

MySocLibrary includes primary source readings from classic and contemporary sociologists.

- Read Leo, *American Preschoolers on Ritalin;* Gelles & Cavanaugh, *Association Is Not Causation: Alcohol and Other Drugs Do Not Cause Violence;* MacCoun & Reuter, *Does Europe Do It Better? Lessons from Holland, Britain, and Switzerland*

National Security in the Twenty-First Century

By inspiring legions of anti-American terrorists where there were few, by straining the U.S. military to its breaking point, by alienating traditional and potential allies abroad, by frightening other states into acquiring new weapons and by provoking popular revulsion around the world, the [Iraq] war has undermined our real national security. . . .
—Stephen F. Cohen

The mission of the Department of Defense is to protect the American people and advance the nation's interests (U.S. Department of Defense 2010). Every four years the Pentagon reviews the mission of the military in the light of changes in international and domestic environments. The *2010 Quadrennial Review* provides the current state of U.S. national security: "The United States faces a complex and uncertain security landscape in which the pace of change continues to accelerate" (p. iii). Among the challenges for defending the nation's interests are (U.S. Department of Defense 2010:iii–iv):

- The rise of China and India will continue to shape an international system that is no longer easily defined.

- Globalization has transformed the process of technological innovation while lowering the entry barriers for a wider range of actors to acquire advanced technologies.
- Nonstate actors (i.e., terrorist groups) will continue to gain influence.
- The proliferation of weapons of mass destruction (WMDs) continues to undermine global security. The instability or collapse of a WMD-armed state is among the most troubling concerns.
- Several powerful trends such as demographic pressures, the increasingly limited resources (e.g., arable land, water, oil), the effects of climate change, the emergence of new strains of disease, and rapid urbanization may exacerbate future conflicts.

Reflecting the new realities, the Defense Department states,

The U.S. military must prepare for a combination of humanitarian missions, untraditional threats such as cyberattacks, environmental disasters, terrorist groups seeking weapons of mass destruction and as many as two major conflicts. (The Quadrennial Defense Review, *reported in Youssef 2010:1A*)

These sections of this chapter describe (1) the magnitude of the military establishment, (2) the threat of nuclear weapons, (3) the threat of domestic terrorism, and (4) the threat of international terrorism.

THE U.S. MILITARY ESTABLISHMENT

Nation-states organize to defend their national security by protecting borders, guarding their national interests, and shielding their citizens and businesses abroad with armies, military bases, intelligence networks, embassies, and consulates. National security in the United States is a responsibility of the president and the cabinet members who run the departments of State, Justice, Defense, and Homeland Security.

The Size of the U.S. Military

The size of the U.S. military establishment is enormous. Here are the facts:

- In 2009 there were 1,454,515 active military personnel. This is an all-volunteer military (see the "Speaking to Students" panel). Conscription can be enacted by request of the president and approval of Congress.
- In 2009 there were 848,000 members of the guard and reserve. These are people who can be "called up" by the Defense Department to carry out a number of activities ranging from patrol of our airports to support missions, like guarding prison detainees, and who back up the troops in combat areas such as Afghanistan and Iraq.
- There were 678,025 civilians on the military payroll in 2009. Most of them do clerical work, report writing, and technical jobs.
- The military operates 865 military bases and other facilities in 135 nations located on every continent. About 451,000 of the Defense Department's personnel are overseas or afloat. The United States spends approximately

Speaking to Students

Recruiting an All-Volunteer Military

The Pentagon in 2009 had a $5 billion recruiting budget. In that year the U.S. military met its annual recruiting goals for the first time in thirty-five years. This shift occurred because of three factors. The first was unplanned. That is, the economic downturn (the Great Recession) and rising joblessness led more youths to enlist (Tyson 2009). Pentagon research shows that a 10 percent increase in the national unemployment rate generally translates into a 4 to 6 percent improvement in recruiting (reported in the *Progressive* 2009).

A second reason for the rise in volunteer recruits in 2009 was that recruits were enticed by an average signing bonus of $14,000 compared to $12,000 in 2008.

Third, military recruiters were armed with information on each potential recruit, giving them an edge in gaining rapport and softening them up to the decision to join up.

In the past few years, the military has mounted a virtual invasion into the lives of young Americans. Using data mining, stealth websites, career tests, and sophisticated marketing software, the Pentagon is harvesting and analyzing information on everything from high school students' GPAs and SAT scores to which video games they play. *Before an Army recruiter even picks up the phone to call a prospect, the soldier may know more about the kid's habits than do his own parents* (emphasis added). . . .

To put all of its data to use, the military has enlisted the help of Nielsen Claritas, a research and marketing firm whose clients include BMW, AOL, and Starbucks. Last year, it rolled out a "custom segmentation" program that allows a recruiter armed with address, age, race, and gender of a potential "lead" to call up a wealth of information about young people in the immediate area, including recreation and consumption patterns. The program even suggests pitches that might work while cold-calling teenagers. "It's just a foot in the door for a recruiter to start a relevant conversation with a young person," says Donna Dorminey of the U.S. Army Center for Accessions Research. (Goodman 2009:21–22)

$250 billion annually to maintain troops, equipment, fleets, and bases overseas (Danes 2009).

- The headquarters of the Department of Defense is the Pentagon in Washington, D.C. It is one of the world's largest office buildings, with 17.5 miles of corridors.
- The military has a worldwide satellite network providing constant intelligence, surveillance, and communication.
- The United States has the world's largest navy and air force and the most sophisticated weapons.
- The carbon footprint of the military is huge (e.g., the U.S. armed forces consume about 14 million gallons of oil per day; Johansen 2009).
- The government outsources some military operations to private firms. There are more of these nonmilitary personnel (53 percent) in Iraq and Afghanistan than military personnel. For example, there were more than 218,000 private U.S. contractors in Iraq and Afghanistan in 2009 (Schwartz 2009). The largest of these security companies is Blackwater, which provides security, conducts clandestine raids against suspected insurgents, and transports detainees. These contractors deploy "private forces in a war zone

free of public scrutiny, with the deaths, injuries and crimes of those forces shrouded in secrecy. [They] are shielded from accountability, oversight and legal constraints" (Scahill 2007:13; see also, Scahill 2009).

- In 2008 there were 23.2 million military veterans. Of these veterans, 2.9 million received compensation for service-connected disabilities for a total compensation of $36.2 billion.

The Cost of Maintaining U.S. Military Superiority

Military might has been the typical security strategy of nations. Since World War II, the United States, for example, has spent more than $20 trillion (adjusted for inflation) on military defense. The defense budget, which represents the government's spending plan for the military for fiscal 2011 (which begins on October 1, 2010) was $741 billion. The military budget includes an operating budget of $549 billion, plus funding for the Iraq and Afghanistan wars at $192 billion, including an extra $33 billion for expanding the war in Afghanistan (*Sojourners* 2010). Significantly, for the first time the cost of the war in Afghanistan will exceed the cost in Iraq. Not included in the military budget are the indirect costs of war: veterans benefits, including health care and disability costs, federal debt payments due to military expenditures, covert intelligence operations, federal research on military and space programs, and at least half the budget for the Energy Department (Parenti 2008:78). Taken together, actual military spending for fiscal 2011 will exceed $1 trillion.

The United States with a formal military budget of $741 billion ($2.2 billion a day) outspends all other nations on national security. In fact, the United States spends more than 40 percent of the combined total of worldwide military expenditures. The "military outlay by the U.S. plus its NATO allies accounts for about 70 percent of world military spending. Add in America's other allies and friends, such as South Korea, and the total share of global military outlay hits 80 percent" (Bandow 2010: para 12). Not counting the costs of the Iraq and Afghanistan wars, the U.S. outspends China by five times and ten times that of Russia, and twenty-nine times the combined spending of the six "rogue" states (Cuba, Iran, Libya, North Korea, Sudan, and Syria; Greenwald 2010a).

There are at least four reasons why U.S. defense spending is so high and continues to grow. First, there is the ongoing fear of nuclear weapons. Russia has a huge nuclear arsenal. Russia and other nations of the former Soviet Union, although much less a threat than before 1990, remain a potential threat to U.S. security. Rogue states such as North Korea and Iran pose a significant threat as they join the nuclear club.

Second, the world, even without the Soviet threat, is an unsafe place, where terrorism and aggression occur and must be confronted and contained. Several nations, including regimes with expansionist agendas and hated enemies, have nuclear weapons or soon will have them. They also have chemical and biological weapons. Several nations are suspected of supporting terror and working to develop weapons of mass destruction (nuclear, biological, or chemical weapons capable of large-scale deaths and destruction). Iran, in particular, is a special worry in the tense Middle East, especially for Israel.

Third, defense expenditures bring profits to corporations, create jobs, and generate growth in the economy. For example, many corporations benefited from the wars in Afghanistan and Iraq as Defense Department contracts more than doubled from 2000 to 2005. The five largest contractors in 2009 were Lockheed

Martin ($14.9 billion), Boeing ($10.8 billion), Northrup Grumman ($9.9 billion), General Dynamics ($6.1 billion), and Ratheon ($5.9 billion; *Washington Technology* 2010). (See the Closer Look panel on Lockheed Martin.) With huge contracts available, these corporations spend millions on lobbying. For example, the ten largest defense contractors spent more than $27 million lobbying the federal government in the *last quarter* of 2009, an increase of $7.2 million from the last quarter of 2008 (Hattern 2010). Corporate military contractors are eager for more contracts, for the following reasons (Parenti 2008:80):

- There are few risks. Unlike manufacturers who must worry about selling the goods they produce, defense corporations have a guaranteed contract.
- Almost all contracts are awarded without competitive bidding and at whatever price the corporation sets. If the cost exceeds the bid (cost overruns) then the government picks up the tab.
- The Pentagon directly subsidizes defense contractors with free research and development, public lands, buildings, and renovations.
- Defense spending does not compete with the consumer market. Moreover, the market is virtually limitless, as there are always more advanced weapons systems to develop and obsolete weaponry to replace.

Members of Congress are eager to support an expansive military machine for two reasons. First, no politician would campaign to reduce the military for fear of being labelled unpatriotic and thereby risk defeat in the next election. Second, politicians gain support from their constituents if they bring military money to their corporations, communities, and state. Lawmakers even team up with defense contractors to fight for certain targeted programs even when the Pentagon says that it does not need the weaponry in question.

The C-17 Globemaster offers one illustration of successful opposition to the Obama-Gates [Secretary of Defense] push for control of weapons spending. C-17s are large cargo planes produced by Boeing that cost $250 million apiece. They have been used heavily since 1993 to transport troops, tanks, and supplies. Every year since 2006, the Pentagon has said that it has enough C-17s. And every year, Congress overrules the military and authorizes funds for additional planes. In October the Senate approved $2.5 billion in the 2010 budget for 10 more C-17s, which would bring the fleet to 215. (Elgin and Epstein 2009:47)

The 2011 Obama budget proposal excluded funds for additional C-17s.

In 2009, California led the way with defense contract expenditures in that state totaling $27.9 billion, followed by Virginia ($23.4 billion) and Texas ($21.1 billion; *StateMaster* n.d.). As an example, consider the consequences for military spending in Massachusetts, which received $8.3 billion in 2006, almost $1,300 for every person living in that state. The money was spread among twenty-seven communities and was the fifth-largest source of jobs in the state (Belkin 2006). Even a small state such as Kansas has three major bases, has 40,000 members in the military, and receives a military boost to the economy of $7.7 billion (Milburn 2009). In sum, business, labor, the states, Congress, and academia combine to present a unified voice supporting massive and increasing military expenditures. Opposing this behemoth are only faint voices from individuals and groups seeking to reduce the huge costs of the military-industrial complex.

Finally, the disproportionate amount that the United States appropriates for war is based on the assumption that by having the world's costliest military force and being so far ahead of other nations in military strength and technology,

A CLOSER LOOK

LOCKHEED MARTIN

- Government contracts 2009: $14,983,515,367 (*Washington Technology* 2010)
- Total lobbying expenditures in 2009: $13,533.782 (Schouten 2010)
- Campaign contributions to federal candidates through PACs in 2008: $1,623,944 (*SourceWatch* 2009)

Lockheed Martin was formed in 1995 with the merger of two of the world's premier technology companies—Lockheed Corporation and Martin Marietta Corporation. The company employs about 140,000 people worldwide.

It has 1,000 facilities in 500 cities, 46 states, and in 75 nations and territories. Lockheed Martin is the world's number one military contractor, as well as the world's largest arms exporter. It dominates the fighter aircraft sector and is heavily involved in transport aircraft, missiles, and space systems.

In addition to lobbying and campaign contributions, Lockheed Martin has links with the government and the Pentagon that make it easier to obtain government contracts. For example, its board of directors includes a number of former high-ranking government officials: the former head of the U.S. Strategic Command, former vice president of the Joint Chiefs of Staff, former deputy Secretary of Homeland Security, former Secretary of Commerce, and a former Secretary of Defense (Derysh 2009). One of the above, former Secretary of Defense Pete Aldridge, in the month before he left the Pentagon to join Lockheed's board, approved a $3 billion contract to build 20 Lockheed planes. Furthermore, while on Lockheed's Board of Directors, Aldridge was appointed by President George W. Bush, to chair the president's commission on space exploration—a possible conflict of interest (*SourceWatch* 2008).

Lockheed has also been able to exercise its influence in a larger way—in support of the invasion of Iraq. The company's former vice president, Bruce Jackson, chaired the Coalition for the Liberation of Iraq, a bipartisan group formed to promote Bush's plan for war in Iraq. Jackson was also involved in corralling the support for the war from Eastern European countries, going so far as helping to write their letter of endorsement for military intervention. Not surprisingly, Lockheed also has business relations with these countries.

In the last few years, the SEC has investigated Lockheed for insider trading and falsifying its accounts. Lockheed Martin leads all defense contractors with 50 instances of misconduct from 1995 to 2008 (American Project on Government Oversight [POGO] 2009). These instances include age, race, and sex discrimination, contract fraud, unfair business practices, contractor kickbacks, federal election law violation, environ-mental violations, improper charges, nuclear safety violations, pricing irregularities, and overcharges. In 2010, the Secretary of Defense, Robert Gates, fined the military officer overseeing the Pentagon's new F-35 stealth-fighter-jet program for cost overruns and technical failures and punished Lockheed Martin by withholding $615 million in fees. Despite the ongoing cases of misconduct (a serious example of corporate recidivism), Lockheed Martin continues to be the number one supplier of military goods to the government.

no one would dare challenge us militarily. Although other nations may have more people (China and India), they do not have the United States' sophisticated weaponry, weapons delivery systems, and nuclear stockpile. The United States chooses to retain this superiority because its leaders believe there is "peace through strength."

This strategy succeeded for the most part during the Cold War years, as the United States and the Soviet Union engaged in an expensive arms race to strike first if necessary and to scare the other side into not attacking first. The attacks on the World Trade Center and the Pentagon showed that this rationale does not hold for the terrorism that we confront in the twenty-first century.

"Oh, that's good, sir, that's very good—'What if they gave a war and nobody profited.'"

> *It [the U.S. military machine] is probably the most effective conventional-war fighting force in history. But the basic assumptions, the culture, of the military-intelligence complex seem suddenly anachronistic. The nexus of national defense and intelligence agencies may be as unsuited for a long-term offensive anti-terrorist campaign as they were to defend New York and Washington against the aerial attacks of September 11th. (Klein 2001:44)*

THE THREAT OF NUCLEAR WEAPONS

Nuclear weapons involve the most destructive technology on Earth. During the Cold War (the intense tension and arms race between the United States and the Soviet Union that lasted from the end of World War II until 1990), the two superpowers had most of the nuclear weapons. The United States and Russia in 2009 possessed 96 percent of the world's nuclear warheads. Other nuclear power holders were France, Britain, China, Israel, Pakistan, India, and North Korea (*Guardian* 2009). The year 1998 was a turning point, as the world entered a new nuclear era when India tested five bombs, followed two weeks later by its rival neighbor, Pakistan.

> *The second nuclear era, unlike the dawn of the first nuclear age in 1945, is characterized by a world of porous national borders, rapid communications that facilitate the spread of technical knowledge, and expanded commerce in potentially dangerous dual-use technologies and materials. (Bulletin of the Atomic Scientists 2007:67)*

Thus, in this globalized world, we face a threatening situation in which as many as forty countries have the capacity to develop nuclear weapons in a very short time span. Two nations, designated by President George W. Bush as part of the "axis of evil," are in this group: North Korea tested a bomb in 2006, and Iran is believed to be close to developing nuclear weapons.

What we have now is not a tight club of nuclear powers with interlocking interests and an appreciation for the brutal doctrine of "mutually assured destruction" but an unpredictable host of potential Bomb throwers: a Stalinist Bomb out of unstable North Korea; a Shiite Bomb out of Iran; a Sunni Bomb out of Pakistan; and, down the road, possibly out of Egypt and Saudi Arabia as well; and, of course, an al-Qaeda Bomb out of nowhere. (Powell 2006:32)

The newcomers to the nuclear club, unlike the charter members, are not governed by elaborate rules and sophisticated technology designed to prevent accidents and firing in haste. Instead, they are dealing with the savagery of ethnic strife, intense religious differences, and insecure nations. Moreover, there is the danger of nuclear weapons or weapons-grade materials falling into the hands of terrorists—"the one enemy we know would probably not hesitate to use them" (Keller 2003:51).

Nuclear technology is expected to accelerate as nations turn to atomic power for their domestic energy requirements. This technology gives them the ability to make reactor fuel, or with the same equipment and a little more effort, bomb fuel (Broad and Sanger 2006). Thus, the tension and the threat will continue to accelerate.

THE TERRORIST THREAT

Terrorism is a major national security threat, as the United States experienced with the ramming of hijacked planes into the World Trade Center and the Pentagon on September 11, 2001. Terrorism is any act intended to cause death or serious injury to civilians or noncombatants to intimidate a population and weaken their will or draw attention to the perpetrator's cause. Thus, terrorist acts are political acts. In the case of the September 11 terrorist attack, al-Qaeda, Osama bin Laden's organization, sought to show the vulnerability of the United States and to rally other extremist Islamists in a war against—in their words—"the Great Satan." So, too, was the bombing of the federal building in Oklahoma City by ex-soldier Timothy McVeigh, who had grievances with the U.S. government. Also, when Joseph Stack flew an airplane into a building housing Internal Revenue Service offices in Austin, Texas, to advance his political grievances, it was an act of terrorism (Greenwald 2010b). Similarly, the killing of abortion doctors and the bombing of abortion clinics are terrorist acts, making a political statement.

Terrorism is "not an enemy; it is a methodology of using violence to gain political objectives" (Greider 2004:11). It is a tactic used historically by groups against governments and organizations viewed as unjust and oppressive. Terrorists believe that they are legitimate combatants, fighting for a just cause, by whatever means possible. The warfare is asymmetric—that is, terrorism is the method of less well-armed and less powerful opponents. Because, typically, they do not have sophisticated weapons, terrorists use what is cheap and available. Instead of guided missiles, they use suicide bombers—"the poor man's air force" (Davis 2006). Because they do not have weapons of mass destruction, they use "weapons of mass disruption" such as arson, infecting computers with viruses (cyberterrorism), and disrupting mass transit. They instill fear through kidnapping, raping, and torturing victims and even showing the beheading of these victims on television. Note that terrorism as a method of asymmetric warfare is not exclusively a Muslim or al-Qaeda method but also a method used, for example, by the American revolutionaries, the Irish Republican Army, the Viet Cong, and antidictatorial forces in Latin America.

Terrorism is a social construction (Turk 2004). That is, what is defined as terrorism and who is labeled a terrorist are matters of interpretation of events and their presumed causes. Consider the different meanings for these words: terrorist/freedom fighter or suicide bomber/martyr.

> *The powerful conflict parties, especially governments, generally succeed in labeling their more threatening (i.e., violent) opponents as terrorists, whereas attempts by opponents to label officially sanctioned violence as "state terrorism" have little chance of success unless supported by powerful third parties (e.g., the United Nations). (Turk 2004:272)*

Most of the remainder of this chapter is devoted to international terrorism, but let us begin with a brief account of the internal terrorist threat: attacks by Americans on Americans.

DOMESTIC TERRORISM

Typically, we typically think of terrorism as deadly acts committed by foreigners, usually Islamic fundamentalists from the Middle East. Thus, when a bomb destroyed the federal building in Oklahoma City in 1995, killing 168, the immediate suspects were Muslim extremists. But Timothy McVeigh and Terry Nichols, two American ex-military men, were convicted of that crime. (McVeigh received the death penalty for detonating the bomb and was executed in 2001; Nichols was sentenced to life imprisonment for his involvement in planning the attack.) As extreme as the Oklahoma City bombing was, the act of an American detonating a bomb to harm other Americans is not unusual because there are about 2,000 illegal bombings annually within the United States (National Academies 1998).

Foreigners acting alone or as agents of their organization or government killing Americans is relatively easy to understand, but Americans killing Americans is more difficult to comprehend. The history of the United States, however, is full of examples of various dissident groups that have used violence against their neighbors to achieve their aims (Hewitt 2003). Colonists, farmers, settlers, Native Americans, immigrants, slaves, slaveholders, laborers, strike breakers, anarchists, vigilantes, the Ku Klux Klan and other White supremacist organizations, antiwar protesters, radical environmentalists, and prolife extremists have acted outside the law to accomplish their ends.* Just in recent years antiabortion terrorists have bombed abortion clinics and murdered abortion doctors. One of those doctors, George Tiller, was wounded in 1993, his clinic was bombed and vandalized, and then in 2009 he was killed by an antiabortion zealot. Also, various extremists have bombed African American churches,

---

*It is important to note that the law can be a friend or an enemy. The agents of government (e.g., police, FBI, military, national guard, and the courts) defend the law even with force but what if a group considers the law immoral, as do prolife supporters or Martin Luther King, Jr., who led protests against the Jim Crow laws in the South? Is it appropriate for them to use unlawful acts to overturn what they consider a bad law?

By Mike Smith. *Las Vegas Sun.* United Features Syndicate.

Mike Smith Edt (new) © King Features Syndicate.

Jewish synagogues, and Islamic mosques throughout the United States, U.S. Bureau of Land Management and Forest Service offices, and the 1996 Olympic games in Atlanta. In addition to bombings, there have been acts of arson, beatings, killings, and letters/packages with bombs or anthrax addressed to political targets.

Extreme actions by the government have persuaded some individuals to become part of extremist groups. The government's actions in conducting the Vietnam War and its reactions to protesters (e.g., the killing of Kent State students by the National Guard) led some groups such as the "Weathermen" to use violence to further their cause. Two events in the 1990s energized the Patriot movement. In 1992 the Bureau of Alcohol, Tobacco, and Firearms (ATF) attacked Randy Weaver, a White supremacist in Idaho, for gun violations. In the process Weaver's wife and son were killed by ATF snipers. The second event was the 1993 assault by ATF on David Koresh and the Branch Davidians near Waco, Texas. This siege, again over guns violations, ended with the deaths of 86 men, women, and children. Those in the Patriot movement interpreted these acts as government run amok, using its power to take away the liberties that individuals are granted by the Constitution. Thus, the membership in this movement, "far from thinking itself outside the law, believes it is the critical force making for a restoration of the Constitution" (Wills 1995:52). See the "Voices" panel for a letter from Timothy McVeigh, airing his grievances with the U.S. government.

The Patriot movement faded somewhat in the late 1990s, although pockets remained. But ten years later the momentum was revived. In 2009 the number of hate groups rose to 932, up 54 percent since 2000. In 2009 another 50 new right-wing militia groups emerged (Southern Poverty Law Center, reported in D'Oro 2009). The U.S. Department of Homeland Security issued a report warning that current political and economic conditions resembled those of the early 1990s, when there was an upsurge in right-wing extremism that culminated in the Oklahoma City bombing (Blow 2009; Krugman 2009a).

VOICES

A LETTER FROM TIMOTHY McVEIGH

Three years before he ignited a bomb that destroyed the federal building in Oklahoma City, killing 168 people, Timothy McVeigh wrote a letter to his hometown newspaper, the Lockport (N.Y.) *Union-Sun & Journal*, listing his concerns about the government.

Crime is out of control. Criminals have no fear of punishment. Prisons are overcrowded so they know they will not be imprisoned long. . . .

Taxes are a joke. Regardless of what a political candidate "promises," they will increase taxes. More taxes are always the answer to government mismanagement. . . .

The "American Dream" of the middle class has all but disappeared, substituted with people struggling just to buy next week's groceries. Heaven forbid the car breaks down! . . .

Politicians are out of control. Their yearly salaries are more than an average person will see in a lifetime. They have been entrusted with the power to regulate their own salaries, and have grossly violated that trust to live in their own luxury. . . .

Who is to blame for the mess? At a point when the world has seen communism falter as an imperfect system to manage people, democracy seems to be headed down the same road. No one is seeing the "big" picture. . . .

What is it going to take to open up the eyes of our elected officials? AMERICA IS IN SERIOUS DECLINE.

We have no proverbial tea to dump; should we instead sink a ship full of Japanese imports? Is a Civil War imminent? Do we have to shed blood to reform the current system? I hope it doesn't come to that. But it might.

There was a resurgence of populist anger, coinciding with the Great Recession, that emerged in 2009. Leading the charge was the Tea Party movement (there is some dispute over the name's origin: was it taken from the 1773 tax revolt, or is it an acronym for "taxed enough already"?). This movement is a platform for conservative populist discontent. It embodies a brand of politics historically associated with libertarians, populists, and those on the fringe: militia groups, hate groups, and anti-immigration advocates. Tea Party activists, although divided on a number of issues, agree that "government is too big. Spending is out of control. Individual freedom is at risk. And President Barack Obama's policies are making it all worse" (Associated Press 2010: para 1). The catalyst was the election of Barack Hussein Obama, the first African American president. This raised two fears for some in the movement: that he was African American and that he was a Muslim. There is more than a hint of racism here. "For some white Americans of a certain age and background, the sight of a black man in the Oval Office, even one who went to Harvard Law School and conducts himself in the manner of an aloof WASP aristocrat, is an affront" (Cassidy 2010: para 2). Also, there is an anti-Islam strain among some in the movement. Fanning these flames, the *Washington Times* ran an article declaring that President Obama "not only identifies with Muslims, but actually may be one himself" (quoted in Krugman 2009a: para 8). One segment of the movement—the Birthers—questioned the legitimacy of Obama to be president because, they argued, his birth certificate was bogus and his father was an African. These fears were fomented by conservative talk show hosts on radio and cable television, who "have gone out of their way to provide a platform for conspiracy theories and apocalyptic rhetoric" (Krugman 2009a: para 5). Most significant, under Obama and the Democrats, broad federal programs were initiated, such as attempted national health care; bailouts of Wall Street banks (actually begun

The Tea Party Movement is a platform for conservative populist discontent. They are enraged by an expanding federal government and liberal government programs and policies.

© Jim West/The Image Works

by President Bush), General Motors, and Chrysler; the $787 billion stimulus (TARP); and an immense and rapidly growing national debt. These were interpreted as moving the nation toward a totalitarian socialist state, with subsequent loss of freedoms, again fueled by talk show rhetoric. Fox News's Glenn Beck, for example, warned viewers that the Federal Emergency Management Agency (FEMA) "might be building concentration camps as part of the Obama administration's 'totalitarian' agenda" (Krugman 2009a: para 7). Obama, by the way, receives on average of 30 death threats a day (a 400 percent increase from the number received by President George W. Bush; Harnden 2009).

Obama's government programs were not only perceived as centralizing authority (an orchestrated "power grab") but also that they benefit the wealthy and educated elites but not average people (see the Closer Look panel airing the grievances of the Texas Suicide Flyer). And many of these average people were suffering in the bad economy. They were worried about their jobs, their retirement incomes, and their mortgages and paying for their children's education. Some were concerned that Whites were losing their numerical majority to non-Whites. For them, immigration, especially illegal immigration, has to be stopped. As Bill O'Reilly of Fox News complained to Senator John McCain about the number of undocumented Latino immigrants:

> *"Do you understand what the* New York Times *wants, and the far-left want? They want to break down the white, Christian, male power structure, of which you're a part and so am I. They hate America, and they hate it because it's run primarily by white, Christian men. They want to bring in millions of foreign nationals to basically break down the structure that we have." (quoted in Benjamin 2009: para 5)*

The Tea Party movement is difficult to define because there is no single Tea Party. "This is an amorphous, factionalized uprising with no clear leadership and no central structure" (Barstow 2010: para 15). Comprised within the movement are a number of local groups, often focusing on different issues. Some followers are gun rights activists, some rally against taxes, some want state sovereignty, some are White Supremacists, whereas others are concerned about

A CLOSER LOOK

THE TEXAS SUICIDE FLYER'S SUICIDE MANIFESTO

Reminiscent of the 9/11 attack, on February 18, 2010, Joseph Stack flew his single-engine plane into an Austin, Texas, office building that housed the Internal Revenue Service, killing two and injuring thirteen. He left behind a manifesto listing his grievances against Big Government and Big Business. Specifically, he railed against (Benjamin 2010):

- A crippled economy dominated by political and corporate potentates
- A campaign and election system rotted by special interests and money
- Government bailouts of corporate and banking interests, paid for with taxes from the "little guy"
- Excessively complicated tax laws that baffle small business owners and individuals

Stack's manifesto calls for a citizen's movement to change this foul system, and to change it through violence:

> I know I'm hardly the first one to decide I have had all I can stand.

It has always been a myth that people have stopped dying for their freedom in this country, and it isn't limited to the blacks, and poor immigrants. I know there have been countless before me and there are sure to be as many after. But I also know that by not adding my body to the count, I insure nothing will change. I choose to not keep looking over my shoulder at "big brother" while he strips my carcass. I choose not to ignore what is going on all round me. I choose not to pretend that business as usual won't continue. I have just had enough.

I can only hope that the numbers quickly get too big to be whitewashed and ignored that the American zombies wake up and revolt; it will take nothing less. I would only hope that by striking a nerve that stimulates the inevitable double standard, knee-jerk government reaction that results in more stupid draconian restrictions people wake up and begin to see

the pompous political thugs and their mindless minions for what they are. Sadly, though I spent my entire life trying to believe it wasn't so, *but violence not only is the answer, it is the only answer.* (emphasis added; Stack 2010: para. 32–33)

Rich Benjamin argues that Stach's complaints echo the issues raised by the Tea Party movement and should be taken seriously because they resonate with the protestations of so many.

Deplorable though he might be. Stack is not quite a "random bad apple." His act might be uncommon, but his jumbled populism is not. His crime is in no way excusable, but it spotlights a larger problem that both political and corporate elites like to caricature or dismiss: visceral populist anger. Stack may have suffered from mental illness, but he is also an acute symptom of this nation's neglected wounds. (Benjamin 2010: para. 16)

the federal government's interference in their freedoms. Connecting the disparate issues that preoccupy many Tea Party supporters is the strong feeling of impending governmental tyranny. This theme permeates the far right's commentary, the Tea Party websites, Facebook pages, Twitter feeds, and YouTube videos (Barstow 2010). Although many of these are relatively benign, some are not. In fact, the Simon Wiesenthal Center (Jewish human rights organization) noted that there was a 25 percent rise from 2008 to 2009 in the number of "problematic" social networking groups on the Internet. The report found that there are over 10,000 networking groups, portals, blogs, chat rooms, and videos on the Internet that promote racial violence, anti-Semitism, homophobia, hate music, and terrorism (cited in Parsons 2009).

This movement represents a passionate rebellion that has the potential to change the political landscape. It is important to note, that although most Tea

Partiers are nonviolent, there is a violent edge to the movement, fueled by frustration, anxiety, fear, and anger. Research shows that in difficult economic times, extremist groups emerge and flourish—groups such as Skinheads, neo-Nazis, militias, White Supremacists, and "Sovereign citizens," who believe that they do not have to pay taxes or obey most other laws, such as having a driver's license. (When Scott Roeder, the convicted killer of abortionist Dr. George Tiller, was arrested, sheriff deputies stopped his car because it had no license plate. Instead there was a tag declaring him a "sovereign" and immune from state law.) During hard times membership in these extremist groups increases, and the number of hate crimes (against gays, Muslims, recent immigrants, and people of color) rises dramatically.

At Tea Party rallies there are occasional placards that incite violence. There are pictures of Obama, redrawn as Hitler, the use of Nazi symbols such as swastikas, and signs reading "Death to Obama" and "Death to Michelle and her two stupid kids."

To reiterate: not all Tea Partiers are violent. They are angry and upset; they feel threatened. The movement represents a genuine backlash against current trends (Berlet 2010). And for some this backlash includes the seeds for violence by some individuals and groups.

INTERNATIONAL TERRORISM

The context for terrorist activity in today's world varies. The terrorists may be seeking separation from the dominant group by establishing an independent state, which is the goal of the Basques in Spain, the Chechnyans in Russia, and Northern Ireland, which seeks independence from Great Britain. They may be rival religious groups such as the Protestants and Catholics in Northern Ireland or Sunnis and Shiites, warring Muslim sects in the Middle East. Ethnic/religious groups in the former Yugoslavia—Serbs (Eastern Orthodox), Croatians (Catholics), and Bosnians (Muslims)—have fought each other with brutal tactics for centuries. Palestinian terrorists attack the Israeli government that keeps them in secondary status. Israeli extremists attack the Israeli government (e.g., the assassination of a moderate leader) when they believe that it will compromise with the Palestinians, as do Palestinian extremists who fear their leaders are not being militant enough with Israel. Various African countries have warring tribes seeking control through ethnic cleansing, and governments such as in Sudan use ethnic militias to terrorize through killings, rapes, and destruction of villages and farms to quell rebellious groups.

Globalization has quickened the pace, scale, and fear of terrorism. As nations become all the more connected, they are increasingly vulnerable to terrorist attacks. The United States, in particular, is relatively unprotected from terrorist attacks because it is a mobile, open society with porous borders that are difficult to police. Every day, over a million people enter the country legally (and many others illegally), as do almost 3,000 aircraft and over 16,000 containers on 600 ships. Satellite communications give the world an instant look at the consequences of terrorist acts. This capability heightens the motivation of terrorists, who seek to dramatize their grievances to a wide audience. Modern societies provide a huge array of possible targets for terrorists. The United States, for example, has 60,000 chemical plants and 103 nuclear plants that could be sabotaged. So, too, could hydroelectric dams, power grids, oil refineries, oil and natural gas pipelines, water treatment plants, and factories. Transportation systems (planes, trains, cargo ships) can be easily disrupted with explosions or computer glitches.

Clearly, humankind lives in an increasingly dangerous world—the context in which nations must seek national security. This section broadly outlines the challenges to the United States by the new terrorism; the U.S. response to terrorism, using the wars in Afghanistan and Iraq as the case study; and the consequences of this response for these nations, the United States, and the world.

U.S. NATIONAL SECURITY AND THE WAR ON TERROR

The U.S. attacks on Afghanistan and Iraq were the result of a number of historical events that converged to bring about the response of war.

Precursors to the 9/11 Attacks

Horrible and incomprehensible as the 9/11 attacks were, terrorism by Islamic radicals against the United States and its citizens was not born on that day. A chronology of terrorist acts directed at the United States by Islamic groups before 9/11 includes the following:

- In 1983, Shiite Muslim suicide bombers destroyed U.S. Marine and French paratrooper barracks in Lebanon, killing 299, including 241 Americans.
- In 1988, terrorists linked to Libya bombed a Pan Am 747 headed for the United States over Lockerbie, Scotland, killing 270 passengers and residents of the town.
- In 1993, a truck bomb was detonated in the garage of the World Trade Center, killing 6 and injuring more than 1,000.
- In 1995, the Army training headquarters in Riyadh, Saudi Arabia, was bombed, killing 5 Americans and wounding 31.
- In 1996, 19 U.S. soldiers were killed and 372 Americans injured by an attack on military housing in Dhahran, Saudi Arabia.
- In 1998, car bombs, organized by al-Qaeda, exploded outside U.S. embassies in Tanzania and Kenya, killing 224 people, including 12 Americans.
- In 2000, the USS *Cole* was attacked in a Yemen harbor by al-Qaeda suicide bombers in a small boat, killing 17 sailors and injuring 39.
- On September 10, 2001, the National Security Agency intercepted messages that said, "The match is about to begin" and "Tomorrow is zero hour." These messages were not translated until September 12 (Dickinson and Stein 2006).

The history of U.S. involvement in the Middle East, Afghanistan, and Iraq in the twentieth century helps to explain why the United States initiated wars after 9/11 and why it is having difficulty winning those wars.

A Brief History of U.S. Involvement in the Middle East.   Before World War II, the United States had only a very limited role in the Middle East. Following that war, three factors prompted U.S. involvement there—the great reserves of oil in the Middle East, the Cold War, and Israel. Because of the need for Middle East oil, the United States sought relationships with the leadership, especially in Saudi Arabia, Kuwait, and Iran, which often has meant siding with antidemocratic despots. In the case of Iran, the CIA backed the coup that overthrew Mossadegh in 1953 and installed the Shah of Iran. Under the Shah's despotic rule, the United States was actively involved in Iran. However, the Shah was forced to flee his nation in 1979 and was replaced by Ayatollah Ruhollah Khomeini, a very anti-American and highly revered spiritual leader. Also in that year, Islamic militants seized the U.S. embassy in Tehran and took sixty-six diplomats hostage.

This region was deemed strategic in the Cold War, as evidenced by the Eisenhower Doctrine, which declared that the United States would use economic and military aid and armed forces to stop the spread of communism in the Middle East. Under President Nixon, this doctrine was reinforced when the United States saw Israel as an anti-Soviet asset, made a military alliance with it, and supported it with massive military aid. Previously, in 1967, the United States backed Israel in its defeat of Egypt and Syria in the Six Day War, and Israel gained control of the West Bank, Gaza, and East Jerusalem. Since then, the Palestinians have lived under Israeli occupation. The rest of the Middle East sided with Palestine, bitterly opposing the Israeli occupation, thus sowing the seeds for the bitter feelings against the United States in the region today. Although the Cold War is over, the U.S. policy toward Israel remains totally pro-Israel, which inflames anti-U.S. actions in the Middle East.

- **A Brief History of Modern Afghanistan.** Afghanistan is a rural, mountainous country, with warlord-led tribal groups controlling various regions. The population is primarily Sunni Muslim. In 1979, the Soviet Union invaded and set up a local government (the following chronology is from BBC News n.d.). The Soviets were resisted by the mujahedin (Afghan freedom fighters), who were supplied with money, supplies, and arms by the United States, Pakistan, China, Iran, and Saudi Arabia. Beginning in 1986, the United States supplied the mujahedin with Stinger missiles (over 1,000 in a three-year period), enabling them to shoot down Soviet helicopters. Among the mujahedin leaders was a Saudi exile, Osama bin Laden. The Stinger missiles and bin Laden's organization—al-Qaeda—were later used against the United States. This is an example of blowback (the unintended consequences of a government's policies, whereby supplies and support given to a presumed ally are later used by the recipient against the benefactor, in this case, the United States; Johnson 2000).

  In 1989, the last Soviet troops left Afghanistan, but civil war continued as rival militias competed for influence and control. Eventually, a government was formed, but in 1996, the Taliban seized control, introducing and enforcing an extreme fundamentalist version of Islam. In 1997, the Taliban was recognized as legitimate by Pakistan and Saudi Arabia. In 1998, the United States launched missile strikes at suspected bases of Osama bin Laden because of al-Qaeda's bombing of embassies in Africa. Beginning in 1999, the United Nations imposed an embargo and financial sanctions in an effort to force Afghanistan to hand over bin Laden for trial. In October 2001, the United States and Britain launched air strikes against Afghanistan after the Taliban refused to give up bin Laden, who was held responsible for the September 11, 2001 attacks on the United States.

- **A Brief History of Modern Iraq.** When Iraq was created in 1920, yet under British control, the boundaries were made without taking into account the different ethnic and religious groups within the territory. Thus, three major divisions currently plague Iraq: The Kurds are fiercely independent Sunnis residing in the north, where much of the oil is located (Iraq has the second or third greatest oil reserves in the world); the Shiites are mainly in the southeast; and the

Sunnis occupy the rest. These differences in ethnicity and religion are not trivial. Although the Shiites and Sunnis share the same Koran, they fundamentally differ in who they believe was the legitimate successor to the prophet Muhammad, who died in 632. This disagreement is a serious schism that divides the Muslim world, often resulting in violence (Ghosh 2007). Complicating these divisions today in Iraq is that although the Shiites are a majority, the Sunnis have historically had the power. Their power began when the British supported Sunni leadership, a tradition later followed by Saddam Hussein. So, although the Sunnis are a numerical minority, they have kept the Shiites in a relatively powerless position since 1932. This balance changed in postwar Iraq with the election of a Shiite-controlled government.

The British mandate ended in 1932, giving independence to Iraq. Iraq was ruled by King Faisal from 1935 to 1958. In 1961, Kuwait gained independence from Britain, and Iraq claimed sovereignty over Kuwait. Britain objected and sent troops to deter Iraq's territorial expansionist claims. Iraq backed down. In 1979, Iraq's president resigned, and his chosen successor was Saddam Hussein. Saddam ruled Iraq with an iron hand, suppressing dissidents through torture and death, even engaging in mass killings of alleged rivals. Under Saddam's leadership, Iraq engaged in a war with Shiite-dominated Iran (1980–1988). This effort was supported by the United States with arms shipments (another instance of blowback, as Iraq later used these weapons against the United States).

In 1990, Iraq again invaded Kuwait. The United Nations condemned the Iraqi invasion and imposed an economic embargo on Iraq. Later it authorized member states to use military action against Iraqi forces occupying Kuwait. In 1991, allied troops from twenty-eight countries, led by the United States, launched an aerial bombardment on Baghdad. The war, Operation Desert Storm, lasted only 6 weeks and ended in the defeat of Iraq. Significantly, President George H. W. Bush chose to limit the war to freeing Kuwait, to not invade Baghdad, and to leave Saddam in power. Some of the president's advisors felt that without removing Saddam and occupying the country, the war was incomplete. Some of these advisors joined Bush's son's administration when he became president.

In 1993, there was an alleged assassination attempt on former President George H. W. Bush by Iraqi agents. President Clinton responded by targeting Iraqi intelligence headquarters in Baghdad with Tomahawk cruise missiles.

The sanctions imposed by the United Nations continued through the 1990s because it was unclear whether Iraq had removed its weapons of mass destruction.

The Precipitating Event

On the morning of September 11, 2001, four commercial planes left East Coast airports loaded with passengers and fuel for cross-country flights. These flights were taken over by hijackers who piloted the planes to new destinations, and the course of history was changed. The first plane left Boston for Los Angeles but headed instead for New York City, where it rammed into the World Trade Center's north tower, setting its upper floors ablaze. Fifteen minutes later, a second plane, scheduled for a Boston to Los Angeles flight, steered into the south tower of the World Trade Center. Within the next hour, both towers, each 110 stories high, melted from the intense heat and collapsed. A third plane departed from Washington, D.C., for Los Angeles, but turned around and plunged into the Pentagon. The fourth plane left Newark for San Francisco, changed direction, but, possibly because of heroic passengers attacking the hijackers, failed in its mission, presumably to dive into the White House or Capitol Hill, crashing instead in rural Pennsylvania. Thus, within about 2 hours, these four planes, commandeered by terrorists in synchronized suicide missions, had attacked two symbols of the United States—the World Trade Center, the hub of U.S. capitalism, and the Pentagon, the headquarters of the world's greatest military—killing nearly 3,000 people, about the same number of Americans who died at Pearl Harbor. "Not since the Civil War have we seen as much bloodshed on our soil. Never in our history did so many innocents perish on a single day" (Gergen 2001:60).

A Rush to War

Responding to the acts of terrorism against the United States that took place on September 11, 2001, President Bush, just nine days later, declared the war on terror. The president could have declared the 9/11 events a criminal act, limiting the response to capturing the criminals and bringing them to justice. The decision, however, was to declare a war. Moves against al-Qaeda—the terrorist group that carried out the 9/11 attacks—would begin the war, he said, but the war would not end "until every terrorist group of global reach has been found, stopped, and defeated." The president advised Americans to expect "a lengthy campaign, unlike any other we have ever seen." He explained,

> We will starve terrorists of funding, turn them one against another, drive them from place to place, until there is no refuge or no rest. And we will pursue nations that provide aid or safe haven to terrorism. Every nation, in every region, now has a decision to make. Either you are with us, or you are with the terrorists. From this day forward, any nation that continues to harbor or support terrorism will be regarded by the United States as a hostile regime. (Bush 2001a:3)

- **A War Like No Other.**   This "war on terror" was to be a war like no other. In the twentieth century, wars were fought by nations over land, resources, and ideology. But the terrorists of 9/11 did not represent a nation, and they were not intent on occupying territories. Terrorists do not have battleships and airfields to be targeted. Instead of an organized army, they are loosely organized through small groups with embedded "cells" to carry out terrorist activities. Containment, the strategy of the Cold War, was no longer possible when there are, as the U.S. State Department noted, thirty-seven foreign terrorist organizations with bases in at least twenty-five nations and the Palestinian territories. These terrorists located around the globe do not wear uniforms but rather live in their host countries as students or workers, just as other residents. If the leaders are identified and killed, others will take their place. Combat includes the use of conventional force as well as car bombs and suicide bombers (the "guided missiles" of the poor). In this new warfare, the combatants will not know victory. "There's no land to seize, no government to topple, no surrender that will bring closure" (Parrish 2001:2). Finally, in this new kind of warfare, great advantages in military technology, as demonstrated by the successful attacks on the World Trade Center and Pentagon, do not make a nation safe.

- **The War in Afghanistan.**   With broad international support, Operation Enduring Freedom launched the war on October 7, 2001, as President Bush had promised, against the Taliban of Afghanistan, which supported al-Qaeda. The immediate war offensive moved rapidly so that control of all the major cities of Afghanistan had been wrested from Taliban control within 2 months of the beginning of combat. A year after starting the operation, the U.S. government claimed that "al-Qaeda went on the run . . . losing their power, their safe havens and much of their leadership. . . . They are fragmented and their leaders are missing, captured, killed or on the run" (The White House 2002a:1).

This optimistic view proved to be wrong. At the beginning of 2007, more than five years after the war began, the Taliban terrorists had not been defeated. Actually, beginning in mid-2006, there has been a resurgence of the Taliban and violence in Afghanistan. Meanwhile, bin Laden and the al-Qaeda leadership had not been found. Incidentally, the main agricultural crop in Afghanistan continues to be poppies, which provides the world with as much as 90 percent of its heroin supply.

- **The Bush Doctrine.** Believing in the rightness of their cause and the evil of the terrorists, the Bush administration developed guidelines for U.S. military actions in the war on terror and the longer-range plan for national security in the twenty-first century. This policy, known as the Bush Doctrine, has its roots in a particular vision about America's role in the world.

> *The great struggles of the twentieth century between liberty and totalitarianism ended with a decisive victory for the forces of freedom—and a single sustainable model for national success: freedom, democracy, and free enterprise. . . . These values of freedom are right and true for every person, in every society—and the duty of protecting these values against their enemies is the common calling of freedom-loving people across the globe and across the ages. . . . Today, the United States enjoys a position of unparalleled military strength and great economic and political influence. We seek . . . to create a balance of power that favors human freedom: conditions in which all nations and all societies can choose for themselves the rewards and challenges of political and economic liberty. (The White House 2002b:i)*

From this vision flow the strategic principles that guide U.S. military actions in the war on terror.

The Line in the Sand. Addressing the nation on the day of 9/11, President Bush said, "We will make no distinction between the terrorists who committed these acts and those who harbor them" (Bush 2001b:1). He clarified later that the United States was drawing a line in the sand, and that all world nations had a "decision to make." "Either you are with us, or you are with the terrorists," the president proclaimed (Bush 2001a:3). Later, that binary principle of "us versus them" led the president to his now famous designation of Iraq, Iran, and North Korea as an "axis of evil" and his denunciation of our allies such as France and Germany when they chose not to join in the Iraq war.

Unbounded U.S. Military Superiority. A second principle of the Bush Doctrine calls for building a military "beyond challenge" and for "experimentation with new approaches to warfare" to give the United States the "capability to defeat any attempt by any enemy" and "dissuade potential adversaries . . . with hopes of surpassing, or equaling, the power of the United States" (The White House 2002b:29–30). In a separate classified policy statement, the Bush Doctrine policy makers even declared that the United States reserves the right to respond to danger with overwhelming force—including potentially nuclear weapons—if necessary (*Washington Times* 2003).

Unilateral Preventive War and Regime Change. The Bush administration asserted the right of the United States to carry out preventive wars unilaterally to remove governments (regime change) that it deems to be engaged in long-range plans to develop weapons of mass destruction (WMDs) and to support terrorism. This pillar of the Bush Doctrine, an astonishing departure from U.S. practice and tradition, was first conveyed by the president in a graduation speech to West Point cadets. "We must take the battle to the enemy, disrupt his plans, and confront the worst threats before they emerge. If we wait for threats to fully materialize, we will have waited too long" (quoted in Ricks 2006:38). "We cannot let our enemies strike first. The overlap between states that sponsor terror and those that pursue WMD compels us to action. . . . To forestall or prevent such hostile acts by our adversaries, the United States will, if necessary act preemptively" (quoted in Ricks 2006:62).

The Bush Doctrine includes the assertion that the United States can engage in a **preventive war** as well as a **preemptive war**. The late historian Arthur Schlesinger notes the differences in these two principles.

> *The distinction between "pre-emptive" and "preventive" is well worth preserving. It is the distinction between legality and illegality. "Pre-emptive" war refers to a direct, immediate, specific threat that must be crushed at once; in the words of the Department of Defense manual, "an attack initiated on the basis of incontrovertible evidence that an enemy attack is imminent." "Preventive" war refers to potential, future, therefore speculative threats. (quoted in Singh 2006:18–19)*

Using this distinction, Robert Singh said, "The Iraq war was as clear an instance of preventive war—illegal under the U.N. Charter—as possible" (Singh 2006:19).

The Bush Doctrine does not require imminent threat for the United States to swing into full offensive military force; it requires only distant threat as determined by U.S. leaders. This is the "One Percent Solution," as enunciated by Vice President Cheney (hence, also known as the "Cheney Doctrine"): "If there was even a one percent chance of terrorists getting a weapon of mass destruction . . . the United States must now act as if it were a certainty" (quoted in Suskind 2006:62). In March 2003, Operation Iraqi Freedom became the first proof of U.S. commitment to this principle for national security in the war on terror.

The Spread of Democracy. The assumption is that the national interests of the United States are best pursued by spreading democratic forms of governance. As President Bush said in his 2004 speech at West Point,

> *"Some who call themselves 'realists' question whether the spread of democracy in the Middle East should be any concern of ours. But the realists in this case have lost contact with a fundamental reality. America has always been less secure when freedom is in retreat. America is always more secure when freedom is on the march" (quoted in Singh 2006:20).*

The War in Iraq

With the early defeat of the Taliban in Afghanistan, the Bush administration's attention turned to Iraq. The Bush administration justified a preventive war against Iraq because its leader, Saddam Hussein, was guilty of mass murder against his own people, but also because, it was alleged, he was amassing weapons of mass destruction (nuclear, chemical, and biological), and there was a strong connection between Saddam Hussein and al-Qaeda's terrorism. A debate rages as to whether these last two charges are factual, as claimed by the Bush administration. An editorial in the *Los Angeles Times* asked: "Did President Bush and his aides completely trump up the case for war and then set out to discredit anyone who called them on it? Did they instead allow themselves to be convinced too easily by evidence that tended to show them what they wanted to see? Or was the president acting reasonably on information that appeared solid at the time?" (quoted in *USA Today* 2007b:13A). Historians will eventually provide a definitive answer to this crucial debate that during the war and postwar years was so highly politicized.

Operation Iraqi Freedom began in March 2003 without a clear United Nations mandate. As in the war in Afghanistan, the initial offensive moved swiftly. Some 340,000 U.S. military personnel were deployed in the Persian Gulf region, along with more than 47,000 British troops and smaller numbers from a few other nations, to carry out the initial invasion of Iraq. After just 25 days, the United States and coalition forces were in some degree of control of all major Iraqi cities. President Bush declared an end to major combat operations on May 1, 2003. No weapons of mass destruction were found, and the rationale for the war shifted to bring democracy to Iraq, which would serve as a model for democracy for other nations in the Middle East to adopt.

Although military victory was achieved, the aftermath of the war proved more complicated and very costly for the United States. Coalition military forces faced significant problems of restoring civil order and the infrastructure and providing basic services because they were challenged by a persistent Iraqi resistance movement. Most significant, sectarian violence between the Shiite majority, which, for the first time since 1932, controlled the new government and the Sunni minority erupted. This had all the earmarks of a civil war with the United States in the middle.

The Iraq War—an Evaluation

The political objectives of the United States in its war with Iraq were bold and ambitious, as summarized by Michael R. Gordon and General Bernard E. Trainor:

> *The military operation was intended to strike a blow at terrorism by ousting a long-standing adversary, eliminating Iraq's weapons of mass destruction, and implanting a moderate and pro-American state in the heart of the Arab world. It was also to be a powerful demonstration of American power and an object lesson—for Iran, Syria, and other would-be foes—of the potential consequences of supporting terrorist groups and pursuing nuclear, biological, and chemical arms. The United States would not just defeat a dictator. It would transform a region and send the message that the American intervention in Afghanistan was not the end but just the beginning of Washington's "global war on terror." (Gordon and Trainor 2006:497)*

The Bush Doctrine was the first attempt at a grand strategy since the end of the Cold War. But did it work? Did it eliminate the threat from terrorist networks and rogue states? Did it spread democracy to the Middle East?

Ultimately these goals may be achieved, but as this is written in early 2010 (at the seven-year anniversary of the invasion of Iraq), the U.S. mission did not succeed. Supporters of the war argued that Saddam Hussein had been captured, tried, and executed as were his sons. The Shia became the majority. A semblance of democracy was established. Opponents argued that the war was not a success. The United States remained the power "behind the throne," and civil unrest was rampant.

A number of errors promoted division and civil war in Iraq, actually increased the numbers of terrorists in Iraq, and led to ever greater anti-U.S. sentiments among the population. Foremost, there was a failure to understand the seriousness of Iraq's ethnic and sectarian differences and a failure to anticipate the threat of insurgency (Cordesman 2006:xxi–xxii). As a result, the United States has been ineffective as Sunni and Shiite militias continuously attack each other's neighborhoods and holy places. Both sides in this struggle use car bombs, suicide bombers, roadside bombs, and guerrilla-style ambushes. The U.S. forces have been caught in the middle of this civil war.

> Neither the United States nor the Shiite militias can defeat the Sunni forces in their home areas, and the Sunnis cannot hope to defeat the majority Shiites, but horrific ethnic cleansing is underway in mixed areas—a grinding and bloody stalemate, with U.S. troops in the middle. (Dreyfuss and Gilson 2007:61)

U.S. interests were undermined when the soldiers finally tried to enforce order, as they engaged in house-to-house raids that terrified and embittered the Iraqi citizens. A government survey found that 10 percent of U.S. troops in Iraq reported that they had mistreated civilians in Iraq, such as kicking them or needlessly damaging their possessions (reported in Ricks and Tyson 2007:33). Adding to the bitterness were the occasional incidents of rapes by American soldiers, the deliberate killing of innocents, and U.S. accidents that killed civilians (Bacevich 2006). Furthermore, the United States did not realize "the disastrous symbolic potential of detaining thousands of suspects at the same Abu Ghraib prison that had been Saddam Hussein's torture center, and through either negligence or intention letting it become a site of abuse and torture again" (Fallows 2006:220).

The war had destroyed much of Iraq's infrastructure (e.g., roads, bridges, buildings, private homes, and the means for providing essential services such as electricity and water). The United States was held responsible for this destruction, which was compounded by the slow rebuilding of the infrastructure because of terrorist acts, bureaucratic mismanagement, scandal, profiteering, and insufficient of funds. All these factors resulted in the quick erosion of U.S. prestige.

Amid the chaos and because of the porous borders, extremists infiltrated from neighboring countries, most notably Iran and Syria, to engage in terrorist activities aimed at exploiting the sectarian divide and to increase anti-American fervor. Moreover, the sectarian schism has led Shiite Muslims in Iran to lend support to Shiites in Iraq and Sunni Muslims in Saudi Arabia to aid Sunnis in Iraq. Ironically, then, Iraq, which initially was not part of the terrorist network, became part of the network *because* of the U.S. "war on terror."

In time there was an election, and Iraqis were trained to eventually take the place of the U.S. military. A drawdown of U.S. troops was completed by the summer of 2010, with a contingent left to back up the Iraqi troops. Meanwhile, almost daily bombs exploded in marketplaces, on transportation, and elsewhere. The Iraqi government was ineffective in bringing the country together.

As troops were withdrawn from Iraq, President Obama ordered an increase in the U.S. military in Afghanistan, which will rise to 98,000. President Obama's plan is to start drawing down troops in July 2011, handing over security responsibilities to Afghan soldiers and police, which are currently under U.S. tutelage.

CONSEQUENCES OF THE U.S. RESPONSES TO 9/11

The United States chose to respond to the 9/11 terrorist attacks by invading Afghanistan and later Iraq. This response has had enormous consequences for the United States, for the people of Afghanistan and Iraq, for the Middle East, and for international relations. Recognizing that the U.S. involvement in the Middle East continues and the end results are unknown, this section outlines the immediate costs of the wars and speculates on the long-term legacy of U.S. actions.

The Costs of the Iraq and Afghanistan Wars

- **Loss of Human Life.** As of June 2009, the deaths from both wars surpassed 5,000 U.S. soldiers (see the "Voices" panel).

  In addition to the deaths of U.S. military personnel, there were deaths of other coalition soldiers, Iraqi and Afghani soldiers/police, U.S. defense contractors, journalists, and civilians. The number of civilian deaths in Iraq is unknown, with estimates varying from 100,000 to 600,000 deaths.

  As for the deaths of Afghans, the numbers rise with the acceleration of the war. According to the United Nations, bombs killed over 2,000 civilians in 2008,

VOICES

ARMY MAJ. DAVID G. TAYLOR, JR., AUG. 9, BAGHDAD
(Journal for His Newborn Son)

It occurred to me again that I don't know how old you'll be when you read this. It wouldn't do to write things an 18-year-old might understand if you read this when you're five. I think I'll assume you're young when you read this. Anything you don't understand, we can talk about when you're older.

That was on my mind the other night when I was sitting in my HMMWV [Humvee] on a street in Baghdad, waiting for one of our companies to raid a suspected militia warehouse. It's a bad part of town. It was 0300, I was tired, and I started thinking of some of the more complicated aspects of this fight here.

[. . .] We were raiding a place reputed to be where one of the Shia militias stores rockets, IEDs, and small-arms weapons. We were the Shia's saviors when we arrived in 2003. Back then, only disgruntled Sunnis who were loyal to Saddam attacked us. Now it's kind of the other way around.

Shia militias kill Sunnis. Sunni militias kill Shia. Foreign terrorists kill them both to incite more Shia/Sunni violence, hoping for a civil war. All of them target U.S. forces, but the Shia and Sunni aren't bold enough yet to admit they do it. [. . .] It's annoyingly complicated [. . .]

So what does all this have to do with you? Well, in my sleep-deprived frame of mind the other night, not knowing if we were about to get into a fight, I thought it was going to be very important for your mom and me to help you through the moral and ethical ambiguities in the world. Everything seems to be more complicated as time goes by. It's probably hard for some people to not just throw up their hands and go with whatever "everyone" else thinks on a complicated moral question. It's our job to arm you to know the right thing to [do], in all situations [. . .]

But how do you live those things in a place like this? Being gentle gets you killed here. [. . .]

Major Taylor was killed by an improvised explosive device (IED) on October 22, 2006.

Source: "Voices of the Fallen." 2007. *Newsweek* (April 2): 50–51.

up 40 percent from 2007. From 2004 to 2007 the bomb tonnage dropped in Afghanistan rose dramatically from 163 tons to 1,956 tons (reported in DeGennaro 2009). In April 2009 alone the U.S. military dropped 438 bombs in Afghanistan. With the military surge beginning in 2010, the killing of Afghans will continue to accelerate.

- **The Injured.** For every U.S. service member killed in Iraq, fifteen more have been wounded, injured, or contracted a serious illness. More than 80,000 were injured or wounded, and another 300,000 required medical treatment. Taking care of these veterans is going to cost at least $59 billion (Bilmes and Stiglitz 2009). Because of better protective equipment and improvements in medical trauma care, more injured troops are surviving the war in Iraq than in any previous war. Although this is good news, the downside is that because of the terrible force of explosions the combat soldiers experience, more are surviving with brain injuries (Bazell 2006).

In addition, the trauma of war is haunting many soldiers when they return home. More than 17 percent of returning soldiers suffer from posttraumatic stress disorder, with symptoms of flashbacks, nightmares, feelings of detachment, irritability, trouble concentrating, and sleeplessness. Those who have been deployed more than once have a 50 percent increase in acute combat stress over those who have been deployed only once (Thompson 2007).

Indicative of the higher stress levels felt by wartime troops, in 2007 five U.S. soldiers tried to kill themselves every day, up from one attempt a day before the Iraq war began (CNN 2009).

Often overlooked in the injuries of war are the consequences of long separations and psychological trauma on the intimate lives of soldiers and their spouses, resulting in a rising divorce rate. Their divorce rate for fiscal 2009 was 3.6 percent, up from 3.4 percent a year earlier, and a full percentage point above the 2.6 percent in 2001, when the United States began sending troops to Afghanistan (Jelinek 2009). The incidence of spouse abuse within military couples has also increased as the war progressed.

More than 80,000 troops were injured or wounded in the Iraq War.

Brooks Kraft/Corbis

Many Iraqis, who fear bombs, raids, and death, suffer various forms of trauma. A study of Iraqi children by the Iraqi Ministry of Health found that around 70 percent of primary school students suffered symptoms of trauma-related stress such as bed-wetting, stuttering, voluntary muteness, and increased aggressive behavior (Palmer 2007).

- **The Displaced.** Of Iraq's total population of about 28 million, 4.5 million are displaced, with more than half of them having fled the country (*Nation* 2009).

- **The Monetary Costs of the Iraq and Afghanistan Wars.** Before the invasion of Iraq, the Bush administration estimated that combat operations there would cost about $50 billion. Seven years later (at the beginning of 2010) the amount allocated to both wars was $1.05 trillion, not including the funds to support the "surge" of 30,000 additional troops to Afghanistan (likely an additional cost of $30 billion; National Priorities Project 2010). Nobel laureate Joseph Stiglitz and former chair of the Council of Economic Advisors Linda Bilmes states that in addition to the more than $1 trillion spent on military operations

  > It will cost perhaps $2 trillion more to repay the war debt, replenish military equipment and provide care and treatment for U.S. veterans back home. Many of the wounded will require indefinite care for brain and spinal injuries. Disability payments are ramping up and will grow higher for decades. (Stiglitz and Bilmes 2009: para. 4).

  New York Times columnist Bob Herbert interviewed Professor Stiglitz, asking how that money might have been better spent. Stiglitz replied,

  > About $560 billion, which is a little more than half of the study's conservative estimate of the cost of the war, would have been enough to "fix" Social Security for the next 75 years. If one were thinking in terms of promoting democracy in the Middle East, the money being spent on the war would have been enough to finance a mega-mega-mega-Marshall Plan, which would have been so much more effective than the invasion of Iraq. (quoted in Herbert 2006, para. 12)

  The Social Policy panel, "What $1.2 Trillion Can Buy," provides some further suggestions for social spending rather than military spending, using a middle estimate of $1.2 trillion for the cost of the war.

- **Who Makes the Sacrifice to Conduct the War?** The Bush administration decided to conduct the war with a volunteer military instead of a draft. The volunteers tend to come from economically struggling areas, mostly rural, with few job opportunities. For example, the death rate for rural soldiers is 24 per million adults, a rate 60 percent higher than the death rate for soldiers from cities and suburbs (15 deaths per million; Engelhardt 2007). Because the military offers educational opportunities and financial inducements, youth from poor and working-class families are overrepresented. For example, 75 percent of those killed came from U.S. towns where the per capita income was below the national average (*Newsweek* 2007). As a result, most Americans do not have family members in the fight. They are not really in the war emotionally.

  Typically, during wartime the government reevaluates tax and spending policies to add revenue and to shift resources from less vital pursuits to pay the additional costs of conducting and winning the war. Not so in this war, as the president and Congress, for the first time in modern history, went into a major war by *reducing the tax burden on the wealthy* (Borosage 2003). Moreover,

SOCIAL POLICY

WHAT $1.2 TRILLION CAN BUY

The human mind isn't very well equipped to make sense of a figure like $1.2 trillion. We don't deal with a trillion of anything in our daily lives, and so when we come across such a big number, it is hard to distinguish it from any other big number. Millions, billions, a trillion—they all start to sound the same.

The way to come to grips with $1.2 trillion is to forget about the number itself and think instead about what you could buy with the money. When you do that, a trillion stops sounding anything like millions or billions.

For starters, $1.2 trillion would pay for an unprecedented public health campaign—a doubling of cancer research funding, treatment for every American whose diabetes or heart disease is now going unmanaged, and a global immunization campaign to save millions of children's lives.

Combined, the cost of running those programs for a decade wouldn't use up even half our money pot. So we could then turn to poverty and education, starting with universal preschool for every 3- and 4-year-old child across the country. The city of New Orleans could also receive a huge increase in reconstruction funds.

The final big chunk of the money could go to national security. The recommendations of the 9/11 Commission that have not been put in place—better baggage and cargo screening, stronger measures against nuclear proliferation—could be enacted. Financing for the war in Afghanistan could be increased to beat back the Taliban's recent gains, and a peacekeeping force could put a stop to the genocide in Darfur.

All that would be one way to spend $1.2 trillion. Here would be another: The war in Iraq.

Source: David Leonhardt, "What $1.2 trillion Can Buy." *New York Times* (January 17, 2007). Copyright © 2007 by the New York Times Co. Reprinted with permission.

the poor were unequally disadvantaged because programs to help them (e.g., food stamps, subsidized housing) have been cut to aid the war effort. In the long run, the cost of the war will be a burden for this and succeeding generations. If the war costs $2 trillion, then that comes to $18,000 per household (Dorrien 2006).

The Legacy of the War

The long-term consequences of the U.S. military interventions in Afghanistan and Iraq appear to be serious and far reaching. We do not know the full extent of the ramifications, but we have some clues. We begin with the successful scenario, followed by a number of negative possibilities.

- **The Effort Is Successful.** Vice President Cheney gave this optimistic prediction:

> *Ten years from now, we'll look back on this period of time and see that liberating 50 million people in Afghanistan and Iraq really did represent a major, fundamental shift, obviously, in U.S. policy in terms of how we dealt with the emerging terrorist threat—and that we'll have fundamentally changed circumstances in that part of the world (quoted in Nye, 2006, paragraph 2).*

Cheney is correct on two counts. First, the U.S. effort freed Iraq from the tyranny of Saddam Hussein. But are the Iraqis better off? Will democracy get a foothold there and spread across the Middle East as apologists for the war believe? Seven years after the war in Iraq began, the answers to these questions are negative. Long term, these are questions for historians to answer. And, second, Cheney asserted that the Middle East will be fundamentally changed by

U.S. efforts. He was correct, but will the U.S. war on terror bring about beneficial changes for that region? Or will they be overwhelmingly detrimental?

- **Iraqis and Afghans Turn against the United States.** The United States did liberate Iraq from the oppressive Saddam Hussein regime, but in the process, much of Iraq was destroyed, rebuilding has been slow and ineffective, and violence is rampant. As the *New York Times* editorialized,

  > *Washington's disgraceful failure to deliver on its promises to restore electricity, water and oil distribution, and to rebuild education and health facilities, turned millions of once sympathetic Iraqis against the American presence. Their discovery that the world's richest, most technologically advanced country could not restore basic services to minimum prewar levels left an impression of American weakness and worse, of indifference to the well-being of ordinary Iraqis. That further poisoned a situation already soured by White House intelligence breakdowns, military misjudgments and political blunders. (New York Times 2006: para. 2)*

  The war and the ensuing violence have propelled an estimated 2.3 million Iraqis to flee to neighboring countries, mostly to Syria and Jordan. In addition, more than 2 million are displaced within Iraq. Clearly, Iraq is not safe, and the blame is no longer on Saddam Hussein but on the occupying force of the United States, which cannot keep order.

- **The Civil War in Iraq Is Polarizing the Sunni–Shiite Schism Worldwide.** Ethnic and regional political divisions in Iraq have been exacerbated by the war, and these resulting sectarian schisms are increasing tensions in the Muslim world. Iraqi Sunni militias bomb Shiite neighborhoods and their holy places. Shiites retaliate by lobbing mortars into Sunni districts and kidnapping Sunni men. These actions are viewed by Arabs on regional television across the region, inflaming sectarian passions and resulting in similar clashes between Sunnis and Shiites in Egypt, Pakistan, Saudi Arabia, and elsewhere. Even in Muslim neighborhoods in the United States, these tensions are felt as, for example, when Shiite shopkeepers were victims of arson, presumably perpetrated by Sunnis, in Dearborn, Michigan.

  Of the world's 1.3 billion Muslims, 85 percent are Sunni. Shiites are a majority in five countries, most notably Iran and Iraq. These Shiite nations form a crescent from Iran to Lebanon. The Sunnis fear the growing power influence of Iran and the new Shiite government in Iraq brought to power by the war. Ironically, the United States finds itself favoring the Shiite government in Iraq but favors Sunni leaders everywhere else, which angers both sides (Feldman 2007).

  Shiite leaders sense that the United States incites sectarianism as a way of blunting Iran's influence:

  > *The growing Sunni–Shiite divide is roiling an Arab world as unsettled as at any time in a generation. Fought in speeches, newspaper columns, rumors swirling through cafes and the Internet, and occasional bursts of strife, the conflict is predominantly shaped by politics: a disintegrating Iraq, an ascendant Iran, a sense of Arab powerlessness and a persistent suspicion of American intentions. (Shadid 2007:6)*

- **Loss of U.S. Image and Credibility in the Arab World.** A goal of the Iraq war was to install a pro-U.S. democracy there with the intention that this model would eventually spread democracy and freedom throughout the Arab world. The war and the occupation, however, turned more and more people in that region against the United States. Gallup polls comparing results from 2002 and

2006 found that the percentage holding "an unfavorable view" of the United States had risen from

- 64 percent to 79 percent in Saudi Arabia
- 33 percent to 62 percent in Turkey
- 41 percent to 49 percent in Morocco.

Another polling organization—Zogby International—found in a 2005 survey of six basically U.S.-friendly Muslim countries (Egypt, Jordan, Lebanon, Morocco, Saudi Arabia, and the United Arab Emirates) that only 12 percent of those surveyed expressed favorable attitudes toward the United States. In addition, the respondents believed that the war in Iraq had created more, not fewer, terrorists, and 86 percent believed that there has been "less peace" in the region since the removal of Saddam Hussein (reported in Regan 2007; see also the BBC World Service poll, reported in *Time* 2007a).

Indicative of the shifting Arab attitude against the United States, in 2007, King Abdullah of Saudi Arabia, a staunch ally and close friend of the Bush family, characterized U.S. troops in Iraq as an "illegitimate foreign occupation" before the Arab summit (quoted in Associated Press 2007a).

Among the reasons Muslims have less regard for the United States since the Iraq war are the preventive attack on Iraq, the subsequent chaos in Iraq, the assumption that the United States is involved because of oil and to weaken the Muslim world, the secret prisons, and the torture of Muslims (per the images of prisoners at Abu Ghraib and Guantanamo Bay, Cuba; Sweig 2006).

- **Inhumane Treatment of Suspected Terrorists Aids the Cause of the Terrorists.** The Geneva Conventions are international agreements on humane treatment of combatants and civilians by opposing governments and military forces during times of war. The first of these treaties dates back to 1864, and since then, the agreements evolved so that nearly every nation (188 of them) was a signatory to the Geneva Conventions at the beginning of the war on terror. Although the Bush administration never suggested that the United States withdraw from these core provisions of international law, there has been a pattern of circumventing them. The pattern began after the 2001 military campaign in Afghanistan, which netted thousands of captive Taliban supporters and suspected al-Qaeda operatives, many of whom were imprisoned and subjected to sometimes barbaric treatment in "defiance of American and international law" (Conason 2007:12). This practice continued with the war in Iraq, as suspects were kidnapped and taken to prisons around the world for months and years at a time. Under American law, these acts were illegal.

  In 2006, Congress passed the Military Commissions Act. When President Bush signed this act, he announced: "In memory of the victims of September 11, it is my honor to sign [this Act] into law" (quoted in Sussman 2007:7). This act (Herman 2006):

  - Significantly broadens the definition of "enemy combatant" and makes it a matter of presidential discretion. An "enemy combatant" is defined as a person who is designated by the commander-in-chief as someone who has engaged in hostilities against the United States.
  - Removes habeas corpus rights of noncitizens. Habeas corpus, a human right considered fundamental to the western world since the Magna Carta (ce. 1215), prevents the police from arresting and holding someone without

"The terrorist barriers seem to be working."

cause. In other words, enemy combatants are denied the right to challenge their detentions in civil courts.

- Permits aggressive interrogations in secret prisons. The act does not list acceptable and unacceptable "methods of interrogation." The legislation keeps methods open-ended and subject to the president's interpretation of the Geneva Conventions.
- Suspension of normal rules of evidence and due process. The act, unlike the procedures in U.S. courts, permits the use of hearsay and coerced evidence and evidence obtained in warrantless searches, and it fails to allow prisoners on trial ensured access to the evidence against them.

The Military Commissions Act may eventually be declared unconstitutional by the Supreme Court because it violates our judicial heritage (e.g., the Bill of Rights). But in the meantime, the U.S. reaction to terrorism was a "five-year transformation from beacon of freedom to autocratic torture state" (Rall 2006:19).

- **The Erosion of Civil Liberties at Home.** Faced with the threat of terrorism, the president sought, and Congress passed, the USA Patriot Act of 2001 (Uniting and Strengthening America by Providing Appropriate Tools Required to Intercept and Obstruct Terrorism). This act was hailed by supporters as a crucial piece of legislation giving the nation's law enforcement and intelligence-gathering personnel the "tools they need" to catch terrorists and stop another 9/11. The provisions of the USA Patriot Act:

  - Expanded the ability of law enforcement personnel to conduct secret searches and conduct phone and Internet surveillance and to access a wide range of personal financial, medical, mental health, and student records. Government monitoring of communication between federal detainees and their lawyers is allowed. Judicial oversight of these investigation activities is reduced by the act.
  - Expanded the legal definition of terrorism beyond previous laws in a manner that subjects ordinary political and religious organizations to surveillance, wiretapping, and criminal action without any evidence of wrongdoing.

- Allowed FBI agents to investigate any American citizen without probable cause of crime if they say it is for "intelligence purposes." As a result, some American citizens, mostly of Arab and South Asian origin, have been held in secret federal custody for weeks or months, many without any charges filed against them and without access to lawyers.
- Allowed noncitizens to be jailed based on suspicion, even without evidence. Suspects can be detained indefinitely without judicial review, and hundreds have been detained. Immigration hearings for post-9/11 noncitizen detainees are conducted in secret.

Some argue that ordinary law-abiding folks have nothing to fear from laws like the USA Patriot Act unless they are involved in some kind of clandestine activity. But this reaction misses the point according to critics. The USA Patriot Act is only one of hundreds of laws and legal regulations rewritten by the Bush administration to create barriers to the possibility of terrorists penetrating U.S. borders. More than any other legal change, it points out the uncanny contradiction of the war on terror policies. Under the Bush Doctrine, the United States has conducted aggressive military campaigns to liberate Afghans and Iraqis and bring democracy to "the greater Middle East." Yet, the actions of the government have restricted civil liberties that are the foundation of the U.S. Constitution and democracy. How can we expand democracy in the wider world when we do not practice it in fortress America?

Senator Russ Feingold from Wisconsin was the only senator to vote against the Patriot Act. His rationale delivered to his colleagues was,

> There is no doubt that if we lived in a police state, it would be easier to catch terrorists. If we lived in a country where the police were allowed to search your home at any time for any reason; if we lived in a country where the government was entitled to open your mail, eavesdrop on your phone conversations, or intercept your e-mail communications; if we lived in a country where people could be held in jail indefinitely based on what they write or think, or based on mere suspicion that they were up to no good, the government would probably discover and arrest more terrorists, or would-be terrorists, just as it would find more lawbreakers generally. But that would not be a country in which we would want to live, and it would not be a country for which we could, in good conscience, ask our young people to fight and die. In short, that country would not be America. (Feingold 2001:2)

To conduct the war on terror, domestic surveillance programs have been conducted by the FBI, the Defense Department, Homeland Security, and the National Security Agency (all of which are justified as inherent in the "wartime" powers of the president). Here are some examples of domestic spying:

- Surveillance by the FBI and local police of domestic activist organizations (e.g., American Friends Service Committee, Greenpeace, and United for Peace and Justice; Dunn 2006).
- The departments of Justice, State, and Homeland Security buy commercial databases that track Americans' finances, phone numbers, and biographical information (Woellert and Kopecki 2006).
- Using a "national security letter," the FBI can demand that an Internet provider, bank, or phone company turn over records of who you call and e-mail; where you work, fly, and vacation; and the like. No judge has to approve the demand. Moreover, the individual under surveillance is unaware of what is happening because it is classified (*USA Today* 2005).
- The Department of Homeland Security recruited utility and telephone workers, cable TV installers, postal workers, delivery drivers, and others

who regularly enter private homes to become federal informants, informing of suspicious persons, activities, and items that they observed (Conason 2007:194).

- To qualify for federal homeland security grants, states must assemble lists of "potential threat elements"—individuals or groups suspected of possible terrorist activity (Kaplan 2006).
- The Justice Department funded a private contractor, Matrix (Multistate Anti-Terrorism Information Exchange), which used "data mining" technology to search public records and matched them with police files to identify some 120,000 "suspects" with "high terrorist factor" scores.

Proponents argue that the dangers are serious, and these and other security measures are needed to make the nation secure by making it easier to identify, prevent, and punish terrorists.

Critics, on the other hand, argue that these measures go too far in expanding the government's abilities to intrude on citizens' lives, thereby weakening individual rights. Citizens have guarantees from the Constitution that protect them from government surveillance, reading the mail, and listening to phone conversations of its citizens—in short, Americans have the right to privacy and freedom from unreasonable search and seizure. Moreover, there is a high probability that the invasion of privacy will not be randomly distributed but more likely will be directed to noncitizens, Muslims, and people who look "Middle Eastern."

There is a fine line between what is needed for security and protecting the freedoms that characterize the United States. If we stray too far toward restricted freedoms, we end up, ironically, terrorizing ourselves. Another irony is that President Bush declared on the night of the assault on the World Trade Center and Pentagon that "America is the brightest beacon for freedom in the world and no one will keep that light from shining," yet the domestic antiterrorism actions taken by the government "darken that very beacon of freedom by making a new attack on our own people's already-endangered civil liberties" (Hightower 2001:1).

STRATEGIES TO COMBAT THE NEW TERRORISM

The strategies employed to achieve national security in the post-9/11 world do not resemble those used during the Cold War. Unmatched military might is not answer. Nor is a missile shield or other military technology the answer. The enemy is not a nation or alliance of nations. This time it is different. How, then, do we address the problem of terrorism by a relatively small, militarily weak, shadowy network of people and groups willing to blow up themselves and innocent others for a cause greater than themselves? Although terrorism is possible from many sources, we concentrate here on ways to neutralize the current and future threat from Islamic extremists. What follows are some ideas from which to develop strategies organized around lessons that we know.

Lesson 1: Military Might Alone Does Not Make a Nation Secure

Overwhelming military and economic superiority did not protect the United States from nineteen men who hijacked four planes with plastic knives, turning them into guided missiles. Moreover, the immense firepower of the United

States and its worldwide network of military bases appears to others as evidence of imperialist goals.

Lesson 2: Vengeance Is Self-Defeating

Responding to attacks with similar attacks ("an eye for an eye and a tooth for a tooth") may make the combatants feel better, but it fuels existing hatreds that extend from generation to generation in a never-ending cycle of violence. As proof, consider the history of the Sunni–Shiite atrocities or the Israeli–Palestinian conflict. The response to attacks must be limited to seeking justice, not revenge.

Vengeance is also self-defeating because it plays into the hands of the terrorists. A noted military scholar, Sir Michael Howard of Oxford University, traced examples of terrorism over the last 130 years and concluded that one of the principal aims of terrorists has always been to provoke savage acts of retaliation to win sympathy for their cause (cited in B. Lewis 2001). If the United States wreaks a holocaust in Arab countries such as Afghanistan or Iraq, or Iran, or Syria, then bin Laden or whomever replaces him will have accomplished his goal of bringing most of the world's 1.3 billion Muslims into a *jihad* against the West.

Lesson 3: The Solution to Terrorism Is to Address Its Root Causes

The United States should take seriously the grievances of the Muslim people in the Middle East. First, the Israeli–Palestinian conflict must be resolved equitably. While ensuring security for Israel, a Palestinian state must be established, with a multinational peacekeeping force placed between the two nations. Further, this Palestinian homeland must be provided with ample aid to bolster its economy, provide jobs for its people, and provide the necessary infrastructure (e.g., housing, schools, irrigation systems, roads, and sewage treatment). As it is, the Muslim world only sees the United States bolstering Israel militarily and economically while the Palestinians languish in refugee camps or as second-class citizens.

Second, U.S. troops and bases must be removed from Saudi Arabia, Egypt, Oman, and other Arab states in the region, thus eliminating the U.S. military, the symbol of domination, from the cradle of Islam.

Third, most societies in the Middle East, for example, have a few very rich people, a small middle class, and a huge population of very poor people. The vast majority suffer from hunger, disease, and hopelessness. This poverty extends across many countries to form the setting where the seeds of terrorism flourish. If the affluent West were to provide investment, aid, technical assistance, and technology to these countries, then their people would thrive, and the attractiveness of the terrorist cause would diminish. The safety of the world can be enhanced appreciably. The United States must adapt to a shrinking world, where all nations are increasingly interdependent. This means that unless the United States and the developed nations find ways to help those left behind in the developing nations, they will be in serious trouble.

Lesson 4: In Planning for War, the Question Guiding the Plan Must Be, How Does the Conflict End?

Implied in this is another question: What will be the definition of success? The generally accepted appraisal is that the United States did not enter the Iraq war with answers to these crucial questions raised by the *Washington Post*: "How

Iraq will be secured and governed after a war that removes Saddam Hussein, and what the U.S. commitment to that effort will be. . . . Who will rule Iraq, and how? Who will provide security? How long will U.S. troops remain?" (*Washington Post* 2007a:24). These questions were not answered inside the administration before the war, but eventually, after considerable meandering, they were. President Obama, in contrast, has laid down a specific plan for concluding the war in Afghanistan. The United States will start drawing down troops in July 2011, handing over more and more security responsibilities to Afghan soldiers until they are in control.

Lesson 5: The U.S. Goal of Spreading Democracy in the Middle East Will Likely Fail

The nations of the Middle East have no history of democracy. Iraq and Afghanistan may, in time, develop democratic institutions, but surely this will not happen because an occupying power imposes them. Some of the countries in the Middle East, including some U.S. allies, are governed by tyrants. It is hypocritical, then, for the United States to depose one despot (Saddam Hussein) while allowing others in Saudi Arabia and Kuwait, for example, to be untouched by us because they are our allies (and, not so incidentally, they supply the United States with oil). Spreading our way of life is also viewed by others as a form of imperialism.

Most important, the United States will fail to plant the seeds of democracy if it is not itself democratic. The conduct of the Iraq war reveals a fundamental contradiction: The Bush administration's goal was to export democracy, yet policies have systematically undermined civil liberties at home by using a variety of tactics to invade the privacy of citizens, by rounding up thousands of American Muslims without evidence and incarcerating hundreds of them without charges, by restricting habeas corpus, and by asserting the power to ignore hundreds of duly enacted laws—all because of an open-ended "war on terror" (Green 2007:20–21). To elaborate, in response to the terrorist threat, the United States has been restructured in undemocratic ways. The presidency, using its war powers, took more and more power from Congress, thereby removing the checks and balances between the executive and the legislative branches. For example, the Constitution requires the president to "take care that the laws are faithfully executed." If a president does not like a bill, he is supposed to veto it. A way around this is through signing statements, whereby the president lists exceptions, allowing him to eviscerate the legislation. President Bush did this to over 750 statutes. "Through signing statements, the president has repeatedly signaled his contempt for Congress and his intention to flout the law on matters ranging from torture to the protection of executive branch whistle-blowers" (Brooks 2006: para. 9).

Moreover, the executive branch engaged in secrecy, claiming national security would be breached if documents were made public. Thus, the public's right to know was thwarted by a government bent on keeping secret the existence of CIA prisons, that it conducted illegal wiretaps, and the like (*USA Today* 2007c).

Lesson 6: The Path to the Moral High Ground Goes through International Organizations and International Law

The United States undermined the possibility of success in its war on terror when, in violation of the U.N. Charter, it invoked preventive war, condoned torture, and denied basic rights to prisoners. To right these wrongs, the United States must revoke these actions and must join the nations of the world in seeking peaceful solutions to such vexing problems as the Palestinian–Israeli conflict; the trouble between India and Pakistan; the threats of Iran, Syria, and North Korea; genocide in Africa; and a variety of unstable political situations in Latin American nations such as Colombia and Peru. In the long run, rather than seeking unbounded military supremacy, the United States should be promoting greater democracy in world bodies such as the United Nations, the World Bank, the International Monetary Fund, the World Trade Organization, and others. Presently, only the votes of a few nations in these and other global venues count, and the U.S. vote is foremost. Reforming the United Nations and other multilateral organizations to allow more equal participation and influence by other nations, especially the poor and developing countries, is not against American interests. It is a matter of promoting democracy and freedom in a globalized world.

If we do not solve national security problems, then the other social problems discussed in this text are immaterial. These global social problems, although seemingly far away and removed from everyday life, hold the ultimate consequences to our individual and collective security.

■ CHAPTER REVIEW

1. Military might, to be second to none in power, is the principle guiding national security in the United States. The U.S. military is the largest and most expensive in the world. Military spending is high because (a) of the fear of nuclear weapons held by others; (b) there are nations with expansionist agendas; (c) defense spending benefits business, labor, the states, the members of Congress, and academia; and (d) outspending others is said to give the United States "peace through strength."

2. Nuclear weapons are the most destructive weapons on earth. The United States and Russia possess 96 percent of the world's nuclear warheads. As many as forty countries have the capacity to develop nuclear weapons.

3. Terrorism is a strategy of using violence to gain political advantage. It is a social construction. That is, what is defined as terrorism and who is labeled a terrorist are matters of interpretation.

4. Domestic terrorism (Americans killing Americans) has occurred throughout U.S. history. The current threats come from individuals and groups focusing on particular issues such as abortion or gun control or a more generalized fear of government overreach and government mistakes, as well as feeling powerless against not only by big government but also big banks and big Wall Street. The Tea Party movement embodies these fears and is a source of unrest. Most movement followers are not violent, but the seeds of violence are.

5. The war on international terror is like no other war because terrorists do not represent a nation but are loosely organized and are willing to use tactics such as suicide bombers.

6. The Bush Doctrine that emerged to guide national security in response to the September 11, 2001, attacks included the following principles: (a) the right of the United States to engage unilaterally in preventive wars and to change governments it deems to be dangerous; (b) the spread of democracy; (c) the building of a military beyond challenge; and (d) dividing nations into those who are with us and those who are against us.

7. The war on terror has been very costly in human life, injury, and treasure. The costs to the United States in conducting this war are not evenly distributed. The soldiers come disproportionately from minorities, the working and lower classes, and rural areas.

8. The possible long-term negative consequences of these wars include (a) the loss of Iraqi and Afghani support; (b) the polarizing of the Sunni– Shiite schism worldwide; (c) the loss of U.S. image and credibility in the Arab world; (d) unintended support for the cause of the terrorists through U.S. actions against suspected terrorists; and (e) the loss of civil liberties in the United States.

9. There are lessons to be learned from conducting this new kind of war: (a) military might does not bring security; (b) vengeance is self-defeating; (c) occupiers rarely succeed in imposing their

way of life on the locals—in this case the United States will likely fail in its efforts to plant democracy; (d) the planning for war must include an endgame; (e) if terrorism is to be diminished, its root causes must be addressed; and (f) the United States will not succeed unless it acts within the framework of international organizations and international law.

■ KEY TERMS

National security. The ways nations organize to protect borders, guard their national interests, and shield their citizens and businesses abroad with armies, military bases, intelligence networks, embassies, and consulates.

Defense budget. The government's spending plan for maintaining and upgrading the military defenses of the United States.

Weapons of mass destruction (WMDs). Nuclear, biological, and chemical weapons capable of large-scale death and destruction.

Cold War. The tension and arms race between the United States and the Soviet Union from World War II until 1990.

Terrorism. A methodology of using violence to gain political objectives.

Blowback. The unintended consequences of policies whereby supplies and support given to a presumed ally are later used by that entity against the original benefactor.

Bush Doctrine. The policy guiding U.S. military actions in the "war on terror" and the long-range plan for national security in the twenty-first century.

Preventive war. A war in response to a presumed future threat.

Preemptive war. A war in response to a direct, immediate, and specific threat.

Habeas corpus. A basic human right in the Western world that prevents the police (or government) from arresting and holding someone without cause.

■ SUCCEED WITH PEARSON mysoclab www.mysoclab.com

Experience, Discover, Observe, Evaluate
MySocLab is designed just for you. This chapter features a pre-test and post-test to help you learn and review key concepts and terms.

Experience sociology in action with dynamic visual activities, videos, and readings to enhance your learning experience. Complete the following activities at www.mysoclab.com.

Social Explorer is an interactive application that allows you to explore Census data through interactive maps.

- Explore the Social Explorer Map: *The Population in the Military*

The Core Concepts in Sociology video clips offer a real-world perspective on sociological concepts.

- Watch *PBS American Experience: The Living Weapon*

MySocLibrary includes primary source readings from classic and contemporary sociologists.

- Read Derber, *The Wilding of America: Iraq and the War Against Terrorism*; Nguyen, *We Are All Suspects Now: Untold Stories from Immigrant Communities after 9/11*; Hoffman, *Why Don't They Like Us*

Index

Cultural diversity, 162
culture, 10, 15-16, 28, 36, 75, 106, 119, 123, 132-133,
    136, 151-152, 159-160, 166, 172, 178, 180,
    183, 187, 247, 250, 259
Culture of poverty, 132, 183
cultures, 15, 165, 180
Currency, 59
Curriculum, 15, 19, 125, 127-130, 134, 142, 147, 151,
    194-195
Currie, Elliott, 249
Custody, 282

D

Darfur, 278
Darwin, Charles, 18
Darwinism, 17-18, 28
Data, 3, 9, 19-22, 24-26, 28-29, 35, 40, 48, 61, 71, 85,
    90, 106-107, 114, 119, 128, 130, 132-133,
    135, 145, 152, 158, 161-162, 164, 174, 184,
    187, 205, 218, 227, 243, 251, 255, 283, 287
Davis, 16, 115, 260
Day care, 13, 193
Death, 7, 67, 74-75, 91, 95, 97, 170, 177, 202, 228,
    231, 233, 260-261, 264, 266, 269, 277, 287
Death penalty, 261
death rates, 67, 97
Debt, 35, 42, 60, 76-77, 79, 83-85, 116, 256, 264, 277
Debt bondage, 76-77, 84
Decision making, 45, 50, 202
Declaration of Independence, 127, 215
Decline, 2, 5, 19, 57, 67-68, 85, 89, 91, 107, 216, 230,
    263
Decriminalization, 245, 247-248, 250
Deferred gratification, 109
Definitions, 8-9, 28, 156, 200, 220-221, 225, 231, 250
Deforestation, 88, 90, 103-104, 117
Degradation, 26, 71, 92-93, 100, 102, 117
Dehumanize, 201
Delinquents, 25
Delirium, 233
democracy, 7, 9, 14, 36, 43-44, 46-47, 49, 52, 58-61,
    263, 271-274, 277-279, 282, 285-287
Democratic principles, 46
Democrats, 44, 47, 49, 59, 178, 263
Demographic transition, 67-68, 71, 84-85
Demographic trends, 145
Demography, 183
Denmark, 6, 65, 116-117, 129
Denominations, 202-203
density, 6, 77, 232
Department of Education, 128, 132, 139, 144, 173,
    180
Department of Health, 177
Department of Homeland Security, 262, 282
Dependency, 16, 23, 79, 84-85, 166
dependent variable, 25, 29
Dependent variables, 26
Depersonalization, 25
Depressants, 228
Depression, 3, 42, 53-54, 175, 227-230, 236-237
Deprivation, 15, 28, 132, 152, 168
desegregation, 141, 182
Developed countries, 66-68, 71, 83, 97, 101, 115, 117,
    236
Developed nations, 6, 66, 71, 78, 81, 84-85, 115, 284
Developing countries, 66-67, 72, 74, 77-79, 101,
    117-118, 155, 286
development, 6, 18, 33, 54, 65, 67, 72, 75, 78, 82, 84,
    92-93, 98, 102, 110-111, 117, 131, 137, 140,
    146, 176, 181, 191, 197, 213, 215-217, 257
Deviance, 8, 10-12, 21, 26-28, 223, 242, 249
Diabetes, 278
Diamond, Jared, 90-91
Diet, 72, 74, 187, 237
differentiation, 110, 186-187, 189, 217
Direct benefits, 56
Disabilities, 93, 137, 256
Disability, 26, 201, 256, 277
Disabled, 23
Disasters, 23, 72, 110-111, 175, 180-181, 254
Discipline, 12, 125, 143
Discouraged workers, 174
Discoveries, 90, 118
Discrimination, 4, 130, 159-161, 163-170, 173, 175,
    179, 182-184, 185, 194, 203, 209-211,
    213-216, 258
    institutional, 167-168, 182-184, 203
    politics and, 185
Diseases, 7, 71, 74, 83, 91, 97, 100, 105-106, 176,

195, 231, 236
Disinvestment, 39
Disney, Walt, 36-37
disparity, 135, 185, 243
Disrespect, 242
distribution system, 72, 241
districts, 19, 47, 127-128, 134-138, 141-142, 145-147,
    149, 151, 279
Diversion, 72
diversity, 59, 104, 107, 149, 162-164, 177-178, 200
Division of labor, 187-189, 213
Divorce, 19-20, 27, 166, 202, 276
    community, 27
    consequences of, 276
    patterns, 19, 166
    psychic, 27
    trends, 19
Divorce rate, 19, 276
    types, 19
DNA, 156
Documents, 71, 73, 127, 285
Dominant group, 155, 158, 166, 183, 266
dominant groups, 182
dominant society, 157, 191
domination, 32, 35, 65, 78, 156, 189, 284
Double standard, 244, 265
Downsizing, 42, 175
Drinking water, 64, 95, 97
Driving, 91-92, 162, 170, 179, 244, 246
Dropping out, 22, 131, 133
Drug abuse, 224, 226-229
    addiction, 229
Drug Abuse Warning Network, 228
Drug addiction, 12, 222, 249
Drug companies, 236
Drug dealers, 245
Drug Enforcement Administration, 226-227, 244
Drug Policy Alliance, 243
Drug use, 27, 148, 220-223, 225-226, 231-235,
    238-239, 243-245, 247-250
Drugs, 11, 17, 23, 55, 75, 219-251
    hallucinogens, 226-227
    illicit, 221, 224, 226, 234-235, 239, 242-243,
        246-248, 250
    types of, 75, 221, 238, 247
Dual labor market, 211
Dual labor market theory, 211
Due process, 46, 281
Dying, 72, 89, 169, 265
dysfunction, 236
Dysfunctional families, 132

E

Earnings, 40, 45, 131-132, 139, 146, 171, 183,
    207-210, 212, 216-217
Ebola, 7, 74
Ecology, 117
economic conditions, 73, 160, 178, 183, 262
economic development, 54, 67, 72, 78, 84, 117, 216
Economic elites, 33
Economic forces, 180
Economic inequality, 71, 85, 175
    power, 71
Economic Policy Institute, 146
Economic problems, 13, 34, 57, 60
economic system, 14, 33-34, 51, 109-110, 112,
    114-115
Economic systems, 51
Economics, 56, 82, 103, 175, 205, 211
economy, 3, 5, 13-14, 16, 22, 26-27, 32-36, 38-39, 42,
    52-53, 56-57, 59, 73, 79, 81, 84, 89, 92,
    101-102, 110, 112, 114-115, 130, 148,
    150-151, 168, 175, 180-181, 185, 188-189,
    206-207, 213-214, 217, 256-257, 264-265,
    284
economy and, 13, 168, 180
Ecosystem, 89, 110
Ecosystems, 89, 92, 119
Ecstasy, 228-229
Ecuador, 239
Education, 1, 6, 8, 10, 13, 19, 26-27, 31, 34, 37, 41,
    58, 63-64, 70-71, 75, 79, 81-83, 85, 87, 109,
    121-152, 153, 155, 164-166, 168-169,
    171-173, 180-181, 183-184, 185, 194-197,
    203, 207-211, 217-218, 219, 231-232, 234,
    246, 249-250, 253, 264, 278-279
    academic achievement, 132, 146-147
    adult, 6, 231-232
    among African Americans, 180, 194

charter schools, 125-126
college level, 141
computers and, 135-136, 143
elementary, 128, 134, 136-137, 141, 143, 146, 197,
    207-208
hidden curriculum, 194
learning and, 139
literacy rate, 6, 70
marriage and, 71
myths, 123, 155
of African Americans, 169, 181
outcomes, 129, 131-132, 146, 151
racial stratification, 155, 169, 183-184
sex, 126, 132, 145, 171-172, 195-196, 203,
    209-211, 217
social class and, 132, 134, 141-142, 210, 234
social structure and, 217
society, 8, 10, 19, 26-27, 34, 41, 70, 75, 122-123,
    126, 130, 132, 134, 139, 144-146,
    149-151, 155, 164-166, 168, 180-181,
    183, 185, 195-196, 217, 234, 246,
    249-250
South Korea, 148
worldwide, 71, 79, 85, 181, 185, 279
Educational attainment, 24, 64, 124, 130-131, 140,
    145, 172, 181
educational reform, 124
educators, 125, 136, 149, 151, 172
efficiency, 102
ego, 196
Egypt, 82, 157, 260, 268, 279-280, 284
Eighteenth Amendment, 222
Eisenhower Doctrine, 268
Elderly, 4, 126, 181
    families, 126
    poverty in, 181
elections, 43, 46-49, 52, 58-59, 204-205
elementary schools, 137
Elite, 46, 50-53, 60, 73, 138-140, 144, 224
Elites, 18, 33, 47, 58, 78, 83-84, 90, 101, 264-265
E-mail, 107, 178, 237, 282
Emancipation, 215
Emergence, 27, 254
Empathy, 228
Emphysema, 99, 227, 231
Empirical evidence, 182
employment, 5, 16-17, 50, 57-58, 77, 84, 111, 114,
    142, 160, 165, 171, 174, 180-182, 203,
    206-208, 210-212, 215
    Affirmative Action, 182, 203, 208
    labor force, 171, 174, 206-207, 210-211
    status of, 203
    Title VII of the 1964 Civil Rights Act, 203
Employment inequality, 211
Enarson, Elaine, 198
Energy, 6, 52, 55, 57, 74, 89, 91-92, 98-102, 108,
    110-117, 212, 215, 230, 238, 256, 260
Engels, Friedrich, 189
England, 9, 148
English language, 198
Enjoyment, 196
Environment, 6, 17, 28, 52, 81, 87-119, 136-137, 139,
    141, 246
    impact, 6, 89-90, 92, 115
    movement, 94
    pollution problems, 94
    population and, 28, 81
Environmental classism, 112, 119
Environmental crisis, 109, 115, 118
environmental justice, 94, 119
Environmental problems, 89, 91, 106, 110-113, 116,
    118
Environmental protection, 39, 81, 94-95, 111
    agency (EPA), 94, 111
Environmental Protection Agency, 81, 94-95, 111
Environmental Protection Agency (EPA), 94, 111
environmental racism, 94, 112, 119, 175, 184
Environmentalists, 261
EPA, 94-95, 97, 99-100, 111
    protection agency, 94-95, 111
Epidemic, 74, 85, 230-231
Epidemics, 71
Equal Employment Opportunity Commission, 210
equal opportunity, 41, 134, 147
Equal Pay Act, 203, 210
equality, 9, 41, 43, 46, 130, 145-146, 150-151, 159,
    169, 182, 186, 197, 203, 207, 215-216, 218
equality of opportunity, 9, 130, 145-146, 150-151
equilibrium, 104